Political Parties, Campaigns, and Elections

POLITICAL PARTIES, CAMPAIGNS, AND ELECTIONS

Robert E. DiClerico

West Virginia University

PRENTICE HALL
Upper Saddle River, New Jersey 07458

Library of Congress Cataloging-in-Publication Data

DiClerico, Robert E
Political parties, campaigns, and elections / Robert E. DiClerico
p. cm.
ISBN 0-13-040030-0
1 Electioneering— United States 2. Elections—United States. I Title

JK2281 D53 2000
324 7'0973 —dc21   99-048852

VP, Editorial Director: Laura Pearson
Executive Editor: Beth Gillett Mejia
Project Manager: Merrill Peterson
Prepress and Manufacturing Buyer: Ben Smith
Electronic Art Manager: Guy Ruggiero
Electronic Art Creation: Mirella Signoretto
Cover Director: Jayne Conte
Cover Designer: Bruce Kenselaar
Cover Photo: Bob Child/AP/Wide World Photos
Senior Marketing Manager: Christopher DeJohn
Editorial Assistant: Beth Murtha

This book was set in 10/12 Times by Stratford Publishing Services
and was printed and bound by Courier Companies, Inc.
The cover was printed by Phoenix Color Corp.

Printed in the United States of America

10 9 8 7 6 5 4 3 2 1

ISBN 0-13-040030-0

PRENTICE-HALL INTERNATIONAL (UK) LIMITED, London
PRENTICE-HALL OF AUSTRALIA PTY. LIMITED, Sydney
PRENTICE-HALL CANADA INC., Toronto
PRENTICE-HALL HISPANOAMERICANA, S.A., Mexico
PRENTICE-HALL OF INDIA PRIVATE LIMITED, New Delhi
PRENTICE-HALL OF JAPAN, INC., Tokyo
PEARSON EDUCATION ASIA PTE. LTD., Singapore
EDITORA PRENTICE-HALL DO BRASIL, LTDA., Rio de Janeiro

Contents

━━━━━━━━━━━━━━━ CHAPTER SEVEN ━━━━━━━━━━━━━━━

Parties, Elections, and Governance   249

Preface

The readings in this book focus on seven major subjects related to elections (primarily presidential) and political parties. These topics address the mechanics of nominating presidential candidates and the consequences for the parties and the candidates (Ch. 1); the role of money in elections and the efficacy of attempts to regulate it (Ch. 2); the role of the media in covering election campaigns and as a vehicle for campaign advertising (Ch. 3); the matter of who votes, who does not, and what impact the level of voting participation has on election outcomes and the political process more generally (Ch. 4); the considerations that enter into the voting decision, and how well voters manage the information environment that surrounds them in election campaigns (Ch. 5); what recent election outcomes (1994, 1996) suggest about the relative strength of the two major parties, and the prospects for realignment (Ch. 6); and finally, how elections impact on governing as it pertains to the president, the behavior within our political parties, and the relationship between the two elected branches in an era of divided government (Ch. 7).

Each of the chapter topics contains three selections. The first two have a more specific focus related to the topic, while the third is designed to provide students with a more general overview. Each article, moreover, was selected not only because it speaks to an important issue(s) related to elections but also because it does so at a level that is accessible to students.

I would like to express my deep appreciation to Merrill Peterson for his always prudent editorial judgment and to Joan Stone, who had overall responsibility for this project.

Robert E. DiClerico
West Virginia University, Morgantown

Political Parties, Campaigns, and Elections

The Nominating Process

The noted practitioner of the political art, Boss Tweed, was fond of reminding his compatriots, "I don't care who does the electin', so long as I do the nominatin'." His was an astute, if not eloquent, observation. For to the extent that the nominating process structures the choices for president that confront us on election day, it may be viewed as the most critical stage in the process of selecting a president.

Over the last thirty years the presidential nominating process has been subject to as much sustained criticism as any feature of the American political system. Indeed, scholars, journalists and public officials alike have repeatedly warned that there is much wrong with the way we choose our presidents. One noted political scientist, for example, asserts that "Perhaps the weakest of our electoral institutions is the presidential nominating system. . . ."[1] The dean of American political journalists (David Broder), sees the process as a "recklessly haphazard way to choose the candidates for that demanding office."[2] And the late Terry Sanford, a one-time governor, U.S. senator, and presidential candidate, observed that ". . . we expect to pick our president . . . by participatory disorder that knows no equal in American society"[3]

The root of the problem, as the critics see it, lies in moving away from a system in which most delegates to our national conventions were chosen in party-controlled caucus-conventions, to one that is now dominated by primaries. Although the wide-ranging party reforms begun in the early 1970s never mandated primaries as a mechanism for selecting delegates, for a growing number of states the primary had a certain appeal. For one thing, the reforms themselves were designed to open up the nominating process. Consequently, to the extent that primaries allowed for broader participation by the rank and file, they were seen as consistent with the spirit of the reforms. In addition, states saw a greater economic payoff by switching to the primary, since it typically attracted more media attention than a caucus, and required candidates to expend considerably more money to run.

1

In the view of many, however, these benefits have come at a high cost—one that is addressed by James Lengle *et. al* in the first selection. Arguing that primaries are inherently more divisive than caucuses as a mechanism for choosing delegates, these authors consider how this divisiveness affects a party's ability to carry primary states in the general election.

Although caucuses are no longer the preferred method of choosing convention delegates, they are still used in roughly 20 percent of the states, the most famous of which is Iowa. In the second selection James W. Davis explains how this complex process works in the Republican and Democratic parties and argues that the caucus affords a more deliberative process for choosing nominees and is more invigorating for the parties as well.

In the final selection, John Haskell offers an overall assessment of our thirty-year experience with the president-by-primary process. He suggests that the process ought be judged by whether it is fair; affords voters a sufficient opportunity to learn about the candidates, and they about the public; makes it possible for the public to reconsider its judgment during the process; and avoids placing obstacles to entry that are so onerous as to discourage otherwise capable public officials from running. Though acknowledging that the current president-by-primary process has some definite strengths, nevertheless, on balance he finds it wanting.

NOTES

1. James MacGregor Burns, *The Power To Lead: The Crisis of The American Presidency* (New York: Simon and Schuster, 1984), p. 157.
2. *The Washington Post,* June 8, 1980, p. B7.
3. Terry Sanford, *A Danger To Democracy* (Boulder, CO: Westview Press, 1981), p. 101.

Divisive Nominating Mechanisms and Democratic Party Electoral Prospects

James I. Lengle, Diana Owen, and Molly W. Sonner

INTRODUCTION

For more than 30 years, political analysts and practitioners have debated the question of whether divisive primary campaigns—where the margin of victory between the winner and loser is narrow—are detrimental to a political party's chances of winning in general elections (Hacker 1965; Lengle 1980, 1981; Stone 1984, 1986; Buell 1986; Southwell 1986; Kenney and Rice 1984, 1987; Stone, Atkenson, and Rapoport 1992; Johnson and Gibson 1974; Comer 1976; Bernstein 1977; Born 1981; Abramowitz 1988; Kenney 1988; Piereson and Smith 1975; Miller, Jewell, and Sigelman 1988).

While inconsistent findings abound in the general research on primaries, the conclusion that divisive *presidential* primaries hurt Democratic contenders' chances of winning *presidential* elections has been consistently supported using both aggregate (Lengle 1980, 1981; Kenney and Rice 1987) and individual (Lengle 1980; Southwell 1986; Stone 1986) level data. These studies employ a variety of measures of divisiveness, control variables, and statistical methodologies to reach similar conclusions. With this study we join the debate by presenting the most comprehensive investigation to date of the effects of nominating mechanisms on presidential election outcomes.

DIVISIVE PRIMARIES REVISITED

Our study differs from, and builds upon, previous research in several notable ways. First, we employ the most expansive data set ever used in this kind of analysis—the entire population of state-level election data from 1932 to 1992.

Next, we restrict our analysis to the Democratic party only. The existing literature suggests that primary divisiveness is more consequential for Democratic candidates than Republican candidates. The pluralistic base, cross-cutting cleavages, and wide ideological range that have been characteristic of the Democratic party since its transformation from minority to majority party status in the 1930s sow the seeds of

Source· James I. Lengle, Diana Owen, and Molly W. Sonner. "Divisive Primaries and Democratic Electoral Prospects," *Journal of Politics, 57* (May 1995), pp. 370–383.

James I. Lengle is professor of political science at Georgetown University and author of *Representation and Presidential Primaries.* Diana Owen is an assistant professor at the same institution. Molly W. Sonner is a research assistant with the Pew Research Center.

conflict among the party elite as well as between the elite and the mass membership over the rules, role, priorities, and direction of the party. The minority status, homogeneous membership, and philosophical coherence of the GOP inoculate it to some degree from the effects of divisiveness. We begin our own study with the 1932 presidential election to test for the effects of divisiveness during this entire period of Democratic ascendancy.

Third, we have expanded the scope of the inquiry by comparing the effects of two types of presidential nominating mechanisms—presidential primaries and caucuses—on party success rates in general elections. Previous research focused on primaries exclusively.

To remain consistent with the literature, we have borrowed the dichotomous indicator of divisiveness initially devised by Bernstein (1977) to study congressional elections and used by Lengle (1980, 1981) to study presidential elections. Under this classification scheme, a primary is considered divisive if the margin of victory between the winner and runner-up is 20% or less. Just as in previous studies at the aggregate level, our work includes controls for the effects of incumbency and state party orientation.

Finally, we have extended earlier research in another major respect. The original studies employed multivariate contingency table analysis. We follow up this research by using probit to estimate the probability of a state voting Republican as a function of divisiveness, incumbency, and party orientation.

NOMINATING MECHANISMS, DIVISIVENESS, AND ELECTORAL OUTCOMES

One major limitation of the current literature is that the relationship between divisiveness and election outcomes is tested for one type of nominating mechanism only—the direct primary. The exclusive focus on primaries in the literature is understandable. Primaries are the nominating method of choice at the congressional, state, and local level. We believe, however, that divisiveness varies reliably by nominating mechanism. Different nominating systems, by virtue of their inherent characteristics, are susceptible to greater or lesser degrees of divisiveness. A nominating process that is quick, less visible, party-centered, and elite controlled, for instance, is likely to be less polarizing, and hence, less divisive, than a method which is protracted, more visible, candidate-centered, and mass controlled. Direct primaries fit the latter type. The focus on presidential elections allows us to compare the effects of two types of nominating mechanisms—presidential primary and caucus—on general election outcomes.

Caucuses by their very nature are likely to be less divisive than primaries for a number of reasons. Campaigns in caucus states are less visible to the party membership than those in primary states. With the exception of the Iowa caucuses, fewer candidates participate, less money is spent, fewer ads are run, and less media coverage is generated. As a result, the party membership in caucus states compared with primary states tends to be less interested, less attentive, less actively involved, and less likely to develop strong emotional and political attachments to candidates. In sum, they are less willing to participate in the process at all. On this last point, the historical record is quite clear: turnout in caucuses is much lower than in primaries. Only 1%–3% of the voting-age population participate in caucuses, whereas 20%–25% vote in primaries (Ranney 1972, 1977; Lengle 1992).

More importantly, however, there is a fundamental difference in the function of primaries and caucuses. For most of the twentieth century, caucuses were responsible, primarily, for conducting party business and, secondarily, for selecting delegates. Party members who attended caucuses may have preferred different candidates for president, but the caucus was a forum to set party rules, plot campaign strategy, disseminate information, choose party officeholders, and select party leaders to the next round of caucuses—not to decide upon a presidential nominee.

The responsibility for choosing the nominee in a caucus-based nominating process rested with the national convention. Thus, if divisiveness arose during the nominating campaign, it arose at the national convention where avenues existed to resolve the conflict and unite the party. Losing factions were offered patronage, pork barrel, policy concessions, or the vice presidency by the winning faction in return for their support in the general election. Divisiveness was reduced through the bargaining and negotiating inherent in a deliberative nominating mechanism.

The purpose of primaries, however, is to measure popular support for presidential contenders. By their very nature, therefore, primaries invite internal party dissension if not civil war. They compel candidates to criticize and malign one another before a statewide and national audience and encourage party members to divide themselves into opposing camps. Negative and deceptive advertising blankets the airwaves and reinforces voter loyalty and antipathy toward candidates. In a presidential primary, the price of victory for the winner is a tarnished image and a split party, and there is no consolation prize for losers. Our argument is not that divisiveness is absent in caucuses and present in primaries, but that the magnitude of the problem is less and the number of party members affected is fewer in caucuses than in primaries.

The effect of different nominating mechanisms on party (dis)harmony and electoral outcomes is an especially interesting question given the recent changes in the presidential nominating process over the last 20 years. Before 1972, an overwhelming majority of states used caucuses to select delegates to the Democratic National Convention, and a small minority used primaries. Since 1972, the ratio of caucuses to primaries has been reversed. In 1992, 38 states used primaries and only 12 states used caucuses. The proliferation of primaries and demise of caucuses was one of the unintended consequences of the McGovern-Fraser Commission reforms adopted by the Democratic party in 1971 (Shafer 1983, 1988; Polsby 1983; Lengle 1987). See figure 1.

One simple test of our hypothesis that nominating mechanisms matter is to compare Democratic party success during the prereform and postreform eras. From 1932 to 1968, when delegates were selected by caucuses and nominees were chosen by national conventions, the Democratic party won seven of 10 presidential elections. Since the inception of the primary-based system, Democrats have lost four of six elections. Obviously, other factors contributed to Democratic party successes and failures from 1932–1992. We believe, however, that it is more than coincidental that victories and defeats are so strongly tied to structural changes in leadership recruitment.

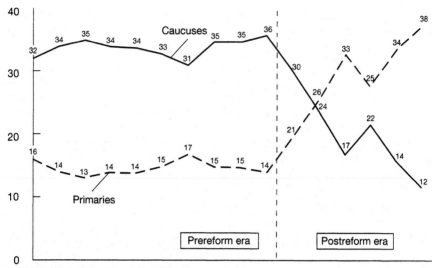

FIGURE 1   *Number of Democratic Primaries and Caucuses, 1932–1992*

Although a direct test of the hypothesis that primaries are more divisive than caucuses is impossible using aggregate data, an indirect test is available. If divisiveness hurts, and if primaries are more divisive than caucuses, then the Democratic party should lose more primary states than caucus states in presidential elections. Moreover, if divisiveness matters, then states with divisive Democratic primaries should be more likely to vote Republican, and states with nondivisive primaries should be more likely to vote Democratic. Consequently, if our inference about the less divisive nature of caucuses is correct, then caucus states should be more supportive of Democratic nominees than either divisive or nondivisive primary states.

Table 1 crosstabulates party choice of states in general elections by type of delegate selection mechanism employed by states and, if states used a presidential primary, by whether the primary was divisive or not.

TABLE 1   *Candidate Choice by Divisiveness of Democratic Delegate Selection Mechanism 1932–1992**

	Divisive Democratic Primaries	Nondivisive Democratic Primaries	Caucuses
Democrat	23%	49%	51%
Republican	77%	51%	49%
	100%	100%	100%
	(105)	(220)	(451)

Chi-square $p \leq .00$; Phi = .19.

*The total number of caucuses in these tables is 451 due to inclusion of Alaska and Hawaii for their first three election cycles.

Outcomes are related to both nominating mechanisms and to divisiveness. From 1932 to 1992, Democrats *lost* 60% of those states that held a presidential primary but *won* 51% of those states that held a caucus. However, when divisiveness is taken into account, the dynamics of this relationship change substantially. As table 1 indicates, Democrats lost 77% of those states that experienced divisive primaries. The party is almost equally successful among those states with nondivisive primaries, losing only 51% of the time, and caucuses, losing 49%. Thus, the evidence points to divisiveness as being a more important determinant of Democratic success than nominating mechanism alone.

The relationship uncovered in table 1 may be a function of state party orientation rather than divisiveness. If traditionally Republican states use primaries and traditionally Democratic states use caucuses, then the relationship found in table 1 between nominating mechanism and success is spurious, a product of the relationship between nominating method and state party orientation.

There is some reason to believe that nominating mechanisms might be tied to state party orientation. States with strong state and local Democratic parties might opt for caucuses because caucuses give state and local party leaders greater control over delegate selection and greater influence at national conventions. States with weak Democratic parties, on the other hand, would be more likely to succumb to populist or progressive pressure for more mass democracy in the form of presidential primaries. In fact, direct primaries sprouted first in those states with weak party organizations. If strength of Democratic party organization is related to nominating method, we would find a tendency for caucus states to vote Democratic, not because caucuses are less divisive, but because the Democratic party in caucus states tends to be stronger. We also would find a tendency for primary states to vote Republican, not because primaries are more divisive, but because the Democratic party in primary states tends to be weaker.

In addition, we also must control for the effects of state party orientation when examining the relationship between divisiveness and success. Since most caucus/convention systems of delegate selection in the past were tightly controlled by state and local party organizations, candidates needed strong party ties to win the nomination. Candidates without these ties had only one strategy—to compete for Democratic delegates in states where their own party's organization was weakest. Such strategic considerations by candidates would produce divisive Democratic primaries in traditionally Republican states. Thus, state party orientation, not divisiveness, would explain the poor performance of Democratic nominees in divisive primary states.

To test for these possible sources of spuriousness, table 2 presents the relationship between nominating mechanism, divisiveness, and party success controlling for traditional state party orientation.

As table 2 shows, the effects of divisiveness remain regardless of state political culture, while the effect of nominating mechanism is somewhat muted. In traditionally Democratic states, the Democratic party *loses* 53% of the divisive primary states but *wins* 78% of the nondivisive primary and caucus states.

The effect in traditionally two-party competitive states is equally dramatic. Democrats *lose* 79% of the two-party competitive states that underwent a divisive primary but *capture* 51% of the nondivisive primary states and 52% of the caucus states.

TABLE 2 Candidate Choice by Divisiveness of Democratic Delegate Selection Mechanism Controlling for State Party Orientation, 1932–1992*

| | Traditionally Democratic | | |
	Divisive Primary	Nondivisive Primary	Caucus
Democrat	47%	78%	78%
Republican	53%	22%	22%
	100%	100%	100%
	(17)	(32)	(120)

Chi-square: $p \le .01$; Phi = 22.

| | Traditionally Competitive | | |
	Divisive Primary	Nondivisive Primary	Caucus
Democrat	21%	51%	52%
Republican	79%	49%	48%
	100%	100%	100%
	(66)	(113)	(193)

Chi-square: $p \le .00$; Phi = 23.

| | Traditionally Republican | | |
	Divisive Primary	Nondivisive Primary	Caucus
Democrat	9%	32%	24%
Republican	91%	68%	77%
	100%	100%	101%**
	(22)	(75)	(132)

Chi-square: $p \le .07$; Phi = .15

*The total number of caucuses in these tables is 445 instead of 451 because the state party orientation for Alaska and Hawaii could not be determined for their first three election cycles.

** Due to rounding

Among traditionally Republican states, the relationship still exists although in a weakened form. Democrats lose traditionally Republican states generally but do far worse among divisive primary states, losing 91%, and significantly better among nondivisive primary or caucus states, losing 68% and 77% respectively.

Our findings in table 1 could be spurious for another reason. The current era of the presidential primary parallels the recent string of Republican presidents. We argue that party success and failure is related to the type of nominating method employed and the degree of divisiveness experienced by the party during these periods. Others, however, could argue just as easily that incumbency accounts for the relationship between nominating mechanism and success. Caucus states voted Democratic because caucuses coincided with Democratic incumbents. Primary states voted Republican for the same reason--primaries proliferated during an extended period of Republican presidents.

Incumbency also might explain the relationship between divisiveness and electoral success. The party out of office is likely to experience divisive primaries because its nomination is open and also more likely to lose the general election because it does not control the resources of the Oval Office. The incumbent party, on the other hand, would have fewer contested nominations and more general election success. Over time the result would be the same for the Democratic party: more nondivisive primaries and more victories when competing as the incumbent party, and more divisive primaries and losses when competing as the out-party. The explanation for failure and success would be incumbency, not divisiveness.

To test for this possibility, table 3 controls our findings for the effects of incumbency. As table 3 shows, divisiveness takes its toll regardless of incumbency. while

TABLE 3 *Candidate Choice by Divisiveness of Delegate Selection Mechanism Controlling for Incumbency, 1932–1992**

	Democratic Incumbent		
	Divisive Primary	*Nondivisive Primary*	*Caucus*
Democrat	12%	69%	74%
Republican	88%	31%	26%
	100%	100%	100%
	(17)	(85)	(186)

Chi-square $p \le .00$; Phi = .31.

	No Incumbent		
	Divisive Primary	*Nondivisive Primary*	*Caucus*
Democrat	15%	25%	34%
Republican	85%	75%	66%
	100%	100%	100%
	(26)	(52)	(114)

Chi-square. $p < .25$; Phi = 10

	Republican Incumbent		
	Divisive Primary	*Nondivisive Primary*	*Caucus*
Democrat	29%	42%	35%
Republican	71%	58%	65%
	100%	100%	100%
	(62)	(83)	(151)

Chi-square: $p \le .12$; Phi = .12.
*See note for table 1

caucuses benefit the party in two of three instances. In election years with Democratic incumbents, divisiveness severely handicaps the party. Democrats *lose* 88% of the divisive primary states, but *win* 69% of the nondivisive primary and 74% of the caucus states. In years with no incumbents, Democrats lose 85% of the divisive primary states, but only 75% of nondivisive states and 66% of caucus states. During election years with Republican incumbent, Democrats lose 71% of the divisive primary states but fare far better in the nondivisive primary and caucus states.

PROBIT ANALYSIS OF STATE VOTE CHOICE

We now take an additional step in our analysis by estimating a probit model (a statistical test—Ed.) to determine the influence of type of nominating mechanism/divisiveness, state party orientation, and incumbency on presidential vote choice.

Table 4 presents the results of the analysis . . . and further supports our con-

TABLE 4   *Probit Analysis*

State Party Orientation	Party Incumbency	Probability of Voting Republican		
		Divisive Primary	*Nondivisive Primary*	*Caucus*
Democratic	Democratic	.29	.11	.08
Democratic	Republican	.63	.40	.38
Democratic	Open	.58	.32	.29
Republican	Democratic	.83	.59	.55
Republican	Republican	.97	.89	87
Republican	Open	.95	.83	.81
Competitive	Democratic	.51	.26	.24
Competitive	Republican	.95	.62	.60
Competitive	Open	.78	.52	.49

Model Statistics

	coeff	se	*coeff*/se	*sign* t
Div. primary	.88	.15	5.84	.00
Nondiv. prim.	.31	.10	3.00	00
Caucus	.20	.09	2.13	.03
Dem SPO	−.72	.13	5.50	.00
Rep SPO	.79	.12	6.58	.00
Competitive	.55	.12	4.61	.00
Dem. incumb.	−.87	.11	7.42	.00
Rep. incumb.	.29	09	3.19	.00
Open seat	.17	.12	1.30	.19
Constant	.51			

$N = 780$; correctly classified = 71%; cases in modal category = 53% ($n = 414$); chi-square = 224.33; $df =$ 5; pseudo $R^2 = .26$; asymptotic $F = 44.87$; significance = .00; $PRE = 45$.

tention that divisive Democratic primaries help elect Republicans, and caucuses help elect Democrats even after controlling for state party orientation and incumbency. As table 4 demonstrates, the probability of voting Republican is highest for divisive primary states and lowest for caucus states for every combination of state party orientation and incumbency. Again, we find that divisiveness is the factor that renders primaries damaging to the Democrats, as the differences in the probability of losing nondivisive primaries and caucuses are small.

Although Democrats do best in "friendly" states in elections with Democratic incumbents, the effect of nominating mechanism on performance is nonetheless dramatic. A Democratic incumbent has a 29% chance of *losing* a "friendly" state after a divisive primary, and only an 8% chance of *losing* a "friendly state" which employs a caucus system.

The worst scenario for Democrats occurs in "hostile" states with a predominantly Republican culture. Democrats *lose* "hostile" states 97% of the time when a divisive primary has occurred, compared with 87% when a caucus has been held. The Democratic party does not fare well when a divisive primary has taken place in a competitive state holding an election for an open seat. Democrats *lose* 78% of the time under these conditions. However, they face a 51% chance of *winning* if a caucus is held.

CONCLUSION

The relationships uncovered in this study should not be surprising to students of political parties, generally, and of party reform, specifically. Historically, party success has been intricately tied to formal institutional mechanisms and procedures for selecting party nominees (Ranney 1975; Cesar 1979; Heale 1982; McCormick 1982; Cavala 1974; Lengle and Shafer 1976; Polsby 1983; Lengle 1987). Consequently, any changes in these rules and mechanisms affect the legitimacy of the decision, the quality of the nominees, the attitudes and loyalty of party members, the power of groups and states within the party coalition, and, ultimately, the competitiveness of the party in the electoral arena. . . .

While our study answers conclusively one important question using aggregate-level data, it also raises many other related ones at the individual level. Obviously, our findings suggest that political loyalties, attitudes, and perceptions of voters in nominating campaigns are influenced enormously by the structure and intensity of the competition fostered by nominating mechanisms. The voters' psychological and political reaction to bitterly fought nominating campaigns does not disappear after the national convention. Instead, it remains with the voters and becomes part of the mindset that influences their behavior in general elections. Issues concerning the relationship of divisive primaries to the development of voters' short- and long-term attitudes toward candidates, political parties, and the political process, their willingness to work for the presidential nominee, and their propensity to turn out in the general election need to be explored. Only when such studies have been conducted can we hope to understand more fully the divisive primary phenomenon.

REFERENCES

Abramowitz, Alan I. 1988. "Explaining Senate Election Outcomes." *American Political Science Review* 82:385–403.

Atkenson, Lonna Rae. 1992. "Moving Toward Unity: An Experimental Look at Attitude Change During a Presidential Election." Presented at the annual meeting of the American Political Science Association, Chicago.

Bartels, Larry M. 1988. *Presidential Primaries and the Dynamics of Public Choice.* Princeton, NJ: Princeton University Press.

Bernstein, Robert A. 1977. "Divisive Primaries Do Hurt: U.S. Senate Races, 1956–1972." *American Political Science Review* 71:540–55.

Born, Richard. 1981. "The Influence of House Primary Election Divisiveness on General Election Margins, 1962–76." *Journal of Politics* 43:640–61.

Boyd, Richard. 1989. "The Effects of Primaries and Statewide Races on Voter Turnout." *Journal of Politics* 51:730–39.

Buell, Jr., Emmett H. 1986. "Divisive Primaries and Participation in Fall Presidential Campaigns: A Study of 1984 New Hampshire Primary Activists." *American Politics Quarterly* 14:376–90.

Cavala, William. 1974. "Changing the Rules, Changes the Game." *American Political Science Review* 68:27–42.

Ceaser, James. 1979. *Presidential Selection: Theory and Development.* Princeton, NJ: Princeton University Press.

Comer, John. 1976. "Another Look at the Effects of the Divisive Primary: A Research Note." *American Politics Quarterly* 4:121–28.

Crotty, William. 1983. *Party Reform.* New York: Longman.

Epstein, Leon. 1986. *Political Parties in the American Mold.* Madison: University of Wisconsin Press.

Hacker, Andrew. 1965. "Does a 'Divisive' Primary Harm a Candidate's Election Chances?" *American Political Science Review* 59:105–10.

Hanushek, Eric A., and John E. Jackson. 1977. *Statistical Methods for Social Scientists.* New York: Academic.

Heale, M. J. 1982. *The Presidential Quest.* New York: Longman.

Johnson, Donald Bruce, and James R. Gibson. 1974. "Divisive Primary Revisited: Activists in Iowa." *American Political Science Review* 68:67–77.

Kenney, Patrick J. 1988. "Sorting Out the Effects of Primary Divisiveness in Congressional and Senatorial Elections." *Western Political Quarterly* 41:765–77.

Kenney, Patrick J., and Tom W. Rice. 1984. "The Effect of Primary Divisiveness in Gubernatorial and Senatorial Elections." *Journal of Politics* 46:904–15.

Kenney, Patrick J., and Tom W. Rice. 1987. "The Relationship between Divisive Primaries and General Election Outcomes." *American Journal of Political Science* 31:31–44.

Key, V. O. 1964. *Politics, Parties, & Pressure Groups.* (5th ed.). New York: Crowell.

Lengle, James I. 1980. "Divisive Presidential Primaries and Party Electoral Prospects, 1932–1976." *American Politics Quarterly* 8:261–77.

Lengle, James I. 1981. *Representation and Presidential Primaries: The Democratic Party in the Post-Reform Era.* Westport, CT: Greenwood.

Lengle, James I. 1987. "Democratic Party Reforms: The Past as Prologue to the 1988 Campaign." *Journal of Law & Politics* 4:223–73.

Lengle, James I. 1992. "Reforming the Presidential Nominating Process." In *The Quest for National Office,* ed. Stephen Wayne and Clyde Wilcox. New York: St. Martin's Press.

Lengle, James I., and Byron E. Shafer. 1976. "Primary Rules, Political Power, and Social Change." *American Political Science Review* 70:25–40.

McCormick, Richard. 1982. *The Presidential Game.* New York: Oxford University Press.

Miller, Penny M., Malcolm E. Jewell, and Lee Sigelman. 1988. "Divisive Primaries and Party Activists: Kentucky, 1979 and 1983." *Journal of Politics* 50:459–70.

Piereson, James E., and Terry B. Smith. 1975. "Primary Divisiveness and General Election Success: A Re-examination." *Journal of Politics* 37:555–62.

Polsby, Nelson. 1983. *The Consequences of Party Reform.* New York: Oxford University Press.

Pomper, Gerald. 1981. *Party Renewal in America.* New York: Praeger.

Ranney, Austin. 1972. "Turnout and Representation in Presidential Primary Elections." *American Political Science Review* 66:21–37.

Ranney, Austin. 1975. *Curing the Mischiefs of Factions: Party Reform in America.* Berkeley: University of California Press.

Ranney, Austin. 1977. *Participation in American Presidential Nominations.* Washington, DC: American Enterprise Institute.

Southwell, Priscilla L. 1986. "The Politics of Disgruntlement: Nonvoting and Defection among Supporters of Nomination Losers, 1968–1984." *Political Behavior* 8:81–95.

Shafer, Byron. 1983. *Quiet Revolution.* New York: Sage Foundation.

Shafer, Byron. 1988. *Bifurcated Politics.* Cambridge: Harvard University Press.

Stone, Walter J. 1984. "Prenomination Candidate Choice and General Election Behavior: Iowa Presidential Activists in 1980." *American Journal of Political Science* 28:361–78.

Stone, Walter J. 1986. "The Carryover Effect in Presidential Elections." *American Political Science Review* 80:271–79.

Stone. Walter J., Lonna Rae Atkenson, and Ronald B. Rapoport. 1992. "Turning On or Turning Off? Mobilization and Demobilization Effects of Participation in Presidential Nomination Campaigns." *American Journal of Political Science* 36:665–91.

Ware, Alan. 1979. "Divisive Primaries: The Important Questions." *British Journal of Political Science* 9:381–84.

Caucus-Convention System:
A Tradition Worth Preserving

James W. Davis

The caucus-convention system, still used in a dozen or more states to select national convention delegates, is the least understood aspect of the presidential nominating process. Yet precinct caucuses and county, congressional district, and state conventions have been an integral part of the presidential nominating system since the birth of national nominating conventions in the 1830s. In this article the operation of the caucus-convention system will be discussed in detail. The level of party member participation in the caucus-convention system and the costs of campaigning in this party-sponsored system will be compared with voter participation and costs in the presidential primary states. The arguments in favor of the caucus-convention system will also be carefully analyzed. Finally, the prospects for the possible return of the caucus-convention system to a number of states will be assessed.

WHAT IS A CAUCUS?

According to one source,

> the caucus or some equivalent has become an indispensable adjunct of party government, and it may now be defined as a meeting of the majority of electors belonging to the same party in any political or legislative body held preliminary to a meeting thereof, for the purpose of selecting candidates to be voted for, or for the purpose of determining the course of the party at a meeting of the whole body.[1]

Caucuses are older than the Republic. Indeed, precinct caucus meetings antedate the founding of the United States Constitution. In New England the term generally applied to any small group of political leaders who met to plan campaign strategy and to conduct political business. Historians consider the party caucus an outgrowth of the Sons of Liberty and Committees of Correspondence, who fanned the flames of independence during the Revolutionary War period. John Adams, our second president, has given us a colorful description of the political activities conducted at the Boston "Caucus Club," certainly the best known of the pre-revolutionary American patriotic societies:

James W. Davis is professor emeritus at Western Washington University. He is author of several books, including *Presidential Primaries: the Road to the White House,* and *Leadership Selection in Six Western Democracies.*

This day learned that the Caucus Club meets at certain times in the garret of Tom Dawes, the Adjutant of the Boston regiment. He has a large house, and he has a moveable partition in his garret which he takes down, and the whole club meets in one room. There they smoke tobacco till you cannot see from one end of the room to the other. There they drink flip, I suppose, and they choose a moderator who puts the questions to the vote regularly; and selectmen, assessors, collectors, firewardens, and representatives are regularly chosen before they are chosen in the town.[2]

GROWTH OF THE CAUCUS SYSTEM

The caucus system, which enjoyed the greatest popularity in the New England states, continued to prosper after the Revolutionary War. Indeed, the size of the caucus meetings expanded rapidly. These mass meetings or caucuses at the local level served as the foundation for the establishment of county conventions by the Jeffersonian Republicans shortly after 1800. County conventions were designed primarily as the nominating mechanism for the selection of candidates at the local level. County conventions consisted of delegates chosen in the local precinct caucuses. Once the national nominating convention was established in the 1830s and 1840s the county convention's duties included the selection of delegates to congressional district conventions for the purpose of electing national convention delegates. (Most national convention delegates are still selected at this level.) Throughout the nineteenth century the caucus-convention system remained the standard procedure for selecting local candidates. State conventions nominated statewide candidates. In the twentieth century, however, the spread of the direct primary displaced the caucus-convention system's nominating function for state and county officers. Presidential nominations, however, remained the province of the party.

PARTY RETAINS CONTROL OF PRESIDENTIAL NOMINATIONS

National conventions consisted of delegates selected from all the states—and several territories—in the Union.[3] For more than 150 years, these quadrennial conclaves have been conducted by the major parties to select presidential nominees.

Prior to the McGovern-Fraser party reforms of the early 1970s, only fifteen states relied on presidential primaries to select national convention delegates. Approximately two-thirds of the states continued to use the traditional caucus-convention system for delegate selection. But the McGovern-Fraser reforms spawned the rapid spread of presidential primaries so that by 1980 nearly two dozen states had shifted from the caucus-convention system to presidential primaries. It is this wholesale shift to primaries that has relegated the caucus-convention system to a secondary role in the nominating process. Nevertheless, the caucus-convention system remains an integral part of the unique American presidential nominating system and merits careful examination.

Unlike presidential primary elections, which are conducted by state and local officials, the caucus-convention system is managed by each of the two major parties. Although both the state governments conducting the presidential primaries and the political parties are involved in the selection of national convention delegates, the party-controlled national conventions are the final decision-making bodies that pick the parties' presidential nominees. Our attention here, however, will be focused chiefly on the caucus-convention system.

The precinct caucus system, like the state presidential primaries, varies somewhat from state to state on such matters as delegate apportionment and the number of stages in the process. Unlike the Republicans, the state Democratic caucuses are closely regulated by the Democratic National Committee's selection rules.

OVERSHADOWED CAUCUS-CONVENTION SYSTEM STILL AN INTEGRAL PART OF PRESIDENTIAL NOMINATING SYSTEM

In the prereform era before 1968, three-quarters of the states used the caucus-convention system to select national convention delegates. However, the rapid spread of presidential primaries to nearly three dozen states in the 1970s sharply reduced the number of caucus-convention states to slightly more than a dozen. Still, major presidential contenders do not neglect delegate-hunting in the caucus-convention states because in a close nominating race the delegates picked up in the caucus-convention states can provide the margin of victory at the national convention. Indeed, the postreform delegate selection rules have made it imperative for presidential contenders to campaign actively in nearly all of the states.

Beyond doubt, the Democratic party adoption of proportional representation for the allocation of delegates in 1974 has enhanced the value of campaigning in the caucus-convention states—a presidential candidate can expect to pick up at least a handful of delegates, even if he loses the state, assuming, of course, he or she has exceeded the 15 percent threshold rule. Under the new Democratic delegate selection rules any candidate collecting more than 15 percent of the vote at the precinct, county, or congressional level would add some delegates to his delegate total.

Presidential candidate-centered campaign organizations also have expanded operations in the caucus-convention states. By making alliances with some state party officials or special interest groups, the presidential candidate can launch a competitive campaign. Candidates with strong ties to labor unions or teacher groups, for example, enjoy an initial advantage over their rivals in terms of volunteers and delegate hunters. Thus, in 1984, former Vice President Walter Mondale's close ties with labor unions over the years helped him mount delegate drives in key states with extensive phone campaigning and organizational work at the local level. In return, leaders of these interest groups expect to have a major voice in selecting delegates to the convention. These delegates also expect to promote the interest of the labor unions at the state and national conventions. In some caucus-convention states an active minority of caucus delegates often remain uncommitted. In Missouri, for example, 39 percent of the Democratic precinct delegates in 1984 were uncommitted, and in Alaska the uncommitted delegates totaled 34.7 percent.[4]

In 1984 the Democratic nominating race featured an intense contest between Mondale and Senator Gary Hart in the caucus-convention states. Approximately one-third of the national convention delegates were selected in twenty-seven caucus contests. Surprisingly, Senator Gary Hart, who lost the Democratic nomination to Mondale, won thirteen out of the twenty-seven caucus races to Mondale's ten states. Uncommitted delegates captured four caucus states—Hawaii, Mississippi, South Carolina, and Kentucky.

Although Senator Hart won more caucus states, his victories were mostly in the thinly populated states. All told, Mondale won 242 more pledged delegates than Hart in the caucus states.

In 1992 Governor Bill Clinton fared decidedly better in the presidential primary states than in the caucus-convention states. Clinton won twenty-eight of the thirty-five states (including the District of Columbia) in which delegates were chosen in primaries. But he won only four of sixteen states in which national convention delegates were chosen in a caucus-convention system. In fact, Clinton did no better than former Massachusetts Senator Paul Tsongas in the caucus states. What accounted for Clinton's weak showing in the caucus states? Most of the caucuses were held fairly early, before Clinton had become the front-runner. Tsongas, former California governor Jerry Brown, and Iowa Senator Tom Harkin all had strengths that appealed to special interest groups in the caucus states—for example, Harkin had strong labor union support.[5]

Clinton, however, won the Democratic nomination with an impressive drive down the homestretch. After a narrow loss to former California governor Jerry Brown in the Connecticut primary. Clinton won twenty-two straight primary victories to clinch the nomination.[6]

PRECINCT CAUCUSES: FIRST STEP IN THE NOMINATING PROCESS

In Iowa, Minnesota, and Washington, for example, the caucus-convention system is based on a three- or four-tier voting process starting at the precinct level. (Precincts are the basic administrative unit for conducting elections; generally, precincts contain approximately 600 to 900 citizens.) This process is spread over several months and is usually not completed until early June. Democratic National Committee rule changes in 1969 required each state party to separate the stages in the delegate-selection process by at least thirty days. Furthermore, all stages of a state's delegate-selection process had to be completed during the first six months of the election year.

Delegates elected in the first-round precinct caucuses next participate in the county convention. Delegates at the county conventions, in turn, select a smaller number of delegates to the congressional-district caucuses or conventions. These same delegates also serve at the state conventions (usually held in late May or early June), which select delegates-at-large to the national convention. In no state do precinct caucuses directly select delegates to the national conventions.

In the caucus-convention system the key to success lies at the precinct level. If a presidential candidate wins control of the delegates at the precinct level, he will thereby control the delegate selection in the county, congressional-district, and state conventions.[7]

Under the caucus-convention system a presidential candidate cannot hope to win control of the state delegation if he starts campaigning for delegates at the county level. It's already too late, because his rivals will have elected all of their pledged delegates in the precinct caucuses, thereby gaining control of the selection process in the county conventions. Consequently, the chief objective of a presidential candidate and his managers is to get a big turnout of supporters at the precinct caucuses in order to influence the selection process all the way to the state and national conventions.

Flexibility is the hallmark of the caucus-convention system. Delegates, whether uncommitted or pledged, can shift to another candidate easily. In the Democratic party, for example, former Georgia governor Jimmy Carter won only 28 percent of the January 1976 Iowa caucuses, but by the time the Iowa state convention was held in late May, Carter had collected over 50 percent of the state delegate vote. The tally showed that Carter had won 25 delegates to 20 for Morris Udall, 1 for Jerry Brown, and 1 for Senator Ted Kennedy.[8] Clearly, a number of the uncommitted delegates had moved into the Carter camp. In 1984, former Vice President Walter F. Mondale received 48 percent of the Iowa caucus vote and approximately 64 percent of Iowa's national convention vote. Once again, several uncommitted members moved over to the Mondale team during the 5-month hiatus between the February caucuses and the national convention in July.

CAUCUS PARTICIPATION

Party reforms in the early 1970s, especially within the Democratic party, required open caucuses. This reform had the effect of making caucuses more like miniature primaries. Indeed, former Senator Howard Baker, a presidential challenger in the 1980 GOP race, described the Iowa caucuses as "the functional equivalent of a primary."[9] In 1980 approximately 120,000 GOP voters and over 100,000 Democratic voters—approximately 10 percent of the voting age population—participated in the Iowa caucuses. This turnout was higher than that of several state primaries.

Candidates visit Iowa throughout the pre-primary election cycle almost as frequently as they tour New Hampshire before its first-in-the-nation primary. Congressman Richard Gephardt, winner of the 1988 Iowa Democratic caucuses, spent 87 days campaigning in Iowa before the 1988 caucuses. Former Arizona governor Bruce Babbitt devoted 80 days to campaigning in the Hawkeye State before the 1988 Democratic caucuses. Republicans, however, have not spent as much time in Iowa as the Democrats. Still, former Delaware governor Pierre DuPont spent 62 days in Iowa before the 1988 GOP caucuses. Senator Bob Dole, the winner of the 1988 GOP caucuses, devoted 31 days to campaigning in Iowa before the caucuses (see Table 1).

TABLE 1   *Number of Days Spent by Presidential Candidates in Iowa, 1987–1988*

Candidate/Republican	Number of Days	Candidate/Democrat	Number of Days
Bush	16	Babbitt	80
Dole	31	Dukakis	46
DuPont	62	Gephardt	87
Haig	21	Gore	26
Kemp	49	Jackson	30
Robertson	22	Simon	53
MEAN	50	**MEAN**	78

Source: Peverill Squire, "Iowa and the Nomination Process," in Peverill Squire, ed., *The Iowa Caucuses and the Presidential Nominating Process* (Boulder, CO: Westview Press, 1989). p. 5.

In Iowa the pre-caucus debates, sponsored by the *Des Moines Register,* have all the standard aspects of a primary state debate. Media coverage of the Iowa caucuses now matches the amount of time given to New Hampshire by the TV networks and the national press.

Beyond Iowa, however, it is an overstatement to say that most state caucuses are the functional equivalent of a primary. Voter turnout in the caucus-convention states has always been much lower than in the presidential primary states. Political scientist Austin Ranney compiled figures in 1976 for twenty-one states using caucuses and a combined voting age population of 33,389,000. or over one-fifth of the national voting age population. According to Ranney, "The mean proportion of the voting age population attending caucuses was 1.9 percent, while the mean of the voting age population voting in the Democratic primaries in closed primary states . . . was 18.6 percent—nearly ten times higher."[10] Since then, participation in the Democratic and Republican caucuses has not varied significantly from Ranney's findings. To be sure, approximately 12 percent of the Democratic and 11 percent of the Republican party activists turned out for the first-round Iowa caucuses in 1988, but turnout in most states (1976–1992) seldom exceeded 3 percent.[11]

Who are the party activists who participate in the caucuses?

Profile of Caucus Participants.   Data on the profiles of participants in the caucus states are much thinner than in the primary states. However, in a 1988 three-state survey (Iowa, Michigan and Virginia) of caucus participants, William G. Mayer found that they are demographically different from the general public.

- *Education.* Among Republican caucus participants in the three states, between 40 and 60 percent were college graduates. Among Democratic caucus attendees, 38 percent were college graduates.
- *Age.* Analysis of the age factor revealed that less than 7 percent of the Democratic and Republican participants were under thirty years old. Almost one-third of caucus attendees were sixty-five years or older.

- *Income.* Over 50 percent of Republican attendees in 1988 earned on average more than $50,000 per year, approximately 30 percent of Democratic participants earned $40,000 or more.

- *Ideology.* Mayer also found that "caucus participants in both parties do have a pronounced ideological tilt to them, far more so than primary voters or party identifiers." Among Republican caucus participants, at least 83 percent of the attendees described themselves as some variety of conservatives—approximately fifteen percentage points higher than Republican voters and identifiers. Among Democratic caucuses, approximately 65 percent said that they were liberals, as compared to about 40 percent of Democratic voters and party identifiers.

- *Party activity.* Among Republican caucus participants, approximately 70 percent reported they were members of a local GOP committee; almost two-thirds said they had been delegates to a previous state convention. Almost 90 percent of the GOP participants had worked in the state party for at least five years. Among Democratic participants, approximately 55 percent said that they had been active in their state party for at least ten years. Another 15 to 20 percent of the Democrats reported that they had been active for five years or more.[12] As Thomas R. Marshall has noted "Many—perhaps most—caucus attendees are persons with previous party or interest group experience and require little prodding by candidates to attend."[13]

CAMPAIGN SPENDING IN CAUCUSES AND PRIMARIES

Most presidential candidates allocate far more resources to primaries than caucuses. Generally, the candidate's strategic goals of maximizing the collection of delegates and maximizing media coverage dictate that more money be allocated to the primary states. On average in multi-candidate campaigns 1976–1988, according to Paul-Henri Gurian, presidential candidates spent more than three times as much per primary as they did in the caucuses.[14] Why? Primaries and caucuses require a different style of campaigning and different resources. Because only a small segment of the electorate (1 to 5 percent) participate in caucuses, candidates allocate less money to mass media advertising in the caucus states. Because primary campaigns are waged chiefly through the mass media, television advertising and direct mail costs are much higher. Caucus state campaigns, by contrast, are based heavily on grass roots mobilization of party activists. If organized interest groups—labor unions, teachers, the Christian Coalition, etc.—are supporting a specific candidate, his or her campaign costs can be expected to be even less.

Generally, presidential candidates spend more money in primaries than in caucuses because primary states usually have more voters and attract more media coverage than the caucus states. Paul-Henri Gurian found that from 1976–1988 mean spending across all primaries was $237,675 and mean spending across caucus states was $70,561—less than one-third the cost of primaries.[15] Mean spending in proportional primaries was $177,396 and $312,504 in nonproportional primaries. As a further means of comparing campaign costs in two states—Oklahoma and Missouri—the parties used the caucus system in 1980 and then switched to presidential primaries in

1988. Candidates spent an average of $44,000 and $20,000, respectively, in the 1980 Oklahoma and Missouri caucuses. In the 1988 primaries, candidates spent an average of $156,000 in Oklahoma and $206,000 in the Missouri primary.[16] Clearly, presidential primary campaigns require a much larger war chest, if the candidates are to be competitive.

DEMOCRATIC PRECINCT CAUCUS SYSTEM IN OPERATION

Presidential precinct caucuses in recent years have become well-publicized events. Party rules in both major parties and state laws now require that the date, time, and place of the caucuses be published in the local press. Formerly, local party leaders were prone to call "snap" caucuses to select delegates to the county conventions, without letting their rivals know about the precinct meetings. But since the McGovern-Fraser party reforms of the early 1970s, Democratic caucus rules have been clearly delineated—no secret meetings, no proxies, no slate-making, etc. In recent years the Republicans have followed almost all of the same rules.

Attendance at a typical precinct caucus in Iowa, Maine, or any other state may vary from a handful of activists to more than one hundred participants. In most caucus-convention states precinct caucuses are held simultaneously in all precincts throughout the state. In a few states the first-level meetings may occur at the town/city or county level or by legislative districts. Generally, the official precinct meeting starts at 8 pm, though members have already been affixing their signatures to the precinct sign-up sheet and listing their presidential preference (or uncommitted status). Once the meeting is convened by the temporary chair, the first order of business is to elect a permanent chairman (usually the temporary convener). The next order of business often calls for messages from county and state officials, speeches from supporters of the various contenders, and pep talks about the need for party unity in the general election.

Meanwhile, the task of certifying all the attendees must be completed before any formal votes can be taken. Democratic party rules prescribe that the caucus must be open to "all voters who wish to participate as Democrats." This stipulation means that the caucus must be open to any Democrat who wants to participate in the caucus. Also, this rule puts some burden on the state parties to discourage participation by independents, unaffiliated voters, or those whose principal attachment is to another party. In states that have party registration, the state parties decree that only registered Democrats may participate in the Democratic caucuses. Once the speech-making is finished, the supporters of the various contenders gather in their "affinity" or candidate preference groups in various corners of the school building, fire hall, or private home to nominate and elect their precinct delegates to the county conventions.[17] In the Republican party no special groups form because delegates are elected by secret ballot.

The Democrats operate under a 15 percent threshold rule, meaning a delegate candidate must have the support of at least 15 percent of the participants within the caucus to qualify for a delegate slot. Adopted in 1976, the threshold rule requires the allocation of a delegate slot to the supporter of any presidential candidate who collects as little as 15 percent support in the Democratic caucus or primary.[18] Critics argue that the threshold rule encourages multiple candidacies, factionalizes the party, and provides an incentive for long-shot contenders without national experience, or even party ties, to run. Proponents argue that the threshold rule gives unknown candidates an opportunity to win delegates, gain national recognition, and use this recognition to build a following and become a national figure.

PROPORTIONAL REPRESENTATION

The Democratic Party, it should be noted, also operates under a system of proportional representation. In other words, precinct delegates and ultimately national convention delegates must be allocated on a proportional basis. Thus, if a candidate receives 35 percent of the vote in the caucus or primary, he or she shall be entitled to 35 percent of the delegates. In the Republican party, only when state law requires proportional representation in the allocation of presidential primary delegates does the GOP adhere to proportional representation. Instead, the Republicans give wide latitude to the state parties and permit winner-take-all primaries and caucuses. The impact of winner-take-all caucuses or primaries should not be underestimated. In 1988, for example, Vice President George Bush won 59 percent of the vote in states with some kind of winner-take-all voting system on Super Tuesday, but won 97 percent of the delegates, handing him an almost insurmountable lead over his chief opponent, Senator Bob Dole.[19]

Within the Democratic caucuses the number of delegates allocated to each precinct is generally based on the presidential or gubernatorial vote in the previous general election. Thus, six hundred votes cast in the previous general election in the precinct will generate six delegates on the basis of one delegate for each one hundred votes cast for the party's presidential or gubernatorial candidate.

If there is a crowded field of candidates, the dickering and bargaining between the various contenders will have some of the trappings of a Middle Eastern bazaar. Backers of candidates with less than 15 percent support must disband and shop around desperately to join supporters of a viable candidate. Failure to find an alternate candidate group will result in their complete elimination from the contest because they have failed to reach the required 15 percent threshold. Sometimes joining the uncommitted delegates will offer the safest landing spot.

As soon as the designated time for balloting and vote counting is completed, the formal allocation of delegates is announced, based on the percentages of votes obtained by each viable candidate. Since 1978, the Democratic party's affirmative action rules have also required that delegate seats be shared equally between men and women.

For the remainder of the precinct meeting, the members discuss the major issues of the day and pass resolutions on these issues for transmittal to the county convention. In Iowa, for example, the heated discussions may extend beyond midnight. All in all, the balloting and issue discussion help reinforce the party-building function. Not all of the delegates will be satisfied with the outcome, but all of the attendees know that the party's future depends upon a united front against the opposition party in November.

REPUBLICAN CAUCUSES

Rules governing Republican caucus participation are similar to those used by the Democrats. Republican national rules, however, allow state GOP parties to be more restrictive in determining who can participate in their caucuses. GOP rules, for example, limit participation to "legal or qualified voters who are deemed to be Republican by state law or party rules." Furthermore, the GOP rules allow governing Republican committees of each state "to prescribe additional qualifications not inconsistent with the state law."[20]

As a result of this rule, a number of GOP state parties, especially in the West, limit their caucuses to members who are party officials or functionaries.[21] In Arizona and Montana, for example, only precinct committeemen and precinct committeewomen elected in the Republican primary held two years earlier are permitted to participate in the first-round caucuses. Wyoming Republican rules prescribe that all registered Republicans are eligible to participate in the precinct caucuses, which elect delegates to the GOP county conventions. However, all Republican committeemen and committeewomen are automatic delegates.[22]

Republican state bylaws and delegate selection procedure manuals say relatively little about how GOP caucuses select national convention delegates. The Republicans, for example, do not have a proportional representation rule. Indeed, the Republicans permit winner-take-all rules so that minority members supporting their candidate may be frozen out of the proceedings without any delegates. Under Republican rules, the national media have a difficult time keeping score of how many delegates each presidential candidate has acquired in the first-round caucuses. In Iowa, for example, Republican leaders, recognizing that the national media want to know the winners and losers in the first-round, have contrived to conduct a nonbinding "straw poll" among caucus participants to respond to the media's insistence on knowing the results. Thus, in 1980 these straw poll results allowed the national media to declare George Bush the upset winner over Governor Ronald Reagan.[23]

Within the Republican Party, state and local party officials determine how many precinct delegates are to be selected in each county and precinct caucus. In Iowa, for example, the county chairmen in the 99 counties determine the size of each county convention and the number of precinct delegates to be selected, based on the GOP Presidential vote received in each precinct in the last election. In the state of Washington, which selects half of its national convention delegates by the caucus-convention system (and half by a presidential primary), county chairmen have the option of using the number of registered voters in each precinct (Washington does not register voters by party) or using the combined vote for president, governor, attorney-general, and state representative to calculate the number of delegates allocated to each precinct.[24]

PRO-CAUCUS ARGUMENTS

Although the number of caucus states has shrunk by over half since 1968, the caucus system can still claim strong adherents. Supporters maintain that citizens can have more serious and sustained influence over the selection of presidential nominees through the caucus system by participating and discussing with fellow party members the merits of the various candidates, than by simply casting a ballot in a presidential primary.

Arguments frequently cited in favor of the caucus system include

1. the provision of a recruitment mechanism to attract party workers and the easier identification of party activists through person-to-person contact;
2. the promotion of greater party unity in the general election;
3. reduced costs in the selection process since the major emphasis is on personal contact rather than mass communication advertising;
4. the greater opportunity for caucus participants to develop knowledge about the candidates, thereby encouraging candidate selection on the basis of issues and the candidate's credentials, not their personalities; and
5. the encouragement of a greater sense of personal accountability between the officeholders and the caucus participants.[25]

Defenders of the caucus-convention system are not easy to find these days. James MacGregor Burns remains one of the most ardent defenders of the caucus-convention system. In Burns' view,

> The caucus system must be the party's answer—indeed, it is the only feasible answer—to that great institutional enemy of parties, the primary system for choosing party nominees. . . . If primaries appear to bring a measure of intraparty democracy to nomination politics, the caucuses could supply a far superior kind of democracy, measured by intensive voter participation, thorough canvassing of candidates and issues and careful consideration of the present and potential link between would-be nominee and the party.[26]

Participatory democracy adherents who favor presidential primaries have far more public support than defenders of the caucus-convention system. Since the McGovern-Fraser reforms in the early 1970s, the unmistakable trend has been to favor popular participation over deliberation. In other words, the reformers believe that involving a greater number of party supporters in presidential primaries to pick nominees is preferable to a caucus-convention system which is based upon deliberation by party activists. But numbers alone, it can be argued, do not determine the quality of presidential candidates. As Wilson Carey McWilliams observed some years ago,

> primaries give special weight to initial support for candidates who enter early, they advantage ideological followers, and they emphasize media image. They discourage considered judgment and place no particular value on party coalitions. They violate all the requirements of deliberation in precisely that aspect of our electoral process—the choosing of nominees—where deliberateness is most needed.[27]

Defenders of the presidential primary system, preoccupied with the doctrine of greater popular democracy in the nominating process, should be reminded of E.E. Schattschneider's well-turned aphorism, uttered more than a half-century ago: "Democracy is not to be found *in* the parties but *between* the parties."[28]

Pressure for return to the caucus-convention system in a number of states is still at a low level. In some respects the process is similar to the proverbial task of putting the toothpaste back in the tube. Easier said than done. Widespread usage of the presidential primary system in over three-quarters of the states has made it the standard method for picking most national convention delegates. Proposed adoption of a single national presidential primary also has enjoyed popular support. Gallup polls conducted throughout the 1980s showed that approximately two-thirds of the respondents favored a national primary.[29] No polls were taken on the question: Should the country return to the caucus-convention system?

Proponents of the caucus-convention system, however, have recently pointed to a small ray of hope on the horizon. Indeed, the dynamics of the presidential selection process may produce at least modest change in the year 2000 nominating campaign.

THE NEW CALIFORNIA "OPEN" PRESIDENTIAL PRIMARY LAW

In California, the largest state in the union, for example, the huge national convention delegates of both parties may be chosen through the caucus-convention system, not the presidential primary, because the California voters refused to repeal the recently-approved "open" primary law, enacted in 1996.[30] California's open primary law now requires that all candidates, including all presidential contenders, must be listed on one "broadsheet" ballot without regard to party affiliation. Since the Democratic national party rules—and now the Republican rules—require that all delegates elected in primaries must be selected in a closed primary system, the California voters' refusal to repeal their open primary could mean that all California national convention delegates will have to be chosen by party members in caucus-conventions.

In the latest development, however, California Governor Gray Davis signed a new "open" presidential primary law in early May 1999 that state officials believe will not violate national party rules that forbid such primaries.[31]

The new California law mandates an open primary—that is, voters may cross party lines casting their ballot for whomever they choose, regardless of party registration. The results will be counted and then forwarded to state party headquarters.

But, unlike earlier laws, the ballots will be coded so that separate tallies can be kept in all instances in which Republicans vote Republican and Democrats vote Democratic and so forth. These vote tallies will also be forwarded to state party headquarters.

Party officials, who helped design the new law, plan to ignore the tallies produced from the voting. While this tallying will respond to the mandate contained in the recently passed citizen initiative for an open primary, both major parties are confident that they can legally pick their own rules for tallying votes and thereby be under no obligation to accept the open primary results.

Instead, they plan to rely on the results from the coded ballots to pick primary winners. If they do not follow this carefully planned process, the state officials warn that the state's delegations to the national nominating conventions will most likely not be seated.[32]

How the Democratic and Republican national committees will rule on this innovative open primary in the most populous state in the Union is still an open question as the nation draws closer to the year 2000 presidential nominating race. But there can be little doubt that no matter which way the two national committees rule, the California open primary decision will have a far-reaching impact on the presidential nominating process in the years ahead.

With the largest state delegations in the nation—more than 400 delegates attended the 1996 Democratic convention and 163 delegates attended the smaller GOP convention—California is the most powerful state in the presidential nominating process. For decades California has been the nation's pacesetter in education, environmental, and social welfare reform. Perhaps, with the possible return of the caucus-convention system in the year 2000, California will serve as a model of reform of the presidential nominating process.

FEW DEFENDERS OF TRADITIONAL CAUCUS-CONVENTION SYSTEM

Why have so many officeholders refused to come to the rescue of the caucus-convention system? The reasons are not difficult to uncover.

No presidential candidate can afford to criticize the presidential primary system directly because to argue against popular participation in the nominating process is "anti-democratic" and "elitist." No candidate for the White House wants to be put in the position of being "against the people" in this era of "direct democracy." Since the Progressive era early in the twentieth century, reformers have campaigned to give the public, not the legislature, the right to decide virtually every major controversial issue by initiative measures. On the state level the initiative process is used in twenty-four states to give citizens the opportunity to circumvent the state legislature and vote directly to enact specific legislative proposals. In 1998 the state of Colorado, for example, had ten initiative measures on the ballot.

H. Ross Perot, the Reform Party candidate for president in 1996 and the leader of the "United We Stand" movement in the 1992 presidential race, has urged the country to turn to "electronic democracy" to give the electorate the right to register their views via their computers, modems, and faxes, e-mail or two-way interactive TV on every major issue facing the nation.[33] Perot, however, has not been critical of the presidential nominating system since he nominated himself in 1992 and used the Perot-dominated Reform Party convention in 1996 to obtain renomination.

Political scientist John Aldrich reminds us "no nominating system generates strong or weak candidates systematically."[34] But our argument here is that caucuses (with a liberal sprinkling of primaries) provide a better mechanism through which established party organizations can maintain at least some measure of influence over the selection of the presidential ticket.[35] To be sure, the charge is made that caucus participants do not represent a typical cross-section of America. Overall, however, caucus participants, regardless of their demographic characteristics, are more likely to consider the long-term needs and benefits of the party, and for that reason, ultimately are likely to be in a better position to reflect rank-and-file opinions and preferences than the larger body of casually interested voters in the primaries. In 1980, for example, monthly surveys conducted by the *New York Times* and CBS News found that only 15 percent of the respondents said that they paid "a lot" of attention to the presidential campaign during January and February of the election year. Three times as many respondents reported that they paid "not much attention." In March, April, and June the proportion of the public that could be considered highly attentive varied between one out of four and one out of five.[36]

Critics may charge that caucuses are not representative bodies, but they certainly can provide participants with the opportunity for far more involvement in the nominating race than rank-and-file members of the electorate. Any party activist will attest to the fact that nominating and general election campaign activity can be time-consuming and costly. Party participation is an expensive hobby. The party does not underwrite hotel bills, meals, or travel costs; the participant picks up the tab. Voters in the primary states, on the other hand, merely have to go to the local polls and cast their ballots—a task that can be handled in a matter of minutes.

Is the movement for the spread of presidential primaries to all fifty states unstoppable? It is perhaps too soon to say. To be sure, the authority of state and local parties has been undermined by the primary movement. Also, the parties have had to contend with boosters and special interest groups—the innkeepers, the restaurant owners, and the tourist agencies promoting travel within the state—who support primaries because they generate revenue and publicity. State legislators, in turn, frequently receive political contributions from those special interest groups, so why shouldn't they be receptive to the passage of presidential primary legislation? Unfortunately, party supporters of the caucus-convention system are far less vocal in their defense of the party-managed caucus-convention system. Unless the repercussions from the heavily front-loaded primary schedule provokes a backlash after the year 2000 primary season, the demand for a national presidential primary may be irresistible.

What are the prospects for a return to the caucus-convention system in a number of states that formerly used this system? The odds are not high.

David E. Price, executive director of the Democratic Hunt Commission and later a member of the House of Representatives from North Carolina, does not hold out much hope for the return of the caucus-convention system to many states. The last serious party effort to push for the revival of the caucus-convention system was undertaken by the Hunt Commission in 1982. According to Price, "Repealing primary laws was a very difficult and costly political prospect in most places and few commissioners relished the attempt to impose constraints on the states sufficient to induce them to take such action."[37] Furthermore, Price concluded, "A 'freeze' that forbade new primaries would risk numerous challenges and might actually 'lock in' states fearful of abandoning their primary lest they lose any possibility of reinstating it in the future."[38]

In its final report, the Hunt Commission stated that the national party should "use whatever incentives and persuasive power at its disposal to encourage more states to shift from primaries to caucuses so that a better balance might result."[39]

Since then, however, neither the Democratic or Republican national parties have made a serious attempt to persuade states to repeal their presidential primary laws and return to the caucus-convention system. However, the stampede created by the front-loaded presidential primary system in the year 2000 campaign may trigger a reexamination of the nominating process by the national parties.

Also, the high cost of running for president—at least $20 million in the bank before the primary season opens—threatens to exclude many well-qualified candidates from seeking the presidency. The fact that the cost of campaigning in the caucus-convention states (except in Iowa) is less than one-third the cost of campaigning in the primary states might induce the national and state party leaders to persuade their state legislatures to repeal the state's presidential primary laws. While the proposed reduction of the number of primaries is far more a hope than a promise, it should not be forgotten that the history of the presidential nominating system has sometimes been unpredictable. Few analysts, for example, would have predicted in the early 1970s that the McGovern-Fraser reforms would have spawned the rapid proliferation of presidential primaries to more than 36 states by 1980. This type of unanticipated consequence could occur again in the presidential nominating process.

The virtues of the caucus-convention system have been well summarized by political scientists Scott Keeter and Cliff Zukin.

> Advocates of caucuses believe that they can ultimately be more representative than primaries precisely because decision-making in them is not atomistic or individual; the caucus participants may be forced at least to consider the broader interests of the party before making a decision and in this sense the needs and desires of non-participants get more consideration.[40]

Although greatly outnumbered, the defenders of the caucus-convention system maintain that the traditional mixed caucus-convention–primary system will, on balance, select more experienced nominees with the necessary coalition-building skills to work effectively with Congress than the current plebiscitarian primary-centered nominating process.

NOTES

1. *The Caucus System in American Politics* (New York: Arno Press, 1974) p. 3.

2. Entry in John Adams' journal, quoted in M I. Ostrogorski, *Democracy and the Organization of Political Parties,* trans. Frederick Clark (New York: Macmillan Company, 1902) Vol 2, p. 4; cited in Austin Ranney and Willmore Kendall, *Democracy and the American Party System* (New York: Harcourt, Brace and Company, 1956), p. 101.

3. Paul T. David, Ralph M. Goldman, and Richard C. Bain, *The Politics of National Party Conventions* (Washington, DC: Brookings, 1960).

4. Gary R. Orren, "The Nomination Process: Vicissitudes of Candidate Selection," in Michael Nelson, ed., *The Elections of 1984* (Washington, DC: CQ Press, 1985), pp. 38–40.

5. Paul R. Abrahamson, John H. Aldrich and David Rohde, *Change Continuity in the 1992 Elections* (Washington, DC: CQ Press, 1994), p. 33.

6. *Ibid.*

7. See Jules Witcover, "Early Caucuses," in Jules Witcover, *Marathon: the Pursuit of the Presidency 1972–1976* (New York: Viking, 1977), pp. 194–221.

8. *Ibid.*, p. 214, note 2.

9. Jack W. Germond and Jules Witcover, *Blue Smoke and Mirrors: How Reagan Won and Why Carter Lost the 1980 Election* (New York: Viking, 1981), p. 96.

10. Austin Ranney, *Participation in American Presidential Nominations* (Washington, DC: American Enterprise Institute, 1977), p. 15; Thomas R. Marshall, "Turnout and Representation: Caucuses Versus Primaries," *American Journal of Political Science,* 22 (February 1978), pp. 169–182.

11. William G. Mayer, "Caucuses: How They Work, What Difference They Make," in William G. Mayer, *In Pursuit of the White House* (Chatham, NJ: Chatham House Publishers, 1996), pp. 126–128.

12. *Ibid.*, pp. 145–146; see also William Crotty and John S. Jackson III, *Presidential Primaries and Nominations* (Washington, DC: CQ Press, 1985), pp 95–97.

13. Thomas R. Marshall, "Caucuses and Primaries: Measuring Reform in the Presidential Nominating Process," *American Politics Quarterly,* 7 (April 1979), p. 158.

14. Paul-Henri Gurian, "Primaries versus Caucuses: Strategic Considerations of Presidential Candidates," *Social Science Quarterly,* 74 (June 1993), p. 312.

15. *Ibid.*, p. 313; see also Thomas R. Marshall, "Caucuses and Primaries," pp. 157–159.

16. *Ibid.*, p. 319.

17. Discussion in this section is based heavily on the author's participation in precinct caucuses in Minnesota, Michigan, and the state of Washington during the period 1952–1998.

18. *Democrats All: Commission on Party Structure and Delegate Selection* (The Mikulski Commission) (Washington, DC: Democratic National Committee, 1973), pp. 15–24.

19. Stephen J. Wayne, *The Road to the White House 1996* (New York: St. Martin's Press, 1996), p. 101.

20. William G. Mayer, "Caucuses: How They Work, What Difference They Make," p. 116.

21. *Ibid.*

22. *Ibid.*, pp. 116–117.

23. *Ibid.*, p. 118.

24. Sources: Mr. Kevin Murphy, Legal Counsul's Office, Republican National Committee; Caroline McGoldrick, Iowa Republican State Central Committee; and Arlene Hilmer, Vice-Chair, Washington Republican State Central Committee.

25. *The Presidential Nominating System: A Primer* (Cambridge, MA: Institute of Politics, John F. Kennedy School of Government, 1979), p. 17.

26. James MacGregor Burns, "Party Renewal: The Need for Intellectual Leadership," in Gerald M. Pomper, ed., *Party Renewal in America* (New York: Praeger, 1981), pp. 198–199.

27. Wilson Carey McWilliams, "The Meaning of the Election," in Gerald M. Pomper, ed., *The Election of 1980* (Chatham, NJ: Chatham House, 1981), p. 174.

28. E.E. Schattschneider, *Party Government* (New York: Rınehart, 1942), p. 60.

29. See James W. Davis, *U.S. Presidential Primaries and the Caucus-Convention System: A Sourcebook* (Westport, CT: Greenwood Press, 1998), Table 15.1, p. 196.

30. B. Drummond Ayers, Jr., *The New York Tımes,* November 15, 1980.

31. *The New York Times,* May 7, 1999.

32. *Ibid.*

33. See Philip Elmer Dewitt, "Dial D. for Democracy," *Time,* 39 (June 8, 1992), pp. 42–45.

34. John Aldrich, "Methods and Actions: The Relationship of Process to Candidates," ın Alexander Heard and Michael Nelson, eds., *Presidential Selection* (Durham, NC: Duke University Press, 1987), p. 182.

35. William G. Mayer, "Caucuses: How They Work, What Difference They Make," p. 130.

36. Scott Keeter and Cliff Zukin, *Unınformed Choice: The Failure of the New Presidential Nomınating System* (New York: Praeger, 1983), p. 57.

37. David E. Price, *Bring Back the Parties* (Washington, DC: CQ Press, 1984), p. 180.

38. *Ibid.*

39. *Ibıd.*

40. Scott Keeter and Cliff Zukın, *Uninformed Choice,* p. 186.

A Quarter Century of Direct Democracy in Presidential Nomination Campaigns: What's the Verdict?

John Haskell

The presidential nomination process has evolved into what may be the wildest democratic political bazaar in the world. Contributing to the excitement is the fact that the stakes are so high. For 140 years every American president has been either a Democrat or a Republican. And while the president may not be able to get what he wants on tax reform, health care, or other domestic issues, as commander-in-chief of the only superpower, with the authority to bring to bear its military force, he is the most powerful man on earth.

Oddly enough, while the public directly determines the nominees of the parties, almost no one understands the process. The parade of straw polls, fundraisers, precinct caucuses, forums, media events, and the byzantine delegate selection rules confuse even the most seasoned observers of American politics.

I. THE DEVELOPMENT OF THE PRESIDENTIAL NOMINATION PROCESS

The fundamentals of the presidential nomination process are deceptively simple. They can be summarized by three points.

- To win the nomination of a major party, a candidate must receive the vote of a majority (fifty percent plus one) of his party's delegates at the quadrennial national convention, held the summer of the presidential election year.
- The national convention is comprised of fifty state party delegations and delegations from the District of Columbia and some of the territories. (Democrats also have a small group of nationally selected officials who serve as delegates.)
- The state parties determine how to select and instruct their delegates to the national conventions, subject to national party rules.[1]

The action during the nomination process revolves around the selection of the delegates and how these delegates decide (or are instructed) to vote at the convention.

Traditionally, dating back to the first political party conventions in the 1830s, the delegates were handpicked by powerful politicians or party leaders in the states. A mayor or governor or state party chairman was likely to have control over which

John Haskell is assistant professor of political science at Drake University. He is the author of *Fundamentally Flawed: Understanding and Reforming Presidential Primaries.*

candidate his state's delegates would support. The conventions and the period leading up to them involved bargaining, negotiating, and horse-trading among influential party leaders in so-called "smoke-filled rooms," where the party platforms were crafted and the presidential and vice presidential nominees were determined.

The parties underwent major changes during the Progressive Era in the early 1900s. Heavy-handed party leaders, some of whom were thoroughly corrupt, were attacked by journalistic muckrakers and other active citizens. These party leaders had a great deal of authority. Perhaps their most important power was control over the nominating procedures for public offices. This gave them control over public officials, essentially giving them a death grip on political power, particularly in cities and states where one party dominated over the other. In fact, in those days, most states and localities did not have vigorous two-party competition.

One of the aims of reformers of that era was to take the power to nominate away from the party leaders by instituting primary elections, which were adopted in many places to choose nominees for state, local, or federal offices. Primaries opened up politics, putting ordinary citizens in a position to select the Democratic or Republican nominee for many offices.

Many states took this idea to presidential politics in the 1910s and used primaries to select delegates to the national convention. Candidates, for the first time, could win delegates to the national convention through politicking in primary election campaigns in the spring of the presidential election year. However, presidential primaries fell out of favor in most states by the 1920s, and up until 1972 the majority of state parties chose not to select delegates in that way, preferring instead to use the caucus-convention system. These meetings were more or less closed to public participation depending on the state, although the trend during the course of the century was toward a gradual opening of these events to activists who wanted to get involved in presidential politics. Still, in some states these procedures remained tightly controlled by party leaders, and there continued to be old-fashioned wheeling and dealing at the conventions.

In the 1960s, while delegate selection was more open to the public in many states than it had been earlier in the century, the selection of nominees was clearly still considered an affair of the parties and not a public matter. Delegates would convene at the conventions, some under the control of party leaders, to select a candidate bearing the party label for the general election. The theory was that, while some party officials and delegates might consult public opinion polls or be influenced by the outcome of a primary in their state, the ultimate responsibility rested with the party to select a worthy standard-bearer. The public played some role in the process, but its principal function in presidential politics was to weigh in on Election Day in November, choosing between the major party candidates and any viable third-party alternatives.

But a second spate of reform in the 1960s and '70s extended the trend in the direction of more citizen participation in nomination politics (already widespread for other federal offices and for many state and local positions, as we have seen) to the presidential level. After a tumultuous convention in 1968, jealously controlled by party leaders, the Democrats decided to open up the selection of delegates for 1972. The new rules stated that whether state parties used primaries or the caucus-convention system, the method had to be openly advertised and the results of those events had to be linked to the selection of delegates for the national convention. This was interpreted to mean that the delegates selected in public events were to reflect the wishes of voters participating. The Republicans have, for all intents and purposes, followed suit.

The new theory was that, whenever there is more than one candidate for a party's nomination, it is fairer to let the public determine the nominee. Voters were to select delegates aligned with one or the other of the candidates in the primaries and caucuses (by the mid-1970s more than 30 states held primaries), essentially pre-determining the convention outcome. Every nominee since 1972 in both parties has been determined by the public in primaries and caucuses. Even when several candidates have contested for the nomination, one has emerged with a majority, usually because so many of his rivals have not been able financially to sustain their campaigns during the grueling period leading up to and during the primaries. By 2000, about forty states will have primaries to select and instruct delegates to the conventions, with more than 80 percent of the convention delegates to be chosen in that way.

What has resulted is a nomination process unique among the world's democracies. Everywhere else party leaders and activists take the responsibility for nominating candidates; here, a plebiscitary expectation has become deeply ingrained—an expectation that the public by means of a vote will determine the parties' nominees.

Perhaps the most peculiar characteristic of this public method of nominating presidential candidates is its *serialized* arrangement. Instead of a one-day primary to determine the nominee, as is done for every other office, the primaries are spread out over four months starting in February and ending the first week or so of June. This characteristic affects the dynamics of the race for the nomination profoundly. Candidates can gather or lose momentum; voters in later states can overturn the decisions of voters in earlier states; and the field of candidates changes, usually getting smaller, as the campaign progresses.

The most important recent development is something called *frontloading*. For many years the early states, particularly Iowa and New Hampshire, have gotten the most attention from the candidates and the press. The Iowa precinct caucuses and the New Hampshire primary are in February, and nearly every serious candidate spends a great deal of time in those states in the year or so prior to the events. Both parties have gone out of their way to protect these states' "first in the nation" status. However, in the last fifteen years or so other states have succumbed to the temptation to try to get the same sort of attention and have moved their primary or precinct caucus dates up from April, May, or even June into March or late February, as Table 1 indicates. In particular, some of the biggest states, including California, New York, and Pennsylvania, will hold primaries within the first two weeks of March in 2000.

Instead of a nomination campaign with primaries spread fairly evenly from February until the first of June, now most delegates will be selected within just a few

TABLE 1   *Frontloading of Presidential Primaries and Caucuses*

Number of delegate selection events held by: *

	March 14	March 31
1980	15	19
1984	15	29
1988	22	30
1992	24	30
1996	30	38
2000**	32	35

Percentage of delegates selected by: ***

	March 14	March 31
1992	36%	44%
1996	49%	75%
2000****	67%	80%

*including District of Columbia and Puerto Rico

**not including District of Columbia and Puerto Rico, and some dates tentative as of this writing

***all these figures are estimates—it is impossible to give precise figures due to variations among the states' delegate selection rules

****about 50% of the delegates will be selected by March 7, 2000

Source. This is an updated and modified version of a chart which first appeared in John Haskell, "Reforming Presidential Primaries: Three Steps for Improving the Campaign Environment," *Presidential Studies Quarterly,* Summer 1996.

weeks after the Iowa caucuses and the New Hampshire primary. This *frontloading* of the nomination process has had profound implications for the way we go about selecting presidential candidates. We look at these effects at some length in the next section.

II. ASSESSING THE PROCESS

There has been a lively and vigorous debate over the last thirty years among scholars and journalists about the strengths and weaknesses of the presidential nomination process. The very notion that plebiscitary methods are used in internal party politics when so much is a stake is extremely controversial. As mentioned earlier, no other country in the world opens up its chief executive nominating process to the public and allows candidates to, in a sense, "self-nominate."[2] Only in America can a person without any national political experience and who is unknown to most of the public less than a year before the election make himself a serious candidate and even get elected. Twice in the last twenty-five years, in the cases of Jimmy Carter and Bill Clinton, a novice and an unknown in national politics has become president due to the open and plebiscitary character of the selection process.

For years most informed observers decried this development, but no one was able to do anything about it. People inside and outside of the parties complained that there was no peer review—no opportunity for those "in the know" to vet potential candidates—like in the old days. Previously, party leaders were in a position to weigh in at the convention if their party was about to make a big mistake. In the 1970s that rapidly became impossible, as candidates were, for the first time, able to sew up the nomination on the basis of winning delegates in primaries and caucuses. The candidates were in control of their own delegates; party officials in the states found their power to influence delegates slipping away.

Much of the debate in the '70s and early '80s centered on whether it would be wiser to turn back the clock to the party-controlled system of years past. The Democrats even tried to achieve this by fiat in the 1980s with the institution of so-called "superdelegates," a group of party officials who would remain officially uncommitted to any candidate until the convention. In theory, they would hang back during the primary season and then exercise their power at the convention if the people made a mistake in the primaries. This did not work, as most of the party officials often took sides with declared candidates even before the primaries started. They seemed to act as handicappers, jumping on the bandwagon of well-financed candidates, as opposed to kingmakers or wise statesmen. What was clear was that the public nature of the campaign could not be changed.

Today, any serious assessment of the process takes for granted its plebiscitary, open, and public character. For better or worse, the days of party control are long past. For that reason, the most important issue is whether the presidential nomination process enables the public to participate and decide in a fair environment and in an informed and responsible fashion. The following criteria will guide us in assessing the strengths and weaknesses of this process:

1. The process of delegate selection in the primaries and caucuses should be fair and democratic.

2. Given the typically large field of candidates, the public should have a reasonable opportunity to learn about the issue positions, accomplishments, and character of the people running. Candidates, too, should have a reasonable opportunity to learn the concerns of the public.

3. Given the high stakes, the process should not permit hastily made judgments without the possibility for the public to reconsider them.

4. The process should not have obstacles to entry that are so burdensome that they discourage the candidacies of well-qualified public officials.[3]

The Process Should Be Fair and Democratic

The presidential nomination process has become much fairer in one important sense. No longer are there gatekeepers who might be in a position to rule out candidates based on informal requirements of race, gender, or ethnicity. While it is true that there have been relatively few other-than-Christian-white-male candidates, the openness of the process does not exclude anyone on the basis of most demographic characteristics. (Of course, the Constitution stipulates that candidates must be 35 years old and born in the United States.) African-American activist and preacher Jesse Jackson became a serious contender for the Democratic nomination in 1988, winning several primaries and caucuses; some think he may well have won the nomination in 1992 had he chosen to run against the weak field of Democratic candidates that year. Elizabeth Dole may prove to be the first truly viable female candidate for a major party nomination as she battles for attention in a crowded Republican field in the early going of the 2000 race.

In short, the process is more inclusive and fair than it used to be. It has also become considerably more inclusive with regard to the delegates who are sent to vote and hammer out the party platforms at the conventions. Republican conventions include nearly equal numbers of men and women in the delegations, and the Democrats abide by gender quotas and have delegations that are roughly representative of the states' rank-and-file in terms of race and ethnicity. This is very different from decades past when the convention delegations were mostly white and male.

But there are other important ways in which the process is not fair and democratic. Two states—Iowa since 1976 and New Hampshire since 1952—take on importance way out of proportion to their population. These states that lead the process have only something under 2 percent of the nation's population, they both have tiny minority populations, are disproportionately rural, and have relatively little diversity of economic interests. Yet the field of serious candidates every four years is essentially determined by the outcomes of the Iowa precinct caucuses (for the Iowa GOP the vote is actually just a straw poll that has little bearing on delegate selection) and the New Hampshire primary in February. While the two states do not determine the nominees, since 1976 they have served to winnow the field to a few major contenders. In addition, the winners in these states usually increase their viability substantially. Obviously, there is a bias in having states so unrepresentative playing such a critical role.

There is a yet trickier problem inherent in placing so much importance on these states. The field of candidates is sometimes quite large, anywhere from five to ten contenders some years. This means that the winner of these states often tallies only about a quarter of the votes. Does this sort of performance indicate wide support worthy of the sort of media attention and momentum candidates receive on the basis of winning one of these two early events?

Consider that Pat Buchanan emerged as Bob Dole's main competition on the Republican side in 1996 based on a 26 percent plurality win in New Hampshire. And back in 1976 Jimmy Carter got his break that led him to the White House in these first two states based on similar tiny pluralities. Would Bob Dole have survived had another candidate with broader support come out on top? Let us look at a hypothetical Republican New Hampshire primary between three of the top candidates that year. Our primary, to keep it simple, will be comprised of twelve voters, and we will be privy to their preferences among three candidates: Dole, Buchanan, and Lamar Alexander.

Five of these voters, represented as V 1–5, liked Buchanan best, Lamar Alexander

TABLE 2   *Order of Preference*

Voters	1	2	3
V 1–5	Buchanan	Alexander	Dole
V 6–9	Dole	Alexander	Buchanan
V 10–12	Alexander	Dole	Buchanan

second best, and Bob Dole third. Four voters, V 6–9, liked Dole best, followed by Alexander and Buchanan in that order. Three voters, V 10–12, liked Alexander best, Dole second, and Buchanan third. We can depict these preferences like this:

Voters, of course, only get to express their first preference in a primary, so the final tally is five votes for Buchanan, four for Dole, and three for Alexander. But if we look carefully, we can see that Alexander, were he to be paired only against Buchanan, would get Dole's four supporters who prefer him to Buchanan, and win 7–5. Similarly, if Dole were paired against Buchanan he would win 7–5, since Alexander's supporters prefer Dole to Buchanan. And if Alexander were paired against Dole with Buchanan out of the race, then Alexander would win 8–4, as he is the preferred alternative to Dole among Buchanan supporters. In sum, Buchanan is actually the least favored candidate on the basis of his inability to defeat his two challengers in head-to-head competition (as might actually have been the case), yet he is able to win the primary and become a major player. Alexander, who is clearly preferred to Buchanan (and even to Dole in our hypothetical), goes home with a third-place finish and may not be able to sustain his campaign.

There are a couple of lessons in this plausible scenario. (In fact, many close observers inside and outside the campaigns believe the dynamics may have been just as depicted above.) One is that extreme candidates—Buchanan is considered the most conservative of Republicans—can win in multicandidate fields. The other is that candidates who are more broadly favored by voters, as Alexander is in this hypothetical, can suffer a debilitating defeat.

The upshot is that key decisions in presidential nominations are made when the field of candidates is still large. Political scientists and economists have known for years that the results of multicandidate races can be, and probably often are, bizarre and unfair.[4] This endemic problem with multicandidate races is a serious defect in the presidential nomination process when so much rides on the outcome of these early states.

On the flip side, in later states the field of candidates is usually narrowed down to two, as most candidates cannot continue to finance their campaigns indefinitely. At that point only candidates with broad support can win, which is as it should be. Dole did defeat Buchanan easily in 1996 when it came down to just those two candidates, probably because Buchanan only appealed to a narrow band of the Republican primary electorate. But we can never know whether a more broadly supported opponent, had he done well in New Hampshire and Iowa, would have made it tougher for Dole to succeed in the end.

Does the Public Learn About the Candidates?
Do Candidates Learn the Concerns of the Voters?

John Kennedy, running for president long before the incredible rigors of the contemporary campaign, was said to have learned about the lives of coal miners in West Virginia during the primary there. While some say that the race for the White House involves an interminably long and degrading trial, Jimmy Carter spoke about how much he valued the opportunity to connect with ordinary people while running. He thought such a process was indispensable for the only person required to represent all of the people. Candidates ranging from Pat Buchanan to Bill Clinton, who otherwise would be cloistered in Washington or their home state, get the opportunity to learn things about people all over the country, to experience voters' lives in ways that probably prove very useful, particularly since, as president, the winner will have to live in a virtual cocoon for security reasons.

The constant campaign is also an effective test of the media skills the president will need so badly while in office. A candidate's aptitude in front of the camera, his ability to connect with people in forums, on television, and in videoconferences, is a key factor for success in the primaries. While in office, the president will need those skills in a variety of ways. In a crisis, a president must communicate with the people in order to rally support. And if a president wishes to realize his domestic policy goals, he will need to use the bully pulpit to set the agenda, something he is better positioned to do than anyone else in the political system. How well he does these things depends in large measure on his media skills.

The constant campaign also gives the public the opportunity to learn about the contenders for president. Particularly in the crucial early states of Iowa and New Hampshire, where most candidates spend a great deal of time, voters get to know the candidates, and they can make a decision that is less colored by television advertising and sound bites. The candidates have to build networks, meet people, and address their concerns. This is in sharp contrast to the sort of politicking that takes place in most of the remaining states, which are far larger and in which candidates spend relatively little time, sometimes just travelling from one media event on the airport tarmac to another.

More generally, over the whole course of primaries, studies by political scientists have indicated that, given time, the voting public learns a good deal about candidates, even those new faces among them.[5] During the first few weeks after the New Hampshire primary, voters know little about the ideological disposition of obscure candidates, and next to nothing of these candidates' accomplishments. Obviously, voters are in no position at this point to make informed judgments about a little-known candidate's character. Obscure candidates who attract early attention due to a surprisingly high finish in Iowa or New Hampshire sometimes benefit from a burst of momentum—an increase in support in subsequent primaries as voters jump on their bandwagon. Some voters apparently project good qualities on these new fresh faces, and voters across the ideological spectrum rally to them, particularly if they have a beef with the consensus front-runner.

An interesting thing gradually happens. Given some time—maybe six to eight weeks or more—voters in later states prove to learn a good deal of relevant information about candidates. Eventually voters can place them on an ideological spectrum and learn specific information about them. At this point, people may even be in a position to make the character judgments that are so important when choosing a president. Larry Bartels found evidence of these sorts of phenomena with little-known (at that time) 1980 GOP contender George Bush and with Gary Hart in 1984, who came out of the blue that year to be front-runner Walter Mondale's most prominent challenger for the Democratic nomination.[6] Both benefited, after early victories, from a burst of support that was unrelated to issues or other more substantive judgments. But the public did, given time, end up learning a good deal about them. Voters in later states were able to make more informed judgments as a result.

Naturally there are some candidates who need no introduction. Well-known candidates—Ronald Reagan in 1980, who had been in the public eye for about forty years at that point, or Al Gore in 2000, who as vice president has been a national figure for about a decade, for example—are relatively easy for voters to assess compared to a new face. But voters can, *given a reasonable amount of time,* learn important and relevant information even about those contenders who were previously unknown to them.

However, the increased frontloading of the process described earlier has thrown a wrench into the voters' learning process. In the 2000 campaign, half of the delegates may be selected within about two weeks of New Hampshire, and nearly all of the delegates by the end of March, only about six weeks after the first primary. The upshot is that voters will not have the time they have shown they need to digest information regarding newly emerging candidates. While the candidates are raising money and lining up support among activists and consultants and courting the press for a year or more prior to New Hampshire, the ordinary citizen isn't paying the least bit of attention. People begin to focus on the campaign after the first events, when there is real news about who is viable and who won delegates in early states. But in 2000, the nomination will likely be sewn up before most voters have had the chance to develop an informed opinion about the candidates. Voters are being asked to do an impossible task.

Frontloading puts most of the primaries and caucuses in a very short time span. In most of the country, candidates will have to rely on media campaigns exclusively and only airport visits to many states. (When there are ten primaries in one week, there is no time for face-to-face campaigning almost anywhere.) The positive effects of retail politicking, where there is real interaction with the public, are not realized, and the opportunity for the public to make informed judgments is severely hampered in the frontloaded process.

Reconsidering Hastily Made Judgments

One of the benefits of a serialized nomination process is that the public, when viewed as a whole, has the opportunity to reconsider the decisions made by voters in early states. New information can come out about candidates, particularly those who were not well known before the race. While some voters in early states may jump on the bandwagon of a successful fresh face, voters in later states can make more sober judgments after having the opportunity to reflect on a more rounded picture of the candidate as it emerges. In fact, as the presidential nomination process progresses, voters do tend to vote for more rational reasons often related to the issue positions and accomplishments of the candidates, as described earlier. If the public is to have a determinative role, it is certainly wise to have a serialized process rather than a one-day national primary.

Once again, however, frontloading presents a problem with regard to the public's ability to reflect, reconsider, and make sober judgments about all the candidates. In the 2000 race, it is likely that a final decision on the nominee of both parties will be made in the first three or four weeks. Voters will not have been in a position to place candidates on the issues, and surely they will not have had the opportunity to make any sort of intelligent judgment about the character of the eventual nominee if he is not already well known. For a process of public choice of such significance, it is extremely unwise to permit a final decision to be made without giving voters a reasonable time to assess and then reassess the qualities of the candidates. While the process remains serialized for the 2000 race, the benefit of that serialization—the opportunity gradually and soberly to assess the candidates and make a considered judgment as the field of candidates narrows down to two or three—is lost.

There is another related problem with the process as it is currently arranged. The hectic, frontloaded schedule will make it easier for candidates to finesse issues. They may be able to avoid forums and probing questions from the press long enough to secure the nomination. This sort of strategy will be much easier to pull off today than it was in the 1970s and early '80s when the race for the nomination often lasted several months. It is more likely today that gimmicks and demagoguery can win the day than previously when candidates were under the public microscope for a longer time while the nomination was still in doubt.

Are Obstacles to Running Too Burdensome?

The Democratic and Republican parties have dominated American politics for 140 years. But both parties were riven by severe factionalism in the 1960s during acrimonious nomination races, the GOP in 1964 and the Democrats in 1968. As we have seen, the parties subsequently moved to open up their races for the nomination, partly as a way to heal the divisions. Now insurgent candidates, those not necessarily favored by the most powerful party leaders, can compete successfully for nominations, and serious insurgencies are regular fare in presidential politics today. The parties probably maintained their hegemony in American politics because of their willingness to open up. Fringe candidates like Jesse Jackson, Pat Robertson, Pat Buchanan, and Jerry Brown don't have to form third parties in order to stage a run for the White House. They can do so as Republicans or Democrats. They are given a fair shot in the primaries and caucuses. Such candidates, while not winning the race, have made their point and, most importantly, had an important impact on their parties.

Two choices are simply not enough in a country as large and diverse as this one. While the parties once served to limit choice, they are now the vehicles for providing more choices. Obviously, the parties' openness doesn't preclude third-party candidacies (witness Ross Perot's efforts in 1992 and 1996), but it probably has reduced them and enabled the parties to continue their dominance.

There is another benefit to the multitude of choices voters now have in presidential politics. One of the raps against the party leaders was that, left to their own devices, they tended to nominate safe, inoffensive candidates. Today the public benefits from the smorgasbord of choices, some of which may not be safe and inoffensive—which may be what the people want.

The most common criticism of the presidential campaign—perhaps the most common criticism of all of American electoral politics—centers on the burdensome fundraising requirements for prospective candidates. For 2000, candidates may need to raise well over ten million dollars during 1999 in preparation for the primaries. Vice President Gore and Texas governor George Bush intend to try to raise somewhere in the neighborhood of fifty million dollars in 1999. If that kind of money, whether ten million, fifty million, or somewhere in between, is required to compete in the three-week window when most of the delegates will be selected, then the process is not really as open as it used to be.

In the 1970s up through the 1984 campaign, candidates could do well in an early state and have time to raise money for later states based on their new-found notoriety. This possibility probably disappeared in 1988 when frontloading reached a critical point. Of course, the huge obstacles haven't seemed to quell interest in running in 2000, at least on the Republican side (at least ten people seem poised and ready to go). It remains to be seen whether the less endowed ones really have a legitimate chance to win the nomination.

While the presidential race attracts many candidates, even with the incredible financial burdens, it may be that potentially good candidates are discouraged for a different reason. The exhaustive campaigning in the year or more leading up to the race is much harder to do if one is gainfully employed. There are eleven Republicans running in 2000 at this writing. Five have never held public office (and have quit their current line of work in order to run), and two of the remaining six are not currently in office and have been running for president full time for most of the 1990s, in the case of Lamar Alexander, and for at least a few years in the case of Dan Quayle. On the Democratic side, Bill Bradley is not currently in office, and Gore is vice president, which is a position that, to say the least, gives a person considerable flexibility in his pursuits. (The vice president has only one constitutional duty: to preside over the Senate. This is a duty which vice presidents by custom rarely fulfill.) Bill Clinton is the only new president elected since John F. Kennedy who was not either vice president or unemployed before running. There seems to be a distinct advantage to not holding public office if one wants to be president. A committee chair or any powerful member of the House or Senate would have to shirk his work in order to run.

The presidential nomination process rewards a pure, single-minded form of ambition. Candidates must put together great enterprises in order to compete, enterprises that may literally take years to form. It is an open question whether the all-consuming ambition required to get elected is conducive to constitutional government in a system of separated powers and checks and balances. The distinguished political scientist Merle Black once wryly commented that the 25th Amendment to the Constitution stipulated procedures for removing a president who has become unstable or has diminished mental faculties, but anyone who wants to do what it takes to be president has to be crazy.[7]

III. SUMMARY AND CONCLUSION

Presidential nomination politics has dramatically opened up, by necessity, in the last few decades. The opportunity to run is there for anyone in a position to put together a campaign. And the public has been given the responsibility to determine who among the candidates will be the parties' standard-bearers. The parties entrusted the people with this responsibility because they had to, not necessarily because they wanted to. The public demanded openness in presidential nomination politics, and the parties gave it to them. The two parties' hegemony in American politics, and perhaps their very survival, depended on it. This new party system, as described by political scientists Richard Niemi and John Aldrich, is a candidate-centered system in which the parties serve as auxiliary institutions to facilitate and serve the ambitions of the candidates.[8] Two *closed* parties, that maintained control over presidential nomination politics, could not have survived the reform period of the 1960s and early 1970s.

And in some ways we are fortunate that the parties proved so flexible. While the scholarly debates rage on as to exactly why through most of American history two parties have dominated, the fact is that, in the main, this has been a good thing. Politics in democracies is, by its nature, fractious, disputatious, and contentious. Our society is populated by people and groups with differing and sometimes irreconcilable interests—we are probably as diverse as any country in the world. Our parties have a long heritage of accommodating and moderating those differences—that is, moderating our politics. The alternative might be a splintered multi-party system and a debilitating immoderation and divisiveness. The Democrats and Republicans have proven to have the flexibility and vibrancy to accommodate differences, even in the most divisive periods of American history. The open presidential nomination process, for all of its flaws, probably preserved the two-party system.

But there is a price to be paid for this candidate-centered party system. As political scientist Theodore Lowi and others have warned, today's president comes into office strictly on the basis of his own herculean campaign efforts and his own popularity.[9] Our presidents have a purely plebiscitary mandate. Every successful presidential candidate has had to forge his own constituency. He cannot rely on others to bring him across the finish line. He doesn't share his success with anyone.

What this means is that there is no party latticework to save him from a fall; there is no shared responsibility institutionalized in the electoral system as there is in parliamentary systems and as there used to be in the United States. In other countries, the chief executive owes the party for his or her nomination, and the executive's success or failure in office is inextricably intertwined with the party; in the United States, the president has gotten to where he is by the sheer force of his own will and ambition, and he is in many ways alone in having to protect his power and his office. His is a *personal* presidency, as Lowi writes. He is *personally* responsible for his branch of government and even, in the view of many, including all of our recent presidents, the fate of the nation itself.

It is not wise to invest this sort of authority in one man in an office that wields unprecedented power. Lowi, Nelson Polsby, and others believe it would be far preferable if presidential candidates were answerable to elites in their parties during the nomination process.[10] There would then be shared responsibility in the executive branch, a far more stable situation than placing the great burden of the office of the presidency on the shoulders of just one person.

The candidate-centered party system leaves all politicians to fend for themselves. The stakes just happen to be greater for the presidency than for an individual member of the House or for a Senator. But there do not seem to be any realistic prospects for changing the party system. This leaves us with the public determining the candidates. The crucial question is whether the public is in a position to make reasonably good choices among the self-proclaimed contenders.

As it is currently configured, the process is far too frontloaded. Voters, charged with the momentous decision of nominating presidential candidates, simply do not have a reasonable opportunity to consider their options intelligently and thoughtfully. To reduce the risks of uninformed choice, voters must be given both the opportunity to assess the candidates over a longer primary season and the chance in later states to reassess judgments made in early primaries, before people had access to some information and a sufficient opportunity to digest it. Simply put, the parties need to devise rules to spread the primaries more evenly over at least two and preferably three to four months. The multiplicity of candidates and the huge stakes cry out for a more rational process.

It is also important for people to understand the limits to what should be interpreted from the results of states like Iowa and New Hampshire. Candidates often win these events with small pluralities, which may disguise meaningless or deceptive results. At the very least, a process that is less frontloaded can give time for the momentum from early victories to simmer down, and give voters the chance to assess more carefully the results from those states.

In the end, we must recognize that the political parties have evolved in ways that the public likes—in the direction of more access and more openness and more democracy. This has its drawbacks, but it is so deeply in keeping with American political cultural traditions and trends that it is absurd to suggest that we can somehow turn back the clock. A more muscular Congress has proved able, in some circumstances, to rein in presidents who have become too big for their breeches. It would certainly be preferable if so much pressure and power were not centered on one man, but so far our institutions have been up to the task of preserving a reasonable balance.

NOTES

1 John Haskell, *Fundamentally Flawed: Understanding and Reforming Presidential Primaries* (Lanham, MD: Rowman & Littlefield, 1996), p. 12.

2. See Alan Ehrenhalt, *The United States of Ambition* (New York: Times Books, 1991).

3. Haskell, *Fundamentally Flawed*, p. 72.

4. Scholars rediscovered this problem with aggregating voters' preferences in the 1950s. In particular, see Kenneth Arrow, *Social Choice and Individual Values* (New Haven: Yale University Press, 1963) and William Riker, *Liberalism Against Populism* (San Francisco, W.H. Freeman, 1982). For extensive computer simulations exploring this problem, see Samuel Merrill, *Making Multicandidate Elections More Democratic* (Princeton: Princeton University Press, 1988).

5. Larry Bartels, *Presidential Primaries and the Dynamics of Public Choice* (Princeton: Princeton University Press, 1988).

6 Bartels, *Presidential Primaries and the Dynamics of Public Choice.*

7. Informal conversation with Merle Black.

8. John H. Aldrich and Richard G. Niemi, "The Sixth American Party System: Electoral Change, 1952–1992," in Stephen C. Craig, ed., *Broken Contract: Changing Relationships Between Americans and Their Government* (Boulder, CO: Westview Press, 1996), pp. 87–109

9. For a good discussion of the development and the effects of the candidate-centered campaign environment in presidential politics, see Theodore Lowi, *The Personal President* (Ithaca, NY: Cornell University Press, 1985) and James Ceaser, *Presidential Selection* (Princeton: Princeton University Press, 1979).

10. For a thorough examination of the problems presidents may have governing without parties, see Nelson Polsby, *Consequences of Party Reform* (New York: Oxford University Press, 1983).

Money
and Campaigns

Apart from his own time and talents, the volunteers he is able to attract, and whatever free media coverage comes his way, virtually everything else associated with a candidate's run for the presidency will require money—staff, consultants, travel, lodging, headquarters, TV ads, fundraising, polls, speaker systems, buttons, signs, and bumper stickers. Money is, in short, the fuel that drives the engine of election campaigns.

There have been three longstanding concerns about the role of money in elections; namely, that it exerts an undue influence over 1) access to the electoral process, 2) election outcomes, and 3) decisions on public policy. The extent of its influence in each of these areas continues to be the subject of considerable debate.

The first mild attempt to regulate money in elections dates all the way back to 1867, when Congress passed a naval appropriations bill stipulating that no naval officer or federal employee could solicit contributions in the navy yards. The next hundred years were punctuated by the passage of several laws intended in one way or another to curb the influence of money in elections. The seriousness of these efforts is open to question, however, for not only were the enforcement mechanisms weak, but the restrictions themselves left open numerous ways by which resourceful presidential candidates, private citizens, and organizations could circumvent the letter and spirit of the laws. Not until the 1970s did Congress pass legislation that seriously addressed the problem of money in presidential elections. These regulations came in the form of the Revenue Act and the Federal Election Campaign Act (FECA), both passed into law in 1971. In response to the scandals of Watergate, they were followed by amendments to FECA in 1974. Taken together, these statutes

1. limited contributions by individuals and groups
2. established overall spending limits

3. provided for partial public financing of presidential nomination campaigns and full public funding of general election campaigns

4. established an enforcement mechanism (Federal Election Commission) to monitor compliance.

That even these regulations did not achieve all that was hoped for is evident by the spirited calls we now hear for another round of campaign finance reform.

Given the important role that money plays in elections, there is a natural inclination to blame any failed election campaign on insufficient funds. Thus, the first article by Michael Robinson, Clyde Wilcox, and Paul Marshall serves as a useful reminder that such is not always the case. Using the 1988 presidential primaries and general election campaigns as a case study, they argue that other factors often count for more than money and suggest that the influence of money on election outcomes is likely to be determined by how the electoral environment is structured.

For Stanley Brubaker, author of the second article, the FECA reforms of the seventies constituted an overreaction which was partially corrected when the Supreme Court stepped in and ruled unconstitutional the provisions imposing spending limits (*Buckley v. Valeo,* 1976). Fearing that we may be moving toward yet another round of intemperate finance reform, he is at pains to point out that the reformers have not yet made a convincing case that money buys either elections or influence. Furthermore, he argues, the curbs that have already been imposed on spending, far from levelling the playing field, have in fact made it more uneven.

The final article reflects the thinking of The Task Force On Campaign Finance Reform, a group created by The Citizens' Research Foundation. In the judgment of these ten scholars, the regulation of money in campaigns is essential but the finance reforms of the seventies are no longer up to the task. In the last fifteen years, campaigns have seen new sources of money and new players who, under the current laws, are regulated little, if at all. As a consequence, there has been an important loss of accountability in the system. In addition, previous reforms have had the unintended consequence of stifling electoral competition rather than encouraging it. The Task Force proposes a number of reforms as correctives, while recognizing that the regulations cannot be made so onerous as to force spenders to go outside the system.

The Presidency: Not for Sale

Michael Robinson, Clyde Wilcox, and Paul Marshall

It's been twenty years since Joe McGinniss first stunned us with his best-selling book, *The Selling of the President.* McGinniss's thesis was simple enough: that political advertising on television had somehow fooled Americans into believing that the Old Nixon of the early 1950s was the New Nixon of the late 1960s. In other words, candidates could buy the presidency by buying television time.

Back in McGinniss's day, money, television, and the campaign industry were already considered slightly sinister. But people generally felt them to be low-grade evils that could be overcome or reformed. Today, that is no longer the case. Money, paid media, and the campaign consultants who orchestrate the two have become *the* national political boogeyman.

Certain types of people are especially likely to be spooked. Losers, for example, invariably blame their defeats on not having had enough money or enough money at the right time. Liberals have always had a special problem with the power of money in all phases of politics. And when losers turn out to be liberals, money and paid media can take on Mephistophelean proportions. In November of 1988 Democrats were willing to believe that the money spent on Roger Ailes and his ads was responsible for George Bush's defeat of Michael Dukakis. In fact, everybody seemed to buy the money-to-vote (MTV) theory as the explanation for Campaign '88. It is true that every candidate needs some money to get started and then more money to prove that he or she's serious. But it would be a mistake to explain the relationship between 1988's candidates and the public by emphasizing money.

Whatever else may have moved voters during the '88 election, it wasn't money *per se.* In fact, our evidence suggests the opposite. The data show that paid media had practically no effect on the race; that campaign expenditures had no greater effect on primaries in 1988 than they had in 1984; that old-fashioned political variables like "home state," "region," and "race" explained more than dollars and cents did. On only one day, and in one party, did money seem to matter.

Source: Michael Robinson, Clyde Wilcox, and Paul Marshall, "The Presidency: Not for Sale," *Public Opinion,* 12 (March/April 1989), pp. 49–53.

Michael Robinson, now retired, was formerly director of the Media Analysis Project at George Washington University and coauthor of *Over the Wire And On TV.* Paul Marshall is a professor of political science and currently with the Institute of Christian Studies, Toronto, Ontario. Clyde Wilcox is a professor of political science at Georgetown University and coauthor of *Serious Money.*

THE MONEY-TO-VOTE THEORY: THE POWER OF MTV IN AUTUMN

How does one measure the power of money-to-voting? It isn't easy. Since 1976 the government has been making it difficult to measure the impact of money in the general election; since then, the federal government has given equal amounts of money to each major party candidate. With everybody getting the same number of dollars, there's no simple way to show how dollars influence the vote.

The fall '88 campaign does provide an interesting test of an important corollary to MTV: paid media *per se*—political advertising—determines vote. In fact, after the '88 campaign ended, pundits insisted that it was George Bush's paid media that made the real difference. Specific ads notwithstanding, we can say that spending *per se* by the Bush campaign on all those ads explains almost nothing about what happened in the polls.

Using KRC/American Political Network daily polling data from the general campaign, and using figures provided by the Bush campaign about how much was spent week by week on ads, we've looked at the statistical relationship between dollars spent and position in the polls for September, October, and the first week in November. We found precious little evidence to support the theory that Bush won votes on the basis of his ads, and practically no evidence that he won votes on the basis of his advertising expenditures.

We correlated Bush's week-by-week paid media buys with four measures of how the race was going in the polls. We correlated the *size* (in dollars) of Bush's weekly ad campaign with: (a) the percent of voters supporting Bush week by week; (b) the percent of voters supporting Dukakis week by week; (c) the *difference* in support for these two candidates week by week; and (d) the *change in the difference* between the two candidates week by week. Overall, the amount Bush spent on all his great ads bore little, if any, relationship with the conditions of the race. The numbers show that Bush's victory cannot be credited to his paid-media effort or campaign.

A correlation measures the extent to which two things change together. Typically, a correlation coefficient can range from as "high" as 1.0 (or −1.0) to as "low" as zero. The "larger" the number (positive or negative), the greater the relationship between the two things (a correlation of 0.00 means no patterned relationship exists between the two factors). So, if Bush's paid media had had much impact on voters, we'd expect to find a large positive correlation between Bush's expenditures for his advertising and the various measures of his support.

But it doesn't work out that way. There is a correlation, week by week, between Bush's paid-media effort and the percentage of those planning to vote for him. The coefficient is +.30, statistically insignificant yet still noteworthy. But that correlation is actually *lower* than the correlation between Bush's paid-media expenditures and the percent of voters intending to vote for Dukakis (+ .35). In other words, using correlation as the test, the more Bush spent on his great media campaign, the *higher* was Dukakis's position in the polls.

The best test of paid-media impact is the correlation between Bush dollars and the difference between Bush and Dukakis support week by week. The correlation between these two factors is .0036, which rounds to zero. No single finding leaves us as unconvinced about the power of paid media as this one—a correlation of zero between the dollar size of Bush's ad campaign and the size of the lead he enjoyed over Dukakis.

An *inverse* relationship existed between Bush's effort and the change in the difference of the size of the lead. When Bush spent more in one week than he had in the previous week, the size of his lead actually grew smaller. In the end the correlations say that Bush's ad campaign was not the major factor in his victory and that money isn't everything in politics, or even close.

THE GENERAL ELECTION

History can make the same point about the influence of money and paid media on the general election.

Because Dukakis formally won his nomination in July of '88, he had a full month's federal funding advantage over George Bush for his fall campaign. Bush, by law, wasn't entitled to his federal money until the end of August.

In fact, some pundits thought that the money advantage might give Dukakis a good chance to expand his post-convention lead over Bush. But Dukakis's lead fell even before the Republican convention. Money proved practically worthless as stories about Dukakis's mental health ate away at his advantage.

Data from the Bush campaign also show that Bush waited until mid-September to start his paid-media effort after he had overcome his fifteen-point deficit in the mid-summer polls. The ad campaign came *after* Bush had taken the lead.

THE PRIMARIES

What about the primaries?

For many reasons it's easy to imagine that big money and paid media might be more powerful in the spring than in the fall. But it didn't happen that way in 1988. What the general election has now revealed about the power of paid media in autumn, the primary campaign tells us about the power of big money early on. Even in primary campaigns money doesn't talk, at least not loudly.

The primaries provide a direct test of the MTV hypothesis: the Federal Election Commission (FEC) keeps close tabs on how much money each candidate spends, by state; and candidates themselves choose to spend different amounts of money among the several states. Although methodological problems also exist with this approach—candidates often fudge on their FEC reports, for example—looking at how much each candidate spent in each caucus or primary and then looking to see how well he did in those campaigns is a good test of the power of money.

THE WINNERS AND LOSERS OF WINTER TO SPRING

MTV was a bigger issue in the primaries than it was in the general election. The specter of MTV set the terms for most of the political questions that were raised back then. "How long can Dole hang on in the campaign now that his money is drying up?" "How far could Jesse Jackson have gone had he had serious financial support from the outset?" "Would Robertson's ready access to money from his evangelical base make him an honest-to-goodness threat?"

What did money really do during the primaries? If money had talked, monied candidates should have won more than the unmonied. But they didn't. As in 1984 the unmonied won more often, and in the more important states.

Consider first those primary or caucus states in which there was a serious dollar effort by *any* candidate—where "serious" is defined as 10 percent of the FEC spending limit for that state. The Democrats—or at least one Democrat—met that test in twenty-seven primary and caucus contests. The Republicans—or a Republican—made a serious effort in thirty-three states. (See table 1)

Setting aside states where the two biggest money people spent equal amounts or where the vote totals were tied among the top two vote getters, there were sixty state contests that had a big spender. And in those sixty big media contests, the big spender won twenty-six times—43 percent of the time.

Given that the average primary or caucus had more than three contestants, one could say that big spenders did better than expected. But they did not do very well— better than chance, but not much better.

Back in 1984 the big spender won 38 percent of the time—slightly less than big spenders were able to achieve in 1988. These two figures are. in fact, statistically almost the same: two victories out of five for the big spender in 1984; two victories out of five for the big spender in 1988. If money is becoming more powerful in determining primary elections, its power is growing slowly enough to be explained by rounding.

Table 1 also contains a delicious irony: although big money had little effect on the Republican primary campaign, it seems to have had some noteworthy effect on the Democratic one.

For the Republicans, starting in Iowa and moving on until Dole's withdrawal from the race, the big spender's success rate was only 36 percent, about what's expected from chance alone in a three-person race. But for the Democrats, the figure was 52 percent—not exactly indicative of money-to-vote politics, but a substantially higher percentage than that for the GOP.

The "party factor" is especially intriguing in those few states where a case can be made that the victory was "bought." A bought state is one in which the big spender outspent his closest competitor by a factor of at least two-to-one and then went on to win the state.

In a few primaries and caucuses, one could argue that money did buy votes in sufficient number to turn a loser into a winner. Excluding home states and those states where nobody made a serious dollar effort, a clear pattern emerges: eight states were "bought" during the primaries, seven by Democrats (Minnesota, Vermont, Maine, Florida, Maryland, Oklahoma, and Kentucky) and only one by a Republican (Connecticut). Even though big spending seems to have made a difference in these, it doesn't contradict our thesis that the MTV theory doesn't hold up. For one thing, our definition of a bought state is shaky. We assume that if the winner outspent his opponents by two to one, then money made the difference. But in a state like Connecticut,

TABLE 1   *Spending and Results: The Republicans*

	Big Spender	Winner	$ Expended by . . . Big spender	Winner (in thousands)	Winner's spending as a percentage of big spender's spending
AL	Dole	Bush	216	88	41%
AK	Bush	Bush	86	86	100
CO	Robertson	Bush	132	102	77
CT	Bush	Bush	143	143	100
FL	Bush	Bush	1118	1118	100
GA	Dole	Bush	291	253	87
HI	Bush	Robertson	86	46	53
IL	Dole	Bush	1098	797	73
IA		TIED EXPENDITURES*			
KS	Dole	Dole	309	309	100
KY	Bush	Bush	115	115	100
LA	Robertson	Bush	259	158	66
ME	Bush	Bush	167	167	100
MD	Dole	Bush	275	115	42
MS	Dole	Bush	1004	906	90
MI	Bush	Bush	976	976	100
MN	Dole	Dole	655	655	100
MS	Bush	Bush	188	188	100
MO	Dole	Bush	423	319	76
NV	Robertson	Bush	98	18	18
NH		TIED EXPENDITURES*			
NC	Dole	Bush	705	204	29
OK	Dole	Bush	306	181	59
RI	Dole	Bush	78	66	85
SC	Bush	Bush	581	581	100
SD	Dole	Dole	253	253	100
TN	Dole	Bush	268	116	43
TX	Robertson	Bush	961	421	44
VT	Dole	Bush	140	105	75
VA	Robertson	Bush	302	55	18
WI	Bush	Bush	140	140	100
WY		TIED VOTE**			
WA	Dole	Robertson	343	100	29

*Winner and big spender spent identical amounts.

**Dole and Bush received same number of votes.

continued

TABLE 1 *Spending and Results: The Democrats (cont.)*

	Big Spender	Winner	$ Expended by... Big spender	Winner (in thousands)	Winner's spending as a percentage of big spender's spending
AL	Gore	Jackson	226	26	12%
AK	Gore	Gore	124	124	100
DC	Dukakıs	Jackson	97	47	48
FL	Dukakis	Dukakis	738	738	100%
GA	Gore	Jackson	239	45	19
IL	Dukakis	Simon	458	321	70
IA		TIED EXPENDITURES*			
KY	Gore	Gore	120	120	100
ME	Dukakis	Dukakis	168	168	100
MD	Dukakis	Dukakis	245	245	100
MA	Dukakis	Dukakis	272	272	100
MI	Gephardt	Jackson	464	78	17
MN	Dukakis	Dukakis	547	547	100
MS	Gore	Jackson	90	22	24
MO	Gephardt	Gephardt	283	283	100
NE	Dukakis	Dukakıs	116	116	100
NH		TIED EXPENDITURES*			
NJ	Dukakis	Dukakis	392	392	100
NY	Gore	Dukakis	980	937	96
NC	Goıe	Gore	355	355	100
OK	Gore	Gore	159	159	100
PA	Jackson	Dukakis	320	305	95
SC	Gore	Jackson	114	41	36
SD	Dukakis	Gephardt	235	101	43
TX(P)	Dukakis	Dukakıs	1069	1069	100
TX(C)	Dukakis	Jackson	1069	74	7
VT	Dukakis	Dukakis	74	74	100
VA	Gore	Jackson	216	21	10
WI	Gore	Dukakıs	516	311	60
WY	Gore	Gore	89	89	100

Note: Texas had a "meaningful" caucus, and a primary. We have included figures for both. Jackson won the caucuses, Dukakis won the primary.

*Winner and big spender spent identical amounts.

one could also attribute Bush's victory over Dole to something other than money—confusion over whether or not Bush was a favorite son, for example. (It sometimes seemed as if most states were his home states.) And two of Dukakis's big-money victories—Maine and Vermont—and Gore's victory in Kentucky could just as easily be explained by regional loyalties as by comparative dollar advantage.

We've identified more than fifty races in which a victory was *not* bought. In thirteen state elections, outspending one's nearest opponent by at least a factor of *two* did not lead to victory. So, once again the MTV thesis falls on its face.

But despite qualifications, the irony remains: the party that has spoken out most against the evils of money in politics is also the party more likely to be influenced by it.

SUPER TUESDAY EFFECTS

Why are Democrats more dollar-sensitive than Republicans? This is best explained structurally—the way the race was organized this time.

The Democratic campaign had an unusual *non*-structure. It had *no* clear front-runner, *no* central issue around which to fight, *no* national incumbent, and *no* palpable issue space between the candidates involved. What the Democrats did have, however, was Super Tuesday. The interaction between these structural factors—the factors they lacked plus Super Tuesday—best explains why the Democrats turned out to be the party of MTV.

If one excludes Super Tuesday states, Democratic voters turn out to be almost as impervious to dollar politics as the Republican electorate. Without Super Tuesday the won/lost ratio for Democratic big spenders is 43 percent, identical to the overall ratio in the primary campaign. On Super Tuesday, however, Democratic big spenders won in 62 percent of the states, a figure high enough to suggest *real* money-to-vote power.

Incredibly enough, for the Republicans it was precisely the opposite. For Bush, Dole, and Robertson, dollar politics had far less effect on Super Tuesday than it had throughout much of the primary campaign. The big spender won in only 24 percent of the Republican contests held on Super Tuesday. On Super Tuesday Dole outspent Bush practically everywhere—in three times as many states as Bush outspent him. Yet Dole lost everywhere.

Among Republicans there was not a single case of "state buying" on Super Tuesday, but lots of examples of states that were not for sale. In Maryland Dole outspent Bush three to one, and Bush wound up with about twice as many votes. In Alabama Pat Robertson outspent Bush by a factor of three and received about one-fifth the popular vote going to the vice president. NOT FOR SALE signs went up in Texas, Oklahoma, North Carolina, and Tennessee—all states in which the big spender outspent his closest opponent by a factor of at least two and still came away a loser.

By Super Tuesday the GOP field had been reduced to two men with fairly well-developed images, both of whom had been national figures for at least a dozen years. In a campaign like that, money per se should have meant very little. Indeed, with all the press attention focusing on Dole and Bush, one might have predicted that the power of money would have been even less than normal, with news overwhelming money and ads as a principal cue for voting. That's precisely what happened.

For the Democrats everything was different. The field was unstructured and the press corps was hard-pressed to cover the four leading, but relatively unknown, candidates. With no real structure—and with so little press attention on each candidate—money should have had more impact than usual. And it did.

WHAT MATTERS MORE?

If MTV didn't determine the outcome of the primaries, and if paid media didn't matter much in the general campaign, then what did matter from spring to fall? The answer is traditional politics.

In the fall, an incumbent party nominated a sitting vice president, who ran during a period of peace and prosperity. And . . . that guy won. Traditional politics.

In the spring, traditional politics also prevailed. Favorite sons—native sons—won everywhere. Dole in Kansas. Gore in Tennessee. Gephardt in Missouri Jackson in South Carolina. Simon in Illinois. And Bush in . . . well, Bush won everywhere he claimed as home. Regionalism worked as well. Gore did best in his center-South, Dukakis in New England, and Jackson in the Deep South.

Race worked, too. Jackson received black votes everywhere he went— in enormous proportions. And he won in Puerto Rico, the Virgin Islands, and D.C.—everywhere blacks were a majority of the Democratic party. So compared to the old standbys like place of birth, region, and race, money was a weak factor.

CONCLUSIONS

In certain circumstances, money does matter in an election, although those circumstances are exceptional. It almost never matters during a general election campaign. The laws of campaign funding and the laws of electoral behavior pretty much ensure that. But during the race for the nomination, it *might* matter: if there is no incumbent, if there are no real policy-related differences among the candidates, if the field of contestants is unrecognized or unrecognizable, or if times are unusually quiescent or divisive. But that's a lot of ifs—and anything other than normal circumstances.

Our last conclusion is that once again the spirit of reform has turned out to be, if not an evil spirit, at least a poltergeist. The issue here is Super Tuesday. Super Tuesday failed to achieve its original goal—the nomination of a conservative (Southern) Democrat. It also gave us the worst of both worlds—worlds in which money counted *too* much among the Democrats, and in which *nothing* counted much among the Republicans.

In the end, then, the problem in Campaign '88 wasn't so much the miseries of money as it was the vagaries of reform. Money didn't do nearly as much damage to the recruitment system as did Super Tuesday. In fact, the Super Tuesday system was the only thing that gave money anything approaching the power most critics assigned to it. So once again, it wasn't big-time money that made presidential politics seem scary or irrational; it was big-time reform.

The Limits of Campaign Spending Limits

Stanley C. Brubaker

Political indignation engenders constitutional excess. Such was the case in 1974 when Congress, hot with anger over Watergate, delivered a beating to First Amendment rights with a set of new provisions to the Federal Election Campaign Act (FECA). The original 1971 act had already set limits on how much of his own money a federal candidate could spend on his own campaign. The new provisions limited how much that campaign as a whole could spend as well as how much any individual or organization working independently to promote a candidate could spend. But, in the 1976 case of *Buckley v. Valeo,* the Supreme Court declared each of these limits on campaign spending unconstitutional.

The *Buckley* court drew a sharp distinction between FECA's limits on campaign spending and its limits on campaign contributions. Contributions, the Court reasoned, convey only a "general expression of support" for a candidate, so limits to them pose no grave threat to free speech (as long as the limits are not so stringent as to prevent one from "amassing the resources necessary for effective advocacy"); further, the danger of corruption or the appearance of corruption posed by unlimited contributions the Court thought significant. Accordingly, it upheld FECA's limits on contributions to campaigns, parties, and political action committees (PACs).

Limits on spending, the Court argued, were an entirely different matter. By restricting how much money an individual, group, or campaign could spend, these laws would restrict "the number of issues discussed, the depth of their exploration, and the size of the audience reached." Further, "these restrictions, while neutral as to the ideas expressed, [would] limit political expression 'at the core of our electoral process and of the First Amendment freedoms.'" Finally, "corruption," the rationale by which the Court upheld limits on contributions, holds little meaning for spending. A candidate cannot corrupt himself by contributing generously to his own campaign. Nor can a campaign corrupt itself by spending a lot of money. And it is barely more plausible to imagine that an individual or group, working independently of the candidate without any coordination of strategy, could corrupt the candidate by advocating his election.

Perhaps anticipating the Court's rejection of the corruption rationale, the government had offered another: Spending limits, it argued, were necessary to "equalize" the ability of individuals and groups to influence the election. This the Court quickly dismissed: "The concept that government may restrict the speech of some elements of our society in order to enhance the relative voice of others is wholly foreign to the

Source: Stanley C. Brubaker. "The Limits of Campaign Spending Limits," *The Public Interest,* 133 (Fall 1988), pp. 33–54.

Stanley C. Brubaker is professor of political science at Colgate University and director of Colgate's Washington Study Group Program.

First Amendment, which was designed to secure 'the widest possible dissemination of information from diverse and antagonistic sources,' and 'to assure unfettered interchange of ideas.'" On this general point, only Justice White dissented.

THE REFORMERS' BRIEF

Today, in the wake of assorted abuses in the 1996 elections, so-called reformers seek to rekindle the scattered embers of cynicism and distrust into a fiery indignation that will sweep in a new regimen of campaign-finance laws. *Buckley* stands as a firewall, limiting such efforts. Some reformers hope to slip past the ban on spending limits by following a route opened by *Buckley* itself when it upheld the system of public funding for presidential elections; that is, though spending limits may not be imposed, candidates may choose to accept them voluntarily—in exchange for certain benefits. Thus, in the legislation urged by Senators John McCain and Russell Feingold, candidates were to be bribed with free TV and postage into accepting spending limits.

But, for more ardent reformers, such proposals are tepid; real change requires the elimination of *Buckley* and its ban on spending limits. That can be achieved in only two ways. One is to change the Constitution. This is the strategy pursued by Senate Minority Leader Tom Daschle and House Minority Leader Richard Gephardt, both of whom made a constitutional amendment permitting Congress and the states to set "reasonable limits" on campaign spending one of their top priorities in the 105th Congress. (It was solidly defeated in the Senate 38 to 61 and appears unlikely to come to the floor in the House.) The other is to have *Buckley* overruled as wrongly decided.

The effort to reverse *Buckley* has an extended front. Attorneys General and Secretaries of State representing 33 states have joined as amicus curiae in a pair of Ohio cases meant to challenge *Buckley*. Joining them are the National Voting Rights Institute in Boston and the Brennan Center for Justice at New York University Law School, both of which are also devoting substantial resources to turning the public against *Buckley*. Over 200 law professors have also signed a petition sponsored by the Brennan Center declaring that *Buckley* was wrongly decided. Even the Clinton administration—giving fresh currency to the old adage that when you're about to get run out of town on a rail, dash to the front and make it look like a parade—has decided, according to the *New York Times,* to ask the Court to reverse *Buckley*.

The tenor, factual premises, and philosophical bearings of this assault on *Buckley* are epitomized in what has become a galvanizing article, "The Curse of American Politics," by legal philosopher Ronald Dworkin. Published in the *New York Review of Books,* in 1996, and widely disseminated by the Brennan Center, the article made several claims, most rather familiar: Today's unlimited campaign spending generates a relentless pursuit of money by politicians, a vast inequality of influence, and a grossly unfair advantage to candidates able to raise lots of money (usually incumbents) or to wealthy candidates able to use their own resources. Thus bad candidates or ideas beat out good ones because the former are heavily bankrolled.

Further, the indictment continues, unlimited spending lies at the root of other problems plaguing American democracy: "Negative, witless, and condescending" campaign ads result from too much money in the hands of candidates. If candidates were sharply limited in their spending, they would have to rely on reporters or events sponsored by nonpartisan groups to get out their message. This plague afflicting American politics can be lifted, Dworkin concludes, only if *Buckley* is reversed. And it should be, he and his fellow reformers argue, because the case was based on a misunderstanding of the fundamental premises of the First Amendment as well as American democracy.

But Dworkin's call, as well as that of others, for campaign-spending limits, relies on a simplistic and distorted view of the role money plays in American politics. Worse, it would insinuate a pernicious premise into the very foundations of our constitutional system.

THE COST OF CAMPAIGNS

Do campaigns cost too much? Campaign costs have indeed risen rapidly over the last several decades. For federal elections, the expenditures grew, in constant dollars, two-and-one-half fold in the two decades prior to the FECA laws of 1974 and an additional threefold in the two decades following it.[1] As the figures suggest, the rise has been fairly long term, but it has not been constant and has never been "out of control," at least no more than it has been in the past. Campaigns are contests, after all, and contestants have always sought the most effective way of gaining the voters' assent, even when this borders on the distasteful. Thus James Madison found it necessary to open the customary rum keg in his election to the state legislature; Whigs to appeal to the less educated voter in their contests with Jacksonian Democrats; and all presidential candidates since Woodrow Wilson to "run" for president rather than to "stand."

Several factors lie behind the escalating costs of elections, most notably the growth in voting population (up 39 percent since 1974), the expanding scope of government, the increasing level of competition in the races, and the changing means and conditions of effective campaigning. For the better part of the twentieth century, the scope of government has grown considerably, affecting an increasing number of interests. As a result, the stakes are greater, as are the differences between the parties and the candidates. In the last several years, the competitiveness of electoral contests—surely a sign of health in a democracy—has also increased. This was especially the case in 1996, since the Democratic lock on the House of Representatives had been broken, as had the Republican lock on the presidency.

Equally important have been the costly advantages afforded by radio and television advertising, the reliance on direct mail, and the supplanting of party volunteers by expensive professionals. Not only are there fewer volunteers to ring doorbells, but home dwellers today are less likely to welcome strangers at the door who tell them how they should cast their ballots. Ads and mailings, while perhaps not always welcome and certainly more expensive, are less irksome. Further, a candidate's ads must compete not only with those of his opponent but with the plethora of commercial and other nonpolitical ads that flood the mail and airwaves, each one pleading for attention. Simply to be noticed against this general din is an expensive undertaking. Finally, it costs money to raise money and to comply with the myriad rules and regulations now surrounding campaign finance. None of these more expensive methods of campaigning would be used if experience had not taught that they work in gaining the voter's support.

All told, $2.2 billion dollars were spent in the 1995–96 election cycle in campaigns for the House, Senate, and presidency.[2] That's a lot of money, but in what sense is it too much? It's less than half of what Americans spent on perfume and cologne over the same period. It equals $11.25 per eligible voter for the two-year election cycle. If recent patterns hold, it's comparable to what other democracies spend either on a per voter basis or as a percent of Gross Domestic Product. But most importantly—setting aside corporate and union contributions to "nonfederal," i.e., soft-money, accounts—it is no more than what individuals, on a voluntary basis, acting alone or through PACs, under the limits established by FECA, have decided to make available to the candidates.

STARVED FOR FUNDS?

Though the "costs too much" thesis is hard to credit in itself, it is used by reformers as the basis for several more plausible charges: Desperate for cash, candidates become vulnerable to, and hence corruptible by, well-endowed special interests; they are forced to spend too much time raising the necessary funds; good people with good ideas are discouraged from running; and wealthy candidates gain an unfair advantage.

Setting aside for the moment the "vulnerable/corruptible" charge, we acknowledge the seriousness of the other problems. They appear to result, however, not from too much money but too little—more specifically, from restrictions in the supply of campaign funds imposed by FECA reforms. By these rules, unchanged since 1974, an individual can contribute only $1,000 to a candidate per election, and a PAC can give only $5,000. Given that the average successful candidate for Congress spent $673,500 in the 1996 elections, it is not surprising that candidates complain of having to spend too much time on the rubber-chicken circuit raising money. Likewise, good people stay out of politics not so much because of the absolute cost of a campaign as the onerous burdens of raising money in this manner.

Similarly, the current advantage enjoyed by wealthy candidates may result less from the high costs of campaigns than the difficulties less affluent candidates face in raising funds. Were it not for the contribution limits of 1974, it has been widely remarked, publisher Steve Forbes, a political novice, might well have placed his considerable sums behind former congressman Jack Kemp rather than his own candidacy in the 1996 presidential contest. Contrast this contemporary regimen of contribution limits with the prereform days, when Senator Eugene J. McCarthy mounted his historic challenge to President Lyndon B. Johnson in the spring of 1968. McCarthy had not needed to canvass the nation for small contributions during the preceding years. And, in any case, Johnson's policy in Vietnam was not at that point objectionable to McCarthy. As it happened, McCarthy gained the backing of Stewart Mott (heir to the General Motors fortune) and Jack Dreyfus, Jr. (a Wall Street banker), whose hefty donations allowed him to get his message out in New Hampshire, delivering a mortal electoral blow to the president.

Inflation provides further reason to believe that the problems result from restrictions in the supply of money, not an "excessive" demand for it. General inflation has reduced the value of contributions to less than a third of what they were worth in 1974; just to keep even, individual contribution limits would need to be raised to $3,000 per election, and PAC contributions to $15,000. But, in addition to general inflation, there has been a more specific campaign inflation. If we use the standard "basket of goods" concept to measure inflation and consider the basket in question to contain a winning campaign for a seat in the House of Representatives, we find that campaign inflation has itself reduced the value of a contribution to roughly a fourth of what it was in 1974. Combining general inflation with campaign specific inflation, we find roughly a twelvefold increase in the cost of campaigns. Thus what $1,000 contributed to a successful House campaign in 1996, as a fraction of that campaign's total cost ($673,500), took only $83 to provide in 1974 (when such a campaign cost $56,500); or what a $1,000 contribution provided in 1974 would take $11,900 to provide today. Though one would be rash to conclude that raising money for a winning campaign has become nearly 12 times more difficult than it was in 1974, one would be willfully blind to ignore restrictions on the supply of money as a source of our problems.

Indeed, it is in light of the restrictions on the supply of money within the system of regulated contributions that we should understand the feverish search for "loopholes," especially soft money.[3] Though soft money accounts for only 12 percent of total campaign expenditures, it underlies virtually all the alleged abuses of any moment in the 1996 elections. The magnitude of many of these contributions, as well as the manner of their solicitation, might justify a limited reform. But the critical point is that this money assumed the unusual importance it did largely because of the difficulty of raising money under the FECA rules.

DOES MONEY BUY ELECTIONS?

What of the claim, set aside above, that money corrupts politicians made vulnerable by the high cost of campaigns? Reformers assume that money buys elections and influence. This claim might appear to have merit. Consider, for instance, the following figures released by the Center for Responsive Politics the day after the 1996 elections: The candidate who spent more money won nine times out of ten in the House of Representatives; eight times out of ten in the Senate. The figures are even more impressive for incumbents. Those who spent more than their opponent won in 95 percent of the races in both the House and the Senate. And in open seats, the top spender still won twice as often as the lower spender. On closer examination, however, there is reason to doubt that the influence of money is either as decisive or sinister as the reformers would claim.

While it is impossible to sort out with precision the independent effect of money among the many other factors affecting congressional elections—e.g., the issues, the quality of the candidates, political parties, state of the economy, incumbency, scandals, and so forth—there can be no doubt that money helps. Indeed, as the *Buckley* Court pointed out, political speech, effective campaigns, and hence self-government would be impossible without it. But the lines of causation are complex and the magnitude of impact varied. For simplicity, I will focus on the House, since the uniform size of its electoral districts, biannual elections, and larger number of seats makes for better comparisons.

To begin with, while money helps to create a strong candidacy, it is the strong candidate who attracts money. A person of intelligence, accomplishment, and political experience, attractive and well-spoken, able to communicate a clear vision that connects with the hopes, fears, and aspirations of the electorate—such a person will attract financial support for many of the same reasons that he or she is likely to attract votes. In a study of challengers in the 1978 House elections, political scientists Donald Philip Green and Jonathan S. Krasno developed an eight-point scale based on such considerations as whether the candidate had previously run for or held political office, whether he was a celebrity or well-connected politically. The authors found a robust relation between the quality of a candidate and his ability to raise money. Challengers with quality scores of 6 or 7 (none in their study attained an 8) were 15 times more likely to raise over $100,000 than those with scores of 0 or 1. (For context, it should be noted that the average incumbent spent $110,000 on his campaign in 1978.) Conversely, of those who rated 6 or 7, not one raised less than $10,000, while such was the case for nearly half of those rating 0 or 1.

If we define a strong candidate as one most likely to win election to the House, we are talking primarily not about challengers, of course, but incumbents—over 90 percent of whom typically win reelection. Since incumbents also outspend their opponents by large margins—nearly three to one over the last decade—reformers conclude that money buys elections. The candidates are "strong," they would claim, primarily because they can outspend their opponents.

In fact, the evidence indicates that the strength of the incumbents has little to do with money. House incumbents were winning elections in excess of 90 percent well before expensive campaigns became a prominent feature of American politics (the incumbent reelection rate averaged 91.7 percent from 1950 to 1970). Quite apart from their ability to raise money, incumbents hold several electoral advantages over challengers, including their ability to send mail free to their constituents, provide them with services and "pork," develop friendly relations with the local media (which unlike the national media, rely on their own congressmen for newsworthy stories), and gain publicity by sponsoring legislation and conducting investigations.

Further, although incumbents raise and spend a lot more money than challengers, it doesn't seem to help them all that much. Campaign efforts, whether monetary or otherwise, are not immune to the law of diminishing returns. Most incumbents enter their campaigns with so much publicity and good will already gained by simple virtue of their incumbency that the additional benefits of campaign spending are small. Indeed, some incumbents spend remarkably little in winning. Congressman William Natcher spent next to nothing on his elections over the 40 years that he represented Kentucky ($6,609 in his final election in 1992). Senator William Proxmire did spend nothing in his final election, in 1982, and only $697 in his preceding election. Few, of course, are willing to go that far in testing the advantage of incumbency. And their reluctance is not irrational. A large "war chest," itself an indication of electoral prowess and prestige, might scare away challengers. And even though the marginal return in electoral support may be slender for the last dollars spent, this may well be the margin of victory in a close race.

Campaign money is worth far more in the hands of challengers, who need it to gain name recognition and positive publicity. Though challengers need money more than do incumbents, they have more trouble raising it. Part of the difficulty comes from the mediocre quality of many challengers. But even a quality challenger will find it hard to gain enough money to run a credible race against an incumbent. While people often give a candidate their vote regardless of his chances of victory, they are more reluctant to give him their money unless he has a decent chance of winning. Thus a vicious cycle sets in: Quality candidates become reluctant to challenge the incumbent, because the grueling sacrifices of fundraising and campaigning are unlikely to be rewarded with victory. Weaker candidates are set in their place; yet they attract even less money; and their weaknesses only serve to increase the incumbent's margin of victory, making it even less likely that first-rate candidates will challenge the incumbent in the future. Disclosure laws add further spin to the cycle, as would-be backers are deterred from advertising to an incumbent their support for a challenger.

Thus we can see that the money-buys-elections theory is not only simplistic but that the proposed "solution" of limiting spending would be perverse. Because money is worth so much more in the hands of challengers, limits on spending (unless set so high as to be ineffectual) would almost certainly further ensconce incumbents. Competitive elections can be furthered by freeing the flow of money to challengers, not by constraining it.

DOES MONEY BUY INFLUENCE?

But if the "money buys elections" thesis is simplistic and the solution of limits perverse—at least as far as furthering competition for office—what about the claim that "money buys influence"? To make their case, reformers point to the many instances where a congressman votes in a way that furthers the interest of a group that has contributed financially to his campaign. From this, they infer that votes follow money, that money buys influence. But logically, the relation could be the reverse; the money could be following the votes. That is, the contributors could be helping the congressman who favors their cause for reasons independent of the contribution—e.g., the interests of his constituency, party politics, personal philosophy, or political ambition.

If we look more closely at the evidence, we see that "political support," rather than "influence buying," best explains contributions. Most money for House candidates (and even more so for Senate candidates) comes from individuals. We know something about who gives—they tend to have higher levels of education and higher incomes; they are more interested in politics, and more likely to see distinctions between the parties than the average American—but we know little about their motivations. We do know that in 1996 small donations (giving less than $200) accounted for a larger share of total federal campaign contributions than did large donations (30.6 percent versus 25 percent), though in the House and Senate races, large donations typically edge out small ones. Since the maximum that an individual may contribute to a candidate is $1,000 per election—or $2,000 per election cycle (primary plus general election)—a so-called large donor could contribute less than one-third of 1 percent of the funds for a winning House race and only four one-hundredths of 1 percent for an average winning Senate race. At that rate, motivations for buying influence are implausible or deluded. Thus, as an ongoing study by political scientists John Green, Paul Herrnson, Lynda Powell, and Clyde Wilcox shows, donors are far more likely to give for ideological reasons.

We can speculate somewhat more confidently about the motivations of PACs, focusing on ideological, labor, corporate, and trade-association PACs. Ideological PACs, of course, give almost entirely to back their friends, not to woo their enemies; indeed, they raise money largely by showing how evil the latter are. Labor PACs too give almost entirely to those with whom they are ideologically attuned. (The $35 million that the AFL-CIO spent attacking 75 House candidates indicates labor's preferred method of dealing with those they oppose.)

With corporate and trade-association PACs, the story is more complicated. Although there is considerable diversity among these PACs, one would expect them to align more with Republicans than Democrats—and, with open seats, that is nearly always the case. But since the early 1980s, among incumbents, these PACs typically favor the party in charge. This is especially true in the House, where in every election from 1978 until 1996, save one (1982), corporate and trade-association PACs gave more to Democrats than to Republicans. When the Republicans took charge of the House after the 1994 elections, corporate and trade PACs adjusted accordingly, but not without significant hedging as they tried to anticipate the next election. Thus, when Republicans were saddled with the blame for the government shutdown, the flow of money began to revert toward the Democrats, only to shift again as the election neared and the GOP's prospects began to brighten.

In this instance, where some distance separates how the congressman might otherwise behave and how the contributor wishes him to behave, there is room for "influence peddling." But who is influencing whom? Though journalists casually throw out the terms "bribery" and "extortion," we should note that these terms point in different directions of influence. In the case of bribery, the contributor has the upper hand: he has the money that the congressman needs and, in exchange for it, gains a benefit that otherwise would not be his. In extortion, it's the congressman who has the upper hand; he has the power to harm an interest, which he will refrain from doing in exchange for a contribution. Though neither of these terms is likely to be appropriate for any but a handful of the thousands of contributions made each year, we might imagine them to occupy the extremes on a continuum that has as its center a point where money would have no effect on public policy. We might ask then, who has the upper hand in the exchange? In which direction does the influence arrow point?

Incumbents typically wish to raise money and lots of it. Though they need the money less than the challengers do, it is not irrational for them to build campaign war chests. At the same time, since the election is basically theirs to lose, and since contributors are to be found on practically any side of most issues, incumbents can easily develop a "diversified" portfolio of contributors, remaining beholden to none. The relative weakness of corporate and trade-association PACs, as well as their fear of incumbents, can be seen in the meager support they gave Republican challengers when the Democrats were in charge of the House. Remarkably, the contributions of such PACs to Republicans never rose above 4 percent of their total House contributions from 1986 to 1992. Indeed, as political scientist Michael J. Malbin has argued, the case for limiting campaign contributions makes the most sense as a means of protecting groups and individuals from pressure by office holders who bear the powers of sword and purse, rather than as a means of preventing contributors from corrupting politicians.

Consider also the motives of congressmen. Few, of course, fail to place a premium on reelection, but the real currency of elections is votes, not money. Money becomes important only if it helps bring in votes. Too much money from the wrong source can even cost votes. An interest representing voters speaks more directly to the congressman's concern for reelection than one representing mere money. Also, most congressmen have aspirations beyond keeping their jobs (there are certainly far easier ways to earn a living): They seek status (and don't wish to be known as the lackey of this or that interest); they seek power on Capitol Hill and good committee assignments (and thus listen to cues given by party leaders); and, contrary to prevailing cynicism, they wish to make what they consider good public policy.

A study by economists Stephen G. Bonors and John R. Lott, Jr., confirms this. They examined the votes of members of the House who had announced the end of their political careers. What they wanted to discover was whether politicians who no longer needed to attract campaign funds changed their voting patterns for the remainder of their time in office. They did not.

Indeed, political scientists consistently find that the interests of constituents, the concerns of political parties, and the politician's political philosophy have more influence on how he votes than do mere campaign contributions. When these other concerns are not present, the statistical correlation between contributions and votes remains relatively small.[4] And even here, it is not clear what independent effect the money is having since the same groups that contribute money also typically shower the congressman with letters, calls, press releases, and policy papers.

And finally, what of the claim, also made by Dworkin, that money is the "root of other problems," in particular, the tendency of candidates to "go negative"? When candidates and their campaign managers employ comparative or negative advertising, they do so for one reason: They think that it works—and often they are right. Whether it is because of our fallen nature, or an inbred trait useful in the perpetuation of the species, or an acquired characteristic, our attention is more readily seized by depictions of vice than of virtue. So negative advertising will continue unless the public turns against it—an end toward which limiting campaign expenditures is unlikely to contribute. With less money, campaigns will rely even more on what is most cost-effective, and that is likely to be negative advertising, especially for challengers.

Further, more high-minded sentiments are unlikely to flow from the reporters into whose hands reformers wish to entrust a greater share of campaign information. News media are hardly immune to the same temptations that lead candidates into negative campaigns. Bad news sells. Reporters, in fact, seem even more willing to go negative than the candidates. In *Good Intentions Make Bad News,* a study of TV coverage of the 1992 campaign, media analyst S. Robert Lichter found that the networks were 40 percent more likely to cover negative ads than the candidates were to run them.

Limiting campaign spending, in short, is a solution in search of a problem, a "solution" likely to entrench incumbents further and to accentuate the negative in campaigns. . . .

NOTES

1. Calculations are made from data in *Buckley v. Valeo* and statistics of the Federal Election Commission. Unless otherwise indicated, campaign data in this essay have been taken or calculated directly from the Federal Election Commission, the Center for Responsive Politics, and Norman J. Ornstein, Thomas E. Mann, and Michael J. Malbin, *Vital Statistics on Congress 1997-1998.*

2 This figure comes from the Center for Responsive Politics. The higher figure of $2.7 billion, often quoted in the media, apparently derives from a raw summation of data supplied by the FEC, not taking into account the double counting that occurs—e.g., when one adds expenditures by PACs, which include their contributions to candidates, with expenditures by candidates, which include the PAC contributions. The $2.2 billion includes soft-money expenditures by the parties (which, as explained below, are technically supposed to aid state and local candidates), but not expenditures for issue ads run by organizations other than the parties (for which disclosure is not legally required). Despite their notoriety, issue ads on TV and radio were estimated by the Annenberg Public Policy Center to have totaled no more than $150 million in the 1996 election, $78 million of which was accounted for by the political parties. Issue ads run by organizations other than parties thus amounted to only 3.3 percent of the total federal campaign expenditures

3 Technically known as "nonfederal" money because the funds are supposed to benefit state and local, rather than federal, candidates, soft money falls outside the FECA regulations in the sense that contributions are unlimited and the sources prohibited from contributing to federal candidates (banks, corporations, and labor unions) may give to these accounts. The money, however, does not fall outside the purview of FECA in the sense that the money may only be used for generic party ads, voter registration, and get-out-the-vote drives. Further, it may only be used when blended with hard money according to

complex formulas designed by the FEC to reflect the benefit going to state and local, as opposed to federal, candidates.

4. Of course, contributions could have an impact on matters short of roll-call votes—for example, access to the congressman, posing of questions at hearings, sharing useful advice and privileged information, and contacting an executive agency. Research has yet to be done on these questions. Nonetheless, the matters in question are fairly small, and there is little reason to believe that money would outweigh the concerns of constituency, party, and philosophy.

New Realities, New Thinking

The Task Force on Campaign Finance Reform

Campaign finance in America has entered a new era, and those who seek reform must now confront the New Realities. For the last generation or more, candidates have controlled their own campaigns as long as they could raise the money necessary to pay for them. In doing so, they effectively supplanted the political party domination of campaigns. However, the candidate-centered campaign no longer occupies center stage. In 1996, we experienced a broad range of actors—political parties, individuals, political action committees (PACs), issue organizations, and others—spending money in campaigns that candidates neither raised nor controlled. In 1996, the campaigns exploded well beyond what we used to think of as their boundaries—at least the boundaries the authors of the Federal Election Campaign Act of 1974 assumed and within which regulation has gone forward.

The blurring of the boundaries of "campaign finance" is indeed at the core of the New Reality in campaign finance. Is it a part of the campaign when the political parties spend soft money on party building and issue advertising in ways intended to affect contests for the Congress or the presidency? When labor unions, business coalitions, and issue groups buy television and radio time to communicate, not only with their members, but with the public at large about particular candidates for office? When the Christian Coalition and environmental groups distribute voter guides intended to influence elections, even the election of specific candidates? We have been moving quickly from an era in which candidates ran their own campaigns to an era of diffusion of both funding and responsibility for the major content and some of the messages of the campaigns.

One crucial aspect of the New Realities results from the interpretation of First Amendment rights, beginning with the Supreme Court's 1976 decision in *Buckley v. Valeo*. At that time, the Court freed candidates from mandatory limits on their campaign spending, holding that any limits had to be voluntarily agreed upon. Moreover, by ruling that money that a candidate gives to his or her own campaign is an expenditure rather than a contribution, it freed wealthy candidates from any limits on the amount of their money that they can spend on their own campaigns. Also, the Court invested independent spending by groups and individuals with First Amendment protections and placed them beyond the regulatory power of the Congress. And in 1996, the Court created a new category of independent expenditures, by political party committees.

Buckley's elaboration of the First Amendment has spawned other related elements of the New Realities. As many states began to reform their campaign funding

---

Source: New Realities, New Thinking. Report of The Task Force on Campaign Finance Reform (Los Angeles: Citizens' Research Foundation, 1997), pp. 1-24.

in the 1980s and 1990s, federal courts drawing on the logic of *Buckley* began to strike down their regulatory innovations. For example, the provisions in the Minnesota statutes increasing the public subsidy for candidates who agree to spending limits and whose opponents do not has been struck down by a Federal Court of Appeals. Moreover, relying on *Buckley*, groups as diverse as business coalitions, the Sierra Club, the AFL-CIO, and the National Republican Senatorial Committee have undertaken "issue advocacy" media campaigns which clearly are intended to influence election outcomes, but which are protected speech beyond the reach of statutory or administrative regulation because they stop short of expressly advocating the election or defeat of a particular, identifiable candidate.

The New Realities, however, spring from roots other than the Court's interpretation of the First Amendment. Increasingly, political sophistication and technological advances in campaigning and communications have dramatically changed campaigning and campaign finance. The grouping of individual contributions— whether by way of the formal bundling by political action committees, such as Emily's List, or via solicitations in informal networks—reflects new levels of organization and motivation among individual contributors. And everywhere one sees the effects of television campaigning or of computer-based arts of direct mail appeals or of Web sites. Beyond much of the precise targeting of messages now possible, of course, lies growing skills in opinion sampling and analysis.

Fundamental changes in the political parties also have contributed to the New Realities. Within the last generation the parties increasingly have centralized their raising of money, so much indeed that national party committees now raise soft money for the grass roots parties in the states and localities to spend at their command. At the same time, legislative parties in the Congress and states are participating in the funding of legislative campaigns, sometimes working with the official state and national party organizations, sometimes not. As money becomes the resource of choice in campaigns, the parties depend less and less on the vanishing volunteers of the grass roots and more and more on the organizational capacity to raise large sums of money.

The cumulative effect of these changes has been an exploding fragmentation of the campaign and the involvement of new groups in it. Whole new categories of campaign activities—such as the bundlers as contributors and the issue advertising groups as spenders—now are presences outside of the 1974 model and its regulatory system. Whole new categories of money and spending, especially the soft money and independent spending by the parties, are subject to disclosure but hardly any other regulation. Indeed, the burgeoning campaigns of issue advocacy test the very question of what the boundaries of campaigning are.

In short, the campaign realities of the 1970s no longer prevail, and the regulatory regime of 1974 created in response to those realities, in which candidates, parties, PACs and independent expenditures are regulated, seems increasingly outdated. The regulatory task is vastly more difficult because the number of players and variety of activities have expanded beyond the boundaries of the required disclosure regulations. Just tracking the raising and spending of money becomes more difficult as activities and interrelationships become more complex.

The devising of policy solutions to identifiable problems similarly becomes more challenging as the political interests involved in reform and change become more complex, and more groups become players. Not surprisingly, political consensus, even a bare majority, for any reform package becomes more and more difficult to mobilize. Above all, the task of reforming the regime of the 1970s, even of patching and rehabilitating it, seems more and more daunting given the judicial shrinking of the regulatory arsenal available to American legislatures.

COURTS, THE CONSTITUTION AND CAMPAIGN REFORM

The Task Force's concern about judicial shrinking of options should not be read as indifference to First Amendment values. We are committed strongly to them, and we deplore reform proposals that play fast and loose with them. The Supreme Court and the Constitution clearly play overarching and essential roles in protecting the rights of political speech and political association of all Americans. Our only concern is that in campaign finance cases the Court has accepted only one narrow definition of a legislature's interest in regulating campaign finance: instances of corruption or the appearance of corruption. We believe that doctrine misspecifies the major issue in campaign finance and that it ignores the legislative interest—and the implicit constitutional imperative—in protecting the integrity of the electoral processes so fundamental to a representative democracy.

The New Realities mean that there is now a wealth of nominally non-campaign-related activity which is intended to influence elections. These New Realities can challenge the integrity of the electoral system without involving quid pro quo corruption. For example, when unions, corporations, and issue organizations spend unlimited and unreported millions of dollars from essentially unknown sources to influence presidential and congressional elections, it is appropriate for government to take notice, even if no candidate literally sells a vote in exchange for such spending.

Courts should recognize the New Realities, the potential for more subtle forms of influence, and the government interest in maintaining the integrity of the electoral system. Specifically, courts should weigh the curtailment of First Amendment rights against the governmental interest in preserving the integrity of the electoral system, while retaining the more narrow "corruption" standard in appropriate cases. There is a "compelling government interest" in such an interpretation in some cases.

Notwithstanding our disagreement with the courts' reasoning in some campaign finance cases, the Task Force members all agree that the judiciary, as an independent branch of government, has a crucial role to play. The Task Force unanimously concludes that extraordinary efforts to work around court rulings through a constitutional amendment are an injudicious way to proceed. The First Amendment requires us to tolerate speech that we would like to silence. While the implications of free speech and of the sheer volume of speech are often unpopular, tinkering with the Constitution would set a bad precedent. The Task Force opposes a constitutional amendment because we do not think the campaign finance situation is so dire or so impervious to improvement that we must resort to such extraordinary means. Finally, we see no simple adjustment that would be of much use, even in the short run. Like most public policy issues these days, campaign reform is complex, triggering many constitutional and other implications. But efforts to solve the problems of campaign finance should go forward—as frustrating as the efforts sometimes seem—without resorting to constitutional amendment.

TROUBLE SPOTS AND NECESSITIES

Because the Task Force believes that reform should address real problems and should be designed with specific goals in mind, our discussion is organized around concerns we have about the current campaign finance system. We have identified six problem areas that inform our recommendations.

Disclosure.   If the American people are to make informed decisions as a result of campaigns, they must have the fullest and most timely information possible about how they are financed. That information must include the sources of campaign money, the amounts raised, and the activities they made possible—whether those were the activities of the candidates or of campaign actors outside of their control. Only full disclosure can provide the data on which the media, public interest groups, academics, and regulatory agencies depend. The goal must be full transparency of the funding of campaigns for public office, undergirded by the "right of the public to know."

Accountability.   If the major participants in campaign finance are to be held accountable, the public must know of their activities as a result of full disclosure. But there also must be a mechanism through which they may be held accountable, and the best such mechanism is the election itself. For that reason, the greater the share of the campaign that is the responsibility of the candidates, the greater the accountability. By the same token, a broadly based political party is more easily held accountable at an election than a narrowly focused interest group. On the other hand, independent spending or issue advertising is much harder to hold accountable.

Competitiveness.   The essence of democracy is free choice among viable alternatives, and if the choices of American elections are to be genuine, the major candidates must be able to mount campaigns that bring them to the consideration of voters. The major challenge to that premise is the ability of incumbent candidates to fund substantial campaigns for reelection while their challengers often can afford only an inadequate campaign. Indeed, the prospect of insufficient funding may impede the recruitment of credible challengers. Even when the challengers have scant chances of success, their campaigns merit essential funding in order to stimulate the democratic dialogue in every state and district of the country.

Adequacy of the Campaigns.   For all of the reasons that support adequate funding for challengers, we also must make sure that the overall level of campaign funding is high enough to support that democratic dialogue. Lowering contribution limits to roll back the amounts of money available will starve campaigns and threatens the health of democratic politics conducted through contests for public office. The candidate needs funding to present qualifications and programs in his or her own words, not as reported by the media or the Internet. We must seek to assure all credible candidates the resources they need to communicate with their electorates. We know that those sums are not insignificant, both because of the costs of campaigning and the numbers of voters in the electorate. The average member of the House of Representatives now represents more than 600,000 residents, and funding for campaigns for that office must reflect such numbers.

Breadth of Participation. As political scientists, we value the democratic process; we celebrate a political system that incorporates individuals and all manner of groups, and we embrace the vibrancy of widespread participation, including financial participation. Idealism aside, our concern with participation is rooted in an understanding of practical politics. Participation spawns legitimacy and we deeply hope that Americans see their governments as legitimate. Financial contributions are a legitimate form of political participation and, while the United States leads the world in the percentage of its citizens making political contributions, we would like to enhance legitimacy by achieving an increase in this form of participation.

Our concern with participation also is associated with the First Amendment's ideals; people are and should be free to speak and to associate with others. In the campaign finance context, this means that citizens should be free to make limited and publicly disclosed contributions to candidates and parties, and they should be allowed to join with other like-minded citizens in making political contributions through political action committees or candidate or party committees.

Regulatory Viability. After a century of struggles, we achieved in the 1970s the most effective scheme of regulation for campaign finance in American history. That system now needs repair and rethinking, but we do not agree that dismantling the regulatory regime should be an option. To achieve viability in a reformed regime requires two major components. First, the legislation governing it must address the New Realities of campaign finance in a logical and integrated way that does not create unreasonable expectations either for the regulated or the regulators. Second, we must assure necessary independence and budgetary support so that regulatory agencies—the Federal Election Commission and state and local boards and commissions—can exercise their responsibilities in a timely and effective way. While urging that federal, state, and local election agencies be structured and funded to facilitate vigorous enforcement, we warn against regulatory overzealousness. There are essential values of free speech, free association, and due process that require vigilance on the part of regulators.

A word about the order of the Task Force's consideration and recommendations:

Since the New Realities raise questions about the traditional basis for accountability, we first take up accountability. Under this heading, we consider aspects of the

New Realities that challenge the electoral system's ability to provide accountability (e.g. soft money, issue advocacy, and independent expenditures). Then, we turn to the more traditional underpinnings of an electoral system that provides accountability, namely, disclosure and enforcement.

Second, we take up competitiveness in the recruitment and funding of candidates. We seek to provide competitiveness by assuring that multiple candidates have the wherewithal to mount adequate campaigns. Under this heading, we discuss individual contributions, limits on individual's total contributions, millionaire candidates, public financing of presidential and congressional campaigns, and spending limits.

Finally, we address issues of participation by considering the sources of funding. Here we look at political parties, political action committees, leadership PACs, bundling, and out-of-district and out-of-state contributions.

Throughout, we are mindful of regulatory viability.

ACCOUNTABILITY

When campaign funds are raised and spent by candidates or by political parties coordinating their activities with candidates, the ballot provides accountability: candidates can be voted out of office and parties can be voted out of control. In order for the ballot to ensure accountability, it is vital that disclosure be comprehensive and timely, and that information be readily available to the media and the public so that voters have access to information they may use in voting.

However, when individuals and groups not formally affiliated with the candidates are engaged in significant spending, such as in independent expenditures and issue advocacy, ensuring accountability is, at the least, more difficult. This is the crux of the fundamental challenge presented by the New Realities of campaign financing.

Soft Money

In the semantics of campaign finance, "hard money" funds are raised in accordance with contribution limits and other provisions of the Federal Election Campaign Act (FECA), as they relate to candidates for federal office and committees supporting them. In contrast, "soft money" is raised and spent outside of these limits and requirements, but is spent in ways that may influence federal elections.

For example, federal law has barred corporations since 1907 and labor unions since 1943 from making hard money contributions in connection with federal elections. However, federal law has been interpreted to allow corporations, unions, and others to make contributions to parties for party building and certain office costs. Contrary to popular wisdom, the provision of the FECA Amendments of 1979 permitting "soft money" was not a legislated loophole, but was requested by the two major parties, and was designed to enhance the role of party organizations by allowing them to engage in certain grass roots volunteer activities (e.g., voter registration and get-out-the-vote activities) without the funds spent on these activities counting against the presidential or other spending limits. Still, we are concerned that the difficulty of tracking the funds creates serious problems of accountability, and that single sources are providing money in amounts so large that the dangers of corruption or the appearance of corruption are real and raise the spectre of excessive influence.

Specifically, we are troubled that in 1996 particularly, the state parties used soft money supplied by national party committees to pay for election year radio and television issue advertising; these advertisements count as "party building" only because the advertisements stop short of expressly advocating the election or defeat or a specific, identifiable candidate. This advertising is not the "party building" envisioned by the authorizing legislation, it augments the soft money circumvention, and it undermines accountability.

Because some states allow political parties to accept corporate and union gifts, both national parties collect large contributions from these sources, as well as from wealthy individuals who have already reached the federal aggregate contribution limit. The national committees then funnel these funds to their state affiliates in unlimited amounts. Where these monies end up is often difficult to determine because federal law does not require a full accounting of monies transferred to the states. The responsibility is left to state law, which is often so inadequate that it is impossible to account for the funds.

Although the Task Force supports the goals of strengthened political parties, and of helping parties to participate in federal campaigns, we propose that soft money be abolished. In operational terms, this means that the national-level party committees should be barred from funneling soft money to state and local party committees, and that federal candidates and their operatives should be barred from soliciting such funds. In effect, this abolishes the differences between federal and non-federal party money, and permits only hard money.

In the interests of federalism, and consistent with devolution to the states, state party committees should continue their fund raising and spending on their party tickets (for registration, get-out-the-vote, canvassing); of course, state parties would remain free to accept hard money transferred from the national party or funds that they raised in accordance with state law for party building and electioneering. Disclosure of hard money transferred to the state party committees should be required at the federal level, so that disbursements can be traced.

Issue Advocacy, Communication with Members

The Federal Election Campaign Act (FECA) provides that a group's or individual's spending does not constitute an independent expenditure and is not subject to disclosure requirements unless it "expressly advocates the election or defeat of a particular, identifiable candidate." And many who communicate their views about candidates avoid this reporting requirement by stopping just short of "express advocacy."

While both campaign finance law and their tax-exempt status bar non-political groups from expressly advocating the election or defeat of a particular, identifiable candidate, these groups can spend unlimited amounts of funds obtained from any source to advocate their issue positions. And such issue advertisements or printed materials can be designed to increase or decrease a given candidate's support.

For example, the Christian Coalition publishes pre-election voter guides which do not endorse or rate candidates but which make it clear which candidates support Christian Coalition positions, and which do not. The resulting guides look like campaign fliers. Yet, because the spending is nominally not election related, groups engaged in issue advocacy are free to spend unlimited amounts from any source, and they need not disclose their spending or the sources of their funds.

Another use of soft money for issue advertising occurred in the 1996 election cycle: it was disbursed as a form of supplementary spending by party organizations to indirectly assist their respective presidential nominees. The parties were thus able to circumvent the contribution and spending limits imposed on presidential campaigns, and spent tens of millions of dollars in hopes of influencing the outcome of the presidential race (This Report recommends raising the presidential prenomination spending limit; see section on Public Financing—Presidential).

Issue advocacy directed at a general audience needs to be distinguished from communication with an organization's restricted class; the restricted class for a corporation consists of its stockholders and executive and administrative employees, and, in the case of a labor union or membership organization, the restricted class consists of the organization's members and their families. While the FECA prohibits both labor unions and corporations from using their treasury funds (from dues or corporate income) to make contributions or expenditures in connection with federal elections, FECA places no limit on the amount of money that unions and corporations can spend on partisan communications directed at their organization's restricted class. As the term suggests, partisan communication includes such activities as endorsing candidates in a newsletter. The costs of such partisan communications must be reported to the FEC if they aggregate to more than $2,000 per election. We view partisan communications with an organization's restricted class as a benign exercise of the basic right of association.

Corporations, unions, trade associations, and issue groups should be required to report expenditures cumulating to $50,000 or more per election for communication with the general public which pictures or names an identifiable federal candidate within six months of an election.

Unions, corporations and trade associations should be barred from paying for issue advocacy with treasury funds obtained from unions dues and corporate profits. Currently, many union members and stockholders are forced to pay for political spending with which they disagree. Instead, corporations, unions and trade associations should be required to pay for issue advocacy with voluntary contributions. These funds should be kept in a separate account, and disclosed to the Federal Election Commission with data similar to other FECA disclosure requirements.

Reform should be designed so that it does not spur increases in issue advocacy. Specifically, reducing contribution limits will increase the incentive to use

alternative channels, such as issue advocacy. Conversely, raising contribution limits will tend to centralize spending under the candidates' reportable expenditures, and thereby increase accountability.

Independent Expenditures

In upholding the First Amendment guarantees of freedom of speech and freedom of association, courts have consistently held that individuals and groups have a right to use independent expenditures to communicate with voters. While the law may limit contributions to a campaign, individuals and groups have the right to spend unlimited amounts of money to advance (or undermine) a given candidacy, so long as they do not coordinate their activities with the campaign.

The Supreme Court's recent decision in *Colorado Republican Federal Campaign Committee and Douglas Jones, Treasurer, v. Federal Election Commission* expanded opportunities enabling political parties to engage in independent expenditures. Specifically, the Court ruled that party organizations that do not coordinate their activities with the party's nominees can engage in unlimited "independent spending" designed to advance the party's nominees. Following this decision, both major parties moved to set up entities to engage in such independent spending, and, in fact, spent independently as much as $16 million in 1996. For our part, we doubt that political parties can operate completely independently of their candidates, nor should they. We do not think that they should try to do so because we value the accountability that parties provide. Parties and candidates should seek to work together, not apart.

While we support the notion that individuals and groups have the right to spend money to advance (or undermine) particular candidacies, we take a dim view of independent expenditures. Our concern has to do with accountability; independent expenditures can shape campaign discourse and popular opinion but, unlike candidates and parties, individuals and groups engaging in independent expenditures do not appear on the ballot and, as a result, cannot be electorally rewarded or punished for their conduct. Thus, despite their disclosure, independent expenditures lack accountability.

In sum, independent expenditures are constitutionally protected, but they undermine accountability. As political scientists concerned about the electoral system, we consider independent expenditures undesirable.

Since federal courts are not sympathetic to legislation designed to curtail independent expenditures, reform should be formulated so that it does not spur increases in these activities. Specifically, lowering contribution limits will encourage individuals and groups to go outside of the conventional candidate and party funding channels. On the other hand, we recommend that the limits on the contributions that individuals can make to candidate committees and to parties be increased so that more funds can flow through candidate and party committees.

Current law stipulates that independent expenditures cannot be coordinated with the campaign of the candidate they are intended to benefit, and it behooves regulatory agencies to ensure that no relationship exists.

Disclosure

Disclosure is one of campaign finance regulation's great, sometimes overlooked, successes; in the past two decades, great strides have been taken to illuminate the roles of money in politics. Disclosure is the cornerstone of regulation and accountability. Disclosure provides voters with the information they need to make judgments on the financial activity of candidates, parties, and other political actors. It also is essential to enforcement of the law; the need to report alerts committees to relevant laws, acts to deter violations, and provides election officials with the information required to determine compliance. Disclosure is most effective when the information is readily available and summarized in ways that make the data meaningful and readily accessible.

Federal law requires disclosure of funds involved in federal elections, and all fifty states require at least some disclosure concerning state and local elections. However, the disclosure requirements in many states are neither comprehensive nor timely, and the staffing levels at most state election agencies are wholly inadequate to provide effective disclosure and enforcement. We urge that disclosure be strengthened both organizationally and statutorily.

Given disclosure's time sensitivity, all disclosed information relating to federal and state elections should be tabulated and made available by election agencies in the form of press releases, direct access to agency computers, optical imaging systems, and over the Internet. To help accomplish these goals and to provide the FEC and state agencies with data needed for timely enforcement, election agencies should be mandated by law to require that the more active political committees file disclosure reports electronically. Specifically, electronic filing should be mandatory for committees that receive or expend more than a reasonable threshold amount per election cycle and that prepare their reports by computer. The threshold should be set low enough to ease access to the most important information, but not so low that it imposes a participation-deterring burden on small committees.

To make it easier for committees to file electronically and for the election agencies to manage this information, election agencies should provide committees with accounting software, free of charge, as the State of Washington and the New York City Campaign Finance Board, among others, do.

Federal law requires that campaign committees report the name, occupation and principal place of business of any contributor who gives more than $200. However, the occupation and place of business data is often missing from committee disclosure filings; committees commonly attribute the absence of this information to the fact that they were not able to collect it, and the FEC tolerates the absence of this information so long as committees have made a good faith effort to obtain it. We urge that campaign committees be barred from accepting contributions in excess of the reporting threshold unless and until they report the contributor's occupation and place of business. Money can be held in an escrow account until the needed information is filed.

To improve effective disclosure, the publicly reviewable filings by federal candidates should contain information on funds that the party spent in coordinated expenditures on behalf of the candidate; the candidates' disclosure forms should indicate how much the party spent on their behalf, and where the party reports of these expenditures can be found in the party committee's filing.

As noted in the section on Soft Money, money transferred from committee to committee should be disclosed in ample ways as to be fully traceable.

Enforcement

In America, the agencies charged with regulating campaign finance suffer from a chronic lack of resources. To varying degrees, they commonly lack adequate funding and enforcement powers, and are saddled with organizational structures that hobble effective action. This situation results chiefly from the sensitive nature of campaign finance enforcement and from legislators' fear of a strong and independent enforcer. Yet, effective enforcement is key to any regulatory regime.

To implement effective disclosure, election agencies must make the raw data available in a useable form, conduct some rudimentary analyses, and enforce the disclosure requirements. The FEC and state election agencies should be provided with the resources needed to computerize, to administer electronic filing, and to rapidly make disclosed information available on the Internet. Appropriations should reflect the fact that implementing new technologies costs money.

Many regulatory programs could seek to assure election agencies of funding and to insulate them from the vagaries of annual budgeting by establishing trust funds with earmarked money. While Congress or state legislatures may undo a trust fund, such arrangements offer some staying power, particularly when made part of a state constitution, as in California.

Although we recognize that the enforcement of campaign finance laws is bound to involve partisan controversy, we believe that the FEC's current bipartisan structure stymies enforcement. The Commission presently consists of three Republicans and three Democrats, with four votes needed to issue an agency ruling or to pursue an enforcement action. This structure virtually guarantees administrative and policy gridlock on important issues.

While noting that enforcement in an area as competitive and partisan as campaigns is bound to involve controversy, we conclude that the structure of the Federal Election Commission is not conducive to effective enforcement.

We urge that FEC commissioners' terms be staggered and that commissioners be limited to one six-year term.

We urge that the FEC be reconstituted so that it contains an odd number of commissioners, appointed and selected less for their partisanship than for their independence, integrity, and knowledge. The six members should choose the seventh member to recommend to the President, who alone can constitutionally make the appointment, which then requires confirmation by the Senate. That person would then be chairman for a limited term of office.

The authority to conduct random audits is important to securing full and accurate disclosure. This audit authority should be available to all election agencies.

Agencies should be allowed to impose fines for technical violations. While courts can review the penalties, the power to impose fines expedites enforcement and allows the agency to target its enforcement efforts more effectively. In contrast, the current requirement that the FEC, for example, must seek a negotiated settlement based on conciliation and, failing that, has an affirmative obligation to persuade a court of the merit of the charge, invites delay.

COMPETITIVENESS

Democratic elections require the presence of multiple candidates mounting credible campaigns. So, as political scientists, we seek to maximize the competitiveness of elections. In particular, we are concerned that campaign finance systems in this country too often tend to discourage competition by advantaging incumbents and wealthy individuals willing to make large contributions to their own campaigns. Specifically, we are troubled when the financial advantage of an incumbent or wealthy individual willing to make large contributions to his or her campaign discourages individuals who might otherwise become credible candidates; and when reporters, other observers, and potential contributors discount a candidacy because of the fundraising advantage that another candidate enjoys by virtue of incumbency or personal wealth. Such events threaten electoral competition and undermine fairness.

Accordingly, in this section, we take up policy issues that bear directly on electoral competitiveness. In each case, our strategy is to encourage competitiveness by assuring that multiple candidates have the wherewithal to mount adequate campaigns.

Limits on Individual Contributions to Candidates

We approach the subject of contribution limits with the understanding that competitive elections require that candidates communicate with voters, that candidate communication costs money, and that this money must come from somewhere. We recognize that contributions from individuals are the least troubling form of private funding because they tend to be idiosyncratic, and because appointments or favors given in exchange for contributions are most easily publicized. Also, recognizing that inflation has reduced the value of the maximum federal contribution by two-thirds in twenty years, we recommend increasing the limit on individuals' contributions to federal candidates, despite the contrary views of most reformers.

Moreover, we reject the drive to decrease limits on individual contributions because we believe that electoral competitiveness is the major issue here, and lower contribution limits will make it harder for challengers to gather the funds they need to contend against well-known, entrenched incumbents. In contrast, higher contribution limits with special provisions to make it easier to raise initial seed money will encourage challengers.

Reducing the limit on contributions to candidates so that middle income individuals can comfortably contribute the maximum would mean that candidates would have to spend more time raising funds, and, due to increased fundraising costs, would end up with less money with which to communicate with voters. It also is likely to produce more self-financed millionaire candidates whose contributions to their own campaigns cannot be limited under U.S. Supreme Court doctrine. In addition, lower contribution limits will mean that some wealthy individuals will spend more on unaccountable independent expenditures, as they find that their ability to channel their financial participation through conventional candidate or party channels is severely limited.

In addition to being unworkable, we believe that attempts at leveling are unnecessary; while we have some concerns about some of the sources of campaign funds (see section on Sources of Funding), we do not believe that elected officials "sell" themselves to the highest bidder. Contributing remains, as it should be, a legal act, and there are laws against bribery and vote selling. Further, we believe that the best way to guard against the danger of abuse is to promote competition among candidates and to adjust the current system so that more of the funds flow directly through regular candidate and party channels and are disclosed fully.

In addition to such policy arguments, there are constitutional problems with low contribution limits. In *Buckley v. Valeo*, the Supreme Court held that campaign speech costs money for amplification. Accordingly, low contribution limits unconstitutionally limit speech. Courts have since applied this doctrine consistently.

We view free speech rights as both an ideal and as a practical reality; attempts to squelch Americans' desire to speak politically will be unsuccessful. If the limit on individual contributions is set too low, the banned money will simply reappear in less desirable forms (e.g., independent expenditures or issue advertising).

The limit on individuals' contributions to candidates for federal office should be increased from $1,000 to $3,000 per candidate per election. This amount is not a random choice but would merely restore the maximum contribution to the value it enjoyed when the FECA's $1,000 limit was established in 1974.

These limits and the others should be indexed for inflation, and rounded to the nearest $100 every two years.

Seed Money

A candidate's ability to mount a credible campaign commonly hinges on his or her ability to raise initial money quickly. A candidate who succeeds in raising considerable funds early in the campaign season is more likely to receive favorable attention from reporters, other observers, and would-be contributors, and, as a result, is in a better position to raise the funds needed to compete. Conversely, the failure to secure early funding tells many observers and prospective contributors that this is not a serious or viable campaign. Campaigns that are not perceived as serious typically have a hard time receiving attention and collecting the funds needed to campaign effectively.

The power of early money generally works to the advantage of incumbents, who often begin their reelection efforts with funds left over from their previous efforts and a well-established base of donors. Accordingly, we have developed a recommendation that will help challengers and those contending for open seats (where there is no incumbent) to collect the early money needed to mount credible campaigns. In this way, we seek to enhance competition and the adequacy of campaigns.

To help candidates raise the initial seed money needed to launch a credible campaign, the contribution limit for individuals should be $10,000 for the first $100,000 raised by House candidates and for the first $500,000 raised by Senate and presidential candidates. Donors of $10,000 seed money contributions cannot contribute in addition the $3,000 limited amount. Funds carried over from previous campaigns should count toward these seed money limits. This recommendation is predicated on the assumption that an effective disclosure system is in operation.

Limits on Individuals' Total Contributions

Currently, federal law stipulates that individuals shall make no more than $25,000 per year in hard money contributions intended to influence federal elections. This ceiling applies to the aggregate of an individual's contributions to national party committees, PACs, and individual candidates. Though inflation has reduced its value by two-thirds, this limit has not been increased since it was first established.

Raising this ceiling will increase electoral competition by increasing funding for challengers. First, it will increase the pool of political funds available to challengers. Second, it will increase the hard money resources available to the political parties, and we can count on parties to allocate these funds to the campaigns where their infusion will make the biggest difference and many of these candidates will be challengers. Also, this additional funding for parties will help to keep parties strong, notwithstanding the abolition of soft money.

In addition, raising the ceiling will open up the conventional party and candidate channels of finance, and decrease the incentive for individuals to use alternative channels (e.g., independent expenditures) where accountability is lacking. Finally, the expanded hard money within this aggregate limit will reduce the amount of time candidates spend raising money.

The limit on an individual's total annual contributions in connection with federal elections should be increased from $25,000 to $100,000. Increasing this limit will not allow individuals to contribute more than they can currently because now there is no limit on soft money contributions. This amount takes into account the Task Force's recommendation tripling the individual contribution limit to candidates.

Self-Financed Millionaire Candidates

The recent incidence of wealthy candidates making large contributions to their own campaigns highlights three disturbing aspects of today's campaign finance regime. First, millionaire candidates undermine electoral competition; high quality potential candidates are discouraged by the presence in the race of a wealthy candidate willing to bankroll his or her own campaign. Moreover, candidates who do opt to run against a self-financed candidate face more than the usual difficulties in raising funds and having their campaigns taken seriously.

Second, self-financed candidacies increase public cynicism about the role of money in campaigns. In this connection, we are particularly troubled by the role that an individual's wealth and willingness to use it to obtain public office plays in candidate recruitment. In varying degrees, both parties on occasion recruit as candidates those who might be willing to spend considerable sums on their own campaigns.

Third, self-financed candidacies have increased owing to a lacuna in the regulatory scheme. While courts, consistent with the *Buckley* decision, have upheld FECA limits on contributions from PACs, parties, and individuals, they have rejected mandatory limits on a candidate's expenditures on his or her own behalf unless those limits are conditions voluntarily accepted in return for public funding. The *Buckley* precedent means a candidate has a right to spend an unlimited amount of his or her own money on a campaign for federal office.

We believe that this is one area in which courts have construed the First Amendment too broadly and governments' interest in regulating campaign finance too narrowly. While a candidate's contributing millions to his or her own campaign may not involve "corruption or the appearance of corruption," self-financed campaigns can undermine the integrity of the election process. The Supreme Court's reading of millionaires' First Amendment rights, and its giving short shrift to the government interest in preserving the integrity of the electoral system, complicate the task of reform. Adoption of the "integrity" standard could be accomplished easily if courts were to view candidates' self-contributions as precisely that, contributions, rather than as expenditures; under current interpretation, contributions can be limited constitutionally.

That said, we oppose a constitutional amendment for the reasons stated above (see the section on Courts, the Constitution, and Campaign Finance Reform). Instead of seeking to amend the constitution, we urge the Court to reconsider the framework it brings to bear in certain campaign finance cases.

A pragmatic way to deal with self-financed candidates is to improve the fundraising capabilities of their opponents. For example, candidates facing self-financed opponents might turn to their party for help and, as discussed below in the section on Political Parties, we advocate abolishing limits on the extent to which parties can support their congressional nominees facing a self-financed opponent. In addition, it may be appropriate to increase public funding for candidates facing wealthy, self-financed opponents. What we should not do is enact "reforms" that will make it harder for candidates to raise funds.

We should increase the fundraising capabilities of candidates facing wealthy, self-financed opponents. Specifically, in the section on Political Parties, we advocate eliminating the limits on the amount of support a party may provide to its nominees; and we advocate increasing public funding for candidates whose opponents are contributing large amounts of money to their own campaigns.

Public Financing—Presidential

Starting in 1976, the United States has experienced six presidential campaigns under a partial public funding system. Overall, this system has been a success. It has practically eliminated the large donor problem (apart from soft money, discussed above), encouraged small contributions to candidates for the nomination, and assured major party nominees of funding sufficient to communicate with voters, while largely freeing them to some extent from the need to focus on fundraising. We applaud these successes, and we reject attempts to dismantle the system of partial public financing of presidential campaigns.

That said, the electoral system we have in place today is very different from that for which the public financing system was designed. Specifically, today's system features many more primaries and caucuses, and the competition among states to have early (and presumably more influential) primaries or caucuses has resulted in a nomination system where the primaries and caucuses are heavily clustered at the early part of the prenomination period. These changes have campaign finance implications; compared with campaigning among party insiders in caucuses in a handful of states, reaching the millions of primary voters across the country requires that candidates spend more money, some of it on expensive media. Also, the frontloading of primaries and caucuses means that it is, at least, much more difficult, and may in fact be impossible, for candidates to use the momentum from surprise showings in the early events to raise the funds needed to compete in the next round. Now, the primaries and caucuses are so concentrated early in the season that it may be impossible for candidates to process funds fast enough to reserve the advertising slots needed to compete in the later primaries.

Raising contribution limits and increasing the limit on the total amount that candidates can spend during the prenomination stage can help adjust for the changes in the electoral system. Higher contribution limits can make up for the value the maximum contribution has lost since it was put in place twenty years ago and can make it easier for candidates to raise funds needed to communicate with the expanded universe of voters.

However, there is a limit to the degree to which campaign finance can address the problems posed by frontloading. Because it takes time to raise the funds needed to communicate with the expanded universe of voters, this frontloading inevitably means that many potential primary or caucus voters who do not happen to live in states with very early contests are deprived of the opportunity to hear messages directly from the candidates campaigning in their states.

There are four other, more technical problems with the presidential public financing system, particularly its funding mechanism. First, the federal tax checkoff no longer provides all of the needed funding. This problem arises because the payouts from the fund have increased with inflation but the income tax checkoff which provides the funding is not indexed. Also contributing to the funding problem is the fact that tax filers are only eligible to participate in the checkoff if they are paying federal taxes, and the percentage of filers paying taxes has decreased. Congress addressed the funding problem in 1993 by increasing the tax checkoff amount from $1 to $3; however, this has not proved adequate and there were temporary shortfalls in the 1996 presidential prenomination period. This problem should be remedied in time for the presidential elections of the year 2000, when the White House will be an open seat, expensive for candidates of both major parties in the prenomination phase.

Second, the threshold for qualifying for matching funds in the prenomination period was not indexed for inflation. Accordingly, two decades of inflation has meant that it is relatively easy to qualify for federal dollars.

Third, the state-by-state limits on spending in the prenomination phase impose significant accounting costs, inspire subterfuge, and advance no important policy goal. Accordingly they should be repealed.

Finally, while the grants for general election expenses were designed to eliminate candidate fundraising during the fall campaign, presidential nominees have subverted this intent by raising soft money. Of course, our previously discussed recommendation that soft money be abolished seeks to solve this problem.

The limit on contributions from individuals to presidential nomination candidates should be increased to $3,000 to adjust for inflation and to make it easier for candidates to raise the funds they need to communicate with voters. In the context of a multi-million dollar campaign with essential disclosure provided by the FEC, a $3,000 contribution is much less than the seed money recommendation of this Task Force, and is consistent with our belief in higher contribution limits.

The prenomination spending limit should be increased to the level of the limit for general election spending—some $61.8 million in 1996. Increasing the limit recognizes that prenomination candidates now compete in elections throughout (most of) the country, and this change would help candidates reach out to more voters in more states. Also, eliminating the separate allowances for fundraising and compliance costs will reduce candidate costs by no longer necessitating the keeping of three sets of figures.

The presidential public financing system needs stable, adequate funding, and accordingly, we recommend raising the amount of the federal income tax checkoff to $5. Minnesota and Rhode Island have had a $5 checkoff and the federal system requires this level of funding as well. Moreover, the checkoff should be indexed to inflation and rounded to the nearest dollar at least every four years.

The threshold for qualifying for matching funds should be raised. In order to receive federal funds, candidates should be required to raise $10,000 in each

of twenty states in amounts of up to $250, rather than the current $5.000 per state.

The state-by-state limits on spending in the prenomination stage should be eliminated.

In keeping with our call for the abolition of soft money, we urge the repeal of FEC regulations that allow special treatment for contributions to host committees in cities holding nominating conventions. If cities seeking political conventions establish host committees with tax-exempt status, then contributions from corporations, labor unions or others would be tax deductible, not in the same category as soft money currently used. Since tax status is regulated by the Internal Revenue Service, it would be desirable to instruct the IRS to adopt regulations requiring disclosure of tax-exempt contributions when donated for purposes of a city holding a national nominating convention.

Public Financing—U.S. Senate and House

In the context of contests for seats in the U.S. Senate and House of Representatives, the paramount campaign finance issue is the recruitment and funding of challengers. Congressional challengers are chronically underfunded, and this reality discourages individuals who might otherwise mount credible electoral challenges.

A system of partial public financing for general election campaigns can address this problem. Public financing can make it easier for congressional challengers to secure the funds they need to mount credible campaigns. Because of its incentive effect, public financing should raise the quality of congressional challengers, further increasing the competitiveness of these races.

Public financing also is an excellent way to confront the problem of wealthy individuals' self-financed campaigns. As explained more fully in the section on Millionaire Candidates above, public financing may encourage wealthy individuals to accept limits on their contributions to their own campaigns—witness Ross Perot in the 1996 presidential elections—and can help candidates who face self-financed opponents to gather the funds they need to mount effective campaigns.

In addition to fostering competition and limiting the problem of self-financed candidacies, a properly structured partial public financing system would promote other goals. It would make everyone—at least taxpayers--a contributor or stakeholder. Also, it would reduce the amount of time candidates need to spend raising funds. Finally, a system of partial public financing would help reduce the role of large contributors and PACs (see section on Sources of Funding).

In supporting public financing, we explicitly reject the view that public financing is "welfare for politicians." We note that candidates are barred from using campaign money for personal purposes. More importantly, we support public financing because we see it as a good way to achieve important goals. We believe that campaigns are vital to American government and politics, and we think it wholly appropriate that public money be used to advance this public good by providing alternative sources of funds.

With one caveat, we are open-minded about the manner in which the public support would be delivered. Specifically, we see three ways of delivering the kind of assistance that would induce candidates to participate in a voluntary program: (1) small individual contributions to participating candidates might be eligible for a partial tax credit; (2) nominated candidates who establish eligibility by raising a specified sum in small contributions might receive lump sum payments for the general election period; (3) participating candidates might receive broadcast vouchers or subsidized postal rates. While this last method promises to provide public funding with little or no funding from the tax-paying public, we are wary of attempts to finance elections on the cheap by shifting costs to the broadcasting industry and the Postal Service.

Experience at the state level has shown that there can be successful public funding systems. However, when primaries are held as late as July, August or September, matching funds are not feasible in the general election period because election commissions cannot turn around late fundraising submissions in time to get public funds to candidates for early spending or even for early strategic planning; accordingly, bloc grants are preferred for general election public funding, as in the presidential public funding system.

Regardless of the mechanism (or combination of mechanisms) for delivering public financing, the assistance should be sufficient to induce the vast majority of candidates to participate in the system; experience at the state level has shown that inadequate funding has caused some systems to be ineffective. That is, if the system does not offer participating candidates sufficient incentive, then significant numbers of candidates may elect not to participate. In that scenario, the system will be ineffective.

We endorse a system of partial public financing for U.S. Senate and House in general election campaigns. Whether aid is delivered by giving a limited tax credit for some contributions, or giving qualified campaigns a lump sum payment, the incentive should be sufficient to induce the vast majority of candidates to participate in the system.

Candidates who agree to participate in the partial public financing system should be required to agree to contribute no more than $50,000 to their own campaigns.

Administering any of these systems would require a considerable administrative apparatus. Therefore, we endorse public funding with the understanding that the FEC will be provided with the resources needed to effectively administer the program.

Spending Limits

For several reasons, public discussions typically link the provision of public funding for campaigns and the acceptance of spending limits by candidates. First, in its *Buckley* decision, the Supreme Court held that spending limits are constitutional only when candidates voluntarily accept them in exchange for public funding. And, second, while public financing is widely thought to be unpopular among the public, spending limits are widely thought to be popular. So, public funding has often been seen as the political price to be paid for spending limits.

We do not accept this framing. Campaign money is not evil *per se*. Rather, it is a necessary instrument for campaign communication. While we recognize that many believe that campaign spending is excessive, we believe that the high cost of campaigns results, not from candidates' buying votes, but from candidates' needs to communicate with voters. Candidates need to sell themselves in their own words, not as mediated by press reports. There is nothing inherently wrong with candidates sending letters to the homes of registered voters, or using television or radio advertisements to deliver campaign messages. On the contrary, we are inclined to see such communication as indicative of a healthy democratic process. And we recognize that, in the market economy in which our politics takes place, such communication costs money.

On a more practical level, our objection to spending limits for congressional campaigns is based on five specific concerns. The first two deal with problems arising from low limits and the remaining three are more general objectives. First, spending limits undermine competition; low ceilings work to the advantage of those candidates who are already known to voters and those candidates typically are incumbents. Putting the point differently, challengers are commonly less well known and low expenditure ceilings will block them from spending the money they need to become known and to mount effective challenges. Limits high enough to avoid this problem will be ineffectual because they will not restrain spending, and will not earn the promised public support.

Second, the Supreme Court has ruled that expenditure limits amount to restrictions on the quantity of candidates' speech and that they cannot be imposed on candidates. Rather, candidates must be offered an incentive (such as public financing) to accept the limits. If the limits are too low or if the incentive is too little, then a significant number of candidates will opt out of the system. We are particularly concerned that wealthy candidates operating self-financed campaigns would be immune from limits and that excessively low limits would encourage more such millionaire candidacies.

Third, in today's environment, imposing spending limits on congressional candidates would mean that more spending would occur under the control of actors outside of the conventional campaign finance channels and without the accountability that the ballot provides. For example, individuals and groups who want to help (or hurt) a given candidate's chances and who are effectively precluded from contributing to the campaign of that candidate (or his or her opponent) are likely to engage in independent expenditures. In *Buckley*, the Supreme Court held that this independent spending cannot be limited, and it is the law of the land.

Fourth, the presence of spending limits would mean that, from the beginning of each campaign, candidates would engage in subversion because they would never be certain whether the limits might constrain them later. The temptation for candidates facing spending limits to skirt the law and to invite surrogates to spend on their behalf increases as election day draws near, the value of spending increases, and the likelihood of being punished before the balloting decreases. This resulting situation would further corrode public trust.

Fifth, we are very concerned about the problem of enforcement. The Federal Election Commission currently has difficulties monitoring ten or fifteen presidential candidates' spending limits. The Commission staff would need to be greatly increased for it to monitor spending limits in hundreds of congressional elections. We see no likelihood that the Congress would sufficiently enlarge the FEC for this purpose.

Notwithstanding these objections to spending limits for congressional campaigns, there are practical reasons for retaining the (increased) spending limits for presidential candidates who participate in that public funding system. First, retaining some cap in the prenomination phase limits the ability of unchallenged presidential incumbents to spend prenomination money to advance their general election prospects.

Second, the presidential public funding system has been in effect over the last six presidential elections. While the spending limits generally have been ineffective, we are willing to change the system in this case only by increasing the spending limits.

Third, the general election grant is intended to limit the major party nominees' concern with fundraising. That is why the money comes in the form of a bloc grant with the proviso that the nominees not raise additional hard money. We seek to keep the presidential financing system intact as much as possible.

Partial public financing of congressional campaigns should be instituted without spending limits. At the same time, the spending limits in the presidential system should be retained, but set at the highest levels that we have suggested for the prenomination period.

SOURCES OF FUNDING

The Task Force values the broad and voluntary participation of Americans in the funding of campaigns for national, state and local offices. In the years of presidential elections at least 5 percent of American adults contribute voluntarily to the funding of campaigns, either by direct contributions to candidates or by contributions to PACs and party committees, a record that no other of the world's democracies can match. Broad-based giving engages millions of Americans in the campaign and its events and encourages voting. It also promotes the representation of diversity and the interplay of interests so crucial for a healthy pluralism of countervailing interests in our politics.

Our concern with participation is also associated with the First Amendment's ideals; people are and should be free to speak and to associate with others. To limit the ability of citizens to direct their money to support ideas they favor is to violate one of our most precious freedoms. In the campaign finance context, this means that citizens should be free to make limited and publicly disclosed contributions to candidates and parties, and they should be allowed to join with other like-minded citizens in making political contributions through political action committees or candidate or party committees.

Our attitude toward financial participation has another basis: a long line of empirical research had persuaded us that campaign contributions do not play as large a role in influencing legislative behavior as many believe. A legislator's principles, his or her constituency, and his or her political party, have consistently been shown to be more influential than are patterns of contributions. Accordingly, we conclude that many reformers, relying on simplistic, unidimensional analyses that fail to consider the numerous factors that influence political behavior, make too much of large contributions.

It is appropriate to highlight a unique aspect of our views and another danger of some popular reform proposals. In our view, campaign money is a necessary instrument for campaign communication, and a way for voters to demonstrate their support for particular candidates. Unlike many reformers, we take the view that starving campaigns of needed funds will not impoverish candidates (who are barred from using campaign money for personal expenses), but it will impoverish the communication on which democratic elections are based.

Competitive elections require that candidates be able to communicate with voters and, in our free market system, such communication requires money. We fear that reform which focuses on driving private money out of the system will produce an electoral system with significantly diminished candidate communication, and hence with reduced competition.

When candidates do not have sufficient money to inform voters about their records, qualifications, and positions on issues, the public loses. In our view, the most expensive election is one in which critical issues and the candidates' important qualities do not receive adequate attention because one or more candidates lack the necessary funds. We believe that the amount spent in elections at all levels of government—federal, state and local—which totalled $4 billion in 1996, is a small price to pay for an open, democratic system.

At the same time, the Task Force is not blindly sanguine about the role of money in politics. By offering groups and wealthy individuals the opportunity to go outside of the conventional campaign finance system, the New Realities of campaign finance now offer to certain sources of funds new and unregulated channels through which their campaign money can flow. We believe that campaign money should be disclosed and regulated with moderate limits.

Political Parties

Political parties seek to win elections by bringing together coalitions of groups and by articulating issues that will resonate with voters. Like political scientists generally, we value this activity as important consensus building in a diverse democracy. Also, using the party as a financial intermediary weakens the potentially corrupting link between contributor and office holder. Accordingly, we wish to strengthen the parties' roles in campaigning.

The Supreme Court decision in the *Colorado* case in 1996 greatly extended the parties' role in campaigns. It treated parties as private associations entitled to engage in unlimited independent expenditures. Thus the Court removed limits on how much parties can spend on a given campaign so long as they do not plan or coordinate those expenditures with their respective candidates. In response, both major parties moved to set up "independent" arms that would allow them to spend unlimited amounts of money to advance the party's nominees. Because we value parties' integrative role, we view this development as unfortunate. We would much prefer that parties do what they are organized to do: encourage candidates to coordinate their activities with the party, and to work together to win election.

Although we value parties, this Report's first recommendation was that soft money be abolished. Clearly, this change would deprive parties of a significant source of funds. Our hope is that a significant share of the additional hard money funds that result from raising the annual limit on individuals' total contributions will flow to parties. In addition, we recommend giving parties greater latitude in their use of hard money.

Currently, federal law stipulates that an individual can contribute to political party committees no more than $20,000 of their annual $25,000 maximum hard money calendar year total. Along with raising to $100,000 the annual limit for individuals contributing in conjunction with federal elections, we recommend abolishing the limit on how much of this money can go to parties. An individual would need to take into consideration his or her total contributions to federal candidates and PACs to determine the remainder within the $100,000 limit that can be donated to party committees.

We recommend the elimination of limits on how much parties and party committees can contribute to congressional candidates or spend on behalf of particular congressional candidates. This change would strengthen parties and the links between parties and their candidates, particularly in the light of the *Colorado* decision which otherwise encourages parties to operate independently of their nominees. Also, this recommendation will allow parties to help their candidates who are faced with millionaire opponents, negative independent expenditures, or negative issue advertising—giving such candidates party help to mount credible campaigns. If there is effective disclosure and enforcement, this change will not increase the risk of money laundering through the parties.

Because the national parties currently funnel the funds to the state parties which actually spend the money, abolishing soft money will deprive state parties of significant revenue. We hope that abolishing soft money will encourage local parties to shift from dependence on soft money transferred from the national headquarters to positions of greater self-reliance.

Political Action Committees

We do not share the animus to PACs that is commonplace among reformers. Rather than rejecting PACs as tools of "special interests," we view them in the context of the larger stream of American political life which, as Alexis de Toqueville observed in the 1830s, has often witnessed the creation of new forms of association to further people's interests and goals. We take the view that such activity inevitably comes with a vibrant democracy. PACs represent an aspect of American pluralist democracy which we must accept, and not solely because the rights of association and speech are protected by the First Amendment. PACs allow individuals to join with others who share their values and to undertake joint action to achieve the political goals they perceive as most important. Some 4,000 PACs are registered with the FEC, and an estimated 12,000 PACs exist at the state level. These numbers are impressive, representing many diverse views and interests that should not be stifled.

PACs are a mechanism for political fundraising that respects the manner in which society is structured. Occupation and professional groups, which some PACs represent, have replaced the neighborhood party wards or precincts as centers of political activity. By allowing individuals to experience the sense of achievement that accompanies taking part in political activity with like-minded persons, PACs increase participation in the political process. By drawing in participants and structuring their participation, PACs allow more voices to be heard in determining who will be elected.

On a more practical level, it is important to note the advantage that PACs offer; with PACs, group-based financial participation in campaigns is disclosed and limited. In this way, PACs contribute to greater accountability in political financing. In particular, PAC participation is preferable to groups engaging in independent expenditures, or asking their members to contribute directly as individuals through bundling.

By providing candidates with funds, PACs also help ensure that candidates are able to inform voters of their views and positions. Further, these contributions make it possible for individuals without wealth to run for office.

One unforeseen consequence of banning PAC contributions, as has been proposed at the federal level, would be that organizations now sponsoring PACs would probably increase their lobbying activities. Despite recent improvements in lobbying registration and disclosure at the federal and state levels, lobbying activities are simply not as accountable as are PAC activities, and so we recognize the advantage of accountable PAC activities over lobbying activities.

One legislative reaction to PAC activity—proposed at the federal level and imposed in some states—has been the effort to limit the total amount each candidate can accept from all PACs. Such aggregate PAC limits raise constitutional questions; aggregate PAC limits are, in effect, receipt limitations, and as such, would force candidates to pick and choose among offered contributions to remain under the ceiling. Those PACs that could give early—likely larger PACs—would fill a candidate's limit and freeze out smaller PACs, which could then charge that their constitutional right to give was being abridged.

The Task Force does not endorse aggregate limits on the amounts congressional candidates may accept from all PACs.

We oppose efforts to ban all PAC contributions and activity. Further, in keeping with our proposal to raise individual contribution limits, we propose that the amounts PACs can contribute at the federal level per candidate per election be increased from $5,000 to $6,000 per candidate per election; and that the annual limit on an individual's contributions to a PAC be increased to $6,000 as well. For an individual contributor, this amount contributed to a PAC or PACs would be a portion of the $100,000 calendar year limit per individual contributor. Corporate,

labor union and other group contributions to political parties could continue to be made by PACs representing these interests. Of course, PAC contribution limits should be indexed.

Leadership PACs

Over the last few election cycles we have experienced the growth of a type of PAC that does concern us. Leadership PACs constitute double dipping by ambitious legislative leaders who appeal for contributions to their own authorized campaign committee and then appeal for contributions to the leadership PAC they administer. Leaders then distribute the leadership PACs' funds to members of their party seeking election or reelection to the legislature. In this way, leadership PACs strengthen the hand of legislative leaders *vis-a-vis* members of their own party, thereby distorting the balance of power in the legislature. In addition, leadership PACs often are ideological or single issue—not party oriented—and seek to advance the leader's personal agenda.

The Task Force supports efforts to ban leadership PACs.

Bundling of Contributions

Some PACs seek to circumvent the limits on the amount of money they are allowed to contribute to a given campaign by having their supporters write checks to that campaign, collecting those checks, and turning them over to the campaign in a bundle so that the candidate perceives the PAC's role in collecting the funds. This practice is known as the bundling of contributions.

Individuals also can bundle to circumvent contribution limits. Whatever the nature of the bundler, the contributions are those of individuals, but the bundler gets its share of political gratitude for organizing the individual collections.

Yet, bundling raises difficult questions because of its similarity to the more benign process of network solicitation, in which a candidate raises money by assigning to various campaign loyalists the responsibility for raising funds from their friends. The difference is that the loyalist fundraiser represents a personal or partisan allegiance to the candidate, not to a group seeking legislative or governmental policies. While the campaign loyalist engages in a kind of bundling, network solicitation is of vital importance to most campaigns and, rather than viewing it as a circumvention of campaign finance laws, we believe that network fund raising is in the great tradition of American volunteerism and that it is a good way for campaigns to raise the funds needed to communicate with voters.

In the end, we view bundling as a serious disclosure issue. Bundlers do not aggregate how much they have bundled for a given candidate. For example, while Emily's List is a registered conduit and it reports separately each check it bundles, it does not report the aggregate value of the contributions it bundles on behalf of each candidate it assists.

Bundlers should be required to report the contributions they bundle and their total bundling activity on behalf of each candidate. As conduits, bundlers must state the political interests they work on behalf of, be responsible for accurate information (names, addresses, occupation) about all individuals whose contributions they bundle, and report total sums bundled per candidate. Attempts to disclose bundling should not impede network solicitation, nor inhibit healthy participation.

Reform attempts should not spur additional bundling by, for example, lowering PAC contribution limits.

Out-of-District Contributions

Campaign finance regulation should not distinguish contributions that come from within an electoral district or state and those that come from beyond the district or state borders. We reject the notion that out-of-district and out-of-state contributions constitute an inappropriate interference with local elections. All politics are not local, and we should not act as though they are. Simply put, individuals' interests in government policy do not stop at the district or state border. The cross-district nature of governance is particularly apparent in virtually all national issues and when struggle for party control of a legislature is at stake.

We also reject the notion that out-of-district and out-of-state contributions are necessarily associated with special interests. Instead, we take a pluralist view that Americans inevitably will organize themselves as they see fit. In fact, out-of-district and out-of-state contributions have distinctive virtues. They are useful for overcoming the parochialism of locally elected legislators, and they help weaken the power of wealthy individuals and interests in the district or state. In addition, they can give voice to interests that are not geographically concentrated.

Finally, special limits on such contributions may not pass constitutional muster; a ban on out-of-district or out-of-state contributions serves as a blanket indictment of all such contributions, yet, because not all such contributions are problematic, courts may well hold that a blanket ban unfairly deprives non-residents of their right to contribute. At the same time, a ban on out-of-district or out-of-state contributions would do nothing to address any problems with contributions from inside the district. In fact, by curtailing outside influence, such a ban would strengthen the hand of contributors from within the district or state. Citizens of this country have a right to make contributions in connection with federal elections, and geography should not serve as the basis for discrimination.

The regulatory scheme should not distinguish between contributions from inside the electoral district and those coming from outside of the district. Regulating outside contributions by banning a certain percentage—50 percent, 60 percent, or 90 percent—does not change the constitutional objection or make such bans desirable.

CONCLUSION

Because no set of reforms will allow us to simultaneously achieve all often conflicting goals, and because there are real costs associated with regulatory overreaching, it is imperative to be smart about reform. Accordingly, in this Report, we have presented a set of reforms designed to address today's campaign finance problems in ways that advance the requisites of democratic government. The changes we recommend would go a long way toward assuring that we would have competitive campaigns with adequate communication from all of the major candidates, that the sources of these funds would do more to enhance democracy than to undermine it, and that voters will have the campaign finance information they need to make informed decisions. At the same time, it is essential not to inhibit or chill legitimate forms of political participation. We have avoided pressing so hard on the lever of regulation that campaign activity would be forced out of the candidate and party channels and extruded in new, and less accountable, shapes.

These are the right reforms and the right amount of reform; seeking less would shortchange democracy, and seeking more is a recipe for disaster.

THREE

The Media
and Campaigns

The presence of the media in American society is pervasive. Seven of ten people read a daily newspaper and two of ten a weekly magazine; the number of radios in use is nearly double the size of the population; 97 percent of the households in the United States have television sets, turned on an average of six hours and forty-four minutes a day; and for 57 percent of the citizenry television is the primary source of information for learning about what is happening in the world. Given their ability to reach a wide audience, presidential candidates have understandably come to see the media, and particularly television, as the key variable in determining whether their run for the presidency succeeds or fails. For this reason, media-related activities typically consume one-half or more of a candidate's budget, and the ranks of his or her staff are heavily populated with individuals whose responsibilities interface with the media in one way or another. These are likely to include a media advance person, radio and TV writer, radio and TV producer, film documentary producer, TV time buyer, newspaper space buyer, and television coach.

In the last twenty-five years or so, television especially has insinuated itself into the presidential selection process more and more. This happened for several reasons. Technological developments such as the TV camera greatly facilitated the media's ability to cover presidential campaigns. Even more important, however, was the decision by the major television networks to expand greatly their commitment to news programming. Beginning in 1963, evening news programs increased their time slot from fifteen to thirty minutes, and local stations followed suit not long after. In 1979 C-SPAN commenced its unedited coverage of public affairs. This was followed in 1980 by the inauguration of CNN's twenty-four hour news programming. In the last twenty years we have also witnessed a proliferation of TV panel and interview public affairs programs, including "Night Line," the "McLaughlin Group," "Washington Week In Review," "Crossfire," and "Capital Gang."

Finally, the growth of television's influence in the presidential selection process is related to the increase in both the number and importance of primaries. Because the president-by-primary process compels candidates to appeal to a much wider audience, they have been forced to rely much more heavily on paid television advertising. Add to this the fact that primaries are precisely the kinds of events that network and cable television like to cover because they involve drama, conflict, and concrete results.

The articles in this chapter focus on the principle means by which the voters learn about presidential candidates, namely, through media coverage of their campaigns and the paid media advertisements that candidates make about themselves and their opponents.

With respect to reporting about presidential candidates, the media have been roundly criticized for trivializing the campaign, focusing not on policy issues, but rather on the "horse race" (i.e., who is winning and losing, and campaign gaffes of no major significance). Media analysts Robert Lichter and Richard Noyes sought to determine whether this approach to campaign coverage was repeated by the television networks during the 1996 campaign. Accordingly, they undertook a content analysis of every campaign story aired on NBC, CBS, and ABC during the primary season. The first article contains an analysis of what they found.

In the second selection, Fred Wertheimer takes on presidential campaign ads, arguing first that this vehicle for conveying information, precisely because it is so costly, has contributed in a major way to the problems of campaign financing. Even more disturbing, in his judgment, is the content of these ads, which in recent presidential elections has become increasingly negative, thereby debasing the campaign discourse and adversely affecting public attitudes about the political process. Believing that neither the cost nor negative content of TV ads can be allowed to continue, he suggests ways to address both problems.

In the third article, William Mayer, calls for a decidedly more tolerant attitude toward negative campaigning. Though he argues against having the media consciously adopt a negative posture in their reportage, he does see real benefits in having candidates zero in on negative aspects of an opponent's issue positions, background, and character. The central question, in his view, is not whether information is negative, but rather is it relevant? If it is, then stressing the negative as well as the positive may serve to sharpen the issues, reduce lies and exaggerations by candidates, and level the playing field.

There They Go Again:
Media Coverage of Campaign '96

S. Robert Lichter and Richard E. Noyes

The scenario for Campaign '96 looked distressingly familiar to viewers of the evening news: none of the Republican presidential candidates was particularly inspiring or interesting; they spent most of their time and resources attacking each other mercilessly; they avoided making difficult choices about America's problems in favor of running on personalities, platitudes, or phony solutions like the flat tax and protectionist trade policies. All in all, the primaries were such a sorry spectacle that it's no wonder voter participation was shamefully low.

At least that was the image of the GOP primaries that we got from the network evening newscasts, where the greatest number of voters still get their information about national politics.[1] But how accurate was this depressing image? After all, most people have no way of comparing the media's highly condensed version of the process to the actual events that occur along the campaign trail. Citizen frustration with the lack of substantive information—one voter told Phil Donahue that "if you listen to anything that's on TV or radio and you try to make your decision that way, it's impossible"[2]—can be seen as a condemnation of the news media as much as the candidates.

There was a self-serving quality to the media's blanket condemnation of Campaign '96. These hard-to-please critics of the campaign trail tableaux gave themselves much more favorable reviews. In a post-mortem on the media's primary performance that aired on CNBC, Tom Brokaw asserted, "this year especially we've done a much better job because we've been much more issue-oriented. . . . We've gotten away from [the candidates'] speeches, looked at the issues, looked at the . . . impact [they're likely to have] as a president."[3] Journalists wore white hats; politicians wore black: "There is enormous reason to sound cynical when reporting on people who so frequently and so blatantly engage in deceitful behavior," asserted *Washington Post* ombudsman Geneva Overholser. "News coverage can't touch the vitriolic effect of TV campaign advertising."[4]

Journalists have come under criticism of late for being too cynical about the way they portray the political process in general and presidential campaigns in particular. Perhaps not coincidentally, finger-pointing has also increased. As Rem Rieder wrote in the editor's column of the *American Journalism Review*, "to blame journalists struggling to make sense of this gumbo for much of the disgust many Americans feel for the political process is a little like issuing an all points bulletin for the

Source: S. Robert Lichter and Richard E. Noyes, *Good Intentions Make Bad News: Why Americans Hate Campaign Journalism* (Lanham, MD: Rowman and Littlefield, 1996), pp. 286–303

S. Robert Lichter is co-director for the Center for Media and Public Affairs. Richard E. Noyes is Political Studies Director for the Center for Media and Public Affairs.

mechanic who tuned up Charles Manson's car."[5] In short, don't blame the messengers, blame the murderers. The point of this hyperbolic simile is not difficult to divine, but Rieder spells it out: "It would do the electorate no favors to cover campaigns C-SPAN style, simply recording utterly disingenuous pronouncements with a straight face, providing no context or truth-squadding."[6]

But how do we know whether television is really serving up the gritty reality of the campaign trail, warts and all, or just producing an exaggerated caricature of politics American-style? One way is by directly comparing the candidates' actual messages from their stump speeches and TV commercials with the tone and substance of news accounts. Only C-SPAN, after all, presents events in toto and without context—the thirty-minute nightly newscasts lack this option. To edit is to choose, as Ben Bradlee once put it, and journalistic choices underlie both the content that goes into each story and the myriad words and deeds that get left out. That's why one viewer's idea of context is another's example of bias. So before we decide whether the networks did the electorate a favor with their hard-nosed campaign coverage, we need to perform our own reality check on the nightly news.

Under the sponsorship of the John and Mary Markle Foundation, we updated our 1992 research with a content analysis of every campaign story broadcast on the ABC, CBS, and NBC evening news programs during the 1996 primary season (January 1 through the March 26 California primary). We examined every topic, source, issue and viewpoint that appeared in the networks' campaign news. Then we used the same techniques to analyze the actual speeches and paid commercials of the major Republican candidates. The findings provide a comprehensive comparison between the candidates' actual messages and the way the networks portrayed them.

All three networks provided extensive campaign coverage during this period, an average of over four and one-half minutes a night on ABC and CBS and three and one-half minutes on NBC. Further, the amount of coverage increased substantially in comparison to the same period in 1992—by 19 percent in terms of the number of stories and 12 percent in total airtime. There is no indication, however, that this increase in the amount of coverage was matched by any improvement in its quality and usefulness. To the contrary, the news agenda was focused on the game rather than the issues, it placed journalists rather than candidates or voters at center stage, and it manifested a pervasive negativism at the very time when many journalists were publicly bemoaning the cynicism of their profession.[7]

The content analysis shows how much of our knowledge of the campaign came from the mouths of journalists, and how little viewers actually heard from the candidates in their own words. As political scientist Larry Sabato put it, "It's not simply that TV is giving candidates slightly shorter sound bites, it's that these celebrities who double as TV journalists are soaking up all the spotlight."[8] Nearly three-quarters (74%) of all campaign news consisted of journalists' stand-ups or voice-overs. The GOP candidates collectively received only 12 percent of the available speaking time, with the rest distributed among other on-air sources. Thus, the nine presidential candidates received only one-sixth as much speaking time as the journalists who covered them (129 minutes vs. 787 minutes). And the candidates were typically heard in only brief snippets of speech: Their average sound bite lasted just over seven seconds. (See Figure 1.)

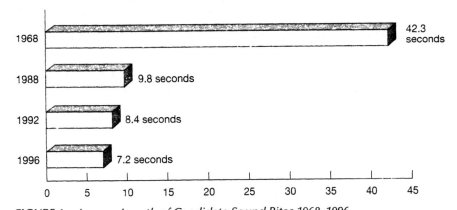

FIGURE 1   *Average Length of Candidate Sound Bites 1968–1996*
Note· ABC, CBS, NBC evening news. 1996 figure is for GOP primaries; others are for general election campaigns

So, what did the networks tell voters about the campaign? The most ubiquitous news topic was the campaign horse race, which made a big comeback in Campaign '96. Prior to the New Hampshire primary, the first crucial benchmark of the race, the number of stories featuring the candidates' standings and prospects *tripled* from their 1992 levels. This increase is all the more striking because the Democratic nomination was not contested in 1996, whereas both parties held hotly contested primaries four years earlier. When reports on the candidates' strategies and tactics are included, "horse race" stories made up a solid majority (61%) of the networks' 1996 primary season news—more than double the proportion (29%) that focused on policy issues or the candidates' qualifications. (See Figure 2.)

The horse race also dominated the media debate over the individual candidates. By the time California voters put the seal on Bob Dole's nomination on March 26, the networks had broadcast more than 3,500 evaluative statements about the various Republican contenders. More than half of these evaluations (54%) assessed the candidates' respective viability; fewer than one in five (19%) evaluated them on their issue stands or past job performance.

This choice of emphasis left voters short of substantive information when it came time for them to choose a nominee. Prior to New Hampshire, only three policy issues (taxes, the budget, and abortion) had been featured in as many as ten network news stories apiece. Such staples of primary campaign rhetoric as immigration reform and anticrime measures each generated fewer than one network news story per week. And some central elements of the "Republican revolution"—among them welfare reform and the devolution of government functions from the federal to the state and local levels—were covered too infrequently to make the networks' "top ten" issues list.

This tally may actually *overstate* the quality of issue information that was available over the airwaves. Even when the candidates' proposals were mentioned, the comments were typically brief and superficial. Only one out of six references

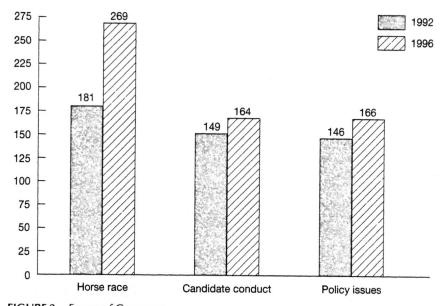

FIGURE 2   *Focus of Coverage*

Note: More than one topic may be coded per story.

to any candidate's policies lasted as long as twenty seconds; only one in seven mentioned any specific detail (e.g., "the Forbes plan . . . suggests a flat tax of 17%"); and just one out of four noted any substantive implications (e.g., "the rich would do better than the middle class").[9] Overall, only four percent of all mentions of policies fulfilled all three criteria for informative issue presentations.

By contrast, a majority (54%) of all policy-oriented discussions included some remark about the political calculations that underlay a proposal or its likely impact on the candidate's prospects (e.g., "the flat tax . . . is powerful political currency.")[10] Thus, the journalistic fascination with the horse race even intruded into airtime that was ostensibly devoted to policy issues. This disparity between substantive and process-oriented issue debate helps to explain how journalists can assert that they deal with "the issues" in campaign reports, even as their critics complain that meaningful issue discussion is missing from the news. It also provides strong support for Thomas Patterson's argument that journalism's traditional fixation on the horse race now pervades all aspects of campaign news.[11]

NEGATIVE NABOBS

When reporters weren't assessing the status of the horse race, they were pointing out the candidates' foibles or denouncing the parlous state of the campaign process. Stories about "candidate issues"—controversies over the campaign trail conduct of the candidates or their staffs—rivalled policy stories in number (each type made up 29% of all campaign stories). Thus, the major "issues" for network reporters often had nothing to do with the policies each candidate might pursue as president. Instead, they focused on the mechanics of the campaign or a candidate's personal behavior. Coverage of these issues often assumed a judgmental quality that would have been ruled out-of-bounds not long ago.

From the outset, the media designated Bob Dole as frontrunner, thereby ensuring that he would be the target of journalists' barbs. As humorist Dave Barry once quipped, the press designates a frontrunner "because we need to have somebody who we can declare is faltering."[12] In 1996, according to the media, Dole "faltered" his way to the GOP nomination. NBC's Lisa Myers dismissed his victory in Iowa as "anemic."[13] After New Hampshire, Dan Rather declared that Dole was in "a fight for survival."[14] Tim Russert, NBC's Washington bureau chief, told his audience that a brokered convention was "a real possibility."[15] Journalists had so hyped the Iowa and New Hampshire contests that they apparently believed those states to be crucial to the nomination. As veteran reporter Christopher Hanson wrote in the *Columbia Journalism Review,* "[Reporters] had to report a horse race, even if it meant turning a blind eye to Dole's advantages."[16] In fact, Iowa and New Hampshire turned out to be glaring exceptions—Dole received a higher percentage of the vote in every subsequent primary and caucus state.

Journalists' doubts about Dole's viability reflected more than their interpretation of the early contests; they also reflected doubts about Dole himself. Reporters panned his response to the president's State of the Union message as "lackluster,"[17] "lame"[18] and "bitter."[19] Dole was the only major candidate to face mostly criticism (68% negative comments) of his campaign ability. "I think his central problem is he's tired," said CBS analyst Kevin Phillips. "He's been running for national office for 20 years, he's 73 before the inauguration, and he shows that wear and tear and that lack of initiative and that lack of spark."[20] ABC's John Cochran agreed that "most of [Dole's] appearances have been as flat as his native Kansas."[21]

Dole's troubles provided a backdrop to the media's endless search for a fresh storyline. Early on, Steve Forbes seemed to provide the best hope for a race, even though some journalists doubted his staying power. Peter Jennings told the *Washington Post* that journalists were focused on Forbes "in order to make it a more interesting race," adding that, "I don't think people really regard Forbes as an absolutely serious possibility to get the nomination."[22] After less than a week of relatively benign "introductory" coverage of this political unknown, Forbes had climbed high enough in the polls for the media to begin a kind of rolling feeding frenzy.

Reporters' main complaints about Forbes's campaign were his "excessive" spending and his negative TV commercials. Overall, network coverage of his campaign conduct was 87 percent negative. Lisa Myers dubbed Forbes "Malcolm the Mudslinger" for his commercials[23] while CBS's Eric Engberg complained that his spending was destroying the mystique of the Iowa caucuses: "The Forbes campaign spurns the vision of Iowa as the last bastion of grassroots, flesh-pressing politics," he charged. "Instead, [he] treats Iowa as just another piece of political property that's up for sale."[24]

Network reporters called Forbes "rich" 102 times, or about twice per day, prior to the New Hampshire primary. Myers was most direct: "Steve Forbes was born not just with the silver spoon in his mouth," she remarked. "He had the entire place setting."[25]

The fact that Forbes attracted such negative coverage suggests that the networks were practicing what Maura Clancey and Michael Robinson dubbed "compensatory journalism"—evening the odds by being tougher on any candidate presumed to have a special or unfair advantage.[26] Clancey and Robinson used this concept to explain the bad press that incumbent presidents typically attract during their re-election campaigns. In the Republican race to challenge the incumbent, however, it showed up in the heavy criticism of Forbes's use of his personal fortune to pay for television commercials against his rivals. Forbes's campaign spending and negative advertising each received more attention than any other controversy surrounding an individual candidate.

As Forbes faded, the media spotlight shifted to Pat Buchanan after the latter's "unexpectedly" strong showings in Alaska, Louisiana and Iowa. Buchanan's coverage was mixed—he was given high marks for his abilities as a campaigner (67% positive), even as reporters deplored the content of his message. NBC's Gwen Ifill gave the devil his due: "He has a clear, provocative message, and he is the best messenger. . . . Pat Buchanan can hit a hot button from a mile away." But she also asserted that Buchanan "treads a fine line between the politics of resentment and outright demagoguery."[27] Meanwhile, CBS's Bob McNamara explored charges that Buchanan is "an extremist who, at the very least, uses code words to attract voters with racist, bigoted views." McNamara allowed that Buchanan's "ideas are now beginning to be judged by the company they keep." He interviewed David Duke, a former leader of the Ku Klux Klan, who boasted that, "if Patrick goes on to win the nomination, I guess part of the credit will have to go to us." A current Klan member added, "just about everything [Buchanan] says, we agree with." McNamara concluded icily: "After calling himself a man who 'says what he means and means what he says,' [Buchanan] must escape the embrace of people who think they know exactly what he's been talking about."[28]

As the New Hampshire primary neared, reporters emptied their notebooks, reminding viewers of Buchanan's controversial statements and associations. We learned that his national campaign co-chairman was an anti-gun-control activist who had spoken before militia and white supremacist groups. The coverage also recalled Buchanan's opposition to the Gulf War, his past newspaper columns questioning the equality of women, and his fiery speech at the 1992 Republican convention, where he asserted that the United States was split by a "religious . . . war for the soul of America."[29] On the eve of the primary, CBS correspondent Phil Jones chronicled Buchanan's rhetorical record before concluding with a rhetorical question of his own: "With some of these views, is he the one the Republican party really wants in '96?"[30]

Such sharp judgments about the candidates clearly reflect the new style of campaign journalism that was introduced on a wide scale in 1992. Prior to New Hampshire, viewers were treated to lopsidedly negative reviews of all the major GOP candidates (63% negative evaluations overall), with heavy criticism of their policies (61% negative), their records (72% negative), and their campaign conduct (78%).

(See Figure 3). For Buchanan and Forbes, positive comments predominated only in general evaluations (such as brief statements of support from voters) and in assessments of their campaign abilities. For Dole, who was often described as an old, tired and uninspiring figure on the campaign trail, only the general evaluations were predominantly positive.

Note especially that *every* major candidate received mainly negative evaluations of his record and proposals, i.e., his qualifications for the presidency. The heaviest criticism was aimed at Forbes's flat tax proposal and Buchanan's views on immigration and economic policy. This kind of issue coverage suggests that the media may actually *encourage* presidential candidates to shy away from running the kind of issue-oriented campaigns whose absence the reporters and voters alike regularly bemoan—in the current media environment, genuinely new and controversial proposals invite sharp scrutiny and heavy criticism. Journalists' rampant negativism provides a strong incentive for candidates to avoid truly bold initiatives until after winning the election.

By no means, however, did journalists confine their criticisms to the candidates: the campaign itself came in for even harsher reviews. By overwhelming margins, the networks portrayed the primaries as negative exercises in big money manipulation of inattentive voters, devoid of substance and dominated by mean and misleading television commercials. "On and on it goes, like a dog chasing its tail," complained CBS's Bob Schieffer. "Any serious discussion of the issues is lost in this maw of 'Yes, you did,' and 'No, you didn't.' "[31] When network reporters discussed the tone of the campaign, they condemned it as overly negative 99 percent of the time. "Forget about the issues," complained Peter Jennings at the start of one ABC broadcast. "There is enough mud being tossed around in the Republican presidential campaign to keep a health spa supplied for a lifetime."[32] Their judgments regarding the candidates' TV commercials were equally one-sided—the ads were attacked 29

FIGURE 3   *Good Press/Bad Press: GOP Candidates*

Note: Evaluations by reporters and nonpartisan sources on ABC, CBS, and NBC evening news election stories.

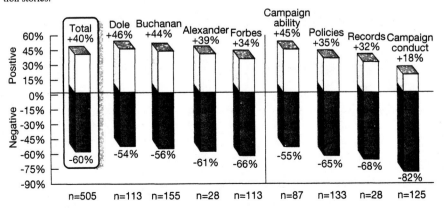

times and defended once (which translates to 97% negative coverage). Campaign '96, the networks bluntly told audiences, was negative and superficial, and the candidates were to blame.

THE REAL WORLD

Was that really the way it was on the campaign trail? To find out, we also examined the candidates' actual messages during the period prior to the New Hampshire primary (January 1 through February 19). We analyzed every line in 28 speeches and 59 different TV commercials produced by the four leading GOP candidates—Alexander, Buchanan, Dole and Forbes. The TV spots were all shown on WMUR-TV, the leading television station in New Hampshire, during the evening local newscasts—prime placement for political advertising. The 59 commercials together received 730 plays during the 36 days leading up to the primary. We examined the candidates' messages using exactly the same procedures we used to analyze the news coverage. The results provide a revealing "reality check" on the media's campaign performance.

The candidates were not relentlessly negative, as they were portrayed on TV. They rarely mentioned their opponents in their speeches, let alone attacked them. On average, a typical speech contained thirteen positive or "self-promoting" remarks and only two negative references to any opponent. As Dole told a Portsmouth Rotary luncheon audience, "I'd rather speak about myself than any of the other candidates."[33] Most of the speeches began and ended with general remarks about the importance of democracy and the greatness of America, along with a general summary of the candidate's proposals, two or three of which were singled out for extensive discussion. In Portsmouth, for example, Dole discussed his positions on the proper role of the federal government and the benefits of a balanced budget:

> We're going to balance the budget, so you'll all have a better life and lower interest rates, whether it's a car loan, home loan, student loan. And the experts tell us that if we set on this path of a balanced budget for seven years, interest rates will drop two percent . . .
>
> And in that balanced budget package, let me just point out a couple of things. Most of the people in this room are in business, small business. We believe one thing we should do is re-reduce the capital gains rate, to reduce your cost of capital. To give you more opportunities to create jobs for the people in New Hampshire and everywhere else . . .
>
> We also know that in nearly every state there are a lot of family held businesses. Maybe one family, maybe two families, maybe three. If someone passes on, you have to liquidate the business to pay the estate tax. We think that's wrong, and we want to raise that credit from $600,000 and in some cases up to $4 million. Not to give you a tax break, but to keep those employees working.[34]

Dole's willingness to address major policy issues in a substantive fashion turned out to be typical of the candidates' campaign discourse. Among the topics that were discussed at least five times in the speeches and ads we reviewed, four out of five (79%) concerned policy issues. By contrast, among the topics discussed in at least five TV election stories, barely one-third (36%) concerned policy issues. Among the issues emphasized by the candidates but downplayed by the networks were welfare reform, education, Social Security, and—Dole's favorite—the devolution of government functions to the state and local level. Only one policy issue got more attention from the media than the candidates—abortion, a controversy that attracted media scrutiny mainly for its potential to create conflicts among the contenders.

As the GOP frontrunner, Dole was the candidate least likely to engage in personal attacks. After all, the conventional frontrunner strategy is to remain above the fray. But Dole's leading challengers also focused mainly on substantive issues. In January, both Alexander and Buchanan delivered major policy addresses at the Heritage Foundation, neither of which was covered on the network evening news shows. Buchanan's speech contained a lengthy critique of the federal judiciary, arguing that federal judges and Supreme Court justices had become involved in issues more properly left to legislatures or individuals. He offered several specific remedies, including appointing judges "for a term of years rather than for life"; allowing voter recall of federal judges; and altering the process of amending the Constitution to "remove Congress from the process."[35] Although the substance of these proposals was potentially quite radical, none of them made the evening news. (The role of the federal judiciary was raised again in April by nominee-presumptive Bob Dole. When he accused President Clinton's appointees of being soft on crime, his charges became front page news.)

Sometimes, journalists' assertions about the candidates' messages were simply wrong. For example, CBS's Phil Jones derided Forbes as a "one-dimensional candidate—Mr. Flat Tax."[36] In fact, Forbes routinely discussed a variety of issues, including congressional term limits, school vouchers, and medical savings accounts. In a speech to the Capital City Rotary Club on the eve of the New Hampshire primary, Forbes offered a detailed plan for revamping Social Security:

> Now, we have to keep the current system for those who are on it—that's only fair. . . . But we know, and especially younger people know, that the current system is not going to be there when they retire. . . . So why not, while we still have time, put in a new system for younger people, where . . . part of their payroll tax that now goes to Washington and subsidizes the national debt at a below market interest rate, would instead go to their own individual savings or retirement account. That way, it takes it out of the hands of Washington, gives young people something to look forward to when they retire.
>
> Let me just give you one hypothetical example of how potent this can be when it's fully implemented. Take a twenty-year-old person today in America. Say this person is making only $10,000 a year. That person's payroll tax is a little over $1,200—almost $24 a week for Social Security. If that $1,200 was all invested in that person's individual savings or retirement account . . . he or she at age sixty-five would have a nest egg totalling almost $1,000,000. Now, politicians who promise to make you millionaires, you're leery of. But this is the American people, by their own productive efforts, making us all millionaires when we retire.[37]

If Forbes's math was wrong, or his solution simplistic, CBS might have challenged him in one of its signature "Reality Checks." These features purport to debunk political rhetoric by comparing a politician's claims with the reporter's version of the "truth." But to call Forbes a one-note candidate belied the breadth and depth of his campaign platform. Of course, the flat tax brought Forbes national attention and provided the leitmotif of his campaign. But he did hit other notes; they were just beyond the range of the evening news. Nor was his coverage unusual in this regard. Overall, the speeches that we reviewed were more than three times as substantive as the media coverage. More than half (54%) of all the statements they contained dealt with policy issues, compared to only one out of six statements (16%) about the candidates on TV news during the same period.

Similarly, the candidates often took the high road in their much-maligned TV spots. Although their commercials were more negative than their speeches, the intense media scrutiny left the false impression that "attack ads" completely dominated the airwaves. Part of the problem was that journalists issued blanket condemnations of "negative advertising" that failed to distinguish between legitimate criticism and dirty politics. As communications scholar Kathleen Hall Jamieson told the *Christian Science Monitor*, the ad-bashers unfairly lump together "ads that lie or distort and those that create a negative image of an opponent by legitimately comparing positions."[38]

But this is not the whole story. When we tallied all the ads that contained every kind of negative message, they turned out to be less frequent than those containing positive claims. In the month that preceded their primary, New Hampshire voters were exposed to seventeen television commercials that relied exclusively on positive messages, and only eleven that were exclusively negative. (The remainder contained a mixture of positive and negative statements.) Measured statement by statement, positive comments in TV spots outweighed negative ones by 57 percent to 43 percent. Nor did the candidates give greater prominence to their negative ads by showing them more frequently than their positive ones. When the totals are weighted to take into account the number of times each ad was broadcast, the percentage of positive messages increases to 60 percent.

Typical of the kinder, gentler genre was an ad in which Lamar Alexander summarized his record: "When I was governor of Tennessee, my goal was to raise family incomes. We did it, by attracting Saturn and growing jobs. . . . I know how to balance a budget. In Tennessee, I did it eight times."[39] Alexander later sought to capitalize on the general outcry against negative ads by touting his own positive approach: "With all the mudballs these other candidates are whipping at each other, I thought I'd take a minute to tell you what I'd actually do as President . . ."[40] By our count, ironically, this ad was partly negative, since Alexander directly criticized his rivals (although not by name). But he was appealing to voter disgust with a process that was only partly created by the other candidates. They, too, ran their share of positive or self-promoting ads; they simply got no credit for doing so from journalists who were fixated on negative ads.

Thus, Bob Dole's campaign featured a sixty-second biographical commercial that included tributes from his wife Elizabeth: "His story is really the 'American story'—triumph over adversity, love of family, commitment to a core set of beliefs that have been tested in the toughest situations imaginable . . ."[41] Pat Buchanan's campaign also offered WMUR viewers a mini-bio, in which the candidate told voters that "the convictions I learned from my parents—work, family, faith, character—have served me well. I've never been afraid to speak my mind. I will never be afraid to lead."[42]

These kinder, gentler campaign messages were by no means limited to personality issues. The candidates also "went positive" in pitching their platforms. For example, the Forbes campaign ran a thirty-second spot on his proposal for medical savings accounts, even quoting a flattering (pre-campaign) NBC News story. The candidate told voters, "Medical savings accounts can improve care, cut waste, and protect Medicare without reducing your benefits. You control your health care, not the politicians."[43] Although the candidates' ads were less substantive than their speeches, they were still far meatier than the newscasts. Forty-four percent of these "paid media" comments were issue-oriented, compared with 16 percent in the "free media."

CONCLUSION: THE MEDIA IN CAMPAIGN '96

Taken as a whole, our findings suggest that the media's "first rough draft of history" in Campaign '96 was rough indeed—rough on the candidates, rough on the viewers, and offering only the roughest approximation of reality. For all the posturing, pandering and prevaricating that sometimes muddied the campaign trail, the news coverage made the process seem far more negative and less substantive than it really was. The candidates did talk about serious issues, and they expended more effort on selling themselves than on sandbagging their rivals. But television reporters often seemed more interested in kibitzing and kvetching about the campaign than in covering it. As *Wall Street Journal* publisher Peter Kann wrote in the aftermath of New Hampshire, "As the public's umbilical cord to the political process, the mass media thrive on filtering out the all too rare nutrients in favor of the all too abundant junk food."[44]

Of course, it isn't only the candidates who suffer from journalism's renewed passion to protect the public from the politicians. Four years earlier the networks promised a new era of campaign journalism, in which voters would benefit from having the public agenda set by journalists rather than candidates. But we found little evidence that this promise has been realized in either the tone or substance of election news. Although coverage of the 1996 primary campaign was more extensive in 1992, it was also more dominated by the horse race. News reports featuring the policy debate were relatively uncommon and tended to be both brief and superficial. In fact, journalists were far more likely to report on the political implications of a policy than any of its details or practical effects.

Further, network airtime was again dominated by the journalists who were covering the campaign rather than the candidates who conducted it or the voters who passed judgment on their appeals. The candidates' messages were typically presented in the words of journalists rather than those of the candidates themselves. When the candidates did speak on-air, they were usually heard only briefly, as the average soundbite length continued to decrease. In practice, material from the candidates' speeches, discussions and debates were sliced into snippets that illustrated whatever themes reporters chose to build their stories around.

Even more disturbing was the relentlessly negative tone of the coverage, which extended not only to the candidates and their records and policies, but to virtually all aspects of the campaign itself. In particular, reporters and other nonpartisan sources cited on television news were nearly unanimous in their frequent complaints about the negative tone of the campaign, its lack of substance, and the candidates' reliance on attack ads. But these complaints don't match the reality of a campaign in which the candidates' ads and speeches were mainly policy-oriented and positive in tone, in marked contrast to the news coverage. These findings raise the question of whether the media outcry over "negative campaigning" might be motivated partly by journalists' desire to enhance their own influence by reserving for themselves the right to interpret the campaign to the public.

Of course, we can't "scientifically" evaluate the truth of any candidate's claims about himself or his opponents. Candidate discourse may be misleading or manipulative even when it is affirmative and substantive. That is why the public depends on journalists for protection against falsehood and demagoguery as well as information about the events of the day. But it is only through the dispassionate and impartial presentation of factual information that journalists earn the credibility that legitimates their activities on the public's behalf. If election news systematically distorts the reality of the campaign trail, journalists cannot expect voters to give much credence to media "truth boxes" and "reality checks."

Some in the profession are already arguing this point. *Time*'s Walter Isaacson told a First Amendment Leadership Breakfast at the Columbia Graduate School of Journalism that "what's happened is that over the past ten, fifteen years we've lost our credibility and our authority."[45] CBS reporter Bernard Goldberg agreed: "There are lots of reasons fewer people are watching network news, and one of them, I'm more convinced than ever, is that our viewers simply don't trust us."[46] If a significant segment of the voting public no longer trusts the accuracy and objectivity of news reports, then even journalists' best efforts become part of a cynical (and ultimately meaningless) election-year game. Chris Hanson described the mindset of many of the reporters who cover presidential campaigns:

> Every four years we enter a chamber where, as in the playroom theatrics of childhood, we create our own reality, change it at whim, alter it to suit our fancy. It's the alcove of the early presidential primaries, where no candidate has yet secured a delegate majority and where we are thus at liberty to project, speculate, and stargaze, with nothing at stake but our credibility. [In 1996] . . . we didn't just kill candidacies off. We resurrected them and killed them again, as in playground wars of old.[47]

The journalism Hanson, Goldberg and Isaacson describe is not one that is particularly useful to voters. It is one that seems intent on squandering what remains of its ability to credibly inform and educate the citizenry. The recent movement to offer free and unfiltered air time to the presidential candidates promises a potentially significant improvement in campaign discourse. But that alone will do little to resolve the underlying problems that beset election news. The social responsibility model that journalists embraced so enthusiastically in 1992 has produced coverage that is superficial and negative. Far from aiding the democratic process, it may further erode public confidence in the political system and in mainstream journalism as well. When the media try to arbitrate an election instead of narrating it, the voters are the real losers.

NOTES

1. According to a Roper survey conducted January–February 1996 for the Freedom Forum, 57 percent of voters said they got most of their information about the presidential election campaign from television news.
2. Quoted on *CBS Evening News*, February 20, 1996.
3. "Politics '96: The Campaign and the Media," CNBC, March 9, 1996.
4. Geneva Overholser, "Candidates and Cynicism," *Washington Post,* February 8, 1996.
5. Rem Rieder, "No Wonder They're Cynical," *American Journalism Review,* April 1996.
6. Ibid.
7. See James Fallows, *Breaking the News: How the Media Undermine American Democracy* (New York: Pantheon, 1996); and Joan Konner, "This Absolutely Wonderful Race," *Columbia Journalism Review,* May/June 1996.
8. Quoted by Stephen Budiansky, "Campaign '96: Rating the Media," *U.S. News & World Report,* April 8, 1996
9. All quotes from an ABC news segment on the flat tax, *World News Tonight,* January 15, 1996.
10. Ibid.
11. Thomas E. Patterson, *Out of Order* (New York: Alfred A. Knopf, 1993), p. 69.
12. Dave Barry, "Agent Soul Sap Charges into the Lead," *Washington Post Magazine,* February 16, 1992.
13. *NBC Nightly News,* February 13, 1996.
14. *CBS Evening News,* February 21, 1996.
15. *NBC Nightly News,* February 21, 1996.
16. Christopher Hanson, "Lost in Never-Never-Land," *Columbia Journalism Review,* May/June 1996.
17. *NBC Nightly News,* January 25, 1996.
18. *CBS Evening News,* January 28, 1996.
19. Ibid.
20. *CBS Evening News,* February 28, 1996.
21. ABC's *World News Tonight,* February 19, 1996.
22. Quoted by Howard Kurtz, "Forbes Leaps Out of Pack and into the Media's Glare," *Washington Post,* January 22, 1996.
23. *NBC Nightly News,* January 30, 1996.
24. *CBS Evening News,* February 2, 1996.
25. *NBC Evening News,* January 17, 1996.
26. Maura Clancey and Michael J. Robinson, "General Election Coverage: Part 1," *Public Opinion,* December/January 1985.
27. *NBC Nightly News,* February 21, 1996.

28. *CBS Evening News,* February 28, 1996.

29. Quoted on *CBS Evening News,* February 19, 1996.

30. Ibid.

31. *CBS Evening News,* February 12, 1996.

32. ABC's *World News Tonight,* February 16, 1996.

33. Dole speech to Portsmouth Rotary luncheon, Portsmouth, NH, delivered February 8, 1996 (as transcribed by Michaleen Driscoll).

34. Ibid.

35. Buchanan speech to the Heritage Foundation, Washington, DC, delivered January 29, 1996 (retrieved from Buchanan for President Website, [http://www.buchanan.org/]).

36. *CBS Evening News,* March 13, 1996.

37. Steve Forbes speech to the Capital City Rotary Club, Manchester, New Hampshire, delivered February 19, 1996 (from C-SPAN broadcast).

38. Quoted by Linda Feldmann, " 'Boom' in Attack Ads Is a Myth," *Christian Science Monitor,* February 28, 1996.

39. Alexander campaign commercial, broadcast on WMUR-TV, January 23, 1996.

40. Alexander campaign commercial, broadcast on WMUR-TV, January 30, 1996.

41. Dole campaign commercial, broadcast on WMUR-TV, January 31, 1996.

42. Buchanan campaign commercial, broadcast on WMUR-TV, January 22, 1996.

43. Forbes campaign commercial, broadcast on WMUR-TV, February 15, 1996.

44. Peter Kann, "A Political Tourist in New Hampshire," *The Wall Street Journal,* February 21, 1996.

45. Remarks excerpted by Joan Konner, "This Absolutely Wonderful Race," *Columbia Journalism Review,* May/June 1996.

46. Bernard Goldberg, "Networks Need a Reality Check," *The Wall Street Journal,* February 13, 1996.

47. Hanson, "Lost in Never-Never-Land."

TV Ad Wars: How to Cut Advertising Costs in Political Campaigns

Fred Wertheimer

[Television,] like the colossus of the ancient world, stands astride our political system, demanding tribute from every candidate for major public office, incumbent or challenger. Its appetite is insatiable, and its impact is unique.

—Senator Edward Kennedy, Senate Committee on Commerce, Hearings, 92nd Congress, 1971

The cost of TV time-buys makes fundraising an enormous entry barrier for candidates for public office, an oppressive burden for incumbents who seek reelection, a continuous threat to the integrity of our political institutions, and a principle cause of the erosion of public respect for public service.

—Reed Hunt, Chairman, Federal Communications Commission, December 5, 1995

We made a huge mistake in dealing with the role of paid television advertising in political campaigns in the United States. We just let nature take its course—and over time, nature has taken an awful course. Among other things, it has imposed enormous financial pressures on our politics and has made the thirty-second negative attack ad the staple of our political communications.

As a result, paid television advertising has had a major impact on the financial cost of our campaigns and on increasing the reliance on influence-seeking contributions to pay for these costs. It also has had a major impact on the social cost of our campaigns—on the lack of confidence that citizens have in their elected leaders and institutions of government, on the high levels of public cynicism and low levels of voter turnout, on the inability of challengers to express their views and run competitive races against incumbents, and on the undue influence that campaign contributors have over government decisions.

Obviously, a number of important factors have contributed to these damaging results. This article, however, focuses on one of them: the price we have paid for letting nature take its course in the world of paid political TV advertising. It does not attempt to address the more comprehensive reforms that are necessary to solve the fundamental campaign finance problems facing the country today.

Source: Fred Wertheimer, "TV Ad Wars: How To Cut Advertising Costs in Political Campaigns," The Harvard International Journal of *Press/Politics,* 2 (Summer 1997), pp. 93–101.

Fred Wertheimer is President of *Democracy 21,* and served as President of Common Cause from 1981 to 1995.

Television is our most powerful and important means of mass communication and will continue to be until sometime early in the twenty-first century, when the Internet is likely to replace it. For some time, polls have shown that most people believe they get their news and their information about politics and government from television. Our national politicians, through their actions, show that they agree with the view once set forth by journalist and author Theodore H. White that "television *is* the political process—it's the playing field of politics."

FINANCIAL COSTS

Television advertising accounts for the lion's share of expenditures in presidential campaigns, and it is the principal expenditure in most Senate races and many House races. As Senator Bill Bradley said, in Senate campaigns "you simply transfer money from contributors to television stations." Studies have shown that presidential contenders are now spending two-thirds or more of their campaign resources on television advertising (West 1993).

In 1996, the Clinton and Dole presidential campaigns each spent some two-thirds of their campaign money on television ads during the general election period. All told, they spent an estimated $70 million and $60 million, respectively, on TV ads from April 1 through the November election.[1] This included tens of millions of dollars spent by the Clinton and Dole campaigns, using their respective political parties as conduits, that exceeded their campaign spending limits and were largely financed by "soft money" contributions not legal for use in presidential campaigns.[2]

According to one study, the Clinton and Dole presidential campaigns and their political parties were responsible for 167,714 ads in the seventy-five top media markets from April 1 through the election. That constitutes fifty-eight days, or 1,397 hours, of political ads.[3] As James Bennett of the *New York Times* reported, "To watch every repetition of every Democratic Presidential commercial broadcast from the beginning of April through [the] election, you would have to sit glued to the set all day and all night, and for an entire month."

Television advertising is also the largest single expense in congressional campaigns. An exhaustive study of campaign spending in the 1992 congressional races found that Senate candidates spent 42 percent of their campaign funds on TV advertising, and House candidates 27 percent—and more than 30 percent in competitive races (Morris and Gamache 1994). The study also found that media consultants received $165 million from congressional candidates in 1992 for candidate time buys and fees, which represented a 42-percent increase over the amount they received in 1990.

It is important to keep in mind that the bulk of the money spent for TV advertising in congressional races was spent for a one-sided conversation by incumbents with the voters: congressional incumbents of both parties greatly outraised their challengers and greatly outspent them on TV ads. The ever-escalating amounts spent on congressional campaigns—from $98 million in 1976 to $621 million in 1994—and on TV ads for these campaigns have, in turn, greatly increased the role of influence-seeking contributions in congressional races.

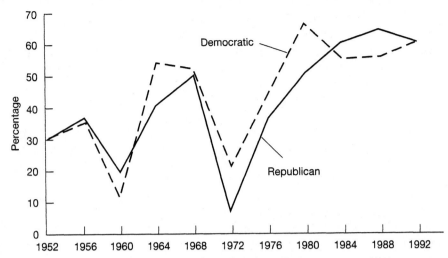

FIGURE 1   *Percentage of Presidential Campaign Budget Spent on Radio and Television Ads, 1952–1992*

Sources: For 1952–1980, Herbert Alexander, *Financing Politics* (Washington, D.C.: CQ Press, 1984), 4–12; for 1984, Stephen Wayne, *The Road to the White House* 3d ed. (New York: St. Martin's, 1988), 28–31; for 1988, Patrick Devlin, "Contrasts in Presidential Campaign Commercials," *American Behavioral Scientist*, 32 (1989): 389–414; for 1992, *Newsweek*, "How He Won," November/December 1992 (special issue).

Reprinted from Darrell M. West, *Air Wars: Television Advertising in Election Campaigns, 1952–1992* (Washington, DC: CQ Press, 1993), p. 8. Copyright 1993, Congressional Quarterly, Inc. Reprinted by permission of the publisher.

Presidential races, meanwhile, have been run under a system of spending limits and public financing since 1976. This has meant that the growth of *legal* spending by presidential campaigns has been limited during the past twenty years to cost-of-living increases incorporated into the spending-limits formula.

The high cost and perceived importance of TV advertising in U.S. politics have nevertheless still had major negative effects on presidential campaigns. Most of the campaign money spent legally by the presidential campaigns has been devoted to TV advertising, leaving little funds for anything else. In addition, millions of dollars have been raised and spent *improperly,* such as the "soft money" raised and spent by the Clinton and Dole presidential campaigns in 1996 to run TV ad campaigns over and above the ones they ran with legal funds.

SOCIAL COSTS

Television advertising is the principal means by which candidates publicly define for the voters their opponents and themselves and the government in which they serve or hope to serve. Television advertising is characterized in the public's mind by one word: *negative.*

Every two years during the fall, and much earlier in presidential election years, a focused, intense, negative message goes out to the American people over the airwaves about how bad the candidates are, how dangerous their ideas are, how their programs don't work, how problems cannot be solved. Obviously, discussing and disagreeing with your opponent's record and views is a normal and necessary part of our political process. It is a key part of informing and educating voters on the choice they have to make. However, our political TV ad campaigns go far beyond traditional comparative advertising.

Although many candidates have some positive things to say in their TV ads, these messages are overwhelmed by the negative attack ads that set the tone and dominate the debate. Because television appeals to our emotions and magnifies and intensifies what it communicates, the impact of the negative message is much more powerful and damaging on television than if the same message were being communicated through print.

Most politicians and their media handlers focus their TV advertising exclusively on one goal: winning on election day. If winning on election day means undermining your own credibility or damaging your ability to govern or breeding public distrust and cynicism or turning large segments of the public away from voting, so be it. Thus we end up with the perverse result that many politicians use TV advertising in their campaigns in ways that ultimately do as much damage to their own credibility as they do to their opponents'.

Regardless of what politicians may believe about negative advertising "working" in their campaigns, it certainly does not work when it comes to doing their jobs and serving the American people as effective and credible representatives. As Stephen Ansolabehere and Shanto Iyengar find in their book, *Going Negative*, "Negative advertising demoralizes the electorate . . . eats away at the individual's sense of civic duty . . . and contribute[s] to the general antipathy towards politicians and parties and the high rates of disapproval and distrust of political institutions" (1996).

Although the candidates bear the principal responsibility for this happening, we cannot underestimate how important the role played by media consultants is in bringing about these enormously damaging results. As a result of the perceived need for consultant expertise to design and produce TV ad campaigns, many candidates abdicate much of the power to define themselves and their opponents to their media consultants. The media consultants have only one objective—winning the election—and this is often equated with negative attack ads. The carnage that is left after the election is over and it is time to govern is someone else's problem.

Media consultants, furthermore, normally receive as part of their fee a percentage of the amount spent to purchase TV advertising time for the campaign, such as 15 percent. This can involve hundreds of thousands of dollars—sometimes even millions of dollars—in fees. It also means that media consultants have a strong personal economic incentive to spend as much money as they can to conduct the negative TV ad campaigns they devise.

Although the thirty-second negative ad has a preeminent role in U.S. politics today, it hasn't always been this way, in terms of either the length or the content of our political ads. During the first twenty years of presidential ads, for example, sixty-second spots were the dominant form of TV advertising. In the 1970s, ads of four minutes and twenty seconds played the dominant role, and starting in the 1980s, the thirty-second spot became dominant in presidential campaigns. Presidential ads also went through a transition, over time, from positive to negative. According to one study, for example, from 1960 to 1988, ads in presidential campaigns were 72 percent positive and 29 percent negative. In 1992, 63 percent of Bill Clinton's ads and 56 percent of George Bush's ads were negative, representing a high-water mark, as of that time, in negative ad emphasis in a presidential campaign (Kaid and Holtz-Bacha 1995).

A PROPOSED SOLUTION

We have let this all go on far too long without seriously challenging the damage being done by political TV advertising to the health of our democracy. We need to reduce the financial costs for candidates to communicate on television to their constituents, and we need to find ways to move candidates away from the negative ad wars that are currently the norm in U.S. politics. There are three basic approaches that can be taken regarding the issue of the costs of candidates' communicating on television.

The first is a marketplace approach. This position is taken by broadcasters and other free-market supporters who argue that the private marketplace should determine the costs of television advertising in campaigns as it does the cost of print advertising and other campaign expenses as well as the cost of commercial television advertising. They argue that to do otherwise would discriminate against broadcasters and would impose an unfair financial burden on them. They also argue that to require broadcasters to provide TV time at anything below the price determined by the marketplace would constitute an unconstitutional taking of their property without just compensation and would also violate broadcasters' due-process and equal-protection rights and the guarantees of free speech and a free press.

The second approach calls for government-mandated requirements for broadcast stations to provide a certain amount of free TV time to candidates, political parties, or both. It is taken by a number of campaign finance reform and communications reform advocates. This approach is based on the proposition that the airwaves belong to the American people and that to place conditions on the use of the public's airwaves by private interests is not taking "their" property. It reflects the view that the government grants broadcast stations valuable exclusive broadcast rights on a particular frequency at no charge and that it is appropriate to require broadcasters in return to provide free TV time to help meet their statutory requirement to serve the public interest. Backers of this approach point to the Supreme Court decision in *Red Lion Broadcasting Co. v. FCC*, 396 U.S. 367 (1969), as supporting the constitutionality of mandated free time, by upholding the public trustee concept for broadcasters and finding that "it is the rights of viewers and listeners, not the right of the broadcasters, which is paramount."

The third approach would require broadcasters to provide candidates with deeply discounted rates for TV time (for a defined time period before an election), such as 50 percent below the lowest unit rate they charge commercial advertisers. (Current law requires broadcasters to provide candidates with their lowest unit rates, although this provision has not been effective in practice and needs to be reformed.) This approach, in effect, splits the difference between the private marketplace and mandated free time. Supporters argue that it balances competing interests, placing less financial responsibility on the broadcasters and leaving the distribution of TV time in the marketplace, rather than requiring a regulatory scheme for its dispersal. Supporters also say that it has been tested in the political marketplace, having passed the U.S. Senate by recorded majority votes in 1992 and 1994, although it has not yet been enacted into law.

Congress should, at a minimum, enact legislation requiring broadcast stations to provide deeply discounted TV rates for federal candidates, such as 50 percent below their lowest unit rate. These rates should be made available only to candidates who agree to constraints on their campaign spending and to use the discounted time for ads of at least one minute or more. Reduced-cost TV time would relieve the fundraising pressures currently facing candidates and would be particularly beneficial to underfinanced challengers, because it would double a candidate's purchasing power to buy TV time. Restraints on spending would help stop the spending arms-race and reduce the role of influence-seeking contributions. It would also help ensure that the discounted TV time did not just result in increased amounts of political TV advertising with no salutary effects.

The Supreme Court in *Buckley v. Valeo,* 424 U.S. 1 (1976), has upheld the constitutionality of a system according to which the government provides campaign resources to candidates who agree to limit their spending, namely the presidential public financing system.

Congress should take away the current government requirement for broadcasters to provide candidates with their lowest unit rates from those candidates who do not enter the new system of discounted TV time and limits on spending. This would provide some financial relief to broadcasters who could then charge these candidates at whatever the market bears while they provide discounted time to those candidates who agree to limit their spending.

Congress should also consider whether it is appropriate to provide broadcasters with further financial relief. This could be accomplished, for example, by allowing broadcasters to take tax deductions or credits to compensate for the discounted TV time they provide or by using funds obtained as part of establishing a spectrum auction or a system of spectrum fees.

It is important to keep in mind, with regard to all of this, that the advent of digital television will lead quickly to new challenges regarding the role of television advertising in political campaigns. We need to pay attention to this now and not repeat the mistake we made when television first came along, when we ignored its impact on political communication and ended up paying a huge price for doing so.

SOCIAL COSTS

A number of proposals have been offered to challenge and break out of the grip of the thirty-second negative attack ad. The most radical proposal would bar all political advertising on TV. Other proposals include requiring that candidates appear on screen the whole time in their campaign TV ads, that whenever a negative charge is made in a campaign TV ad that it be made on screen by the candidate, that all campaign TV ads be five minutes or more in length, and that candidates take greater personal responsibility for their campaign ads.

The issues and choices involved here are very difficult. On the one hand, there is great value to our political process and our democracy in moving away from the political culture embedded in the thirty-second attack ad. On the other hand, regulating, through mandatory requirements, the use and content of political ads raises fundamental First Amendment and policy concerns regarding the ability of citizens to exercise free speech in presenting their candidacies to the American people.

Although TV ad campaigns are causing deep problems for our political system today, it is also important to keep in mind how valuable communicating on TV can be. TV campaign ads allow candidates to communicate their views to mass audiences and to do so unfiltered by any intermediaries, such as the media. Ansolabehere and Iyengar point out the real problem: "It's not the pervasiveness of broadcast advertising that spawns public cynicism; it is instead the tone of the advertising campaign. If campaigns were to become more positive, people would be less embittered about politics as usual and more willing to vote" (1996).

Congress should require that candidates appear on screen at the end of their political ads and state they are responsible for the ads. This would provide clearer public accountability for candidates regarding the messages they present to voters on TV. By having to take personal responsibility for their ads, visually, candidates may become less interested in and less likely to run the kinds of negative attack ads that are common practice today.

Congress should also require TV stations to provide a designated amount of free TV time to political parties for use either by their candidates for their campaigns or by party officials to present party views. The free TV time to the parties could be conditioned on the candidates and party officials appearing on screen to present their messages. Broadcasters could be provided financial relief for this free TV time through tax credits or deductions. (Most democracies provide free TV time for campaigns, and since most of these countries involve parliamentary systems, the free time is given to the political parties.) This would strengthen the role of political parties, providing them with new clean campaign resources to use to support their candidates or present their views. It would also provide the parties with the opportunity to focus new resources on underfinanced challengers, to the extent the parties are willing to assist them as opposed to their incumbent candidates.

CONCLUSION

There *are* ways to reduce the financial and social costs of TV advertising in U.S. campaigns. The policy changes proposed here would greatly reduce the current financial costs to federal candidates of communicating through TV. The changes would also challenge the basic premise that currently drives TV political ad campaigns. Through a combination of incentives and requirements, they would help move us away from the thirty-second negative attack ad without intruding on the candidates' First Amendment free-speech rights.

Changing the culture of American political campaigns is no easy task, needless to say. Citizens, however, are rightly fed up with the current system. The stakes involved here for our politics, our governance, and our country are enormous. Now is the time to begin changing our TV ways.

NOTES

1. Reported in the *New York Times*, Nov. 13, 1996.
2. Letter from Common Cause to Attorney General Janet Reno asking for Justice Department Investigation of Clinton and Dole Presidential Campaigns, Oct. 9, 1996.
3. Study by Competitive Media Reporting, reported in the *New York Times*, Nov. 13, 1996.

REFERENCES

Ansolabehere, Stephen, and Shanto Iyengar. 1996. *Going Negative: How Political Advertisements Shrink and Polarize the Electorate.* New York: Free Press.

Kaid, Lynda Lee, and Christiana Holtz-Bacha, eds. 1995. *Political Advertising in Western Democracies: Parties and Candidates on Television.* London: Sage.

Morris, Dwight, and Murielle E. Gamache. 1994. *Handbook of Campaign Spending: Money in the 1992 Congressional Races.* Washington, DC: Congressional Quarterly.

West, Darrell M. 1993. *Air Wars: Television Advertising in Election Campaigns, 1952–1992.* Washington, DC: Congressional Quarterly.

In Defense of Negative Campaigning

William G. Mayer

There is little doubt that contemporary American election campaigns do fall short of the standards commended in our civics books. But in the laudable desire to improve our campaigns, surprisingly little attention has been paid to the easy, almost reflexive assumption that negative campaigning is bad campaigning: negative speeches and advertising are always morally wrong and damaging to our political system. In part, perhaps, the problem is one of semantics. Negative campaigning certainly sounds bad: it's so, well, you know, negative. But if we move beyond the label, what really is so bad about negative campaigning?

The purpose of this article, as its title indicates, is to challenge the accepted wisdom about negative campaigning. Negative campaigning, in my view, is a necessary and legitimate part of any election; and our politics—and the growing movement to reform our election campaigns—will be a good deal better off when we finally start to acknowledge it.

THE VALUE OF NEGATIVE CAMPAIGNING

What exactly is negative campaigning? Most people who use the term seem to have in mind a definition such as the following: Negative campaigning is campaigning that attacks or is critical of an opposing candidate.[1] Where positive campaigning dwells on the candidate's own strengths and merits, and talks about the beneficial policies he would adopt if elected, negative campaigning focuses on the weaknesses and faults of the opposition: the mistakes they have made, the flaws in their character or performance, the bad policies they would pursue. And the more one focuses on the reality and consequences of such practices, the more clear I think it becomes that negative campaigning is not the plain and unmitigated evil that it is frequently portrayed to be. To the contrary, negative campaigning provides voters with a lot of valuable information that they definitely need to have when deciding how to cast their ballots.

To begin with, any serious, substantive discussion of what a candidate intends to do after the election can only be conducted by talking about the flaws and shortcomings of current policies. If a candidate is arguing for a major change in government policy, his first responsibility is to show that current policies are in some way deficient. If the economy is already growing rapidly with low rates of inflation, if the

Source: William G. Mayer, "In Defense of Negative Campaigning," *Political Science Quarterly,* 111 (Fall 1996), pp. 437–455.

William G. Mayer is professor of political science at Northeastern University and author of *The Divided Democrats: Ideological Unity, Party Reform, and Presidential Elections.*

"environmental crisis" has been greatly exaggerated, if present policies have largely eliminated the possibility that nuclear arms will actually be used, then everything the candidates are proposing in these areas is useless, even dangerous.[2] The need for such proposals becomes clear only when a candidate puts them in the context of present problems—only, that is to say, when a candidate "goes negative."

If you doubt this, go to a bookstore or library and look at any of a dozen or so books that analyze some major current policy issue. Don't select books that are written by public officials, and which might therefore be "tainted" by their ambitions for higher office. Choose the volumes that are written by the top experts in the field, the ones that presumably define the very best we can hope for in the way of intelligent and civilized discourse. What you will find is that almost all of these books organize their argument in the following way: they start by looking at the defects and shortcomings of present policy, and only then do they turn their attention to proposing new policies and solutions. It is no accident that they take this form: this is the way that most of us think about policy issues. Implicitly or explicitly, we adhere to the old adage that if it ain't broke, don't fix it. We only want to institute new policies if the old ones aren't working. Even if we are dealing with a policy area such as welfare, the schools, or the deficit, where there is widespread criticism of current practices and perhaps a consensus that something needs to be done, we would still like to have a better diagnosis than just a vague sense that the present system isn't working. In what specific ways are current policies failing? Why are they failing? What particular aspects of the current policy mix are at fault? It is difficult to imagine anyone producing an intelligent prescription for the future without first answering such questions.

But the information and analysis embodied in negative campaigning are also valuable on their own terms, for they tell us something extremely relevant about the choices we are about to make. We need to find out about the candidates' strengths, it is true, but we also need to learn about their weaknesses: the abilities and virtues they don't have; the mistakes they have made; the problems they haven't dealt with; the issues they would prefer not to talk about; the bad or unrealistic policies they have proposed. If one candidate performed poorly in his last major public office, if another has no clear or viable plan for dealing with the economy, if a third is dishonest, the voters really do need to be informed about such matters. I need hardly add that no candidate is likely to provide a full and frank discussion of his own shortcomings. Such issues will only get a proper hearing if an opponent is allowed to talk about them by engaging in negative campaigning.[3]

Finally, negative campaigning is valuable if for no other reason than its capacity to keep the candidates a bit more honest than they would be otherwise. One doesn't have to have a lot of respect for the truth and intelligence of current campaign practices in order to conclude that things would be a lot worse without negative campaigning. If candidates always knew that their opponents would never say anything critical about them, campaigns would quickly turn into a procession of lies, exaggerations, and unrealistic promises. Candidates could misstate their previous records, present glowing accounts of their abilities, make promises they knew they couldn't keep—all with the smug assurance that no one would challenge their assertions. Every campaign speech could begin with the words, "I think I can say without fear of contradiction. . . ."

THE CHARACTER ISSUE

Given the likely consequences of an attempt to limit or discourage critical comments of any kind, many commentators might want to modify their definition of negative campaigning. Perhaps what they really mean is something more like this: "Critical comments about your opponents' policy proposals are acceptable. But critical comments about your opponents' character, ability, or personal behavior are wrong. That's what negative campaigning is."[4]

This argument, of course, is simply one variant of another common theme in the recent public debate about election campaigns. Whenever a candidate's personal character or behavior are questioned by his opponents or by the media, a number of voices will be heard insisting that such matters have no legitimate place in our elections and that campaigns should stick "strictly to the issues." But this argument, too, is fundamentally mistaken. Its basic flaw is the failure to appreciate the fact that candidates for public office are not computer programs with lengthy sets of preestablished policy subroutines, but flesh-and-blood human beings.

Campaign promises are at best only a rough guide to the actual decisions that a public official will make when in office. Candidates may lie or avoid facing up to hard choices. New issues will arise that were never discussed during the campaign. Old issues will appear within an entirely different context. Whatever the cause, it is striking how many of the most important policy initiatives of the last thirty years were never discussed in the previous campaign, or were taken by presidents who had promised or implied that they would do otherwise. The issue positions assumed during a campaign, in other words, are short-lived and changeable; a better guide to what a candidate will do is often provided by his personality and character.

Once a public official does reach a decision, there is surely no guarantee that it will automatically be promulgated and executed with the full force of law, especially in the highly fragmented environment of American government. Congress must usually agree to pass the proper legislation; the bureaucracy must implement it; interest groups and the public must often be persuaded to cooperate. Officeholders, in short, need to do a lot more than closet themselves away with a big stack of policy reports in order to reach the right decisions. They must also be good managers and political strategists, meet frequently with other elected officials, lead public opinion, persuade the recalcitrant, and attract and retain talented staff. And all of these are matters of ability, temperament, and character.

For both of those reasons, candidate character and behavior are entirely relevant issues, more important than many policy questions. Indeed, if you examine the records of the last few presidents, what strikes you is how their most serious failings— at least in the minds of the voters—were not brought on by their policy views, but by their character flaws: Nixon's dishonesty and vindictiveness, Carter's inability to work with other elected officials, Reagan's management style, Bush's general disinterest in domestic policy. Small wonder, then, that public opinion polls continually show that voters are highly concerned about the personal qualities of the people on the ballot.[5]

After acknowledging this, however, the issues become somewhat murkier. Character matters, but what particular character traits would recommend or disqualify a candidate? Does sexual promiscuity make for a bad president? Does avoiding the draft? Many of the most important character traits, moreover, are remarkably difficult to assess. We now know something about how to determine if a candidate is promiscuous, but how do we "prove" that he is vindictive or paranoid or unintelligent? If a candidate loses his temper at a campaign stop, is this an isolated incident or a sign of a deep-seated mean streak? When a candidate cheats on his wife, is this a regrettable but common human failing, or a symptom of a larger personality disorder?

There are no simple answers to such questions; but particularly in elections for executive offices such as president, governor, or mayor, where character flaws can have such important repercussions, I think we are well advised to cast the net widely.[6] Certainly there is no reason to preclude a priori any discussion of a candidate's sexual behavior or intellectual honesty. More to the point, the criterion one uses to decide whether such matters are worth discussing is not negativity, but relevance. Gary Hart's sexual behavior, for example, should not have been excluded from discussion in the 1988 campaign simply because it was a negative issue that cast him in a bad light. There is a reasonable argument, however (though I am inclined to reject it), that Hart's extramarital affairs were irrelevant to the campaign, because they told us nothing about what kind of president he would have made.

Furthermore, when difficult and border-line cases do arise as to whether particular behavior or character trait is relevant to a candidate's performance in office, the bias should clearly be in favor of reporting and discussing the issue. If many voters believe that such matters are irrelevant, then presumably they can be trusted to ignore the issue when deciding how to cast their own ballots. But the final say should rest with the electorate, not with the reporters, political consultants, or fair campaign practice committees who might wish to screen such matters from public attention.

And if issues of character and behavior should be discussed, then they should be examined in both their positive and negative aspects. If candidates are free to portray themselves as leaders or deep thinkers or good managers or highly moral, then their opponents should be free to contest these claims. If Joseph Biden wanted to project an image as a passionate orator, fine. But the campaign manager for one of his leading opponents should then have been allowed to point out that some of Biden's passion and rhetoric were borrowed.

THE ROLE OF THE MEDIA

Another possible line of reply to the argument presented here is that I have left one important element out of the equation: the news media. If the purpose of negative campaigning is to expose the candidates' weaknesses and shortcomings, and to prevent lies and misrepresentations, then perhaps we can rely on television, newspapers, and magazines to help perform these functions. Equally significant, even if the critics of attack advertising do not actually intend to place the onus of negative campaigning on the media, it seems likely that this would be one practical effect of their proposals. The more difficult candidates find it is to talk about the deficiencies of their opponents, the more it will be left up to reporters and editors to determine whether and which such matters will come to public attention.

But when it comes to the need for negative campaigning, the news media cannot substitute for the candidates. Yes, the media will often be negative—but about the wrong things and in the wrong ways. Two major characteristics of the American news media, amply verified in a long list of studies, make them ill-suited to perform the functions that have traditionally been served by negative campaigning. In the first place, the media have a long-standing aversion to issues of any kind—positive or negative—or to detailed discussions of the candidates' previous performance and governing abilities. As one recent analysis of the media performance literature has noted:

> Countless studies of campaign journalism (both print and broadcast) have shown that the news invariably focuses on the campaign as a contest or race. News reports on the candidates' standing in public opinion polls, their advertising strategies, the size of the crowds at their appearances, their fund-raising efforts, and their electoral prospects far surpass coverage detailing their issue positions, ideology, prior experience, or decision-making style.[7]

This same sort of disproportion can be found in negative articles about the campaign. If a candidate makes a major gaffe, if his poll ratings are slipping, if there is in-fighting among his advisers—all these will be reported promptly and in exhaustive detail. But do not expect such detailed examination of the shortcomings in a candidate's economic policies, his environmental record, or his plans for dealing with the Middle East. The media's past record suggests that they are unlikely to provide it. Studies of campaign advertising, by contrast, usually conclude that political commercials have far more substantive content than is generally appreciated. Moreover, according to a recent study by Darrell West, negative spots usually have more specific and issue-based appeals than positive commercials.[8]

A second obstacle to the media's attempt to "police" an election campaign are the norms of objectivity and nonpartisanship that govern most major American news outlets. What exactly objectivity means, and whether the media always live up to that standard, are complex and difficult questions, but ones that need not concern us here. Within the well-defined arena of election campaigns, these norms have an important impact that has also been confirmed in a substantial number of studies: outside of the editorial page, the media are generally averse to saying anything explicit about the issues that could be construed as judgmental, interpretive, or subjective. As Michael Robinson and Margaret Sheehan found in their study of news coverage during the 1980 election:

> As reluctant as the press is about saying anything explicit concerning the leadership qualities of the candidates, the press is markedly more reluctant to assess or evaluate issues. . . . [We found] an almost total refusal by [CBS and UPI] to

go beyond straightforward description of the candidate's policy positions. During the last ten weeks of Campaign '80, CBS failed to draw a single clear inference or conclusion about a single issue position of a single candidate—UPI as well.[9]

How do the media cover issues, then? The answer is that they report on what the candidates themselves are saying. As Robinson and Sheehan put it, "For all practical purposes, whatever the candidates or their surrogates said about the issues served as issue coverage."[10] As a result, the only kinds of policing of the issues that the media will undertake on their own initiative are questions that can clearly and unambiguously be labeled as matters of fact. If a candidate makes a blatant factual error—by misquoting a report, or claiming that nuclear missiles can be called back after they are launched, or adding items to his resume that never actually occurred—the media will sometimes call him on it. Obvious inconsistencies, where a candidate makes a statement that is clearly in conflict with positions he has taken earlier, may also get reported. Even the recent profusion of ad watches, which represents a more self-consciously aggressive attempt to scrutinize the candidates, generally adheres to these same guidelines.

In most campaigns, however, the most significant issue controversies are not matters of fact, but questions that require a substantial amount of judgment and interpretation. Would George McGovern's proposed defense cuts have left America unprotected? Was Jimmy Carter avoiding the issues in 1976? Was Ronald Reagan a warmonger? Was Walter Mondale too much in hock to special interests? Did George Bush have any vision for America's future? Were Michael Dukakis's social values at odds with those of the mainstream American voter? On these and similar controversies, the media's record is that they will publicize these issues only if a candidate's opponents have talked about them first. During the 1980 campaign, for example, almost the entirety of the mainstream economics profession believed that it was impossible for Reagan to cut taxes, increase defense spending, and still balance the budget. But the media were unwilling to make this charge on their own authority. Negative comments about Reagan's economic proposals, Robinson and Sheehan found, "invariably" came from the other candidates or their supporters, "never" from the journalists themselves.[11] The media's ability to perform their police function, in short, depends on the candidates' ability to engage in negative campaigning.

But even if the news media were to adopt a new set of norms and were willing to police our election campaigns, it is doubtful that we would want to put this burden primarily on their shoulders. The right of any individual or group to criticize, to object, to dissent is one of the signal achievements of American democracy, enshrined in the First Amendment.[12] To say that we should restrict or penalize negative campaigning is to say, in effect, that candidates should now largely abdicate that right and rest content with whatever the media decide to broadcast or publish. If candidates did agree to abide by such strictures, they would thus be renouncing many of the most important duties we have traditionally expected from our best leaders and political heroes: such tasks as articulating grievances; speaking on behalf of the ignored and the forgotten; taking an unappreciated problem, bringing it to public attention, and thereby compelling the system to take action. . . .

WHAT RESTRICTIONS ON NEGATIVE CAMPAIGNING WOULD MEAN FOR AMERICAN POLITICS

Of the proposals discussed for reducing or restricting negative campaigning, it is unclear how many would actually accomplish their intended goal. Take, for example, the bill that would require any candidate who uses radio or television commercials to attack another candidate to deliver the attack in person. The reasoning behind this proposal is that candidates are willing to attack their opponents largely because they can hide behind the relative anonymity of a slickly produced advertisement; they would be much more reluctant to criticize another candidate if they had to do so in person. Perhaps, but as any number of recent campaigns illustrate, lots of very strident negative campaigning is already being done by the candidates themselves, with little or no apparent backlash from the voters. In 1988, for example, George Bush showed no qualms about repeating in his own speeches most of the charges about the furloughing of Willie Horton and Dukakis's veto of a Pledge of Allegiance bill that were also featured in his television ads. So the candidates and their consultants might decide, after some initial hesitation and experimentation, that personally delivered attacks are still quite effective and continue their negative campaigning unabated.

But let us suppose, for a moment, that one or another of these proposals would be effective: it would significantly reduce the volume of negative campaigning and make it considerably more difficult for a candidate to attack or criticize his opponent. What impact would this have on the character of American politics?

The most obvious consequence, of course, is that it would deprive the electorate of a lot of valuable information, and thereby make it that much more difficult for the voters to make intelligent choices about the people they elect to public office. Like our political system generally, our electoral system is based on the belief that good decisions are more likely to result from a full, thorough, and unrestricted discussion of the issues. As the Supreme Court stated in one of the most important free speech cases of the twentieth century, there is

> a profound national commitment to the principle that debate on public issues should be uninhibited, robust, and wide-open, and *that it may well include vehement, caustic, and sometimes unpleasantly sharp attacks on government and public officials.*[13]

Deprived of the important information conveyed in negative campaigning, the voters would be in the position of a blackjack player who must decide how to play his hand without getting to look at his hole card. He may, of course, stumble into the right decision, but the odds are surely better if he knows all the cards he has been dealt.

But beyond this general enfeebling of democracy, any limitation on negative campaigning is likely to have important systemic consequences for our politics. In congressional elections, restrictions on negative campaigning would almost certainly work to the advantage of incumbents, making them even more entrenched and difficult to unseat. As a score of recent studies have shown, incumbent members of the House almost always begin the election campaign with a huge advantage over their opponents.[14] They are better known; they have an established record of service to the district; they have made numerous speeches and sent out hundreds of newsletters and press releases, all designed to show how attentive they are to the voters' interests and opinions and how well they represent the district in Congress.

How can the challenger overcome such a lopsided starting point? The challenger's first task, almost all studies agree, is to make the voters familiar with his own name and qualifications, since the evidence clearly indicates that people won't vote for someone they have never heard of. But there appear to be distinct limits to the effectiveness of this kind of positive campaigning. For virtually anything the challenger pledges will seem hopelessly abstract and insubstantial when compared to the tangible, proven record of the incumbent. The challenger may claim, for example, that he will do wonderful things for the district; but his promises will certainly seem less impressive than what the incumbent (even a very bad incumbent) has already accomplished. The challenger can also promise to represent district opinion and help solve the nation's most pressing problems, but the incumbent will no doubt reply that he is already doing these things, once again reinforcing his position by a long litany of specific bills he has introduced or sponsored, resolutions he has voted for, position papers written by his staff, etc. For all the recent talk about an anti-incumbent mood, there is no evidence that very many voters are so ornery as to throw incumbents out of office for no reason except that they are incumbents, or so risk-seeking as to vote out an acceptable incumbent on the hope that the challenger might prove to be even better. To the contrary, the evidence shows that voters place a strong premium on the value of experience.[15]

In the end, a challenger in a congressional election stands almost no chance of winning unless he "goes negative": unless, in other words, he can succeed in raising doubts about the incumbent's character, voting record, and attention to the district. Particularly worth noting here is Gary Jacobson's analysis of congressional election data from the 1980 and 1982 American National Election Studies (ANES). Incumbents who got reelected and incumbents who lost, Jacobson found, were virtually indistinguishable in terms of how voters assessed their positive qualities. In 1980, for example, 58 percent of the voters in districts with winning incumbents could name something specific they liked about the incumbent, as compared to 59 percent in districts with losing incumbents. Nor was there any difference between winning and losing incumbents in whether the voters could remember anything specific the incumbent had done for the district.

What did distinguish winning and losing incumbents was whether the voters could name anything specific that they disliked about the incumbent. In districts with incumbents who got reelected, only 18 percent of the voters could mention a specific dislike; but in districts with losing incumbents, 46 percent were able to voice a specific grounds for dissatisfaction. As Jacobson concludes:

> Challengers certainly hope to convince people of their own virtues—at minimum, that they are qualified for the office—but they are not likely to get far without directly undermining support for the incumbent. . . . The data indicate that successful challengers do two things: They make voters aware of their own virtues, and they make them aware of the incumbent's shortcomings.[16]

Any move to limit negative campaigning, in short, would just add one more weapon to the already formidable arsenal with which incumbents manage to entrench themselves in office.

What effect a reduction in negative campaigning would have on presidential elections is more difficult to predict, partly because we have fewer cases available to study, partly because it is less easy to generalize about the strategic situation confronting the candidates. Consider, however, two different scenarios:

In three of the last eight presidential elections, a popular incumbent running for reelection began the general election campaign with a huge lead over his opponent. In 1964, Lyndon Johnson led Barry Goldwater in the first Gallup Poll conducted after the conventions by a 65 percent to 29 percent margin: in 1972, Richard Nixon was beating George McGovern by 64 percent to 30 percent as the fall campaign got underway; in 1984, Ronald Reagan's lead over Walter Mondale was 56 percent to 37 percent.

In this kind of situation, it is not clear that either candidate derives a special benefit from a limit on negative campaigning. On the one hand, if the challenger has any hope at all of cutting into the incumbent's lead, he must make some attempt to mount a sustained attack on the incumbent's record in office. Goldwater, McGovern, and Mondale certainly recognized this point, for all three did a substantial amount of negative campaigning during the fall. But the chances are probably very small that these attacks will have much impact on the electorate: If the voters have decided they basically like the incumbent after watching him perform in the Oval Office for three and a half years, they are unlikely to revise this opinion in two and a half months, no matter how skillfully the challenger campaigns. In addition, the challenger will no doubt have his own set of faults and shortcomings, and none of the incumbents listed above was especially shy about bringing these to the attention of the electorate. Perhaps the safest conclusion one can draw about a presidential election of this kind is that when an incumbent is this far ahead by September of the election year, nothing that goes on during the fall campaign is likely to have too much effect on the final outcome.

The situation is very different, however, when the early fall polls show a close, hotly-contested race (as in 1980 and 1988), or when the out-party candidate has opened up a lead over the incumbent (as in 1976 and 1992). In these cases, there is a clear imbalance in the information available to the average voter. Given the tremendous visibility of the presidential office, the failures and shortcomings of the incumbent administration are already a matter of widespread public knowledge. When Gerald Ford faced an uphill battle in 1976, when Jimmy Carter sought reelection in

1980, when George Bush ran as the successor to Ronald Reagan in 1988 and then for a second term of his own in 1992, most Americans knew their records quite well: the poor or uneven performance of the economy, the foreign policy setbacks and trouble spots, the inability to define and implement a program. Incumbent candidates in this position do spend some of their time trying to convince voters that things are better than they seem, but even the most energetic campaign efforts in this direction are not likely to have much payoff. As in the case of the popular incumbent, voters are unlikely to change an assessment they have developed over three and a half years, on the basis of several months of obviously partisan propaganda.

So the only chance such an embattled incumbent has is to raise doubts about his opponent. Especially in the modern era of presidential selection, when the out-party candidate is rarely a prominent national figure prior to winning the nomination, his faults and shortcomings are generally not well-known. Most voters, it appears, knew remarkably little in 1976 about Jimmy Carter's record as governor of Georgia, or about Ronald Reagan's performance in California in 1980, or about the gubernatorial records of Michael Dukakis and Bill Clinton.

Such matters have not received a great deal of attention from survey researchers, but the data that are available suggest, not at all surprisingly, that most Americans do not devote much effort to monitoring the performance of fifty different state governors. In mid-October of 1980, for example, the CBS News/*New York Times* poll asked a national sample of probable voters, "Do you think Ronald Reagan did a good job or not when he was Governor of California, or don't you know enough about that to have an opinion?" Forty-eight percent of the respondents admitted they didn't know enough about the matter; another 4 percent said they weren't sure. A similar result occurred in September of 1988, when a NBC News/*Wall Street Journal* survey asked likely voters, "From what you know, do you think Michael Dukakis has been a good Governor of Massachusetts, or not?" Though the "don't know enough" option was not specifically offered in this case, and though Dukakis's gubernatorial record had by that time become a major issue in the 1988 campaign, 28 percent of the respondents still said they didn't have an opinion. In September 1992, 40 percent of the registered voters in a CBS News/*New York Times* poll were unable to say if they had a "favorable or unfavorable impression of the job Bill Clinton has done as Governor of Arkansas." By way of comparison, when the Gallup Poll asks its standard job performance question about an incumbent president during the late summer or early fall of a presidential election year, only about 8–14 percent of those surveyed give "don't know" responses.[17]

And the more negative campaigning is discouraged or penalized, the more likely it becomes that all voters will ever learn about how the challenger performed in his previous position is the candidate's own highly colored version of that record. Thus, in a close election of this kind, where the campaign could make a difference in the final outcome, limits on negative campaigning would be distinctly to the advantage of the challenger.

It is no accident that when various commentators recommended a moratorium on negative campaigning during the last few weeks of the 1992 presidential race, Bill

Clinton readily agreed to the idea and George Bush tried to resist it.[18] Both major-party campaigns understood quite well that Bush's only chance for victory lay in a negative campaign against Clinton. To be sure, there is something a little sad about an incumbent president whose best argument as to why he should be reelected is to say, in effect, "Sure, I may not have been a very good president—but my opponent would be even worse." But the fact that this argument is sad does not mean that it may not be in some cases entirely valid.

THE SEARCH FOR BETTER CAMPAIGNS

To defend negative campaigning, of course, is not to deny that positive campaigning is also important. What our politics really needs is a mixture of the two. A candidate who is challenging an incumbent should be required to show the weaknesses and short-comings of his opponent, and then to indicate how and why he would do better. An incumbent should defend his own record, and then (since that record is unlikely to be entirely without blemish) should be able to point out the ways in which the challenger would be deficient. The point is that both are valid ways of appealing to and informing the electorate—just as economic affairs and foreign policy are both relevant issues.

The effort to stamp out negative campaigning thus deals a double blow to any attempt to improve the quality of future American election campaigns. It seeks to deny the voters important information that is relevant to their decisions; but it also helps divert attention from the many serious problems that genuinely afflict our campaigns. Most of the practices that are condemned on the grounds of negative campaigning are actually objectionable for very different reasons. Sending a forged letter about one's opponent, as the Nixon people did in 1972, is wrong, not because it is negative campaigning, but because it's a lie. Demanding that your opponent take a drug test isn't objectionable because it's negative, but because the issue it raises is trivial. Calling your opponent "unChristian" is wrong because it is a misuse of religion. Accusing a congressional incumbent of taking too many junkets would be wrong if it takes such incidents out of context. (It may also be a real indication that the incumbent is neglecting his duties and abusing the perquisites of office.)

There is a simple test that can be applied to all of these issues. If you think that a particular campaign practice is wrong because it is an instance of negative campaigning, then it follows that the same behavior would be acceptable just as long as it was done in a positive manner. So, if negative campaigning is the real villain in all of these cases, sending a forged letter that attacks an opponent is wrong, but forging a letter that says positive things about one's own candidate is acceptable. Or: it's wrong to criticize your opponent for failing to take a drug test, but it's okay if you yourself take a drug test and then trumpet the results as proof of your spectacular fitness for office. It's wrong to call your opponent "unChristian," but acceptable to call yourself "the Christian candidate in this election."

Rather than trying to limit or discourage negative campaigning as a generic category, we ought to recognize that some negative campaigning is good and some negative campaigning is bad—and then think more carefully about the kinds of moral criteria that really should make a difference. A full-blown examination of this matter is the subject for another article or book, but the preceding discussion and the examples commonly cited in the negative campaigning literature clearly point in several important directions. Probably the most significant problem with campaign advertising, positive and negative, is that so much of it is misleading, taking votes and actions out of context, or implying connections between events that may be completely unrelated. Many ads also deal with matters of highly questionable relevance that tell us little or nothing about either candidates' ideology or fitness for office. It also seems clear that many voters are troubled by the incivility of many negative ads, the tone of which is frequently harsh and mean-spirited. All of these are real and serious problems, eminently worthy of our best efforts to rectify them. But we will make little progress in this direction by a war against negative campaigning.*

NOTES

1. Not surprisingly, most journalists and political practitioners do not define the term explicitly, but this definition clearly fits the way that they use the term in their speeches and writings. Those sources that do offer an explicit definition, however, almost always provide one similar to that proposed here. See, for example Gina M. Garramone, "Voter Responses to Negative Political Ads," *Journalism Quarterly* 61 (Summer 1984), pp. 250–259; Morton Sipress. "Wisconsin in 1992: The Impact of Negative Campaigns" (paper presented at the annual meeting of the Midwest Political Science Association, Chicago, 1993); Ansolabehere et al.. "Does Attack Advertising Demobilize the Electorate?"; Pfau and Kenski, *Attack Politics.* For a more elaborate attempt to develop a typology of negative ads, which makes the valid point that many so-called positive ads actually include implied references to the opposing candidate, see Karen S. Johnson-Cartee and Gary A. Copeland, *Negative Political Advertising: Coming of Age* (Hillsdale, NJ: Erlbaum, 1991). chap. 2.

2. All of these, I should point out, are positions that have been defended in recent years by serious policy analysts.

3. See the argument of John Stuart Mill that it is not enough to hear unpopular opinions stated by their adversaries; the public "must be able to hear [such arguments] from persons who actually believe them, who defend them in earnest and do their very utmost for them." See Mill, *On Liberty* [1859] (Indianapolis: Library of Liberal Arts. 1956), p. 45.

4. Though no one I am aware of actually defines negative campaigning this way, a number of sources have suggested the need to distinguish between issue-based and personal attacks. See, for example, Donald L. Rheem, " 'Negative' to Negative Ads," *Christian Science Monitor,* March 22, 1988; and Clifford D. May, "Analysts Say Political Mud Can Yield Gold," *New York Times,* November 4, 1988.

5. See Angus Campbell et al., *The American Voter* (New York: Wiley, 1960), esp. pp. 54–59; David P. Glass, "Evaluating Presidential Candidates: Who Focuses on Their Personal Attributes?" *Public Opinion Quarterly* 49 (Winter 1985), pp. 517–534; and Arthur H. Miller, Martin P. Wattenberg, and Oksana Malanchuk, "Schematic Assessments of Presidential Candidates," *American Political Science Review* 80 (June 1986), pp. 521–540.

6. For a more extended discussion of some criteria that might guide media coverage of "character" issues, see Larry J. Sabato, *Feeding Frenzy: How Attack Journalism Has Transformed American Politics* (New York: Free Press, 1991), especially chap. 8.

*The author would like to thank Amy Logan, Hendrik Hertzberg, Chris Bosso, Teresa Celada, Lance Bennett, Gerald Pomper, and Ted Lasher for helpful comments on earlier drafts of this article.

7. Stephen Ansolabehere, Roy Behr, and Shanto Iyengar, *The Media Game* (New York: Macmillan, 1993), pp. 57–58.

8. See, among others, Thomas Patterson and Robert McClure, *The Unseeing Eye* (New York: Putnam, 1976); and Darrell M. West, *Air Wars: Television Advertising in Election Campaigns, 1952–1992* (Washington, DC: Congressional Quarterly, 1993), chap. 3.

9. Michael J. Robinson and Margaret A. Sheehan, *Over the Wire and On TV* (New York: Sage, 1983), p. 46.

10. Ibid.

11. Ibid.

12 It is worth noting that the First Amendment not only guarantees "freedom of speech," but also the right "to petition the Government for a redress of grievances." Given the origins of the American Revolution, I think it no accident that this last proviso is phrased in terms of negative grievances, rather than positive improvements. Anyone who doubts this should try rereading the Declaration of Independence. which is little more than a catalogue of negatively phrased "injuries and usurpations" committed by the British government, with remarkably little discussion of what remedies a new government might provide.

13. *New York Times Co. v. Sullivan,* 376 US 254 (1964) at 270. (Emphasis added.)

14. See Thomas E. Mann, *Unsafe at Any Margin: Interpreting Congressional Elections* (Washington, DC: American Enterprise Institute, 1978), chap. 4; and Gary C. Jacobson, *Money in Congressional Elections* (New Haven: Yale University Press, 1980).

15. The most vivid demonstration of the voters' regard for experience in congressional elections is, of course, the fact that about 95 percent of incumbents get reelected every two years. On the regard for experience in presidential elections, see Campbell et al., *American Voter,* pp. 54–58; and Steven J. Rosenstone, *Forecasting Presidential Elections* (New Haven: Yale University Press, 1983), pp. 58–63 and 86–87.

16. The analysis discussed here may be found in Gary C. Jacobson, *The Politics of Congressional Elections,* 2d ed. (Boston: Little, Brown, 1987), pp. 81–83 and 134–36.

17. Another way to demonstrate this point is to examine the percentage of the electorate that is able to assign the candidates a position on the seven-point issue scales in the American National Election Study (ANES) surveys. The 1980 survey. for example, had nine such scales; in all nine cases, a larger number of respondents were able to provide a rating for Jimmy Carter, the incumbent president, than for Ronald Reagan, even though the latter had an unusually well-defined ideological profile for a challenger. Similarly, the 1984 ANES sample showed a higher number of "don't know" responses for Walter Mondale's issue positions than for President Reagan's on all eleven of the scales used. In 1988, when George Bush was not the incumbent but was closely associated with the incumbent administration. the vice president's issue positions were known to more Americans in nine of nine cases.

18. See, for example, their comments on the matter in the second debate in *New York Times,* October 16, 1992.

Voting: The Matter of Turnout

As one surveys the political behavior habits of the American people, none perhaps attracts greater attention, and oftentimes condemnation, than the rate at which Americans turn out to vote in presidential elections. Since the 1960 presidential election, when turnout was at 63 percent, there has been an almost non-stop decline, with the exception of 1984 when it rose just a few tenths of a percent, and 1992 where it went up a full 5 percent, possibly due to the interest generated by the presidential candidacy of Ross Perot. In 1996, however, it dropped to 49 percent, the lowest turnout figure since 1924, and the biggest single four-year decline since 1920. It was, moreover, a decline that manifested itself in every one of the fifty states.[1] This, despite the fact that 1996 was the first presidential election in which the National Voter Registration Act (1993) went into effect, allowing potential voters to register when they apply for or renew their licenses rather than going through the more cumbersome procedures established in a number of states.

The three articles that follow come at the turnout issue from quite different perspectives. Peter Nardulli, John Dalager, and Donald Greco provide a historical analysis of voting turnout (1828–1992) focusing on the rather substantial variations in turnout by locale types (i.e., cities, suburbs, small towns, rural areas). Recent turnout changes in these locales, they argue, have significant implications for the electoral power of both parties in presidential elections. They also conclude that there is an ebb and flow to turnout, with these changes being conditioned by alterations in the rules of the game, the strength of political parties, and the salience of issues.

In the second selection Arend Lijphart is concerned not with the source of, or variation in, turnout within the United States. He focuses instead on the consequences. Such a low turnout, he argues, raises questions about the legitimacy of the government installed and the undue influence on government policy of those groups who regularly show up at the polls to vote. The most practical way to ensure a high turnout, in his view, is to establish a system of compulsory voting—a change that would not only help to equalize influence on government, but would have the added benefits of lowering the costs of elections and discouraging negative campaigning.

In the final article, Ruy Teixeira examines both the demographics of non-voting and the relationship of non-voting to election outcomes. Focusing on presidential elections from 1972 to 1988, the period which saw the greatest post-1960 decline in turnout, he argues that the stereotype of the non-voter is no longer completely accurate. He also cautions that attempting to selectively mobilize non-voters is far more difficult than it may appear and, in any event, would probably not alter election results; nor, he argues, would a more general mobilization of non-voters lead to election outcomes that favored one particular party over the other.

NOTES

1. Stephen Knack, "Drivers Wanted: Motor Voter and the Election of 1996," *P.S.* 32 (June 1999), p. 237.

Voter Turnout in U.S. Presidential Elections: A Historical View and Some Speculation

Peter F. Nardulli, Jon K. Dalager, and Donald E. Greco

An examination of presidential voting patterns between 1828 and 1992 for all counties and most large cities in the continental U.S. (approximately 135,000 cases altogether) confirms that there has been a decline in turnout rates[1] since 1960, as most commentators have suggested. For the nation as a whole, turnout in presidential elections dropped 20 percent from 64 percent in 1960 to 51 percent in 1988. Turnout rebounded slightly in 1992 to 55 percent, due perhaps in large part to the interest generated by Ross Perot.

As striking as these data appear, they must be put in historical perspective to be properly understood. Figure 1 displays the turnout rate for every presidential election between 1828 and 1992 (see Table 1 for a listing of the actual rates). It shows that while turnout in the presidential election of 1988 was the third lowest since 1828, surpassed only in 1920 and 1924 (with turnout rates of 44 percent in each election), the 1960–1988 decline is not unprecedented in U.S. electoral history. In an earlier 28-year period (1896–1924), turnout rates in presidential elections declined from 72 percent to 44 percent. This is a 39 percent decline in turnout, almost double that experienced between 1960 and 1988.

TABLE 1   *National and Local Turnout Rates*

Year	Nation	Main Center Cities	Suburbs of Main Center Cities	Smaller Center Cities	Suburbs of Smaller Center Cities	Urban Counties	Rural Counties
1828	0.57	0.54	0.57	0.53	0.57	0.55	0.59
1832	0.55	0.51	0.6	0.5	0.567	0.58	0.51
1836	0.54	0.48	0.57	0.54	0.59	0.55	0.53
1840	0.77	0.57	0.77	0.67	0.78	0.78	0.81
1844	0.74	0.53	0.72	0.68	0.79	0.76	0.79
1848	0.67	0.49	0.66	0.6	0.7	0.69	0.72
1852	0.63	0.45	0.6	0.6	0.68	0.67	0.66

continued

Source: Peter F. Nardulli, Jon K. Dalager, and Donald E. Greco, "Voter Turnout in U.S. Presidential Elections: A Historical View and Some Speculation" *P.S.*, 29 (September 1996), pp. 480–490.

Peter F. Nardulli is professor of political science at the University of Illinois at Urbana-Champaign and Director of the Structure of Electoral Change Project. Jon K. Dalager is professor of political science at Georgetown College. Donald E. Greco is professor of political science at Baylor University. Both have been associated with the Structure of Electoral Change Project.

TABLE 1 *National and Local Turnout Rates (cont.)*

Year	Nation	Main Center Cities	Suburbs of Main Center Cities	Smaller Center Cities	Suburbs of Smaller Center Cities	Urban Counties	Rural Counties
1856	0.71	0.52	0.68	0.61	0.7	0.74	0.76
1860	0.72	0.53	0.7	0.64	0.73	0.74	0.77
1864	0.65	0.52	0.65	0.57	0.67	0.69	0.66
1868	0.7	0.6	0.69	0.58	0.67	0.74	0.73
1872	0.65	0.53	0.62	0.59	0.64	0.67	0.68
1876	0.75	0.63	0.72	0.67	0.72	0.78	0.77
1880	0.73	0.64	0.73	0.63	0.71	0.77	0.75
1884	0.71	0.59	0.7	0.6	0.71	0.74	0.75
1888	0.73	0.62	0.7	0.63	0.73	0.74	0.77
1892	0.69	0.61	0.68	0.57	0.71	0.7	0.72
1896	0.72	0.67	0.71	0.61	0.74	0.72	0.75
1900	0.67	0.63	0.66	0.56	0.7	0.67	0.7
1904	0.59	0.56	0.58	0.47	0.59	0.59	0.61
1908	0.58	0.51	0.58	0.47	0.61	0.59	0.61
1912	0.51	0.47	0.52	0.41	0.53	0.51	0.53
1916	0.56	0.49	0.56	0.46	0.57	0.56	0.62
1920	0.44	0.39	0.47	0.39	0.48	0.44	0.47
1924	0.44	0.39	0.49	0.37	0.45	0.45	0.47
1928	0.52	0.5	0.6	0 44	0.51	0.54	0 52
1932	0.53	0.5	0.59	0.43	0.53	0.53	0.55
1936	0.58	0.58	0.64	0.46	0.56	0.57	0.57
1940	0.6	0.62	0.68	0.5	0.58	0.59	0.57
1944	0.54	0.59	0.62	0 44	0.51	0.52	0 49
1948	0.52	0.56	0.59	0.42	0 49	0.5	0.49
1952	0.62	0.63	0.7	0.54	0.61	0.61	0.6
1956	0.6	0.6	0.68	0.52	0.58	0.59	0.59
1960	0.64	0.62	0.72	0.56	0.62	0.63	0.65
1964	0.62	0.6	0.68	0.57	0.61	0.61	0.62
1968	0.61	0.56	0.66	0.57	0.61	0.61	0.63
1972	0.59	0.54	0.64	0.57	0.58	0.59	0.59
1976	0.55	0.59	0.59	0.52	0.55	0.56	0.57
1980	0.53	0.47	0.57	0.51	0.54	0.54	0.55
1984	0.52	0.59	0.55	0.51	0.52	0.52	0.52
1988	0.51	0.45	0.53	0.49	0.52	0.51	0.52
1992	0.55	0.47	0.57	0.54	0.58	0.56	0.57

Figure 1 also shows that while most commentators use the 1960 election as a basis for gauging changes in turnout, it is a somewhat misleading baseline. Turnout in 1960 was 64 percent, which was the highest turnout rate for U.S. presidential elections since 1900. The 1960 election capped a 36-year rise in turnout rates, and represented a 45 percent increase over the low points registered in 1920 and 1924. Indeed, with the exception of 1944 and 1948, when the nation was preoccupied with World War II and its aftermath, the period between 1928 and 1968 shows a steady increase in presidential turnout rates. The period between 1952 and 1968 shows an average turnout rate of 62 percent, which is almost halfway between the historical highs of

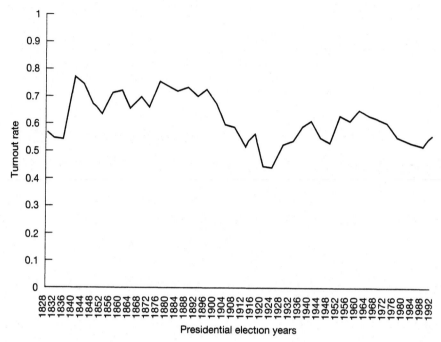

FIGURE 1 *National Turnout Rate for Presidential Elections, 1828–1992*

the last quarter of the nineteenth century (72%) and the historical lows of the first quarter of the twentieth century (54%).

The 1968 election is used as a cut-off here because for most of the country, there is no significant decline in turnout rates until 1972, when the franchise was expanded to include those 18 and older. The nation's turnout rate dropped from 64 percent to 61 percent between 1960 and 1968, about one-quarter of the 13-point decline that occurred between 1960 and 1988. The remaining 10 point drop, which accounts for 77 percent of the 1960–1988 decline, occurred after 18-, 19- and 20-year-olds became part of the eligible voter pool. This does not suggest that the newly enfranchised voters account for all of the decline, but they quite clearly account for a considerable portion of the post-1968 deterioration.

The data also demonstrate that recent trends in turnout differ dramatically across locale types (cities, suburbs, small towns, rural areas). We divided the counties and cities in our study into six different categories: (1) the 32 main, "tier 1" center cities[2] of the twentieth century (New York, Chicago, Philadelphia, Los Angeles, Dallas, etc.);[3] (2) cities and counties that include the suburbs of those 32 main center cities; (3) counties that include 37 smaller, "tier 2" center cities (San Jose, Birmingham, Charlotte, Tampa, El Paso, Austin, Richmond, Sacramento, Des Moines, etc.); (4) counties that include the suburbs of those smaller center cities; (5) smaller urban counties (those that include SMSAs defined by the Census Bureau in the 1990 census, but were not part of the 68 metropolitan areas defined above); and (6) rural counties (all other counties).

The data on turnout for each of these six locales are depicted in Figure 2 (the actual data is reported in Table 1). These data show that in the 32 main metropolitan areas—which are comprised of category (1) and category (2) above—decline in turnout between 1960 and 1988 was twice as great as it was in the rest of the country. In 1990 these metropolitan areas comprised about 40 percent of the nation's population.

Turnout in these metropolitan areas dropped by 18 percent, as opposed to 9 percent elsewhere in the nation. The largest absolute drop (19 points) was experienced in the suburban areas, which went from a turnout rate of 72 percent in 1960 to 53 percent in 1988. Next came the center cities of the 32 largest metropolitan areas, which experienced a 17-point drop from 62 percent to 45 percent. The smallest decline was experienced among the "second tier" center cities. Turnout in these areas dropped 7 points from 56 percent to 49 percent. The other three locales experienced declines in turnout between 10 and 12 points.

An examination of the turnout data by locale also demonstrates that there is no marked downward trend in turnout outside the nation's 32 largest metropolitan areas between 1960 and 1968. Turnout in the 32 largest metropolitan areas dropped 6 points between 1960 and 1968, while it remained unchanged in the second tier of metropolitan areas. Turnout went from 63 percent to 61 percent in the smaller urban counties between 1960 and 1968, but was unchanged in the rural counties. This suggests that while the newly enfranchised younger voters may account for turnout declines in much of the nation after 1972, other forces are at work in the largest metropolitan centers. Moreover, these forces appear to have had an impact in wealthier suburban areas as well as in center cities.

FIGURE 2   *Turnout Rate for Presidential Elections, 1828–1992, by Type of Locale*

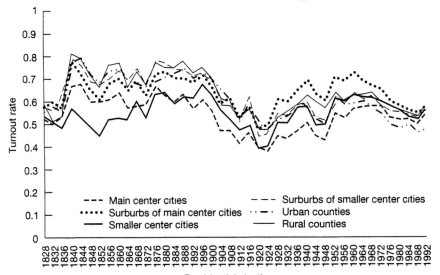

Presidential election years

These differential patterns are significant because they reflect major shifts in electoral power in presidential politics, shifts that could have important policy consequences. These shifts can be seen in Figure 3, which reports the proportion of the total U.S. vote for president, by locale, for all elections since 1828; the actual data is reported in Table 2. Care must be used in interpreting these patterns because the character of locales have evolved greatly over time. What are now smaller urban areas were rural 100 years ago. What we now call suburbs were small towns 50 years ago. Nonetheless, some patterns are well defined and meaningful.

Consider first the 32 major center cities. Beginning at about 7 percent of the national vote in 1828, the electoral power of these cities rose steadily and peaked in 1944 at 27 percent. They have declined steadily since then, constituting only 14 percent of the national vote in 1992—a dramatic decline that is matched in U.S. electoral history only by the decline of rural areas over the first half of the twentieth century.

The suburbs of the 32 main center cities contributed about 10 percent of the national vote between 1828 and 1916. Since then, their share of the national vote for president has risen steadily, reaching a plateau in 1984 at about 23 percent of the national vote.

The share of the national vote contributed by the tier 2 center cities increased only slowly over U.S. electoral history, going from 2 percent in 1828 to 4 percent in 1912. Since then it has doubled. The suburban counties surrounding these smaller

FIGURE 3   *Proportion of National Vote for President, 1828–1992, by Locale*

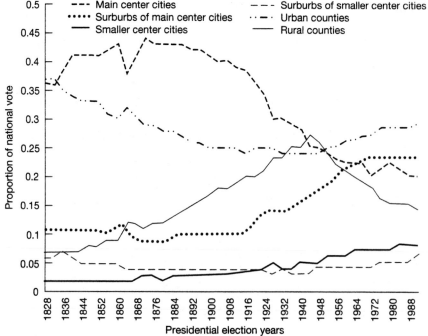

TABLE 2   *Share of National Vote*

Year	Main Center Citites	Suburbs of Main Center Cities	Smaller Center Citites	Suburbs of Smaller Center Cities	Urban Counties	Rural Counties
1828	0.07	0.11	0.02	0.06	0.37	0.36
1832	0.07	0.11	0.02	0.06	0.37	0.36
1836	0.07	0.11	0.02	0.07	0.35	0.38
1840	0 07	0.11	0.02	0.06	0.34	0.41
1844	0.07	0.11	0.02	0.05	0.33	0.41
1848	0.08	0.11	0.02	0.05	0.33	0.41
1852	0.08	0.11	0.02	0.05	0.33	0.41
1856	0.09	0.1	0.02	0.05	0.31	0.42
1860	0.09	0.11	0.02	0.05	0.3	0.43
1864	0.12	0.12	0.02	0.04	0.32	0.38
1868	0.12	0.1	0.02	0.04	0.31	0.41
1872	0.11	0.09	0.03	0.04	0.29	0.44
1876	0.12	0.09	0.03	0.04	0.29	0.43
1880	0.12	0.09	0.02	0.04	0.28	0.43
1884	0.13	0.09	0.03	0.04	0 28	0.43
1888	0.14	0.1	0.03	0.04	0.27	0.43
1892	0.15	0.1	0.03	0.04	0.26	0.42
1896	0.16	0.1	0.03	0.04	0.26	0.42
1900	0.17	0.1	0.03	0.04	0.25	0.41
1904	0.18	0.1	0.03	0.04	0.25	0.4
1908	0.18	0.1	0.03	0.04	0.25	0.4
1912	0.19	0.1	0.04	0.04	0.25	0.39
1916	0.2	0.1	0.04	0.04	0.24	0.38
1920	0.2	0.11	0.04	0.04	0.25	0.36
1924	0 21	0.13	0.04	0.04	0.25	0.34
1928	0.23	0.14	0.05	0.03	0.25	0.3
1932	0.23	0.14	0.04	0.04	0.24	0.3
1936	0 25	0.14	0.04	0.03	0.24	0.29
1940	0.25	0.15	0.05	0.03	0.24	0.28
1944	0.27	0.16	0 05	0.03	0.24	0.25
1948	0.26	0.17	0.05	0.04	0.24	0.25
1952	0.24	0.18	0.06	0.04	0.25	0.24
1956	0.22	0.19	0.06	0.04	0.25	0.23
1960	0.21	0.21	0 06	0.04	0.26	0.22
1964	0.2	0.21	0.07	0.04	0.26	0.22
1968	0.19	0.22	0.07	0.04	0.27	0.22
1972	0.18	0.23	0.07	0.04	0.27	0.2
1976	0.16	0.23	0.07	0.05	0.28	0.21
1980	0.15	0.23	0.07	0.05	0.28	0.22
1984	0.15	0.23	0.08	0.05	0.28	0.21
1988	0.15	0.23	0.08	0.05	0.28	0.2
1992	0.14	0.23	0.08	0.06	0.29	0.2

central cities have accounted for between 3 and 5 percent of the national vote since the Civil War; it was slightly higher in the Jacksonian era.

Smaller urban counties contributed between one-third and one-quarter of the U.S. vote for president throughout much of American electoral history. Since the Depression their share has increased from 24 percent to 29 percent.

The proportion of the national vote cast in rural counties rose slowly between 1828 and 1872, when it peaked at 44 percent. The rural share of the national vote more than halved between 1872 and 1972, when it bottomed out at 20 percent. It has remained between 20 percent and 22 percent of the vote since 1972.

Much of the temporal shifting in the relative share of the national vote across these different locales is due to population change. This can be seen in Figure 4, which reports changes in the proportion of the eligible electorate in each of the locales between 1828 and 1992.

As important as these population shifts are in accounting for trends reflected in Figure 3, they do not tell the whole story. Also important is the **relative propensity to vote**. The relative propensity to vote is measured as: (the proportion of the national vote)/(the proportion of the national electorate). This concept is illustrated by a few examples. In 1980, the tier 1 center cities had 17 percent of the national electorate but only 15 percent of the national vote. Thus, their relative propensity to vote is .88 for 1980. The suburban areas of those tier 1 cities, however, had 21 percent of the national electorate but 23 percent of the national vote. Their relative propensity to vote is 1.10 for 1980. Smaller urban areas had 28 percent of the national electorate and 28 percent of the national vote in 1980, and their relative propensity to vote is 1.00.

Scores above 1 reflect elections in which a locale produced more votes than would be expected by their relative share of the eligible electorate. Scores below "1"

FIGURE 4 *Proportion of Eligible Voters, 1828–1992, by Locale*

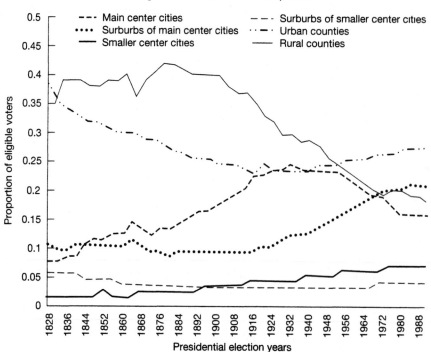

reflect elections in which a locale produced fewer votes than would be expected based on their relative share of the eligible electorate. Over time a locale's relative propensity to vote can change even if its turnout rate is constant—if the turnout rate of other locales is changing more rapidly. Thus, trends in relative voting propensity will indicate how a locale is doing compared to others.

Figure 5a displays these relative propensities to vote for the largest center cities and their suburbs, and the results are revealing (the actual data for all locales is reported in Table 3). Throughout much of American electoral history, the largest U.S. cities had a relative propensity to vote that was below 1.0. The emergence of efficient urban political machines after the Civil War led to relative vote propensities ranging from .85 to .95 between 1868 and 1932. The saliency of politics to urban areas after the Depression and the centrality of these urban areas to the New Deal coalition led to the reinvigoration of the urban machines, producing relative propensities to vote above 1 in large cities for the first time in American electoral history. They peaked at 1.13 in 1944 and remained above 1 through 1952. The decline that began in 1944 remains unabated and stands at .82 in 1992—which represents a 27 percent drop in their relative propensity to vote since 1944. This drop in the relative propensity to vote accounts for almost 40 percent of the loss in voting power experienced by these cities between 1944 and 1992. Based on a drop in the cities' share of the national electorate, they should have dropped only 8 points (from 27 percent to 19 percent)

FIGURE 5A　*Relative Propensity to Vote, 1828–1992*

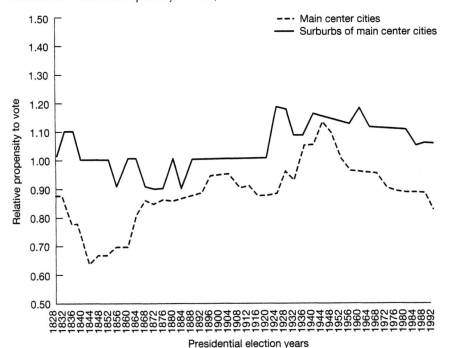

TABLE 3   Relative Propensity to Vote

Year	Main Center Cities	Suburbs of Main Center Cities	Smaller Center Cities	Suburbs of Smaller Center Cities	Urban Counties	Rural Counties
1928	0.88	1 00	1.00	1.00	0.97	1.03
1832	0.88	1.10	1.00	1.00	1.06	0.92
1836	0.78	1.10	1.00	1.17	1.03	0.97
1840	0.78	1.00	1.00	1.00	1.03	1.05
1844	0.64	1.00	1.00	1.00	1.03	1.08
1848	0.67	1.00	1.00	1.00	1.03	1.08
1852	0.67	1.00	0.67	1 00	1.06	1.05
1856	0.69	0.91	1.00	1 00	1.03	1.08
1860	0.69	1.00	1.00	1.25	1.00	1.08
1864	0.80	1.00	1.00	1.00	1.07	1.06
1868	0.86	0.91	0.67	1.00	1.07	1.05
1872	0.85	0.90	1.00	1.00	1.00	1.07
1876	0.86	0.90	1.00	1.00	1.04	1.02
1880	0.86	1.00	0.67	1.00	1.04	1.02
1884	0.87	0.90	1.00	1.00	1.04	1.05
1888	0.88	1.00	1.00	1.00	1.04	1.08
1892	0.88	1.00	1.00	1.00	1.00	1.05
1896	0.94	1.00	0.75	1.00	1.00	1.05
1900	0.94	1.00	0.75	1.00	1.00	1.03
1904	0.95	1.00	0.75	1.00	1.00	1.05
1908	0.90	1.00	0.75	1.00	1.00	1.08
1912	0.90	1.00	1.00	1.00	1.04	1.05
1916	0.87	1.00	0.80	1.00	1.04	1.09
1920	0 87	1.00	0.80	1.00	1.00	1.09
1924	0.88	1.18	0.80	1.00	1.04	1.06
1928	0.96	1.17	1.00	0.75	1.04	1.00
1932	0.92	1.08	0.80	1.00	1.00	1.00
1936	1.04	1.08	0.80	0.75	1.00	1.00
1940	1.04	1.15	0.83	0.75	1.00	0.97
1944	1.13	1.14	0.83	0.75	0.96	0.89
1948	1.08	1.13	0.83	1.00	0.96	0.96
1952	1.00	1.13	1.00	1.00	1.00	0.96
1956	0.96	1.12	0.86	1.00	0.96	0.96
1960	0.95	1.17	0.86	1.00	1.00	0.96
1964	0.95	1.11	1.00	1.00	1.00	1.00
1968	0.95	1.10	1.00	1.00	1.00	1.05
1972	0.90	1.10	1.00	0.80	1.00	1.00
1976	0.89	1.10	0.88	1.00	1.04	1.00
1980	0.88	1.10	0.88	1.00	1.00	1.05
1984	0.88	1.05	1.00	1.00	1.00	1.05
1988	0.88	1.05	1.00	1.00	1.00	1.00
1992	0.82	1.05	1.00	1.20	1.04	1.05

rather than 13 points. Even if these cities had been able to achieve a voting propensity of 1 they would have contributed 17 percent of the national vote in 1992.

The profile of relative voting propensities looks very different for the suburban areas surrounding these major cities (Figure 5a). They hovered around 1 for most of the timeframe studied until 1924. In 1924 their relative vote propensities jumped well above 1 and remained there through the 1980 election. Indeed, most of the relative propensities for these suburbs were between 1.10 and 1.15 between 1924 and 1980. However, since 1960 the relative voting propensity for the suburbs has dropped 10 points. Half of this drop (5 points) occurred after 1980.

Smaller urban and rural counties, in contrast to the main center cities, have seldom had a relative voting propensity less than 1 and usually they have been greater than one (Figure 5b). The relative propensity to vote is slightly higher in rural areas than in smaller urban counties. With the recent declines in turnout in the suburban areas of the largest metropolitan areas, the relative propensity to vote in rural areas has been about 1.05 which is comparable to that in suburban areas in recent elections.

A very different pattern emerges among the tier 2 metropolitan areas (not shown graphically here). While the relative voting propensities for the center cities in these metropolitan areas hovered between .75 and .85 for most of the period between 1896 and 1948, they have ranged between .85 and 1 since 1952. They never experienced the surge that the larger cities did in the 1930s and they have not experienced the decline that the larger cities did beginning in the 1940s. The suburban counties in these metropolitan areas have been close to 1 for most of their history and evidence no recent trends, even though they jumped to a remarkably high 1.20 in 1992.

FIGURE 5B   *Relative Propensity to Vote, 1828–1992*

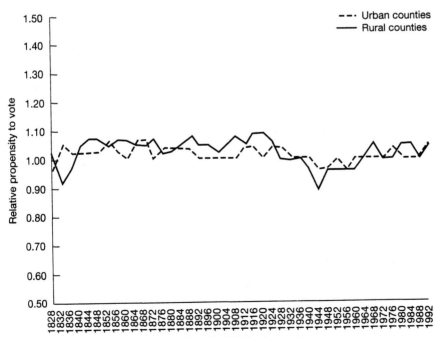

The differences in the relative propensity to vote are important for electoral outcomes because the partisan allegiance differs dramatically across locales. This can be seen by examining the "margin of victory" in presidential elections by locale across the span of American electoral history. Margin of victory is computed by subtracting the Republican proportion of the vote from the Democratic proportion of the vote. Positive numbers on this scale indicate Democratic pluralities and negative numbers indicate Republican pluralities. The closer the number is to 0, the closer the election.

The data on margin of victory, by locale, are reported in Table 4. These data make it clear that the center cities in the 32 largest metropolitan areas have routinely delivered large margins of victory for Democratic presidential candidates since the Roosevelt era, as can be seen in Figure 6. Since 1952, the percent of the vote for the Democratic candidate in these cities has ranged between 15 and 20 points above the nation as a whole. The suburban areas, which have had the largest propensity to vote in the post-war era, regularly return the largest Republican pluralities.

These differences in partisan allegiances are significant because urban cores and their peripheries also differ markedly in their turnout rates, as was seen earlier. The center cities are least likely to vote while their suburban areas are the most likely to vote. . . . What can politicians, pundits, and political scientists glean from these findings? Perhaps the most important insights flow from an examination of Figure 1. It shows that the decline in voter turnout experienced between 1960 and 1988 is not unprecedented. As noted earlier, the decline in turnout for this period is about half

FIGURE 6   *Margin of Victory—The Nation and "Tier One" Center Cities*

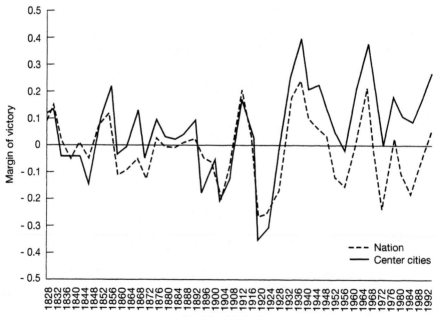

TABLE 4 *Margin of Victory*

Year	Nation	Main Center Cities	Suburbs of Main Center Cities	Smaller Center Cities	Suburbs of Smaller Center Cities	Urban Counties	Rural Counties
1828	0.08	0.11	0.03	−0.01	0.04	0.04	0.13
1832	0.15	0.14	0.14	−0.04	0.07	0.13	0.2
1836	0.02	−0.04	0.03	−0.09	−0.03	0.04	0.02
1840	−0.06	−0.05	−0.05	−0.17	−0.11	−0.05	−0.06
1844	0.01	−0.04	0.01	−0.1	−0.04	0.01	0.04
1848	−0.05	−0.15	−0.04	−0.16	−0.1	−0.05	−0.02
1852	0.07	0.01	0.06	−0.01	0.02	0.05	0.08
1856	0.12	0.22	−0.03	0.18	0.13	0.05	0.18
1860	−0.1	−0.03	−0.18	0	−0.05	−0.17	−0.07
1864	−0.09	0	−0.13	−0.11	−0.06	−0.1	−0.1
1868	−0.05	0.13	−0.09	−0.03	−0.01	−0 09	−0.07
1872	−0.12	−0.05	−0.13	−0.1	−0.01	−0.15	−0.12
1876	0.03	0.09	0.01	0.04	0.03	0	0.04
1880	0	0.03	−0.03	−0.01	0	−0.02	0.01
1884	0	0.02	−0.01	−0.04	0.02	−0.01	0.01
1888	0.01	0.04	−0.02	0	0.03	−0.01	0.01
1892	0.03	0.09	0.01	0.1	0.06	0.02	0.02
1896	−0.04	−0.17	−0.14	0.01	0.05	−0.09	0.04
1900	−0.06	−0.08	−0.12	−0.03	0	−0.09	−0.03
1904	−0.19	−0.2	−0.24	−0.14	−0.09	−0.2	−0.17
1908	−0.08	−0.12	−0.18	−0.03	−0.02	−0.01	−0.05
1912	0.19	0.2	0.15	0.28	0.22	0.16	0.19
1916	0.03	0	−0.08	0.14	0.11	0.02	0.07
1920	−0.26	−0.35	−0.38	−0.09	−0.16	−0.25	−0.21
1924	−0.25	−0.3	−0.41	−0.2	−0.17	−0.28	−0.16
1928	−0.17	−0.01	−0.25	−0.19	−0.25	−0.23	−0.21
1932	0.18	0.25	0.04	0.2	0.18	0.1	0.24
1936	0.24	0.39	0.13	0.35	0.24	0.2	0.19
1940	0 1	0.21	−0.01	0.22	0.13	0.09	0.05
1944	0.07	0.22	−0.03	0.18	0.08	0.05	0
1948	0.04	0.14	−0.08	0.08	0.05	0.03	0.04
1952	−0.11	0.05	−0.2	−0.08	−0.12	−0.14	−0.17
1956	−0.15	−0.02	−0.26	−0.14	−0.18	−0.2	−0 15
1960	0	0.2	0.05	−0.01	−0.06	−0.03	−0.08
1964	0.22	0.38	0.19	0.18	0.18	0.21	0.14
1968	−0.01	0.2	−0.06	−0.01	−0.08	−0.04	−0.09
1972	−0.23	0	−0.26	−0.23	−0.33	−0.27	−0.33
1976	0.02	0.18	−0.07	0.01	−0.04	−0.01	0.04
1980	−0.1	0.11	−0.17	−0.08	−0.17	−0.12	−0.12
1984	−0.18	0.09	−0.24	−0.18	−0.31	−0.22	−0.25
1988	−0.08	0.17	−0.13	−0.07	−0.19	−0.12	−0.12
1992	0.05	0.27	0.03	0.04	−0.06	0.02	0.01

that which occurred between 1896 and 1924, a comparable 28-year period. An equally important point illustrated by Figure 1 is that turnout trends, unlike diamonds, are not forever. While American electoral history has experienced periods of stable turnout rates (particularly in the last half of the nineteenth century), it also is characterized by secular swings. Trends in turnout ebb and flow. . . .

It is fairly well accepted by political scientists—although not rigorously documented—that the decline in turnout around the turn of the century was generated principally by two factors: progressive reforms and a decline in the saliency of politics for most citizens. Progressive reforms attempted, among other things, to reduce vote fraud and political corruption. In so doing, barriers to voting were constructed and political parties were weakened. Between 1896 and 1924, the Australian ballot and voter registration laws became the norm in most states. Residency requirements for voting were established in many states and poll taxes, literacy tests and devices such as the eight box law became part of the voting labyrinth in most of the South. Progressive attacks on party organizations and their bosses also reignited the deep-seated, but long-dormant, American hostility to political parties. The Australian ballot, civil service reform, and the introduction of primary elections loosened party control of the electoral process. Losing control over the ballots cast by voters undermined partisan efforts to mobilize them. Courting the party faithful in low-turnout elections became a better way to insure victory at the polls.

Just as devastating to turnout rates in this period was the fact that long-standing partisan affiliations were upset by the volatile politics of the 1880s and 1890s. Party allegiances dictated by religious affiliations and emotional appeals that dated to the Civil War were jolted by the Bryan-McKinley battle of 1896. Compounding this was the fact that the agendas of the two parties in the early part of the twentieth century were not highly distinct. Electoral politics did not seem very salient to voters, thus encouraging participatory norms that were very different from those prevailing in the latter part of the nineteenth century.

A key factor in reversing the 28-year trend in turnout rates was the increased salience of electoral politics. Al Smith's Catholicism mobilized both Protestant and Catholic voters in 1928, and this election was followed by the Great Depression. Economic hard times led the parties to offer fundamentally different programs, and Roosevelt's class-based appeals mobilized millions of hopeless and anxiety-stricken voters. Moreover, the New Deal program provided tens of thousands of government jobs that were used to strengthen the Democratic party, especially in large cities. This enhanced patronage was useful in stimulating turnout, especially in the largest cities: their turnout rates in the 1940s approached nineteenth century levels (see Figure 2 and Table 1). The impact of the participatory norms generated by the New Deal peaked in 1960.

Our analysis of the 1896–1960 period suggested that three broad types of factors were influential in generating secular changes in turnout: changes in the rules of the game, the strength and interests of political parties, and the saliency of politics to ordinary citizens. We think all three are relevant for understanding the contemporary period as well as for anticipating the near future.

It seems likely, for example, that the most influential factor in generating the recent declines is similar to that which generated the decline in the early part of the century: governmental tinkering with the rules of the game. Most of the post-1960 decline in turnout rates—and all of the sustained, broadly based declines outside the 32 largest metropolitan areas—comes after suffrage was extended to eighteen-year olds in 1970 by the 26th Amendment. While enlarging the size of the electorate is hardly comparable to raising barriers to participation (literacy tests, registration requirements, poll taxes, etc.), the turnout rate has a denominator as well as a numerator. Changes in either can generate marked changes in turnout rate.

There have been governmental attempts during this period to increase the "numerator" of the turnout rate, and some of these have been successful in certain areas of the country: the Voting Rights Act of 1965, increases in the number of polling places, and voting by mail. None of these efforts, however, has been able to overcome the 26th Amendment's impact on turnout rates. However, the recent enactment of the national "motor voter" bill could change this. This law has the potential to significantly expand the pool of registered voters. This, in turn, creates the opportunity for newly registered citizens to be activated by the election campaign or by last-minute political party mobilization efforts. These last two points are relevant because of changes in political parties and the increased salience of politics for citizens resulting from such factors as increased economic uncertainty, concern with the nation's moral climate, or tax burdens.

The institutional restructuring of national and, more recently, state parties along with the availability of "soft money" to promote things such as voter mobilization drives could well lead to considerable success in turning out the millions of new voters registered under the provisions of the "motor voter" law. Modern political parties, regardless of their recent empowerment do not and will not resemble old-time, localized parties that were deeply rooted in the community and nurtured by armies of patronage workers. Nonetheless, the voter mobilization efforts of modern political parties could be enhanced by a combination of modern campaign technologies (television ads, electronic voter lists, mass mailings, etc.). These technologies obviate the need for labor-intensive mobilization efforts. Moreover, they can be effective tools in the party's effort to turn out the vote, even if these more sterile means of political communication are not effective in creating strong partisan attachments. Parties are motivated to use these technologies, even though they may not result in long-term allegiances, simply to counterbalance the mobilization efforts of their competition.

Interacting with the newly empowered political parties are distinctive partisan stands on issues about which voters care deeply. The strength and weave of the social safety net, which is of increasing importance to citizens facing downsizing and economic uncertainty, will be directly affected by the approach used to balance the federal budget and the parties have labored to persuade voters they have distinctive approaches to budget balancing. The same can be said for the moral issues facing the country. The fact that the government must necessarily play a role in some of these matters, along with distinctive partisan views on what that role should be, makes government more salient to citizens than it has been at least since Reagan's time. Many voters who have believed that government was part of the problem, may now begin to see it as part of the solution, promoting a modestly more participatory culture. Apparently Ross Perot energized many new voters in 1992. . . .

In closing, the recent trends in turnout evidenced by the nation's 32 largest metropolitan areas deserve some special comment. The distinctiveness of these trends, and the size and partisan make-up of these metropolitan areas, can provide important insights to partisans concerned with mapping long-term electoral strategies. . . .

These long-term secular shifts are of considerable importance because 1) these metropolitan areas constitute over 40 percent of the national electorate; and 2) the cities and suburbs that compose them are highly partisan. Since 1932 the center cities have returned the largest Democratic margins of victory among the locales studied here; their suburbs have been among the most Republican of these locales since the turn of the century (see Table 4). Because of their size and partisan allegiances, these cities and suburbs have been the key to statewide elections in their respective states for some time.

If we think about the long-term strategic implications of these data, two points are clear. The first is that the Democrats cannot focus solely on mobilizing the center city vote. The combination of declining electorates and voting propensities in these cities suggests that this is not a fruitful strategy, although it may be an important part of a more comprehensive strategy. Even if relative voting propensities in these cities could be increased to 1 (a level which these cities reached only in the New Deal era, but which could possibly be generated by the impact of the "motor voter" bill), . . . this is not likely to change the outcome of future presidential elections. The second point is that the Republicans might begin to think about what is generating the decline in voting propensities in the suburbs, as well as what can be done about it. While these voting propensities are still above 1, the Republicans have long depended upon greater turnouts among their wealthier and better educated adherents. It would be costly to them to lose the "bonus" that their suburban constituents have provided them since 1924.

NOTES

1. The turnout rate used here is computed as: total votes/eligible voters Eligible voters were determined by age, race, and sex determinations on a state-by-state basis. Some states allowed African-American men to vote long before passage of the Civil War Amendments and some states recognized the right of women to vote well before 1920. Finally, a few states allowed people younger than 21 years old to vote before 1970.

   The data set used here was constructed to conduct long-term analyses of U.S. electoral behavior. Because Alaska and Hawaii were not added to the union until 1959, the data set does not include them. All references to U.S. totals should be read as reflecting totals for the continental U.S. only.

2. We felt that the forces affecting turnout would differ significantly across different types of cities both because of historical factors and more recent demographic changes. At the same time it proved challenging to differentiate cities over the period of this study. The size and relative ranking of the nation's largest cities varied over time; what are the largest center cities today were not the largest cities fifty years ago. Cities that have long been at the core of a metropolitan area have had different experiences over the past century than cities that have grown rapidly over the post WWII period.

   To differentiate among these different large cities, we began by looking at populations aggregated over the twentieth century for all cities that had a population of 200,000 or more in 1990, 69 cities altogether. We aggregated both the city and the metropolitan area. Dividing these cities into two equal categories based on aggregated city population gave us a good basis for differentiating among cities. Six cities were eliminated from the tier 1 grouping because their aggregated metropolitan population did not match with the others in that group (San Jose, Birmingham, El Paso, Sacramento, Memphis, Rochester). At the same time several others were added to the top thirty because they had large metropolitan areas (Minneapolis, St. Paul, Seattle, Newark, Denver). Then the two groupings were examined to see if any "mismatches" appeared. Kansas City appeared to be the only "mismatch," just barely missing classification in the tier 1 category. Because it appeared to have more in common with the cities classified as tier 1 it was reclassified. The remaining 37 cities were categorized as tier 2 center cities.

3. We collected actual city data for twenty of these cities, usually as far back as 1860. The exceptions were Phoenix, Oakland, San Diego, Miami, Atlanta, Buffalo, San Antonio, Dallas, Houston, and Fort Worth. In the latter cities we used county totals to represent the city.

Compulsory Voting Is the Best Way to Keep Democracy Strong

Arend Lijphart

Voting is the commonest and most basic way of participating in a democracy, but far too many citizens do not exercise their right to vote, especially in the United States. In the 1988 and 1992 presidential elections, the turnout of registered voters was only 50 and 55 percent, respectively, and in the midterm congressional elections in 1990 and 1994, it was only 33 and 36 percent.

This is a serious problem for two reasons. One is democratic legitimacy: Can a government that has gained power in a low-turnout election really claim to be a representative government? For instance, some Americans questioned President Clinton's mandate because he received only 43 percent of the votes cast and because only 55 percent of those registered to vote actually did so—which meant that he received the support of fewer than 25 percent of all eligible voters in 1992. The other, even more serious problem is that low turnout almost inevitably means that certain groups vote in greater numbers than other groups and hence gain disproportionate influence on the government and its policies.

The only way to solve these problems is to maximize turnout. It may not be realistic to expect everyone to vote, but a turnout of, say, 90 percent is a feasible goal, as the experience of quite a few democracies shows.

On the basis of studies ranging from the 1920s work of Harold F. Gosnell at the University of Chicago to the 1990s research of Robert W. Jackman of the University of California at Davis and Mark N. Franklin of the University of Houston, we know a great deal about the institutional mechanisms that can increase turnout. They include voter-friendly registration procedures; voting on the weekend instead of during the week; easy access to absentee ballots; proportional representation, with multiple lawmakers representing electoral districts instead of the current U.S. system of winner-takes-all elections; and scheduling as many elections as possible—national, state, and local—on the same day.

The evidence suggests that using all of these measures together can produce a voter turnout of around 90 percent. But adopting all of them is a tall order. Only a handful of states have even managed to introduce the minor reform of allowing citizens to register to vote on the same day as the election.

Source: Arend Lijphart, "Compulsory Voting Is The Best Way To Keep Democracy Strong," *The Chronicle of Higher Education* (October 18, 1996), pp. B3, B4.

Arend Lipjhart is emeritus professor of political science at the University of California at San Diego. He is also a past president of the American Political Science Association and author of *Democracy in Plural Societies*.

Fortunately, one other reform, by itself, can maximize turnout as effectively as all of the other methods combined: compulsory voting. In Australia, Belgium, Brazil, Greece, Italy, Venezuela, and several other Latin American democracies, mandatory voting has produced near-universal voter turnout.

It is somewhat surprising that making voting compulsory is so effective, because the penalties for failing to vote are typically minor, usually involving a fine roughly equal to that for a parking violation. Moreover, enforcement tends to be very lax; because of the large numbers of people involved, compulsory voting simply cannot be strictly enforced. (Parking rules tend to be enforced much more strictly.)

For instance, with 10 million eligible voters in Australia, even a typical turnout of 95 percent means that half a million people did not vote, and it obviously is not practical to issue such a large number of fines. Australia is actually among the strictest enforcers of compulsory voting, but even there, only about 4 percent of non-voters end up having to pay the small fines. In Belgium, fewer than one-fourth of 1 percent of non-voters are fined.

Mandatory-voting requirements produce large turnouts, however, even though a government technically cannot compel an actual vote. A government can require citizens to show up at the polls, or even to accept a ballot and then drop it into the ballot box, but it cannot require its citizens to cast a valid vote; secret ballots mean that nobody can be prevented from casting an invalid or blank one.

It is worth emphasizing why low voter turnout is such a serious problem for democracies—one that deserves our attention. Low turnout typically means that privileged citizens (those with better education and greater wealth) vote in significantly larger numbers than less-privileged citizens. This introduces a systematic bias in favor of well-off citizens, because, as the old adage has it, "If you don't vote, you don't count." The already-privileged citizens who vote are further rewarded with government policies favoring their interests.

The socio-economic bias in voter turnout is an especially strong pattern in the United States, where turnout is extremely low. In presidential elections from 1952 to 1988, turnout among the college-educated was 26 percentage points higher than that among the population as a whole; the turnout for people without a high-school diploma was 16 percentage points lower. Unless turnout is very high—about 90 percent—socio-economic biases in voting tend to be a major problem. For instance, low and unequal voter turnout is a major reason why politicians find it so much easier to reduce government aid to the poor than to cut entitlement programs that chiefly benefit the middle class.

The low levels of voter turnout in the United States are often contrasted with turnouts as high as 95 percent in a few other countries. But when we measure turnout in other democracies in the way we usually measure it in the United States—as a percentage of *the voting-age population,* rather than as a percentage of *the registered electorate*—we find very few countries with turnouts above 90 percent, and most of those nations have compulsory voting. According to a study by G. Bingham Powell of the University of Rochester, half of the world's democracies have turnout levels below about 75 percent of the voting-age population. This half includes most of the larger democracies: not only the United States, but also Britain, France, Japan, and India, none of which require citizens to vote.

Even these figures cast turnouts in a deceptively favorable light, because they measure voting in what political scientists call first-order elections—that is, national-level parliamentary or presidential elections. But the vast majority of elections are second-order elections—for lesser posts—which attract less attention from citizens and lower turnouts. In the United States, only presidential elections produce turnouts of more than 50 percent of the voting-age population; turnout in midterm Congressional elections has been only about 35 percent in recent years, and in local elections is closer to 25 percent.

Low turnout is typical for second-order elections in other countries, too. For local elections in Britain, it is only about 40 percent. Even in Australia, it is only about 35 percent, because voting at the local level is not mandatory, as it is for national elections. In the 1994 elections for the European Parliament, another example of a second-order contest, the average turnout in the 12 nations of the European Union was 58 percent. The power of mandatory voting is highlighted by the fact that when it is applied to local elections—as it is in all nations with compulsory voting except Australia—turnout levels are almost the same as those for presidential and parliamentary contests.

It is time that we paid more attention to the issue of voter turnout, because the already low levels of voting in many countries around the world are declining even more. In the United States, voting in presidential elections has fallen to 50 to 55 percent of the voting-age population in the 1980s and '90s, from 60 to 65 percent during the 1950s and '60s. In the presidential contest of 1996, turnout was just under 50 percent.

The biggest advantage of compulsory voting is that, by enhancing voter turnout, it equalizes participation and removes much of the bias against less-privileged citizens. It also has two other significant advantages. One is that mandatory voting can reduce the role of money in politics, since it does away with the need for candidates and political parties to spend large sums on getting voters to the polls. Second, it reduces the incentives for negative advertising.

As the political scientists Stephen Ansolabehere of the Massachusetts Institute of Technology and Shanto Iyengar of the University of California at Los Angeles have shown in *Going Negative: How Attack Ads Shrink and Polarize the Electorate* (Free Press, 1995), attack ads work—indeed, they work all too well. They are effective not because they persuade people to vote *for* the candidate making the attack and *against* the candidate attacked in the ads, but because they raise enough doubts in voters' minds that they decide not to vote at all. So the candidate making the attack has lowered his or her opponent's total vote.

Moreover, attack ads breed general distrust of politicians and cynicism about politics and government. Under mandatory voting, it would be so much harder for attack ads to depress turnout that I believe they would no longer be worth the effort.

The main objection to compulsory voting is that it violates the individual's freedom—the freedom not to vote. This was the main reason it was abolished in the

Netherlands in 1970, for example. It is unlikely, however, that the Dutch would have made this decision had they foreseen the disastrous plunge in their voter turnouts, from about 90 percent in all elections to only 50 percent and 36 percent, respectively, in the most recent elections for provincial offices and for seats in the European Parliament.

In any case, the individual-freedom argument is extremely weak, because—as I've noted—compulsory voting does not actually require a citizen to cast a valid ballot. Besides, mandatory voting entails an extremely small decrease in freedom compared with many other, more onerous tasks that democracies require their citizens to perform, such as serving on juries, paying taxes, and serving in the military.

Some scholars argue that U.S. courts might rule compulsory voting unconstitutional because it restricts individual freedom. Richard L. Hasen, of the Chicago-Kent College of Law at the Illinois Institute of Technology, recently has argued, in "Voting Without Law?" (*University of Pennsylvania Law Review,* May 1996), that the only plausible ground for such a ruling would be the First Amendment's guarantee of freedom of speech. But the Supreme Court has explicitly rejected the notion that voting can be regarded as a form of speech. For instance, in 1992, in *Burdick v. Takushi,* the Court upheld Hawaii's ban on write-in votes, ruling against a voter's claim that the ban deprived him of the right to cast a protest vote for Donald Duck. The Court said an election is about choosing representatives, not about expressing oneself. Of course, even if mandatory voting were to be found unconstitutional, a constitutional amendment permitting it could be adopted—a difficult, but not impossible, prospect.

Probably the most important practical obstacle to compulsory voting in countries that do not have it is the opposition of conservative parties, like the Republican Party in the United States. High turnout is clearly not in their partisan self-interest, because unequal turnout favors privileged voters, who tend to be conservative. But conservative parties generally were also opposed to universal suffrage, which eventually was accepted by all democracies, because it was recognized to be a basic democratic principle. Compulsory voting should be seen as an extension of universal suffrage—which we now all take for granted.

Just How Much Difference Does Turnout Really Make?

Ruy Teixeira

. . . The sheer magnitude of nonvoting—91 million Americans of voting age did not participate on election day in 1988—has produced much critical commentary across the political spectrum. The same questions keep coming up: Does low turnout significantly bias the nature of contemporary U.S. politics? Are differences we see in voting between those with high and with low incomes and between blacks and whites—to name only a few groupings that participate at different rates in elections—large and growing? And finally, do these differences matter?

Many believe that the extent of nonvoting is contributing to biased election outcomes and unrepresentative policy choices. A restatement of this thesis comes from economist John Kenneth Galbraith in his book, *The Culture of Contentment*. Galbraith argues that government policies reflect the preferences of those who vote and that these comfortably situated voters are systematically turning the nation's attention away from pressing social needs.

"In past times, the economically and socially fortunate were a small minority—characteristically a dominant and ruling handful. They are now a majority, though as has been observed a majority not of all citizens but of those who actually vote. They rule under the rich cloak of democracy, a democracy in which the less fortunate do not participate."

Galbraith goes on, "Weapons expenditures, unlike spending for the urban poor, reward a very comfortable constituency," giving voice to a commonly held belief that the preferences of comfortable, affluent voters are different from those who do not vote.

How much truth there is to such claims can be seen by looking first at who votes and who doesn't, then at how those patterns have changed over time, and finally at what difference these patterns make to election outcomes and policy preferences. Underlying all these issues, however, is a larger question: Just how much difference does turnout really make?

THE CLASS GAP IN VOTING: IS IT GETTING LARGER?

Data collected by the Census Bureau after each election show that there are demographic skews in voting in the United States. Table 1 displays some of these differences

Source: Ruy A. Teixeira, "Just How Much Difference Does Turnout Really Make?" *The American Enterprise* (July/August 1992), pp 52–59.

Ruy Teixeira is director of the Politics and Public Opinion Program at the Economic Policy Institute and author of *The Disappearing American Voter.*

in voting rates by race and by key socioeconomic variables, such as income, occupation, and education, and looks at how these differences have changed over time.

Income is the socioeconomic characteristic most people have in mind when they think of class, so this is an appropriate place to begin to look for class divisions in voting. The data here clearly show that affluent Americans are much more likely to turn out to vote than poorer ones. In 1988, 75.4 percent of those with family incomes above $60,000 reported voting, compared to only 39.8 percent of those under $7,500. The data in Table 1 also show that turnout has declined for both low- and high-income groups over time. Still, it is possible that the class gap in turnout may have widened substantially due to a sharper decline among low-income groups. Many believe, for example, that the poor are simply dropping out of politics, leaving elections and policy choices to the affluent; however, the Census Bureau data show only a modest increase in the turnout gap between 1972, when it was 32 percentage points and 1988, when it was 36 points.

We can also define income groups in another way, that is, by their relative position in the income structure, by dividing structure into six equal groups. (About 17 percent of Americans fall in each group.) The advantage of examining income data by equal-sized groups is that the relative position of groups in the income structure remains constant over time.

Once again, however, the Census Bureau data show only a modest increase in the gap between 1972 and 1988. The pattern that applies to the standard income categories is evident here: the gap between low- and high-income earners is large; the magnitude of that gap has changed relatively little over time; and finally, both low- and high-income voters are voting less than they did in the past. The education data show a similar pattern. Like the income data, the turnouts among those at the top of the education hierarchy and those at the bottom have been declining over time. Still, the decline in turnout has been larger among the lowest group in the education distribution. Reflecting this, the gap between voters with higher educations and those with lower ones was 36 points in 1972; in 1992 it was 41 points.

Another measure of socioeconomic status, occupation, also shows a general decline in participation across all groups. In 1972, 55 percent of blue-collar workers (excluding laborers) reported voting; in 1988, only 44.9 percent did. Among those in professional and technical positions in 1972, 82.3 percent reported voting, but only 75.7 percent did in 1988. Still, the decline among those in lower-status occupations has been slightly greater than among those in the higher-status ones.

The weight of evidence, at least for the 1972–1988 time period, does not suggest a dramatically widening class gap in voter participation. Instead, the data are consistent with a moderate increase in the gap, whether class is measured by income, education, or occupation. It could still be argued that if trends could be tracked back to 1960, the increase in the class gap would be much larger, perhaps dramatically so. However, the one data source that does go back to 1960—the University of Michigan's American National Election Studies (NES)—generally shows smaller increases in the class gap between 1960 and 1972 than between 1972 and 1988, which suggests again that overall change in the class gap has been moderate.

The data in Table 1 tell three stories. They are drawn from the Census Bureau surveys conducted in November of every election year (see note below). The first story is that the decline in voter turnout in the last several decades has been pretty much across the board. Between 1972 and 1988, for example, turnout among those in the lowest Census Bureau income category dropped 7.4 points (from 47.2 to 39.8); for those in the highest category, it dropped 3.7 points (from 79.1 to 75.4).

The data here also show that there is a class gap in voting in the United States. In 1988, there was a 36-point gap between those with low and high incomes; a 33-point gap between those in the lowest and the highest income sextile, and a 41-point gap between those with low and high education levels. A gap exists between black and non-Hispanic white voters, but it is much smaller (10 points in 1988), and it has been narrowing over time.

Many believe that the class gap in turnout is widening and causing a turn away from the poor (now allegedly underrepresented) in the policy discourse of the country. But the gap in both income measures above widened only moderately between

TABLE 1 *Turnout Rates by Income, Education, Occupation, and Race*

	1972		1988	
Family income in dollars		**Gap**		**Gap**
$7,500 or less	47.2%	31.9%	39.8%	35.6%
$60,000 or more	79.1		75.4	
Family income by sextile				
Lowest sextile	49.2	29.6	40.7	33.4
Highest sextile	78.8		74.1	
Education				
0–8 years	47.4	36.2	36.7	40.9
College graduate or more	83.6		77.6	
Occupation				
Professional-technical	82.3	27.3	75.7	30.8
Blue collar*	55.0		44.9	
Race				
Non-Hispanic white	65.7	13.5	61.8	9.7
Black	52.2		52.1	

Note: Income figures are in 1988 dollars. Base is voting-age population.

*Excludes laborers.

There are two main sources for data on turnout, the Census Bureau and the University of Michigan's American National Election Studies. The Census Bureau sample of the voting-age population is about 50 times larger than the NES sample, so estimates of relative turnout rates based on the Census data are far more reliable than those based on the NES data. However, the Census Bureau data have the deficiency that data tapes are only available from 1972 on, while NES data tapes are available since 1952. When Americans are asked by Census Bureau interviewers whether they voted, far more Americans say they did than actually participated. Thus, the figures here overstate turnout. They should not be used as absolute numbers, but they do enable us to look with confidence at the relative changes in group participation in elections.

Source: Author's tabulations of Bureau of the Census data.

1972 and 1988, as did the education or occupation gaps. For race, it has actually decreased.

Many people also believe that turnout decline in the United States has been particularly sharp among minorities and that a large racial gap in voting contributes significantly to distorted election and policy outcomes. If many members of minority groups don't vote, the argument goes, the issues of most concern to them can be ignored. But the data do not support these conclusions. Turnout differentials by race continue to exist, but these differentials are not large when compared to voting differentials by class; moreover, they have been declining, not increasing, over time. The gap between non-Hispanic whites and blacks was 14 points in 1972 but only 10 points in 1988. Thus, contrary to the gloomy assessments of many commentators, this is one area of voter participation in which things have actually gotten better, not worse.

WHO VOTES AND WHO DOESN'T

The discussion above has shown that turnout has declined across most demographic categories, swelling the ranks of nonvoters among the affluent as well as the poor, college graduates as well as high school dropouts. Moreover, during this period, the electorate has become more affluent, educated, and white-collar. These factors would lead us to expect a substantial shift over time in the composition of the nonvoting pool away from the very lowest socioeconomic categories and toward a more "middle-class" social composition. There is, in fact, evidence that this is occurring.

Table 2 allows us to examine this issue directly by providing data on the demographic composition of the nonvoting pool, the voting pool, and the entire electorate in 1972 and 1988. Using these data, we can see how these distributions have shifted over time. The data confirm a substantial upgrading of the nonvoting pool, especially in terms of educational levels.

Table 2 compares the demographic profiles of voters and nonvoters and compares them to the demographic makeup of the population. Each category adds to 100 percent vertically. Over the last 16 years, the population (see column labeled "All") has become more educated. In 1972, 11.6 percent of the population were college graduates or more; in 1988 that figure was 19 percent. Like the population as a whole, the pool of nonvoters has also experienced some educational upgrading. In 1972, 29 percent of nonvoters had 0–8 years of education; by 1988, only 16 percent did. The table also shows that the nonvoting pool has become younger, particularly in the 25–44-year-old category, and that it has remained almost the same percentage black.

The composition of the nonvoting pool does not mirror the profile of the population as a whole; it tends to overrepresent "low" or disadvantaged demographic categories and underrepresent "high" ones. However, the nonvoting pool is not a monolith of the disadvantaged and includes many middle-class citizens.

For example, while about three in ten nonvoters in 1972 had eight years or less of education and over half were high school dropouts, by 1988 only 16 percent had eight years or less of education and less than one-third were high school dropouts.

TABLE 2   *Profile of Nonvoters, Voters, and the Population*

	1972			1988		
	Nonvoters	*Voters*	*All*	*Nonvoters*	*Voters*	*All*
Education						
0–8 years	29.2%	15.5%	20.6%	16.0%	6.9%	10.8%
9–11 years	21.2	13.5	16.4	16.3	8.5	11.8
High school graduate	34.8	38.7	37.3	41.8	37.5	39.3
Some college	9.6	16.8	14.1	16.0	21.6	19.2
College graduate or more	5.2	15.5	11.6	9.9	25.5	18.9
Family income in dollars						
under $7,500	15.4	8.0	10.7	16.9	8.2	11.9
$7,500–14,999	22.9	15.3	18.1	22.2	14.6	17.8
$15,000–19,999	14.5	10.2	11.8	20.5	17.6	18.9
$20,000–29,999	20.9	21.7	21.4	16.4	18.4	17.5
$30,000–39,999	15.3	21.0	18.9	13.1	18.7	16.4
$40,000–59,999	6.3	13.5	10.8	5.7	10.8	8.6
$60,000 or more	4.7	10.3	8.2	5.2	11.7	9.0
Age						
18–20 years	11.3	6.2	8.1	9.5	3.5	6.0
21–24 years	13.3	8.0	10.0	12.0	5.6	8.3
25–34 years	21.5	13.5	16.4	29.3	20.0	24.0
35–44 years	14.9	17.2	16.3	18.0	21.1	19.8
45–54 years	13.5	19.3	17.2	10.7	15.8	13.6
55–64 years	11.0	15.6	13.9	8.7	14.6	12.1
65–74 years	8.0	10.0	9.3	6.2	12.6	9 9
75 years old and older	6.6	4.8	5.5	5.6	6.8	6.3
Race						
White	85.4	91.1	89.0	82.4	88.4	85.8
Black	12.8	8.2	9.9	12.6	9.9	11.1
Other	1.8	.7	1 1	5.1	1.7	3.1

Note: Income figures are in 1988 dollars. Base is voting-age population.

Source: Author's tabulations of Census Bureau data for years indicated.

Conversely, in 1972, just 5 percent of nonvoters were college graduates and under 15 percent had attended college at all, but by 1988, 10 percent of nonvoters were college graduates and over one-quarter had attended college. Clearly, the old stereotype of the nonvoter as high school dropout is becoming less and less reliable. Occupational upgrading (not shown in Table 2) of the nonvoting pool is also evident, though less dramatic.

Interestingly, the upgrading described above is not evident when looking at income. For example, the proportion of nonvoters in income categories higher than $40,000 per family remained stable between 1972 and 1988 at about 11 percent. Similarly, the proportion of nonvoters in the categories having less than $15,000 income per family was virtually unchanged (38 percent in 1972 and 39 percent in 1988). What change there was took place in the middle three categories of the income distribution, which included roughly the same proportion of nonvoters in 1988 as in 1972 but shifted downscale toward the lowest of these three categories. To a large extent, this lack of income upgrading for nonvoters probably reflects the population-wide stagnation of family income levels after 1973 (in contrast to the continuation of educational and occupational upgrading after this date).

The data in Table 2 provide two additional items of interest: (1) the nonvoting pool has become substantially younger, chiefly from an increase in the 25–44-year-old group (an age group that was virtually co-terminus with the Baby Boom generation in 1988); and (2) the nonvoting pool has remained almost exactly the same percentage black (about 13 percent) over time. The latter point underscores the extent to which nonvoting is not a racial issue, despite attempts by such politicians as Jesse Jackson to portray it that way. In conclusion then, the nonvoting pool is hardly a monolith of society's disadvantaged. While it is true that nonvoters are poorer, less-educated, more likely to be blue-collar or service workers, and more likely to be members of minority groups, it is also true that many, many nonvoters are middle-class in the most conventional sense of the term.

MOBILIZING NONVOTERS

But what if more nonvoters voted? Would it help Democratic and/or more liberal candidates since individuals in groups with lower voting participation—those of lower socioeconomic status—tend to be more Democratic and liberal?

This reasoning seems clear enough as far as it goes; however, it does not specify *how much* nonvoter mobilization would help Democratic candidates, only that mobilizing nonvoters would be *some kind* of help. (That is, it specifies the *direction* not the *magnitude* of change for the Democratic candidate.) This is a crucial distinction since changing the outcome of an election by expanding the voting pool is far more difficult than generally believed.

To begin with, the nonvoting pool is not an overwhelmingly disadvantaged group, as we have documented. But there are other reasons that the mobilization of more of those in this pool would not change outcomes considerably. One is that partisan differences by demographic group are not large by international standards, and skews in political attitudes are even smaller. In addition nonvoters are particularly likely to disregard partisan and other preferences and surge in the direction of a candidate who appears to be winning. And finally, from the standpoint of simple mathematics, *it is a great deal easier to change an election outcome by switching the preferences of existing voters than by adding new voters.*

The latter point deserves some expansion. The basic idea is that every existing voter who switches, for example, from the Republicans to the Democrats, provides the Democrats with a net of *two* votes (the Democrats have one *more* vote and the Republicans have one *less* vote). In contrast, every additional mobilized nonvoter provides the Democrats with only a fractional net vote equal to the difference in the level of support nonvoters would give the two parties. For example, if the Democrats are supported by 60 percent of nonvoters and the Republicans by 40 percent of non-voters—a fairly high pro-Democratic differential—and if ten are newly mobilized, the new voters would split their votes, six for the Democrat, four for the Republican. That would produce a net gain of two votes (six minus four equals two, or .2 net vote per nonvoter) for the Democrats. Thus, even under a relatively favorable scenario, it still takes 10 nonvoters to generate as many net votes as our vote switcher generates.

Given a plurality for, say, the Republicans among existing voters, that plurality has to be neutralized by the Democrats among the newly mobilized nonvoters. But even under optimistic scenarios, the number of newly mobilized nonvoters will be relatively small compared to the number of existing voters (for example, a 10-percentage-point increase in presidential turnout in 1992 would still be only one-fifth the size of the presidential electorate from 1988, which was 50 percent of the eligible electorate). Because of this, the intensity of support for the Democrats among the smaller number of newly mobilized nonvoters must be much higher than the level of support for the Republicans among the much larger numbers of existing voters, or else the mobilization strategy won't work.

But assumptions of such support levels among nonvoters are typically unrealistic. In the example above (50 percent 1988 turnout, 10-percentage-point increase in 1992), Democratic support among newly mobilized nonvoters, assuming an existing 54–46 percent Republican advantage (approximating the 1988 presidential election results), would have to be 70–30 percent—*five times the percentage-point plurality of the Republicans among existing voters*. To say that this is unlikely to happen is to understate the case considerably.

The only way to avoid such an unrealistic assumption is to posit an even-larger turnout increase—say, 20 percent. But this is also unrealistic. And even here, the level of Democratic support would have to be 60–40 percent among the mobilized nonvoters for the strategy to work—itself not an easy goal to attain.

Thus, the basic dynamics of electoral arithmetic are such that a nonvoter-mobilization strategy typically involves unrealistic assumptions about support levels among nonvoters, or levels of increase in turnout, or both. Conversely, the fact that such unrealistic assumptions are necessary to reverse an electoral outcome suggests that most electoral outcomes are unlikely to change through simple expansion or contraction of the voting pool. These points are further illustrated by considering two types of mobilization scenarios.

WOULD MOBILIZING MORE MINORITIES MAKE A DIFFERENCE IN ELECTION OUTCOMES?

Perhaps the most common scenario for turnout deciding an election outcome is based on the concept of mobilizing nonvoters from key demographic groups that have strong political leanings to the desired party. (I will concentrate on mobilization of Democratic-leaning demographic groups since this is how the argument is typically made.) The basic idea is that certain demographic groups with known Democratic sympathies (blacks, Hispanics, the poor) are also generally known to have relatively low turnout rates. It therefore follows that if their turnout rates could be raised—perhaps just made equal to those of other demographic groups—it should help Democrats and lead to changes in electoral outcomes.

Since the distribution of these demographic groups in the electorate can be measured, we can actually estimate turnout rates for them. We can then see how much these rates would have to increase to match or surpass turnout rates of other groups. Finally, these estimated turnout rate increases can be combined with information on the Democratic proclivities of these groups (for example, from exit polls) to produce fairly concrete estimates of the impact of these turnout increases on Democratic fortunes in any given election.

The 1988 presidential election is a good case study, but the principles are general and apply to most elections . . . The Democrats' defeat in the 1988 presidential election was, as usual, accompanied by relatively low turnout rates among blacks, Hispanics, and the larger group of the poor. As many readers no doubt recall, some people in the Democratic Party (most notably Jesse Jackson) claimed after the election that the defeat could be attributed to these low turnout rates among the Democrats' core constituencies.

The numbers, however, show otherwise. In fact, they show that even very large increases in turnout among blacks, Hispanics, and the poor would still have left Michael Dukakis far behind George Bush. For example, if black turnout had matched turnout of the general population, which would have meant an increase of 6 percentage points, the Democrats would have netted about 865,000 additional votes. If black turnout had matched that of non-Hispanic whites, an increase of 10 points, the net Democratic gain would have been about 1,442,000 votes. And if black turnout had somehow been 10 points higher than turnout among whites (that is, 20 points higher than it was in reality), the Democratic gain would have amounted to about 2,884,000 votes. *But Dukakis lost the election by over 7 million votes.* This suggests that the 1988 election was decided more by overall levels of support among the population than by relative turnout rates of different groups.

Further illustrating this point, if turnout among Hispanic citizens had matched turnout among the general population, the net gain for the Democrats would have been about 292,000 votes. If Hispanic turnout had matched that of whites, the Democrats would have netted about 453,000 votes. Finally, under the unlikely scenario that Hispanic turnout had exceeded white turnout by 10 points, the Democrats would have gained about 776,000 voters. This means that if both Hispanics *and* blacks had voted at rates 10 points higher than whites—a very unlikely scenario—the overall net gain for the Democrats, 3,660,000 votes, would still have fallen far short of the number of additional votes Dukakis needed for victory.

It could still be argued that the Democratic turnout problem in 1988 was not so much a matter of race as of economic class. Supporting this argument is the fact that the turnout rate of the poor in 1988 was 36 points lower than that of the rich (see Table 1). What if the poor had turned out at higher levels?

If turnout among those with less than $12,500 in family income had matched that of the population, the Democrats would have netted about 1,703,000 voters. If poor turnout had matched rich turnout, the net gain would have been about 3,468,000 votes. Finally, if some sort of unprecedented poor people's mobilization had taken place and the poor had turned out at a level 10 points higher than the rich, the Democrats would have gained about 4,449,000 votes—not enough, by itself, to reverse the 1988 electoral verdict.

But what about the entire Rainbow Coalition of blacks, Hispanics, and the poor? Since a substantial fraction of blacks and Hispanics are poor, any attempt to calculate figures for the Coalition must eliminate double-counting. The simplest way to do this is to add up the projected vote increments for Hispanics, blacks, and the white poor (not the poor as a whole). Assuming the highest turnout scenarios (for blacks and Hispanics, 10 points higher than whites; for the white poor, 10 points higher than the white rich), the computations still show only 4,677,000 net additional votes for Dukakis.

These results seem clear enough. However, it could still be argued that if the results of increased turnout were concentrated in a few key states, the electoral college vote could magnify the impact of the mobilization scenarios discussed above. For example, Jesse Jackson claimed after the 1988 election that relatively modest increases in black registration and turnout in 11 key states would have won the election for Dukakis.

Again, such a scenario is relatively easy to test. In fact, I was able to test not only the state-level effects of increased black turnout but also the state-level effects of increased turnout among Hispanics and the white poor. The results are not the good news that advocates of this type of mobilization want to hear.

With a modest 5-percentage-point increase in black turnout, not a single state would have gone from Bush to Dukakis. With a 10-point increase in black turnout in every state that Bush won, only two states would have switched—Maryland and Illinois—for a total of 34 additional electoral votes. Finally, I looked at the effect of a 20-point increase in black turnout, far more than a modest increase, but even here, there is little additional effect: only Pennsylvania is added to the two other states, producing a still-lopsided Dukakis loss of 367–171 in the Electoral College.

Of course, devotees of this kind of mobilization mathematics could go beyond the claim made by Jackson and maintain that if Hispanics and the white poor had been mobilized at the levels just envisioned for blacks, and these turnout increases were mediated by the Electoral College, the results would be quite different. But increasing Hispanic and white poor turnout by 20 points in every state Bush won adds only California to the Democratic column, chiefly due to the state's large Hispanic population and the relative closeness of the election there.

In sum, if turnout among blacks, Hispanics, and the white poor had *all* been 20 points higher in every state Bush won—a mobilization advocate's dream come true—Dukakis still would have lost the 1988 election 320–218 in the Electoral College. That these 20-point increases would have been difficult, if not impossible, to achieve (Republicans would countermobilize other demographic groups generally supportive of the GOP)—and that they wouldn't have changed the outcome anyway—suggests just how difficult it is to change election outcomes through selective mobilization. Conversely, the difficulty of changing outcomes through selective mobilization suggests that most electoral outcomes . . . are not, in any meaningful sense, determined by relative turnout rates.

Now, none of this is to say that mobilizing key demographic groups could not *technically* have won the 1988 election for the Democrats. For example, if *every black* in the United States had voted in 1988 (and not a single additional white), Dukakis would probably have won. Or if turnout among the poor had been 20 points higher, and *every one of these additional poor people had voted Democratic,* this, too, would have been enough to swing the election. But these scenarios are the stuff of political science fiction.

As silly as they seem, however, these scenarios do illustrate an important point. When people say "turnout is the problem" or "if turnout could only be higher," they are usually basing their assessments on just such fantasies. That is, they assume preposterously high turnout increases for a group, preposterously high voting rates for their candidate among new voters, or both. Such assumptions are seldom justified. . . .

WHAT IF ALL AMERICANS VOTED?

Selective mobilization of demographic groups is not only unlikely to change election outcomes, it is quite difficult to achieve in practice. A more plausible mobilization scenario is simply expanding the voting pool through general mobilization of nonvoters. Under this scenario, no one gets to "pick" the nonvoters who are added to the voting pool. They are drawn, more or less at random, from the nonvoting pool without regard to political proclivities or demographic affiliation.

But since, on average, nonvoters are concentrated in demographic groups that are relatively supportive of the Democrats, even random additions of nonvoters should help the Democrats. Or so the story goes. The problem is, however, that there's very little evidence this would actually happen.

This can be seen most clearly by looking at the extreme case of general nonvoter mobilization: 100 percent voter participation. In other words, what if they held an election and everybody came? Would it make a difference? The answer, it appears, is not much.

This basic result is consistent across a number of studies, election years, and data bases. For example, the 1988 CBS/*New York Times* postelection poll shows that if nonvoters had voted, the election result would have been the same—except that Bush would have won by a wider margin! Similarly, a study by Steven Bennett and David Resnick of the University of Cincinnati has found that, according to NES data, complete mobilization of nonvoters in 1980 and 1984 would have produced the same outcome—slightly decreasing Reagan's victory margin in the first instance and slightly *increasing* it in the second. Finally, John Petrocik of UCLA has presented NES-based evidence covering every presidential election from 1952 through 1984 showing that complete mobilization would not have changed the outcome of any of these elections, with the possible exception of 1980. In fact, Petrocik found that the typical effect of complete mobilization would have been to increase the victory margin of the winner.

The relatively minor impact of full nonvoter mobilization on presidential election outcomes is further illustrated by the data in Table 3, which compare the actual presidential votes with the expressed presidential preferences of nonvoters and then combines the two to show the outcome if all Americans had voted. We see that in no instance would the winner have been changed if all nonvoters had voted. This suggests that while nonvoters' candidate preferences can be somewhat different from those of voters, they are not likely to be different enough to change most election outcomes, even under conditions of complete general mobilization.

What would happen to election outcomes if all nonvoters voted? Table 3 provides the answer. These data compare the reported presidential vote of those who turned out and the expressed preference nonvoters gave to survey researchers who asked them how they would have voted. In no instance would the winner have changed if all nonvoters had voted. In every election through 1980, nonvoters were somewhat more Democratic than voters, but this situation reversed itself in the last two elections. In both 1984 and 1988, levels of Republican support among nonvoters were higher than among voters, meaning that the GOP victory margins would probably have gone up, not down, if all nonvoters had decided to vote.

TABLE 3 *Presidential Vote/Preference of Voters and Nonvoters, 1964–88**

	Voters supported	*Nonvoters preferred*	*Voters + Nonvoters*
1964			
Democratic candidate	67.4%	79.7%	70.0%
Republican candidate	32.4	20.3	29.9
1968			
Democratic candidate	40.9	44.6	41.7
Republican candidate	47.6	40.4	46.0
Other candidate	11.5	15.0	12.2
1980			
Democratic candidate	39.4	46.8	41.1
Republican candidate	50.8	45.1	49.5
Other candidate	9.8	8.2	9.4
1984			
Democratic candidate	41.4	38.6	40.8
Republican candidate	57.7	61.2	58.4
1988			
Democratic candidate	46.6	44.4	46.0
Republican candidate	52.3	54.3	52.8

Note: *The NES did not ask about the presidential preference of nonvoters in 1972 and 1976, so these years are not included in the table.

Source: Author's tabulations of University of Michigan's American National Election Studies data for years indicated.

In every election through 1980, nonvoters were somewhat more Democratic-leaning than voters. But . . . in both 1984 and 1988, levels of Republican support among nonvoters were actually *higher* than among voters, meaning that the Republican victory margins would probably have gone up, not down, if all nonvoters had decided to show up at the polls. This suggests that not only is it incorrect to assume that general nonvoter mobilization will substantially help the Democrats (that is, change election outcomes), it may even be incorrect to assume that the Democrats will be helped at all. Supporting this point, a May 1992 NBC News/*Wall Street Journal* nationwide poll of voters and nonvoters found that nonvoters were actually slightly more likely than voters (45–41 percent) to approve of the job President Bush was doing. Moreover, in a three-way presidential matchup, Bush finished first among both voters and nonvoters.

SUMMING UP

Most electoral outcomes are not determined in any meaningful sense by the size of the turnout, and these outcomes are not likely to change as a result of even highly implausible levels of nonvoter mobilization. To put it more bluntly, nonvoting does not, as a rule, make much of a difference. . . .

Does this mean that nonvoting *never* makes a difference to election outcomes—that elections are *never* determined by the level of turnout? No, it just means that very specific, and relatively unusual, conditions have to be met for turnout to play a determining role. These conditions are well summarized by Thomas Cavanagh of Yale University: The election must be very close to begin with, due to partisan balance and/or other political trends; a very large turnout increase can be generated, relative to the normally expected turnout level in that election; and, finally, a large group of nonvoters with very lopsided candidate preferences must be available for mobilization.

These conditions are not likely to obtain often. This is especially true at the state or national level. It is somewhat more likely, however, that these conditions will obtain in local elections, for the simple mathematical reason that base turnout levels are typically very low in these elections. This makes it comparatively easy to generate a turnout increase whose relative weight is large compared to base turnout. For example, the outcome of the 1983 Chicago mayoral election, where there was a tremendous increase in normally low black turnout levels, was probably determined by higher turnout. Blacks had a historically low turnout rate; they increased their participation by 30 percentage points and voted 99 percent for Harold Washington.

The overwhelming majority of U.S. elections do not, and will not, take place in electoral settings where anything resembling these conditions exists.

The Voting Decision

Elections are of interest to political observers because of what they tell us about how voters make their voting decision; the relative overall strength of the parties in the electorate; and the potential impact of the electoral decision on governing. This chapter focuses on the first of these three considerations.

Perhaps no aspect of American political behavior has been subject to more study than the factors that influence how we vote in presidential elections. Across the political science literature on this subject, there is general agreement that the American voter falls well short of the idealized "philosophical citizen," described by one scholar as an informed individual who carefully weighs the relevant issues, and then casts a ballot not on the basis of self-interested considerations, but rather for the common good.[1] On the other hand, there is less agreement on the *relative* impact of those considerations that guide individuals in their voting choices.

In the first article, Martin Wattenberg identifies three major theories that have dominated the study of voting: the sociological, which sees the voting decision as growing out of group affiliations; the psychological, which maintains that party attachment serves as a perceptual screen through which voters evaluate candidates and issues; and the economic, which suggests that voters, uninfluenced by party or social affiliations, rationally calculate which party will provide them with the most benefits. Noting that no single model for explaining voting behavior should be viewed as definitive "for all time," Wattenberg assesses the strengths and weaknesses of each. He goes on to suggest, however, that given the declining importance of party, and the rise of the "candidate-centered campaign," the economic, and to some degree the sociological, model of voting behavior are increasingly applicable in explaining how Americans vote.

A number of scholars and commentators have pointed to the growing number of independents as one of the primary indicators of the declining attachment to parties in the electorate. Indeed, over the last three decades the percentage of Americans calling themselves independents has been reported to range from the mid-twenties to high thirties, at times even exceeding the number of those identified with one of the two major parties. In the second selection, however, Raymond Wolfinger cautions us against accepting those figures at face value. He insists that a full and careful analysis of the voting survey data reveals that the number of true independents is really no greater than it was in the 1950s—roughly fifteen percent. In his view, party identification remains a significant force in influencing voters' perceptions of the political world and their choices on election day.

The final selection focuses on the information environment of elections and how voters make use of it in reaching their voting decisions. Relying on surveys, focus groups, and in-depth interviews of voters in the 1992 presidential election campaign, Marion Just *et. al.* assess how voters responded to the various information formats to which they were exposed, including news, candidate interviews, and political ads. Impressed by voters' ability to judge the quality of information they receive, and the range of factors they bring to bear in evaluating candidates, the authors go on to suggest how the quality of the election campaign information environment could be further enriched.

NOTES

1. Gerald M. Pomper, *Elections in America: Control and Influence in Democratic Politics* (New York: Dodd, Mead, 1968), pp. 70, 74, 75.

Theories of Voting

Martin P. Wattenberg

The subject of voting is one of the most interdisciplinary topics in all of social science. Political science, the natural home for research on voting behavior, has in fact failed to agree on a central paradigm for the analysis of voting. Instead, it has borrowed repeatedly from three related disciplines for a theoretical framework: sociology, psychology, and economics. This chapter examines the scholarly influence of each on voting behavior research over the past four decades, as the literature has undergone a natural progression from initially focusing on fundamental sociological factors, to mediating psychological ties, and finally to assessing short-term economic variables. This scholarly progression makes eminent sense given the transformation from party to candidate-centered politics.

CLASSIC STUDIES OF AMERICAN VOTING BEHAVIOR

Most voting behavior research in the first half of the twentieth century employed the sociological approach. This was largely because the best available data were census data demographics, which could easily be compared to voting patterns. Thus, when the technique of survey research first became available, it was natural that demographic variables were examined first, as their role in shaping voting decisions had already been well established by sociologists. In addition, sociology was the first of the disciplines to embrace survey methodology, which is particularly well-suited to the analysis of individual voting behavior.[1]

The pioneers of survey research in sociology were led by Paul Lazarsfeld at Columbia University's Bureau of Applied Social Research. Lazarsfeld, Bernard Bereleson, and Hazel Gaudet set out to understand how voting intentions changed during a campaign by interviewing a panel of voters repeatedly during the 1940 election year.[2] Finding that relatively few voters switched back and forth, they fell back upon previously established demographic patterns of voting to explain their findings. The stability of voting preferences and relative lack of susceptibility to media influence were said to be the result of political predispositions stemming from social status, religion, and place of residence.

The initial negative findings on vote switching reported in their study, *The People's Choice*, led to a more in-depth investigation of the role of demographic

---

Source: Martin P. Wattenberg, *The Rise of Candidate-Centered Politics* (Boston: Harvard University Press, 1991), pp. 13–30.

Martin P. Wattenberg is professor of political science at the University of California, Irvine and author of the *Decline of American Political Parties, 1953–1996.*

characteristics. Bereleson, Lazarsfeld, and William McPhee's classic 1954 work entitled *Voting* laid out a comprehensive sociological model of the vote decision.[3] The bulk of their data, as the authors put it, related "either directly to primary groups or to clusters of them in the social strata."[4] The basic assumption was that voting is as much conditioned by who one is as by what one believes. In other words, sociological variables create common group interests that shape the party coalitions and define images concerning which party is most attuned to the needs of various types of people.

To the authors of *Voting,* understanding the past was essential to interpreting the present. Their major concern was to explore the roots of stability rather than the forces of change from election to election. Therefore, the concepts of political heritage and community were crucial to the analysis. "In a very real sense," Bereleson and his coauthors wrote, "any particular election is a composite of various elections and various political and social events . . . The vote is thus a kind of 'moving average' of reactions to the political past."[5]

Early studies of voting that adopted this approach left much of the vote unexplained, however, and were unable to account for shifts in the vote from year to year. This was shown most clearly in another work published in 1954 entitled *The Voter Decides.*[6] Based on nationwide survey data collected by the University of Michigan's Survey Research Center, the book concluded,

> The experience of the last two presidential elections has shown us . . . that the simple classification of voters into sociological categories does not have the explanatory power that at first appeared. It has been demonstrated that the application of the Lazarsfeld index to the national electorate in 1948 resulted in a prediction of the vote not remarkably better than chance. In 1952, the great shifts in group preferences . . . would have been very difficult to predict on the basis of previous voting records.[7]

These weaknesses in the sociological approach led the Michigan investigators to focus more directly on the calculus of individual behavior, and hence relevant psychological theories. Demographic characteristics were downplayed in *The Voter Decides,* with the emphasis instead being on party attachment and people's orientations toward the issues and the candidates.

As with the Columbia study, the Michigan center's first treatise on voting behavior was followed by a far more elaborate landmark work, which fully explicated the underlying theory of their disciplinary approach. The publication of *The American Voter* in 1960 introduced an explicitly social psychological model of the vote.[8] The focal point of this theory was the mediating role of long-term psychological predispositions—particularly that of party identification. As the authors stated at the outset, "Our hypothesis is that the partisan choice the individual voter makes depends in an immediate sense on the strength and direction of the elements comprising a field of psychological forces, where these elements are interpreted as attitudes toward the perceived objects of national politics."[9]

Although conceding that sociological characteristics are crucial in the development of party identification, the psychological approach argues that partisanship is more than simply a political reflection of a voter's upbringing and current social status. Correlations between demographic factors and the vote provide interesting information, "yet information pitched at a low level of abstraction."[10] The important theoretical addition of the psychological view is its argument that party identification acts to filter individuals' views of the political world, providing them not only with a means for making voting decisions but also with a means for interpreting short-term issues and candidacies. Thus, far more than sociological characteristics, psychological variables bear a direct relationship to the vote, as they are more proximally involved in the decision-making process.

The disciplinary approach that emphasizes the factors most proximal to the vote is economics. Political commentators have long been highly cognizant of the critical role of economic performance in influencing electoral outcomes. In both *Voting* and *The American Voter*, however, such performance assessments were largely ignored, perhaps being too obvious.

Unlike the classic sociological and psychological contributions to the voting behavior literature, the economic perspective was introduced by a theoretical rather than an empirical treatise. This was Anthony Downs's seminal 1957 book entitled *An Economic Theory of Democracy*.[11] Instead of testing classical notions of democratic practice, Downs reformulates them according to modern economic theory's assumptions of rationality. Thus, rather than examining how politically informed the public is, Downs lays out a set of conditions under which it is rational to be informed—devoting an entire chapter to "how rational citizens reduce information costs."[12] Whereas *Voting* and *The American Voter* investigate the social and psychological correlates of nonvoting, *An Economic Theory of Democracy* discusses the causes and effects of rational abstention.

The fundamental axiom of Downs's theory is that citizens act rationally in politics. When it comes to voting, Downs writes, "this axiom implies that each citizen casts his vote for the party he believes will provide him with more benefits than any other."[13] The key to this decision process is the voter's perception of expected utility. "As a result," Downs asserts, "the most important part of a voter's decision is the size of his *current party differential*, i.e., the difference between the utility income he actually received in period t and the one he would have received if the opposition had been in power."[14]

In sum, Downs's theory of voting asserts that citizens make voting decisions in a rational calculating manner, taking into account party promises as well as government performance. The vote is not predetermined by social groupings, nor is political behavior shaped by partisan predispositions. Rather, the voter is seen as an individual actor capable of evaluating every new situation and judging what will be in his or her best interest.

HOW SCHOLARS "VOTE WITH CITATIONS"

It can therefore be said that the six years from 1954 to 1960 was a truly formative period in American voting behavior research. Three seminal works were published, each of which solidly established a unique disciplinary perspective on the subject of voting. In the three decades since their publication, these works—*Voting, The American Voter,* and *An Economic Theory of Democracy*—have set much of the agenda for scholars of voting behavior.

The level of influence of these three books is demonstrated by the frequency with which they have been cited in scholarly articles. It is often said that students vote with their feet, attending classes with the most appealing reputations. As class sizes grow, so does the professor's influence on campus. Scholars, by contrast, communicate with each other primarily through written rather than oral means. Authors thus "vote with their citations," referring in print to works which have influenced their thinking.

Since 1966 the Social Sciences Citation Index (SSCI) has recorded citations in numerous scholarly journals. Taking the period 1966–1987 as a whole, citations to *An Economic Theory of Democracy* have averaged 74 a year, compared to 72 a year for *The American Voter,* and 31 a year for *Voting.* Yet, as can be seen in Figure 1, these overall figures disguise markedly different patterns of citation over time. Both *The American Voter* and *Voting* apparently reached the peak of their influence in the 1970s. By the 1980s the rate of citation for each had fallen approximately 40 percent.

FIGURE 1 *Average number of citations per year to* Voting *(Berelson),* The American Voter *(Campbell), and* An Economic Theory of Democracy *(Downs).*
Source: Social Sciences Citation Index, 1966–1987.

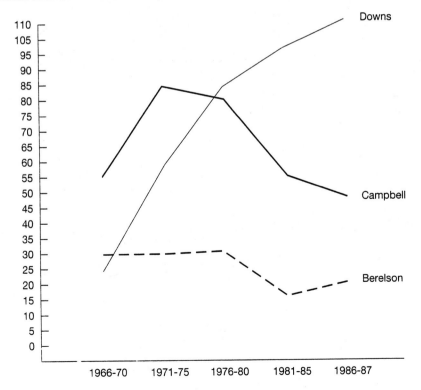

In contrast, citations to Downs's *Economic Theory of Democracy* have risen steadily throughout this whole period. In the late 1960s it was cited slightly less often than *Voting* and half as often as *The American Voter;* now it is cited over four times as often as the former and more than twice as often as the latter.

In his 1965 foreword to the paperback edition of *An Economic Theory of Democracy* Stanley Kelley wrote that years from now he would "be surprised if Downs's work is not recognized as the starting point of a highly important development in the study of politics."[15] The fact that it took eight years for a paperback edition to appear and that Kelley felt compelled to offer such a prediction indicate that the book was slow to catch the attention of scholars. The citation data from 1966 to 1987 not only verify this impression but also make Kelley's statement seem prophetic.

Differences between theoretical and empirical work no doubt account for some of the variation in the citation patterns shown in Figure 1. To begin with, theoretical work is typically far broader in scope. A notable feature of Downs's work, for example, is that it is one of several works that have been instrumental in starting the subdiscipline of public choice. Thus, a possible reason for the increasing number of citations to Downs is that it is now being applied to numerous facets of human behavior in addition to politics.

As a way of checking this hypothesis, the citation data from the last five years were reviewed to determine the number in political science journals.[16] When the scope is narrowed to explicitly political journals, we find that *An Economic Theory of Democracy* has recently averaged 30 citations a year, compared to 22 a year for *The American Voter* and just 6 a year for *Voting*. It is therefore clear that Downs's book has achieved the most prominent place in the political science literature of the three classic works on American voting from the 1950s.

Another key difference between theoretical and empirical presentations is that the latter deal with data from a particular time period. Even if the findings escape the fate of becoming "time-bound," they will eventually be seen as out of date. The result is that over time books such as *The American Voter* and *Voting* will be replaced in citations by more recent demonstrations of similar phenomena. In contrast, theoretical work is not bound to any particular time period. A book such as Downs's can be readily adapted to numerous questions that could never have been imagined at the time of publication. In fact, it is one of the central arguments of this chapter that *An Economic Theory of Democracy* is now much more relevant to the study of American voting behavior than when it was written.

WHY DOWNS IS MORE RELEVANT TO VOTING BEHAVIOR IN THE CANDIDATE-CENTERED AGE

In *The Responsible Electorate* Key outlined a basic model of political behavior known as the "echo chamber" theory. The central idea of this theory was that "the people's verdict can be no more than a selective reflection from among the alternatives and outlooks presented to them."[17] Similarly, scholarly outlooks on voting behavior must reflect how voters present their views during the course of survey interviews. If voters discuss politics in increasingly Downsian terms it should be expected that more analysts will come to rely on Downs's theoretical framework.

As Key argued, the structure of the political debate plays a large role in determining how voters evaluate political issues and make their choices. With the rise of the media and the candidate-centered campaign, much has changed since the 1950s to turn the debate increasingly toward the short-term considerations that Downs focused upon. Whereas candidates were once dependent on the party organizations to get their message out, now they can appeal directly to the electorate via the media. No longer do they have to toe a centrist party line on the issues. They are instead free to craft their own individual appeals tailored specifically to the pressing (as well as the trivial) issues of the day.

Freeing candidates from the parties' control has had the result of turning the focus of the campaign from long-term to short-term issues. Being less tied to the patterns of the past, the American electorate is far more volatile compared to three decades ago, and has grown accustomed to looking directly at the candidates through the mass media. How the candidates have performed in the recent past and what they promise for the not-so-distant future have taken on increased importance. Poll results fluctuate dramatically, as candidates joust with one another over the state of the nation, and the media turn the spotlight from one aspect of the debate to another.

It is probably no accident that as forces which tend to stabilize the vote have declined, academics have come to pay greater attention to economic influences on voting. Downs portrays the average voter as able to assess questions like "What have you done for me lately?" better than the voters portrayed in the Columbia and Michigan studies; and questions of this kind have become increasingly prominent in the last several elections. It is important to note that although *An Economic Theory of Democracy* is framed in terms of the strategies which parties employ during elections, the Downsian model works far better for candidate-centered than for party-centered politics. Parties, as Downs notes, have a rational incentive to converge toward the modal point of opinion when public opinion is distributed in a unimodal fashion—as in the United States. By doing so, however, they make it difficult for voters to apply the decision rules that he focuses upon. As Downs states, "Apparently the more rational political parties are, the less rational voters must be."[18]

A tension thus exists between the rational behavior of parties and voters in the Downsian model. "If either of these is allowed to dominate the other fully, the model may become contradictory; i.e., one of the two sets of agents may cease to behave rationally. Thus if parties succeed in obscuring their policy decisions in a mist of generalities, and voters are unable to discover what their votes really mean, a *rationality crisis* develops."[19] The tension between parties and voters that Downs identified still exists, but the balance has changed dramatically. In particular, the degree to which parties cloud the issues (and thereby impede Downsian type decision making on the part of the voters) has lessened considerably. In several recent elections it has been the parties rather than the voters that have acted contrary to Downs's notions of rationality.

It is important to note, however, that the moribund American party machinery had relatively little to do with the clear-cut choices being offered. Rather the primary and caucus voters have promoted noncentrist candidates to prominence. Numerous studies have found that primary voters are more ideologically inclined than the general electorate.[20] Furthermore, as Byron Shafer remarks, activists in the nomination campaign are especially predisposed to "lean away from the political center due to their lack of concern for a geographically based electorate" and "dedication to a particular group or cause as their principal motive for participation."[21]

Party organizations have not consciously ignored Downs's prescription for electoral success; noncentrist positions have simply been pushed upon them as part of the tension Downs spoke of between voters and parties. Voters want meaningful choices, but parties are naturally wary of giving it to them because of the electoral risk. As control of the nomination process devolved from the party organizations to the primary activists and voters, the pendulum shifted in favor of the alternatives preferred by the latter.

With the institutionalization of the new U.S. nominating process, it is unlikely that the pendulum will shift back in the foreseeable future. Although the congressional party delegations still contain a fair degree of diversity, in 1988 there was little divergence of views among each party's presidential candidates. Howard Baker was the only Republican not firmly associated with conservative causes who even considered running, and he gave up his remote chance at the presidency to accept the position of White House chief of staff. On the Democratic side, the creation of a southern regional primary date provided additional incentive for a conservative to enter the presidential sweepstakes. Nevertheless, such notable conservatives as Senator Sam Nunn stayed on the sidelines, leaving only the moderate Albert Gore to represent the Democratic Party's nonliberal faction. The result was that for the second election in a row the electorate was given a choice between a clear conservative and a clear liberal—something that would have seemed inconceivable three decades ago.

In the 1950s Downs's focus on ideology seemed misplaced to those who studied the average voter, and it quickly became the most criticized aspect of his work. Most notably, Campbell and his coauthors made the case that survey data from the Eisenhower–Stevenson contests showed that few American voters actually employed ideological criteria. First, they noted, the stable aspects of voting behavior emanate from "long-term loyalties to the parties rather than ideological commitments." Second, they argued, forces other than party loyalty "appear almost wholly free of ideological coloration." They concluded that there existed an "absence of overriding public concern to judge the policies of the candidates and their parties against the standards received from well-elaborated political ideologies."[22]

Yet we must realize that *An Economic Theory* and *The American Voter* approached ideology from rather different functional perspectives. The latter conceived of ideology as the most sophisticated method of decision making, involving the collection of much ancillary knowledge. In contrast, the former viewed ideology more as a rational way to reduce information costs. As Downs explains, "With this short cut a voter can save himself the cost of being informed upon a wide range of issues."[23]

Downs's emphasis on voting shortcuts fits well with survey results regarding how little attention most people pay to politics. But his choice of ideology was somewhat questionable given the existence of far easier criteria. As Donald Stokes noted in one of the first critiques of Downs's book, many crucial issues do not involve alternative courses of action. Performance issues, for example, deal merely with questions of who will do best in reaching universally desired goals. Stokes writes, "The machinery of the spatial model will not work if the voters are simply reacting to the association of the parties with some goal or state or symbol that is positively or negatively valued."[24]

Downs does mention performance considerations, but only as secondary considerations in assessing utility income. In his model, "performance ratings enter a voter's decision-making whenever he thinks both parties have the same platforms and current policies."[25] Rational choice theorists who followed Downs have often reversed priorities, concentrating on the lowered information costs associated with performance as opposed to ideological factors. In short, performance-based voting offers people a rational cognitive shortcut for ensuring that unsuccessful policies are dropped and successful policies continued. Through its analysis, scholars have been able to establish how cycles in the economy affect electoral outcomes, and thereby have extended Downs's increasingly relevant theories.

CHANGES IN CANDIDATE EVALUATIONS SINCE DOWNS

One indirect method by which the role of the economy in presidential elections can be traced from the 1950s to the 1980s is through voters' responses to open-ended questions about the candidates. Since the National Election Studies began in 1952 each presidential study has asked a representative cross section of the electorate the following set of questions with regard to each of the major candidates:

> Is there anything in particular about _____ that might make you want to vote *for* him? (If so) What is that? Anything else?

> Is there anything in particular about _____ that might make you want to vote *against* him? (If so) What is that? Anything else?

The responses over the ten presidential elections studied to date provide one of the richest data sources available on the factors determining voting decisions. Such questions allow voters to identify what is most important to them about the candidates, regardless of whether such considerations might occur to the designers of the survey. Thus, the data are uniquely suited for comparing economic, sociological, and psychological factors on the vote over time.

Of course, no technique in survey research is without its drawbacks. Some respondents say little or nothing to the open-ended questions—because they are either reluctant to talk openly or unable to express themselves. Others simply repeat what they have heard recently from friends or observed that day on television. And for those who express a number of comments, each one is necessarily treated equally even though some are in fact more important to the individual than others.[26] Nevertheless, there is little reason to suspect that these problems are any different from one survey to another, and hence for time series purposes they remain virtually ideal. It is almost impossible to write closed-ended questions that will be relevant across many campaigns, but with open-ended questions it is up to the respondents themselves to define what is most relevant.

Figure 2 shows the trends in the percentage of respondents mentioning economic, partisan, and sociological factors as reasons for voting either for or against a presidential candidate. Economic criteria include comments about government intervention in the economy, which were particularly emphasized by Downs,[27] as well as comments about the economy's health (inflation, unemployment, interest rates, and so on).[28] Partisan comments, which were emphasized by the Michigan center's social psychological approach, consist mostly of remarks indicating that the person likes or dislikes the candidate because of his party affiliation or the general party image.[29]

FIGURE 2 *Percentage mentioning economic, partisan, and sociological factors in open-ended candidate evaluations.*
Source: SRC/CPS National Election Studies.

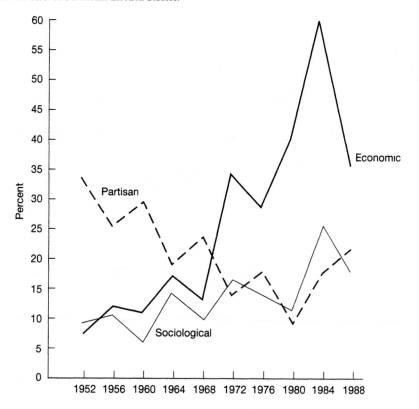

And sociological comments concern which candidate would do best for particular demographic groups, as well as the demographic characteristics of the candidates themselves.[30]

As hypothesized, the open-ended data show a clear increase in the salience of economic evaluations since 1960. In the elections from 1952 to 1960 only about 10 percent of the electorate mentioned an economic factor, compared to an average of 32 percent since 1964, when voters were first faced with a choice between distinct candidates. Most notably, in 1984 this figure reached an all-time high, with nearly 60 percent mentioning an economic issue. The 1984 record can be traced to two major factors: the clearest choice in half a century between a staunch liberal and a staunch conservative; and the frequent comparisons drawn between the results of the Carter-Mondale administration and those of Reagan's first four years in office.

It is probably no coincidence that economic criteria have become more prevalent at the same time that partisan comments have declined. As can also be seen in Figure 2, the percentage of the electorate spontaneously evaluating the candidates along partisan lines has dropped from 30 percent in the period up to 1960 to an average of 17 percent in the period since 1964. This pattern fits nicely with the evidence for dealignment that is presented elsewhere. In the Eisenhower elections, voters typically conceptualized economic issues in terms of which *party* had done the best job in the past.[31] Aside from exceptional times, such as those of 1932, these images remained firm because voters tended to view economic issues through the perceptual screen of partisanship. As short-term economic factors have become less mediated, they have taken on greater significance.

With the decline in the salience of American political parties, one would also expect sociological factors to take on greater importance as alternative political reference points. In 1960 Campbell and his colleagues wrote, "The psychological economy of the individual demands parties as an organizing principle, and if bereft of this, there might be much more straightforward dependence on other groups for guidance."[32] As political parties have lost their relevance over the last several decades, and hence their ability to mobilize the public, interest groups have acquired key resources that have made them more powerful than ever before. For example, direct mail strategies made possible by recent technological advances have enabled groups to better organize potential members, communicate with them about key issues, and raise money for campaigns.

The result has been that presidential candidates have come to rely more on group-based appeals and that voters have reacted accordingly. During the period 1952–1960 an average of just 8.5 percent of those interviewed said they liked or disliked a candidate because of the demographic groups he was for or against. Since 1964 the average has risen to 15.1 percent, with the all-time high of 25.3 percent occurring in 1984, owing to the focus on Mondale's interest group links and concerns about Reagan's ties to the wealthy.

In sum, the decline of long-term party affiliations has opened up possibilities for both short-term economic factors as well as enduring social group attachments to play a far greater part in shaping electoral politics. It should be no surprise, therefore, that Downs's economic model is now being cited more often or that a renaissance of the sociological school is beginning to take place, as witnessed by the recent interest in contextual effects.[33]

The patterns of American voting behavior over the last three decades have, if nothing else, shown that no single theory of voting is best for all time. Rather, each theory is particularly appropriate for a given pattern of behavior. The sociological model fit well when election results showed stability and channels of communication were relatively insular. As the vote started to fluctuate more from year to year, a social psychological theory proved especially useful for separating out sources of stability (partisanship) from those of change (candidates and issues). And as deviations from the "normal vote" became the rule rather than exception, an economic theory emphasizing short-term costs and benefits proved increasingly relevant.

Each of the three major social science approaches thus focuses on different slices of time in the voting decision—from the distant sociological variables, to the mediating psychological ones, to the immediate economic performance factors. Together, a unified theory of voting behavior incorporating all three approaches would look schematically as follows:

**Demographic
Characteristics**

lead to →

**Psychological
Affiliations
and Biases**

which modify/screen →

**Candidate
Performance
Evaluations
and Issues**

which determine →

Voting

As can be seen, psychological variables such as partisanship are at the center of the whole voting process. In an era of declining partisanship, therefore, it is to be expected that short-term economic variables will become more important in guiding political behavior. Without the mediating function of partisanship, voters are more likely to look directly at the candidates, assessing their pluses and minuses.

NOTES

1. Jean M. Converse, *Survey Research in the United States: Roots and Emergence, 1890–1960* (Berkeley: University of California Press, 1987), pp. 402–403.

2. Paul F. Lazarsfeld, Bernard R Berelson, and Hazel Gaudet, *The People's Choice* (New York: Columbia University Press, 1944).

3. Bernard R. Berelson, Paul F. Lazarsfeld, and William N. McPhee. *Voting: A Study of Opinion Formation in a Presidential Campaign* (Chicago: University of Chicago Press, 1954).

4. Ibid., p. 301.

5. Ibid.. p. 316.

6. Angus Campbell, Gerald Gurin, and Warren E. Miller, *The Voter Decides* (Evanston, Ill.: Row, Peterson, and Co., 1954).

7. Ibid., p. 85.

8. Angus Campbell, Philip E. Converse, Warren E. Miller, and Donald E. Stokes, *The American Voter* (New York. Wiley, 1960).

9. Ibid., p. 9.

10. Ibid., p. 36.

11. Anthony Downs, *An Economic Theory of Democracy* (New York: Harper and Row, 1957).

12. Ibid., chap. 12.

13. Ibid., p. 36.

14. Ibid., p. 40.

15. Ibid., p. x.

16. The journals considered as political science are: *American Political Science Review, American Journal of Political Science. Journal of Politics, Western Political Quarterly, European Journal of Political Research, Canadian Journal of Political Science, British Journal of Political Science, Polity, PS. Political Science and Politics, Legislative Studies Quarterly, Comparative Political Studies. Comparative Politics, Political Studies*, and *Political Science Quarterly*.

17 Key, *The Responsible Electorate*, p. 2.

18. Downs, *An Economic Theory*, p. 137.

19. Ibid., p. 139.

20. See James I. Lengle, *Representation and Presidential Primaries: The Democracy Party in the Post-Reform Era* (Westport, Conn.: Greenwood Press, 1981).

21. Byron E. Shafer, *Bifurcated Politics: Evolution and Reform in the National Party Convention* (Cambridge, Mass.: Harvard University Press, 1988).

22. Campbell et al., *The American Voter*, pp. 549–550.

23. Downs, *An Economic Theory*, p. 98.

24. Donald E. Stokes, "Spatial Models of Party Competition," in Angus Campbell et al., *Elections and the Political Order* (New York: Wiley, 1966), p. 170.

25. Downs, *An Economic Theory*, p. 44.

26. The problem of equal weighting of responses is addressed at length in Kelley, *Interpreting Elections*, Appendix 1. Although Kelley finds statistical evidence for the application of differential weights, his conclusion is that "the constraining assumption of the equal weighting of issues makes no difference in one's ability to account for votes."

27. Downs, *An Economic Theory*, p. 116.

28. The economic codes for 1952 to 1968 are as follows: 80–81, 420–460, 490–493, 541–560. For 1972 to 1984 on comparable codes are: 605–606, 805–808, 811–812. 829–831, 837–838, 901–945, 952–961, 965–967, 1001–1003, 1007–1009, 1025–1027.

29. The partisan codes from 1952 to 1968 are 800–820 and 700–711. For 1972 to 1984 the comparable codes are as follows: 53–54, 101–122, 133–134, 500–503. 1202–1206.

30. From 1952 to 1968 the sociological codes are as follows: 251–253, 260–263, 391, 712–790. After 1968 the comparable codes are: 425–426, 455–456, 1207–1297.

31 See Campbell et al., *The American Voter*, pp. 45–48.

32. Ibid., p. 139.

33. See Robert Huckfeldt and John Sprague, "Networks in Context: The Social Flow of Political Information," *American Political Science Review* 81 (1987): 1197–1216; and John Books and Charles Prysby, "Studying Contextual Effects on Political Behavior: A Research Inventory and Agenda," *American Politics Quarterly* 16 (1988): 211–238.

Scholars Misinterpret the Data About Independent Voters

Raymond E. Wolfinger

For more than two decades, political commentators have called attention to a growing decline in voters' identification with our political parties. Scholars and journalists, both liberal and conservative, have argued that the Republican and Democratic Parties are losing their hold on the American electorate. The much-publicized rise of the independent voter has led to predictions of wide swings from election to election among voters' preferences, of growing ineffectiveness of the established parties, and of the increased likelihood of third parties and independent candidacies.

This view may have helped persuade Ross Perot to launch his independent bid for the presidency. But independent or third-party candidates would do well to consider recent research that challenges the conventional wisdom. This research shows that the number of truly uncommitted voters is far lower than commonly thought. The misconception stems from scholars ignoring and misinterpreting available data on citizens' expressed party preferences and voting behavior.

Until the middle of this century, political analysts primarily assessed voters' party commitments by tracing historical voting patterns. Then in 1952, more precise measurement became possible with the advent of academic surveys based on nationwide samples of voting-age citizens: Social scientists began to gauge the party allegiance of individual Americans in the most direct way—by asking.

For a dozen years thereafter, about three-fourths of all respondents called themselves Democrats or Republicans: most of the rest listed themselves as independents, and an infinitesimal number of respondents claimed affiliation with some other party.

Social scientists used these measures of party identification to interpret voter behavior and electoral politics. They explained voting decisions as the interaction of a long-term predisposition—party identification—and short-term forces. Scholars used party identification as a benchmark for ascertaining the effect of transitory issues and particular candidates on voters. They argued that the overwhelming percentage of voters committed to either the Republicans or the Democrats helped explain why third parties found such an inhospitable environment.

The 1960s profoundly disturbed this portrayal of the American voter. Interviewers reported that more and more people claimed to be independents. As early as 1966, survey research showed that independents outnumbered Republicans. By 1974, independents accounted for 37 percent of all the potential voters sampled, only slightly less

Source: Raymond E. Wolfinger, "Scholars Misinterpret the Data About Independent Voters," *Chronicle of Higher Education* (October 14, 1992), p. A44.

Raymond E. Wolfinger is the Heller professor of political science at the University of California, Berkeley, and coauthor of *The Myth of the Independent Voter.*

•

than the 39 percent of respondents who called themselves Democrats. In 1990, Democrats and independents each accounted for 36 percent of the University of Michigan's national sample, and Republicans for 28 percent. There is endless speculation about why more people began calling themselves independents but little evidence.

Scholars and political commentators were not slow to notice this trend, arguing that the Democratic and Republican Parties were becoming irrelevant to large numbers of voters. Political scientist Walter Dean Burnham, in his 1982 book *The Current Crisis in American Politics*, predicted that the apparent decline of parties would cause "political instability and ineffective performance on a scale without recent precedent." The journalist Hedrick Smith, in his 1988 book *The Power Game*, echoed the consensus of the past dozen years when he called the rise of independent voters "the most important phenomenon of American politics in the past quarter century."

Certainly, the many Americans who joined the drive to place Mr. Perot's name on the ballot in 50 states were willing to support an independent candidate. But what are potential voters actually saying when they call themselves independents?

Research that I have conducted with five former graduate students published as *The Myth of the Independent Voter,* shows that the number of genuinely neutral voters is no greater a proportion of voters in presidential elections now than in the 1950s.

Since 1952, data from the University of Michigan's *National Election Studies,* distributed to hundreds of campuses around the country, have been the principal source of most research on party identification and voter choice. Since their inception, the Michigan surveys have set the standard wording used by most polling organizations: "Generally speaking, do you usually think of yourself as a Republican, a Democrat, an independent, or what?" The Michigan surveys have followed up this question with one of two further queries. Respondents who call themselves Republicans or Democrats are asked, "Would you call yourself a strong Republican [Democrat] or a not very strong Republican [Democrat]?" Analysts have used their responses to classify these partisans as "strong" or "weak" Democrats and Republicans.

Respondents who call themselves independents have always been asked, "Do you think of yourself closer to the Republican Party or to the Democratic Party?" Over the years, nearly two-thirds of the people who have initially called themselves independents have conceded that they are closer to one or the other party. But the scholarly literature shows little attention to the responses to this question. The oversight may reflect the precedent set by the published reports of the first Michigan surveys, which treated all self-described independents alike.

That decision may not have seemed important when all three varieties of independents—those who conceded leaning toward the Democrats, toward the Republicans, or who persisted in professing neutrality—amounted to scarcely more than a fifth of any sample. It has become a different story, however, with the increasing proportion of respondents who report themselves to be independents.

Our contribution is simply told. When independents are subdivided into categories, it becomes clear that those who admit being closer to the Democrats or to the Republicans exhibit similar voting behavior to those who identify outright with the parties. In the past ten presidential elections, independents leaning toward the Democratic

Party have voted for the Democratic candidate *slightly more often* than those who call themselves weak Democrats. The same is true on the Republican side. In 1988, Michael Dukakis did better with independents who leaned toward the Democrats than with strong and weak Democrats together.

The similarities are not limited to the way voters choose among presidential candidates. Independents who lean toward the Democrats or the Republicans resemble those voters who identify outright with their party in every measure of partisan feeling we could find in the data—including their votes in presidential primaries and congressional elections, their attitudes toward the two parties, and their positions on a variety of issues.

In short, the number of truly uncommitted citizens has always been wildly exaggerated. In 1988, the people who were truly neutral—not leaning more toward one party or the other—accounted for just 11 percent of the electorate, not the 36 percent that is usually reported when all independents are cited. Even this number overestimates the potential of these "pure independents," because as a group they are much less informed, interested, and active in politics than those who identify with particular parties. Their turnout is so low that, while they constituted 11 percent of the survey sample in 1988, they accounted for just 7 percent of people who actually voted. That behavior was also true in earlier years. From 1952 on, pure independents have never been more than 15 percent of any Michigan sample, nor more than 10 percent of the people who voted.

Moreover, since so-called independents are as ideologically diverse as the entire electorate, there is little reason to assume that they will come together to form a third party or to support a particular independent candidate. This is especially true since those who report leaning toward one party or another are only slightly more likely than outright partisans to switch parties.

We have concluded that all the portentous worry about the declining relevance of parties and the warnings about the growing threat of electoral instability are overblown. They were based on a mistake in the data analysis that began with the first analysts of the Michigan survey data and have been perpetuated by a new generation of scholarly revisionists who held that far fewer voters have been identifying with political parties than in the past. . . . Just as they did 30 and more years ago, parties shape not only most Americans' views of the political scene, but the choices they make on election day.

Discourse and Decision

Marion R. Just, Ann N. Crigler, Dean E. Alger,
Timothy E. Cook, Montague Kern, and Darrell West

Election research has seen cycles of optimism and pessimism, although the particular concerns have varied. Scholars have worried that election campaigns do not produce satisfying discourse because the people do not work hard enough at politics, the candidates mislead them, and the news media fail them. While this study does not contradict the weight of research about inattentive voters, strategizing politicians, or commercial media, by looking at all of the actors simultaneously it presents a different picture. We see the presidential campaign as a dynamic interaction in which each of the participants constrains and influences the others, leading to the election outcome. The interactions of the campaign, as well as who wins or loses, have important consequences for governance and for the robustness of the democratic process.

By examining the crosstalk of the campaign, this study has shown how powerfully the citizens' agenda can constrain candidate discourse, how news values constrain candidate coverage, and how candidates broke through the constraints of news to engage the citizens in new media formats. We have shown that for all of the participants in campaign discourse, the personal is political. And perhaps that is as it should be in a presidential campaign. Our study does not find the citizens to be captives of either the candidates or the journalists, nor even of their own political predispositions. They can reject or reinterpret media messages and consider alternative and even conflicting information. We found, of course, not only constraints but dependency. As citizens build constructs of the candidates, their information environment makes a difference in the range of considerations they bring to bear. The candidate attention to the locale, the resources and editorial choices of the local media outlets, the candidates' ad buys, and the citizens' news habits influence the richness of the process for better or worse. Below we detail our findings and discuss the implications for citizens, candidates, journalists, and democratic governance.

Source: Marion R. Just, Ann N. Crigler, Dean E. Alger, Timothy E. Cook, Montague Kern, and Darrell West, *Crosstalk: Citizens, Candidates and the Media in a Presidential Campaign* (Chicago: University of Chicago Press, 1996), pp. 233–243.

Marion R. Just is professor of political science, Wellesley College; Ann N. Crigler is associate professor of political science, University of Southern California; Dean E. Alger is an independent scholar and political analyst; Timothy E. Cook is professor of political science, Williams College; Montague Kern is assistant professor of journalism, Rutgers University; Darrell M. West is professor of political science, Brown University.

CAMPAIGNS AND CITIZENS

Throughout this book we have seen how campaigns can provide people with an opportunity to see their own personal concerns in the context of the nation's problems. There is ample evidence that the presidential campaign informs people's vote choices and also provides occasions for participation beyond the simple act of voting. Citizens actively interpret communications, engage the attention of candidates and the media, and have opportunities to express their views in surveys, focus groups, town meetings, call-in talk shows, and even in candidate debates. To the extent that citizens believe that they can enter into the campaign discourse and that their concerns are being heard, the presidential election can be an empowering and democratic experience. But even if particular campaigns do not achieve that empowering and legitimizing effect, the campaign discourse sets priorities and expectations that have important consequences for governance.

CONSTRUCTING THE CANDIDATES AS PERSONS

Our findings triangulate evidence from surveys, focus groups, and in-depth interviews to show that voters select candidates as persons. The way voters decide substantially reflects the tendencies of all campaign communications—both news and ads—to focus attention on the personal qualities of the candidates. Our in-depth interviews and focus groups demonstrate, however, that citizens believe assessments of candidates as persons, especially their qualities of character, offer the most reliable indicators of how candidates will perform in office.

Our study of the 1992 presidential election provides persuasive evidence that assessments of candidate character were essentially political. In 1992, George Bush was deemed "out of touch," not merely because he had never seen a supermarket scanner, nor because he blithely boated off the shore at Kennebunkport, nor because he kept looking at his watch during the second debate, but because he would not admit the gravity of the recession and kept trying to steer the debate away from it. Bill Clinton, in turn, was judged caring and empathetic, not merely because he took a bus trip, nor because he hailed from "a place called Hope," but because he kept on addressing the problems that faced Americans in their everyday lives. And Ross Perot was deemed the most honest of the three, not because of his haircut, nor because he appeared on "Larry King Live," but because he talked directly to the public about a serious issue—the deficit—that the other candidates were perceived to be avoiding.

INTERACTIONS WITH THE POLITICAL INFORMATION ENVIRONMENT

In our study we have been impressed by citizens' abilities to make the most of the information available to understand the political world. Our surveys, focus groups, and in-depth interviews all show that people gain information over the course of the campaign.

Surveys showed that respondents were better able to identify the candidates' positions on the issues in the fall than in the spring. Focus group participants and in-depth interviewees increasingly used their own experiences and previous understandings to make sense of new information. And our interviewees in all four communities expressed more considerations about the candidates as the campaign went on.

Our evidence suggests that, at least in a presidential campaign, information is nearly omnipresent, so that people do not need to take information shortcuts. Instead, they can think about and extrapolate the implications of information readily available. As the campaign proceeds, people find new information all around them. Sometimes when they encounter new information, they note it and shrug it off. At other times, they may rebut it by referring to prior knowledge about politics or experiences from their everyday worlds. In dramatic instances, new information may require them to completely rethink the candidates and even to undertake new information searches. We saw this kind of reevaluation in the case of John, an unemployed Vietnam veteran, when he found out that his preferred candidate, Bill Clinton, had resisted the draft. Given the media environment, John did not have to look very far to find out more about Clinton and the draft.

Our examination of four very different information environments shows, however, that relative access to information is an important factor in candidate assessment. At every stage in the campaign, the interviewees with the widest range of considerations about the candidates tended to live in the area with the richest information (Boston), while interviewees who expressed fewer considerations tended to come from information-poor environments such as Winston-Salem. In a fascinating naturally occurring experiment, when Winston-Salem became a richer political information environment as a result of candidate ads and visits to North Carolina in the late fall, there was a corresponding increase in the number of considerations our interviewees brought to bear. As Huckfeldt and Sprague (1988) would have predicted, political discussion is influenced not only by individuals' habits and preferences but also by the supply of political information. Our findings show that the ability and willingness of people to talk about the campaign and the candidates is closely linked to the richness of the political information environment, as measured simply by the amount of news and ads in the locale. Given citizens' haphazard and often inadvertent ways of encountering information, the more information available, the greater the chance it will get through.

Our investigation points out how valuable different kinds of information are to citizens. In focus groups, we compared the discussion that followed exposure to different "forms" of campaign communication. Notably, the standard format of horserace coverage occasioned relatively lackluster discussion in our spring focus groups. By contrast, the discussion that followed a news analysis in the fall not only was more lively, but also allowed the participants to connect the larger political debate with their personal experiences. As far as ad watches were concerned, our focus group discussions made clear that people were suspicious of critiques that emphasized the candidate's strategy or the expected audience impact. But ad watches that focused on the verification of candidates' claims aroused attention and stimulated discussion of the issues. The ad watch format, however, did not completely deflect candidate messages. If the ad being critiqued contained information that resonated with their concerns, people talked about the candidates' messages just as they did after seeing an ad.

The focus group discussions also emphasize the power of the citizens' role in the interpretation of media messages. Focus groups commonly ignored or transformed rather than followed the meaning of messages to which they were exposed. By analyzing the groups' conversational exchanges, we found that discussion often moved away from the point of view of the message or moved on to other subjects. Interestingly, only the candidate interview programs (which, in reality and in our stimuli, tended to feature the challengers) generated discussion on the topic and echoed the point of view of the candidates being interviewed. Candidate interviews were also more effective in getting people to concentrate on actual words and ideas presented than either ads or news. Evidence from our in-depth interviews and surveys suggests that the Perot infomercials had a similar effect. In both cases the format's credibility seemed enhanced by an emphasis on issues that resonated with public concerns, presented with the fewest frills and least packaging.

While individuals in our focus groups and in-depth interviews actively and variously interpreted campaign messages, the polysemy of the interpretation did not mean that there were no patterns of meaning. In fact, our data show that the discourse of the election on the whole reflected the relative frequency with which certain kinds of messages were accepted or rejected. While individuals might have had idiosyncratic interpretations, people generally found some formats more credible than others (interviews, debates), some issues more resonant than others (the economy, rather than peacetime foreign policy), and some candidates more credible than others on certain issues (challengers can call for change more effectively than the incumbent). These overall patterns of interpretation and dynamic interaction shaped the discourse and, ultimately, the outcome of the election.

LESSONS AND PROSPECTS

Anyone who expects performance to the standards of the *Federalist Papers* or the Lincoln–Douglas debates could not fail to be disappointed with the discourse of recent presidential elections. The 1992 presidential campaign was no exception. Key moments in the campaign included a curious assortment—Clinton explaining that he did not inhale; a citizen asking the president what the national debt meant to him personally; Perot claiming Republican dirty tricksters were planning to sabotage his daughter's wedding; Quayle misspelling "potato"; Stockdale wondering in the middle of a nationally televised debate, "Who am I? What am I doing here?"

What made the campaign discourse more salutary than its recent predecessors was *not* that it was somehow more edifying or well mannered, but that this spectacle explicitly involved the American people as key participants. During this campaign, the citizens received ample confirmation of their potential importance and power, not only through the election returns and the polls but also through their vividly displayed interactions with candidates in interview programs and debates. Not surprisingly, public opinion surveys showed that people felt themselves to be more politically effective than in previous elections—a rise that one team of scholars has suggested led directly to the increased turnout in 1992 (Rosenstone et al. 1993). What enabled 1992 to be different from its lamented predecessor, the 1988 presidential election? We set forth our explanations along with lessons that candidates, journalists, and the people might take away from this campaign and this study.

Candidates

Candidates, of course, are preoccupied with one thing above all—winning the election. For them, the function of the campaign is to gain votes. Ads play an important role in getting the candidate's message across. The more resources a candidate can devote to ads, the more likely the message will be heard. Witness the surprisingly successful campaign by the wealthy independent candidate Ross Perot. Evidence in our interviews shows that the sheer repetition of ads can defeat a viewer's defenses and seep into his or her consciousness. For instance, Selma from Boston was a strong Democrat who claimed never to have listened to any Republican ads in the fall, but she was able to describe in detail three Bush ads; Sara from Winston-Salem noted that Bush's "Arkansas Record" ad had been run so many times that she was sick of it, but she also wanted to know whether it was "true."

Our findings suggest, however, that candidates do not have to be altruistic to want to mount substantive and responsive campaigns. Attention to the issues pays off. Evidence from our surveys, focus groups, and in-depth interviews confirms that successful ad campaigns integrate issue information. By "dovetailing" (Kern 1989) visual and verbal cues and integrated issue appeals with references to character, ads provoked focus group discussion that stayed on message. Less well-crafted ads produced confusion and even derision. Bob Kerrey's "hockey rink" ad is a good example of a signal failure. The visuals of the candidate standing on an ice rink in front of a hockey net simply did not match his words about the balance of trade with Japan. Focus group participants and interviewees who remembered seeing the ad were generally puzzled by it. By comparison, it is surely no coincidence that the most successful ad campaigns during the primaries—Buchanan's and Clinton's, whether judged by our survey results, focus groups, or the recollections of interviewees—most effectively integrated sight and sound, issue and character. In fact, most general election ads referred to both issues and character. But ads that referred first and foremost to character were less effective simply because they seemed like mudslinging and politics-as-usual. Bush's attempts to push the message of "trust" in the fall may have increased Clinton's negatives; but the ads did not gain an advantage for Bush because they raised questions about his own integrity.

Our conclusion that effective candidate communications integrate issue and character reminds us of Richard Fenno's (1978) classic insights about how members of Congress communicate with their constituents. Fenno followed a number of legislators around their districts and concluded that their main goal was to establish and reinforce trust. But Fenno noted that in their interactions with constituents, members must talk about *something,* and they generally talk about the issues. Similarly, in an election campaign, even if candidates are fundamentally concerned with presenting themselves as persons, and even if citizens are most interested in making a personal assessment of them, candidates need to talk about the issues. Citizens then use what candidates say to infer not only what they stand for but who they are as persons.

Of course, when candidates talk about issues they need not be specific. It is rational for politicians to be ambiguous, especially with heterogeneous electorates. Page's (1978) exhaustive examination of candidate communications notes how presidential candidates avoid detailed policy proposals and turn instead to broad policy areas, basic values, and consensual appeals. Although such communications may not allow anyone to predict just what a candidate will do if elected, they give people as good a sense as any of the *priorities* that a candidate may bring to the presidency.

Journalists

Journalists are in the information business. But given that the news is a business, journalists are under increasing pressure to make the product salable. In order to gain a large audience, journalists try to produce an impartial, if not objective, product. If they want audiences to watch the news every day, reporters must also find ways of presenting something timely, entertaining, or new. But the sheer necessity of cranking out a news product day in, day out leads journalists to "routinize the unexpected" (Tuchman 1973).

In the case of presidential elections, these news routines focus on the election as a game. By paying attention to who is ahead and who is behind, and what strategies each side is using to stay ahead or to catch up, journalists are assured new developments every day, something that might elude them if they reported for the umpteenth time that a candidate gave the same speech. This "game" mentality has been deplored in virtually every study of election coverage. Not surprisingly, we also find that the "horse race" is a key aspect of media coverage. In fact, the less news outlets cover the campaign, the more they emphasize the horse race; so we might even say that horse-race coverage is the sine qua non of election news. But our content analysis (which coded stories not by particular kind, but by whether they included particular content) shows that horse-race coverage does not push out issue coverage altogether. Just as candidates must talk about the issues in order to present themselves, so journalists must refer to issues when presenting news about candidates' strategies. Even when races are most seriously contested and horse-race news is at its height, there is plenty of information in the news about where the candidates stand.

But journalists might want to rethink the horse-race and strategy emphasis, not because of the scolding of some political scientists, or even because of public criticism of the media's preoccupation with scandal and trivia. Our focus groups reveal that horse-race news is neither useful nor interesting to the public. Judging from the results of our spring focus groups, horse-race news provoked little discussion, did not permit individuals to bring personal experience into their conversation, was difficult to build on as a topic for discussion, and was often perceived as biased. While horse-race news may well be helpful to citizens trying to identify the viable candidates, it is not good for much else. Our focus group participants responded quite differently to another form of news coverage: news analysis, a form represented in our study by the "American Agenda" segment on ABC News. Discussions of "American Agenda" were not only animated, but also enabled voters to bring their personal experiences into the political discussion. It is worth noting that producing such analytic stories may be cheaper for news organizations than sending reporters out on the campaign trail. By keeping reporters at home the news media could perform their tasks in ways that would save them money and produce the kind of journalism that is most desired and best used by the public.

We are somewhat cautious, however, in recommending more news analysis because our results show a significant and consistent tendency in all media for analytic, journalist-initiated stories to have a distinctly negative tone toward the candidates. It seems that journalists equate "enterprise" with "negativity." While we could easily imagine stories instigated by journalists that were positive toward candidates, this rarely occurs. We would argue that being "soft" on candidates across the board is not acceptable; neither is being invariably harsh. Evidence from our in-depth interviews and focus groups suggest that journalists' unrelieved "tough" posture diminishes their credibility and turns people off.

The negative tilt of journalist-initiated stories was one of many commonalities across the news. Our analysis amply confirmed that the coverage in 1992 was as homogeneous as Patterson's description from 1976. Candidates were covered the same way across media and modalities, although the tone across outlets in the same community often varied significantly. In particular, there was clear consensus during the primaries about who was worth covering and who was not, thereby winnowing the field. All news organizations also converged on similar narratives about the three major competitors in the fall. In the process, by sheer repetition for months at a time, the initial hunches people had about the candidates became indisputable facts. Notably, that the economy was in terrible shape and that George Bush was responsible for it might have been open to discussion, but by the end of the campaign in the face of the continuing barrage of news and candidate messages with that storyline, almost none of our interviewees, even those favorable to Bush, disputed it.

Our analysis of news indicates why candidates were stimulated to seek other venues in which to present themselves to the public. The success of the "talk show campaign" illustrates that journalists no longer have a monopoly on providing information to the American public. Some journalists quite reasonably felt threatened when politicians found a way to get around them—for example, shortly after Clinton's inauguration, UPI's Helen Thomas fumed on National Public Radio, "They feel we are expendable, and if they make an end run, they will get a better press, if you will, with the people. Eventually, they should realize the president has to be interrogated, and has to be accountable, and we're the ones to do it" ("Weekend Edition," NPR, January 24, 1993, as quoted in Cook and Ragsdale 1995).

But journalists do not have to be the *only* "ones to do it." While deceptive, ambiguous, or lightweight ads may require journalists to press candidates for more details and substance, interview programs were not deficient in that way. In fact, interviews focused on more substantive matters when ordinary people rather than journalists posed the questions, and provided longer opportunities for the candidates to explain their positions than the news. Our focus groups demonstrated that candidate interviews provoked citizens to grapple with ideas, rather than images, strategies, or personality.

As a result, the candidates' appearances on interview programs is perhaps the most salutary development of the 1992 campaign. By using an entertainment format, candidates found a way to communicate effectively to audiences they might otherwise miss and to present their views on the topics they wanted to emphasize.

Voters

The path-breaking campaign studies conducted at the University of Michigan and reported in *The American Voter* (Campbell et al. 1960) painted a bleak picture of elections as collective events, during which citizens discuss, debate, and deliberate about issues. Many scholars concluded that citizens were simply too inattentive to politics to participate much and could only make sense of the campaign through personal connection to candidates or party identification. Beyond partisanship, the possibility that people could project constrained or even consistent belief systems into the process seemed remote (Converse 1964, 1970).

There have been various attempts to revise *The American Voter*'s conclusions about citizens' capacities to participate in democratic politics. Some scholars have raised serious questions about whether a person who has an ideologically constrained belief system is best equipped for democratic citizenship. Marcus for one, says no (1988; see also Krouse and Marcus 1984). Ideologues may not be able to enter into dialogue with anyone who does not agree with them; it is better, Marcus argues, to have a large stock of open-minded observers who will listen to debates among partisans, note the evidence, and make considered judgments. What might then strike Converse as an example of incoherence and inconsistency is instead an ability to consider more than one possibility and a willingness to listen and be persuaded. Others have found similar evidence of positive ambivalence among the American electorate. Hochschild puts it this way:

> A democracy composed of consistent, tranquil, attitudinally constrained citizens is a democracy full of smug people with no incentive and perhaps no ability to think about their own circumstances. They know who they are, how things fit together—and woe betide anyone who questions or violates the standard pattern. Conversely, a democracy composed of citizens coping with disjunction and ambivalence is full of people who question their own rightness, who may entertain alternative viewpoints, and who, given the right questions, are more driven to resolve problems than ignore them. (1993, 206)

We are impressed with the range of considerations people bring to bear about candidates. People seem to feel no discomfort about wandering and wondering. They wander through the information they run across, sometimes far from where they usually look, including the allegations and charges of opposing camps. And they wonder what its implications might be for their assessments of the candidates and the campaign. Only toward the end of the campaign do people use their initial predispositions—notably, partisanship—to help them craft their considerations into overall assessments of the candidates. The process of consideration that we observed speaks to the capacity of citizens to deliberate at least individually, if not collectively.

Governance

There are several indicators that tell us how well a campaign has succeeded as a democratic instrument: whether the candidates and the news media structured the debate so as to address the issues the people wanted discussed; the amount of information and number of considerations the people take into account in their vote choices; and the degree of satisfaction that the people have with the campaign and the candidates. By those indicators, the 1992 campaign was something of a surprising success. But what did the campaign mean for governance? What mandate did the campaign convey to the new president?

On the surface, our findings seem to show that the campaign mandate is very personal. But our investigation demonstrates that personal assessments of a candidate's character invoke relevant political qualities. The public imputes good character in part to candidates who share their values, priorities, and concerns. Based on the campaign, it was reasonable for the public to expect in Bill Clinton a president who would focus on the economy, be accessible to the people, and empathize with their concerns. When Clinton began his presidency with attention to other issues, the public may have had good reason to register disappointment. As the new president's approval ratings fell, President Clinton learned what George Bush had before him, that campaigns matter. Candidates can be held accountable not only for the most publicized and generalized commitments—"read my lips"—but also for the implicit style of leadership that they conveyed during the campaign. The candidate's campaign construct itself, then, is part of the expectation of governance.

The subsequent trials and tribulations of the victorious candidate in 1992 (see Kumar 1995) should not discourage efforts to make future campaigns meet or exceed the standards of accessible information, high interest, and new popular involvement set in this election. Admittedly, that is no easy task. Election climates and candidates vary. The public will not always be galvanized by a single overriding issue that can set the boundaries of debate. Candidates may not want to expose themselves to the vagaries of television interviews or may face fewer liabilities in "going negative." In the future, journalists may not wish to yield pride of place to the public or less professional media personalities. But if elites trivialize the public's role, they do so at their peril. The downward slide of faith in government, political leadership, and journalism threatens the democratic process itself. The lesson of the 1992 campaign, and this study, is that together citizens, candidates, and the media have the capacity to engage in useful and substantive crosstalk and build mutual confidence in the democratic process.

REFERENCES

Campbell, Angus, Philip E. Converse, Warren E. Miller, and Donald E. Stokes. 1960. *The American Voter.* New York: Wiley.

Cook, Timothy E., and Lyn Ragsdale. 1995. "The President and the Press: Negotiating Newsworthiness at the White House." In *The Presidency and the Political System.* (4th ed.). Edited by Michael Nelson, 297–330. Washington, D.C.: CQ Press.

Converse, Philip E. 1964. "The Nature of Belief Systems in Mass Publics." In *Ideology and Discontent,* edited by David E. Apter, 206–61. New York: Free Press.

———. 1970. "Attitudes and Nonattitudes: Continuation of a Dialogue." In *The Quantitative Analysis of Social Problems,* edited by Edward R. Tufte, 168–89. Reading, MA: Addison-Wesley.

Hochschild, Jennifer L. 1993. "Disjunction and Ambivalence in Citizens' Political Outlooks." In *Reconsidering the Democratic Public,* edited by George E. Marcus and Russell L. Hanson, 187–210. University Park: Pennsylvania State University Press.

Kern, Montague. 1993. "The Advertising-driven 'New' Mass Media Election and the Rhetoric of Policy Issues." In *Mass Media and Public Policy,* edited by Robert Spitzer, 133–52. Westport, CT: Praeger.

———. 1995. "The Focus Group Method, Political Advertising, Campaign News and the Construction of Candidate Images." *Political Communication* 12:127–45.

Krouse, Richard W., and George E. Marcus. 1984. "Electoral Studies and Democratic Theory Reconsidered." *Political Behavior* 6:23–39.

Kumar, Martha Joynt. 1995. "President Clinton Meets the Media: Communications Shaped by Predictable Patterns." In *The Clinton Presidency: Campaigning, Governing, and the Psychology of Leadership,* edited by Stanley A. Renshon, 167–93. Boulder, CO: Westview.

Marcus, George E. 1988. "Democratic Theories and the Study of Public Opinion." *Polity* 21:25–44.

Page, Benjamin I. 1978. *Choices and Echoes in Presidential Elections.* Chicago: University of Chicago Press.

Rosenstone, Steven J., John Mark Hansen, Paul Freedman, and Marguerite Grabanek. 1993. "Voter Turnout: Myth and Reality in the 1992 Election." Paper prepared for presentation at annual meeting of the American Political Science Association, Washington, D.C.

Tuchman, Gaye. 1973. "Making News by Doing Work: Routinizing the Unexpected." *American Journal of Sociology,* 110–31.

Voting:
A Macro-Level View

From time to time in American history the political equivalent of an earthquake occurs; that is, the dominant political party in the electorate loses its hold on a majority of voters and is replaced by the other party. This occurrence, typically precipitated by a focusing event (e.g., a civil war or depression), is signalled by a "realigning election" in which the new majority party in the electorate wins control of the presidency, Congress, and the greatest share of elected offices at the state level. The elections of 1800, 1828, 1860, 1896, and 1932 have been identified as realigning elections, suggesting to some that such events are likely to occur every thirty-two to thirty-six years.[1] Indeed, in 1969 political writer Kevin Phillips wrote a widely discussed book (*The Emerging Republican Majority*) in which he argued that the New Deal Democratic coalition, in the process of decomposing for some time, was about to be replaced by a new realignment. Phillips's prediction, however, proved to be incorrect, or at the very least premature, for neither the 1972 election nor those that followed met the classical definition of a realigning election.

How to interpret political developments of the last thirty years has generated considerable scholarly comment. Some contend that realignment is occurring but in ways different from previous realignments in our history; others maintain that realignment is unlikely in an era when voters do not appear to be strongly attached to political parties; and still others insist that as an explanatory concept, the term realignment is seriously flawed.[2]

In the first of the articles that follow, Everett Carll Ladd attempts to place the 1996 presidential election into the broader context of political forces, arguing that it is consistent with a "philosophical" realignment that has long since occured in the electorate—a realignment in which the pro-government attitude growing out of the New Deal has been replaced by greater skepticism about what government can do. Ladd is quick to acknowledge, however, that this realignment of attitude has not brought with it a new majority party in the electorate and in government. In seeking to account for this apparent anomaly, he suggests that the answers may lie with the leadership of both political parties, the nature of the contemporary electorate, and the manner in which we now conduct our elections.

Alan Abramowitz and Kyle Saunders focus their attention primarily on the 1994 congressional election, which saw Republicans gain control of both Houses for the first time in forty years, and at a time of relative peace and prosperity. In their view, this important midterm election was the culmination of an ideological realignment that has been going on in the electorate during the last several election cycles. They contend that this realignment is rooted in the growing ideological polarization of the two parties, particularly during the Reagan and post-Reagan era. This differentiation, they suggest, made it easier for voters to choose their party identification on the basis of their policy preferences rather than simply adopting the party of their parents. As a consequence of these choices, the Republicans, even though not yet a majority party, have made significant inroads into Democratic Party ranks. This development, in the authors' view, makes it very unlikely that the Democratic Party will be able to dominate Congress as it has in the past.

Daniel Shea, in the third article, holds the view that the American electorate is "dealigned," not realigned. While acknowledging that the elections of the eighties and nineties have had potentially significant implications for the relative strength of the two parties, he nevertheless points out that for every trend suggesting realignment there are counter trends that argue against it. In attempting to account for why the electorate remains "unanchored," he argues that we must look beyond failed presidencies and beyond the impact of various domestic and international events. In his view a crucial factor lies in the service-based approach adopted by the party organizations—an approach that does little to foster voter attachment to our political parties.

NOTES

1. Walter Dean Burnham, "Critical Realignment: Dead or Alive?", in Byron E. Shafer, ed., *The End of Realignment? Interpreting American Electoral, Eras* (Madison: University of Wisconsin Press, 1991), p. 101; Everett Carll Ladd, "Like Waiting for Godot: The Uselessness of 'Realignment' for Understanding Change in Contemporary American Politics," in Shafer, *The End of Realignment*, p. 27.

2. See, for example, Helmut Northpoth, "Underway and Here to Stay: Party Realignment in the 1980's?", *Public Opinion Quarterly,* 51 (Fall 1987), pp. 376–391; James L. Sundquist, *Dynamics of the Party System,* rev. ed (Washington, DC: Brookings Institution, 1983); Shafer, *The End of Realignment*; Edward G. Carmines and James A Stimson, *Issue Evolution: Race and the Transformation of American Politics* (Princeton, NJ Princeton University Press, 1989), pp. 21–26.

1996 Vote: The "No Majority" Realignment Continues

Everett Carll Ladd

In multiple understandings of the term, the 1996 vote was a status-quo election. It was obviously such in the sense that it left control of the government essentially unchanged. The Republicans retained majorities in both the House (where their margin dropped from the thirty-two-seat edge they enjoyed following the 1994 balloting to twenty seats) and the Senate (where they gained two seats, bringing their majority to fifty-five to forty-five). This is the first time the GOP has managed congressional majorities for consecutive terms since 1928. Meanwhile, as Table 1 shows, President Bill Clinton won reelection by a margin similar to the one he gained over George Bush four years earlier. Clinton again won despite persisting doubts about his character because his political skills surpassed his opponent's and because the economy (seen as bad in 1992, good in 1996) was on his side again.

It was a status-quo election, though, in a more fundamental sense. The partisan realignment that ushered in our contemporary system is now fully mature, its essential features set. One large part of this realignment involves a clear and decisive shift in the agenda of politics—what I will call the "philosophical realignment." The other principal element, involving the parties' competitive standings, is more ambiguous. The Democrats have long since lost the majority status they held from the New Deal to the Great Society, but the Republicans have not been able to claim the mantle. Voters again chose in 1996 to divide control of the national government between the two major parties. Finally, 1996 saw the now-familiar patterns of social group voting that began emerging in the late 1960s.

In this article I will discuss some factors peculiar to the 1996 contest and its candidates, but I will concentrate on placing the balloting squarely in the context

TABLE 1   *Vote for President, 1992 and 1996*

	Clinton	Bush and Dole	Perot	Dem. over Rep. Margin
1996	49.2	40.8	8.5	8 4
1992	43.0	37.4	18.9	5 6

Source: Everett Carll Ladd, "1996 Vote: The 'No Majority' Realignment Continues," *Political Science Quarterly*, 112 (Spring 1997), pp. 1–23.

Everett Carll Ladd was professor of political science and director of the Institute for Social Inquiry at the University of Connecticut and executive director of the Roper Center for Public Opinion Research.

of the postindustrial party system. That system is distinguished by the following features:

- a philosophical realignment which sees the electorate significantly more conservative than it was in the preceding era, especially in the sense of being far less inclined to accept claims that *more government* represents progress;
- markedly weakened ties of voters to the political parties;
- television's dominance as the campaign's medium and an institutional setting that is a vast departure from predecessor systems. Candidates lacking television access to voters on a par with their opponents in a very real sense lack political free speech. New political gatekeepers, including television news producers, on-air journalists, and talk show pundits, are a major force in this "electronic democracy."[1]
- In large part due to factors that inhere in the loss of party loyalty and the dominance of television, the contemporary system lacks a majority party and shows little prospect of adopting the "sun and moon," majority party/minority party model that Samuel Lubell described so vividly nearly a half-century ago.[2]
- Divided government does not inevitably follow in a no-majority-party era, but it is naturally more readily obtained in one. Other factors that I will describe below have contributed to persisting split party control, making it a deeply established, far from coincidental feature of contemporary politics.
- Finally, the composition and alignment of social groups that we see today in politics—differing sharply as they do from those of the New Deal years—persist because they reflect central structural features of the postindustrial economy and the group conflicts and cultural tensions of this era.[3]

UNDERSTANDING REALIGNMENT

Each of the major partisan transformations the U.S. has experienced historically has grown out of broad shifts in the country's socioeconomic setting. Once established, the underlying properties of the new system shape subsequent election results in many ways. They do not, obviously, determine who the winners will be in each election. The personal appeal (or lack thereof) of the candidates is always a key independent element, and parties have opportunities to fashion appeals and build majorities whatever the sociopolitical setting.

There was plenty of mystery and uncertainty at the start of the 1996 campaign. It was by no means certain in late 1995 that Bill Clinton would win reelection. He responded boldly to his then-sagging electoral fortunes, adopting or emphasizing positions closer to what conservative majorities in the electorate favored than he did in his first two White House years. From proclaiming that "the era of Big Government is over" in his January 1996 State of the Union Address, to calling for programs that rally the "vital center" in his December speech to the Democratic Leadership Council (DLC), Clinton responded to a changed political environment. We cannot know precisely how much the subsequent rise in his approval ratings and electoral standing accrued from these changes in direction, but it is apparent that Clinton helped himself with the voters.

On the Republican side a variety of important short-term factors hurt the GOP's chances to regain the presidency. Urged by many Republican officials to seek the party's presidential nomination and enjoying a high level of public encouragement (through the polls), Colin Powell nonetheless said no. The GOP found itself with a weak field of candidates and nominated a man who had never, in a long and distinguished political career, shown the ability to rally the nation. Ross Perot, who mounted so formidable a challenge to George Bush's reelection in 1992, had by 1996 lost much of his appeal. Many Americans who had seen the economy in trouble in 1992, had by the 1996 campaign come to feel better about their own economic positions and that of the country. All these factors contributed to Clinton's reelection.

Still, for all the unpredictability which resulted from short-term factors, one can see the imprint of an underlying sociopolitical setting in the election. Movement from one setting to another precipitates shifts in social needs and problems and in the public's thinking about what needs to be done, and it reshapes the contending coalitions of groups and interests. Early in a realigning era these elements are in flux, and we are often startled by departures from predecessor systems, but the mystery vanishes when the transition is largely complete and we have observed the properties of the new sociopolitical era over a series of elections. That was the situation in 1996.

The U.S. has experienced four great sociopolitical eras. The emergence of each has precipitated broad partisan transformations. The first era involved the post-Revolution maturation of a rural republic that was unprecedentedly egalitarian in resource distribution and social relations but which permitted slavery. The Jeffersonian/Jacksonian party system was the creature of this era. The post–Civil War years saw the growing ascendancy of an urban and industrializing order in the population centers of the North, and a South isolated by memories of the war and by its nonparticipation in industrial development. The Republicans assumed leadership of industrial nation building and from this base gradually established a decisive national majority outside the South. The third broad setting emerged with the maturation of the industrial system, which resulted in an America distinguished by institutional scale, interdependence, and complexity. These developments placed new demands on government, and on national government in particular.[4] Over the last several decades, the U.S. has entered a fourth major sociopolitical period that I call, following Daniel Bell's seminal work on the subject, the postindustrial era.[5] Dispersion and decentralization are as distinctive a feature of the technology and economy in this period as increasing scale and centralization were in the preceding era.

Each of these four eras displays features that reach beyond the socioeconomic setting narrowly construed. Each has witnessed, for example, an important redefinition of the thrusts of American individualism, at once extending opportunities and recognition to groups previously excluded and posing new tensions and problems. Each has had its special mix of ethnic groups and its distinctive frontier of ethnic conflict. That the U.S. of the first era was essentially a nation of British ancestry with a large, enslaved minority of African ancestry was enormously important to the politics of the time; these elements were not, however, products of the rural republic setting. Similarly, politics in the 1990s is influenced by current shifts of ethnic make-up—that are not a feature of postindustrialism, though they accompany it. Each of the four eras demarking U.S. politics historically has had, then, along with its distinguishing socioeconomic core, many other important, ancillary elements.

THE PHILOSOPHICAL REALIGNMENT

Calling this change in direction in the public's thinking about government and politics a shift toward "conservatism" is, of course, simplistic—as was describing the New Deal change in terms of "liberalism." In every era, the populace displays considerable variety in political outlook, and many people don't sign on unambiguously and *en masse* to any of the contending positions. Given these qualifications, it makes sense to describe the New Deal setting as liberal and the present one as conservative—as long as the meanings attached to these terms are carefully delineated. In the political era bounded by Franklin Delano Roosevelt's election in 1932 and Lyndon Baines Johnson's Great Society of the mid-1960s, public support for expanding governmental programs and initiatives was high, set against American historical experience. Few thought, for example, that there was too much power in the hands of the national government.

Our postindustrial era is distinguished by far greater skepticism about government, though for most not by hostility toward it. This shift has two different sources. For one thing, it took the creation in the Great Society years of "big government" with its inevitably more visible failings to swing individualist America away from its relatively brief and historically anomalous enthusiasm for expanding national government. The other source comprises the dispersion and decentralization induced by postindustrialism, that have made central national government bureaucracy seem

FIGURE 1

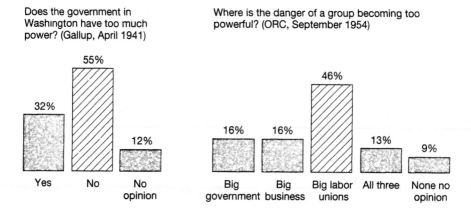

Does the government in Washington have too much power? (Gallup, April 1941)

Where is the danger of a group becoming too powerful? (ORC, September 1954)

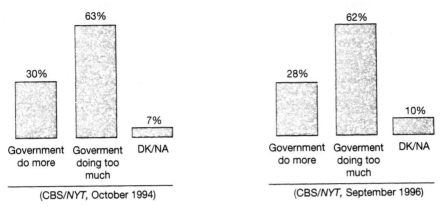

FIGURE 2   *Should government do more to solve national problems or is it doing too much?*

ever more cumbersome and out of phase. Americans have not come to see less government as progress—as some Republicans found to their acute disappointment in the public's response to the work of the 104th Congress in its first year. But we have come rather decidedly to reject the idea that more government is progress.

In the mid-1990s the U.S. is no longer seeing significant year-to-year change in public sentiment about government and its proper role. The 1994 congressional elections were widely taken as a call for a Republican-led "revolution" against the New Deal/Great Society state, although much of the commentary in 1996 had Americans calling off this revolution (if indeed they had ever sought it). But survey data show great continuity over this span in public thinking about government.

The conservative swing indicated by these data has not, of course, occurred evenly across the population. African-Americans give much more support than most other groups to a broader governmental role. Differences by gender are less striking, but women in 1996 continued to provide more support than men for governmental activism—which probably goes far toward explaining the electoral gender gap evident again in the 1996 balloting (Figure 3). The 1996 election day voters' poll taken by Voter News Service (VNS) found big regional differences on how much government is desirable, with Texans at one end of the continuum and New Yorkers at the other (Table 2). Overall, though, questions posed by the opinion polls in 1996 confirmed the electorate's desire to stay with a relatively conservative stance on role-of-government questions.

Two sets of surveys—one taken by the Hart and Teeter research companies for NBC News and the *Wall Street Journal,* the other by Gallup for CNN and *USA Today*—point up the extent to which today's relatively conservative mood reaches beyond role-of-government issues. Hart and Teeter asked respondents which political party they thought would do a better job handling fourteen issues (Table 3). The list is a carefully balanced one reaching across the policy spectrum, including foreign policy, crime, taxes, reforming welfare, Medicare, and education. At this supposed

Question: If you had to choose, would you rather have a smaller government providing fewer services, or a bigger government providing more services?

Question: Do you agree or disagree that the federal government should see to it that every person who wants to work has a job?

Question: Do you think the government in Washington should guarantee medical care for all people who don't have health insurance, or isn't that the responsibility of the government in Washington?

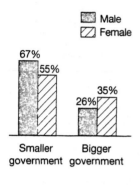

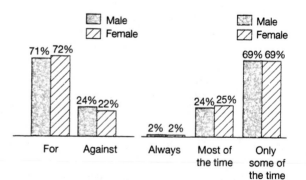

Source: Survey by CBS News/*New York Times,* 22–24 February 1996.

Source: Survey by CBS News/*New York Times,* 22–24 February 1996.

Source: Survey by CBS News/*New York Times,* 22–24 February 1996.

Though Both Sexes Call Government Too Big and Untrustworthy

Question: Which comes closer to your view: Government should do more to solve national problems, or government is doing too many things better left to businesses and individuals?

Question: . . . Please tell me whether you would vote for or against the following propositions. . . . A reduction in the size and budget of all government agencies.

Question: How much of the time do you think you can trust government in Washington to do what is right: just about always, most of the time, or only some of the time?

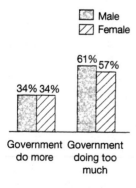

Source: Survey by CBS News/*New York Times,* March 31–April 2, 1996.

Source: Survey by the Gallup Organization, April 23–25, 1996.

Source. Survey by the Gallup Organization for CNN/*USA Today,* May 9–12, 1996.

FIGURE 3 *More Women than Men Support Government Activism*

TABLE 2   *Big State-to-State Differences in Calls for "Less Government"*
(1996 Exit Poll Findings) (in percentages)

Question: Which comes closer to your view: . . . ?

	. . . Gov't is doing too many things better left to business and individuals	*. . . Gov't should do more to solve problems*
National	52	41
Texas	65	31
Oregon	62	33
Maine	61	37
New Hampshire	61	34
Minnesota	60	37
Wisconsin	59	37
California	58	37
Georgia	58	38
Ohio	57	39
Washington	57	38
Connecticut	56	39
North Carolina	55	41
Pennsylvania	55	40
Florida	54	42
Tennessee	54	40
Massachusetts	48	47
New Jersey	46	49
New York	45	50

Note: States shown are only those where the question was asked.
Source: Exit poll by Voter News Service, November 5, 1996.

low point in GOP fortunes, pluralities gave the party the edge on nine of the fourteen. These 1996 assessments can be compared to those made in 1994 just before voters elected Republican majorities to the House and Senate. In May 1996, when Hart and Teeter asked about ten of the fourteen issues they had examined in mid-October 1994, they found no change during this nineteen-month period. Not only did Republicans lead on the same seven (of the ten) in both October 1994 and May 1996, but they led by virtually identical margins. They gained 15 points on the Democrats on controlling government spending, while losing 8 points on health care, but on most issues the shift was minuscule.

In late April 1996, Gallup conducted an opinion referendum for CNN and *USA Today* in which respondents were asked how they would vote, supposing that "on election day this year you could vote on key issues as well as candidates," on twenty-six propositions, including a balanced budget amendment (BBA), prayer in schools, the death penalty for murder, and a ban on assault rifles. As in the Hart-Teeter survey, the overall list was balanced. A few of the propositions, such as doctor-assisted suicide and selling off public lands, don't fit on a liberal-conservative continuum; but by my count twenty of the twenty-six do. On only five of the twenty issues did pluralities come down on the liberal side: banning assault rifles, reducing defense spending,

TABLE 3   *The Parties Hold Their Ground on Issues (in percentages)*

Question: When it comes to [each item], which party do you think would do a better job—the Democratic Party, the Republican Party, both about the same, or neither?

May 1996			*October 1994*	
Republican	*Democrat*		*Republican*	*Democrat*
43	15	Controlling government spending	34	21
43	20	Foreign policy	34	15
36	21	Promoting strong moral values	38	20
31	21	Crime	28	23
34	25	Taxes	38	23
30	26	The economy	30	22
35	31	Reforming the welfare system	31	28
25	34	Abortion	24	31
24	40	Education	21	34
22	42	Healthcare	25	37
35	18	Immigration	—	—
21	19	Drug problem	18*	15
26	45	Medicare	22**	33
17	45	The environment	15*	44

*October 22–26, 1993
**June 2–6, 1995
Source. Surveys by NBC News/*Wall Street Journal,* May 10–14, 1996 and October 14–18, 1994.

raising the minimum wage, (not) reducing social spending, and (not) banning all abortions except to save the life of the mother. On most of the fifteen issues where the conservative side carried, including the BBA, term limits, reducing all government agencies, and school choice, it did so overwhelmingly (Figure 4).

THE REALIGNMENT HAS NOT PRODUCED A NEW MAJORITY PARTY

As noted, although the philosophical side of the postindustrial realignment has come swiftly and decisively, the partisan side has not. The 1996 balloting reflected the general partisan parity that has prevailed since the postindustrial system took clear form a decade and a half ago. Clinton won reelection, and the Republicans retained congressional majorities. Republicans now lead the Democrats in governorships by thirty-two to seventeen (with one independent in Maine), one of their largest margins ever; but the Democrats still lead in state legislative seats, 3,883 to 3,470 (though this margin is down sharply from what it was after the 1992 vote).

National surveys asking about partisan identification typically find a small Democratic edge, on the order of 2-to-4 percentage points. Thirty-nine percent of those interviewed by the VNS on November 5 called themselves Democrats, 35 percent Republicans. There has been no significant movement in party identification distributions since 1984—the point at which Reagan's leadership and Democratic missteps had brought the Republicans back from their deep deficit to parity.

TABLE 4   *State Legislatures: GOP Closing But Democrats Still Lead*

1996		1994		1992	
Republicans	*Democrats*	*Republicans*	*Democrats*	*Republicans*	*Democrats*
Members of State Legislatures					
3470	3883	3491	3846	3005	4342
Control of State Legislative Chambers by Party					
46	50	47	48	29	66
State with Both Legislative House and Governor of Same Party					
12	6	15	7	3	16

Two different explanations may be offered for this state of affairs. One focuses on failures of leadership in both parties, the other on underlying characteristics of the contemporary electorate and the way elections are now conducted. Elements of both may be valid.

Explanation One

At any time, decisions and actions of a party's leaders will be, in varying degrees. helpful or harmful to its standing. Today it may be argued that neither party has produced leaders able to reconcile contending themes and impulses in voters' thinking in anything like the persuasive fashion achieved by Franklin Roosevelt, Theodore Roosevelt, Abraham Lincoln, Andrew Jackson, and Thomas Jefferson. Ronald Reagan did strengthen the Republican party by understanding the extent of the philosophical realignment that was occurring and by being the kind of political personality—sunny and optimistic—Americans persistently seek in presidents. But he has found no successor. Whereas Reagan grew up politically a Roosevelt Democrat, both George Bush and Bob Dole entered Republican politics in an era of Republican failure. Theirs is—in a way the older Reagan's never was—a prerealignment Republicanism. Many postrealignment Republican conservatives have long complained about this. Bush and Dole are clearly in the American conservative tradition, but their roots are in the conservatism-in-retreat era of GOP minority status. The delay in bringing a new generation of Republican leadership to the fore in the presidential party has blunted Republican efforts to expand their base.

Along with these weaknesses in recent Republican presidential leadership, the party's congressional leadership overreached in 1995—mistaking the public's clear rejection of the idea that "more government is progress" for a conclusion it has not reached, that "less government is progress." There may have been an "underreach" in the Republicans' response—one that 1996 presidential hopeful Lamar Alexander discussed in a *Wall Street Journal* op-ed piece following the election. To become the majority, Alexander argued, Republicans need to do more than demonstrate failures of the New Deal/Great Society state. They must offer plausible alternatives to it, ones

Question: Suppose that on election day this year you could vote on key issues as well as candidates. Please tell me whether you would vote for or against each one of the following propositions?

Proposition	%	For/Against	
Balanced budget amendment	83%	For	(14% against)
Racial preferences in jobs/schools	83%	Against	(14% for)
English as the official language	82%	For	(16% against)
Life sentences for drug dealers	80%	For	(17% against)
Death penalty for murder	79%	For	(18% against)
Congressional term limits	74%	For	(23% against)
Legalization of marijuana	73%	Against	(24% for)
Prayer in school amendment	73%	For	(25% against)
Reducing all government agencies	71%	For	(23% against)
2-year cutoff for welfare without work	71%	For	(24% against)
Legalization of gay marriages	67%	Against	(28% for)
School busing for racial balance	62%	Against	(34% for)
School choice	59%	For	(37% against)
Ban on partial birth abortions	57%	For	(39% against)
Ban on assault rifles	57%	For	(42% against)
Reduce defense spending	54%	Against	(42% for)
Federal flat tax system	49%	For	(39% against)
Reduce social spending	42%	For	(54% against)
Ban on all abortions except for life of mother	42%	For	(56% against)
Raising the minimum wage	15%	Against	(83% for)

FIGURE 4   *The 1996 Gallup Opinion Referendum Found a Distinctly Conservative Tilt*

Source: The bars show the percentage of all respondents taking what is conventionally called the more conservative response on the issue. The numbers shown in parentheses after the bars are the percentages taking the opposing response. Included in the referendum but not shown here are the following items: withdrawal of U.S. from UN, five-year freeze on legal immigration, reestablishing relations with Cuba, doctor-assisted suicide, mandatory job retraining, and selling off public lands.

that meet public expectations for a better society. New solutions need to be offered, clearly and positively. Alexander gave the following example of what, he believes, Republican politicians need to say and do: "Nothing is more important to me than making it possible for you to send your child to such a school, one of the best schools in the world—a safe, neighborhood school where every child is expected to behave and learn high standards. I am ready to make the changes necessary to create those schools and give you those opportunities, and the Democrats are not. There will be time to explain the policies—charter schools, high standards, a GI Bill for Kids—*after* we paint the picture."[6]

As the GOP was encountering its problems, national Democratic leaders were trying to respond to criticisms of the failings that had contributed to their party's electoral decline. From the Vietnam War on through the 1980s, the national Democratic party seemed unaware of the extent of the emerging conservative realignment. The party seemed tone deaf. This was the situation in which Bill Clinton and his party found themselves in December 1994 after their "blow-out defeat." Subsequently, though, the president has changed direction. He has been criticized for waffling and lacking firm principles. But it is sometimes hard to tell precisely where waffling and lacking principles leave off and pragmatism and flexibility begin. Since the 1994 debacle, the determinedly centrist thrust of his speeches and such decisions as signing the welfare overhaul bill in 1996 helped Clinton give a new look to the national Democratic party.

The President's December 1996 DLC speech is especially instructive on the reach of his effort to redirect the Democratic party so as to bring it into phase with the philosophical realignment. He called upon the party to mobilize the "vital center" by making six main commitments:

- balance the budget;
- give young people the best education in the world;
- reform welfare by demanding "responsibility of welfare recipients," while avoiding the more "punitive" aspects of Republican approach;
- press the fight against "gangs and guns and drugs and violence;"
- strengthen families; and
- pass "meaningful campaign finance reform legislation and modernize government operations."

While there are liberal elements in such program—e.g., seeking expanded family leave (though "in a very limited way")—his call to the DLC meeting, like much of his 1996 campaign, was largely devoid of a liberal agenda.

Explanation Two

An alternate explanation begins with an entirely different perspective—that the chief reason no party has majority status is that large segments of the electorate are abandoning firm partisan ties. For decades many political scientists and journalists were mesmerized by the New Deal realignment, which had seen a new majority emerge quickly and decisively. *Realignment* became virtually synonymous with *new majority,* but the historical record shows that each of the country's historic realignments followed its own course.[7] Broad changes in social structure, yielding new demographics, new social problems, and new views of government's role and policy needs, need not result in one party's ascendancy for an extended period.

There is strong evidence that the continuing weakening of voter ties to parties is one key dimension of postindustrialism. Growing segments of the electorate are thereby up for grabs in each contest. The postindustrial electorate is more highly educated and more confident of its ability to make political judgments independent of party cues. It draws its information not from party-influenced sources but from independent, adversarial mass media. Surveys such as one the Roper Center conducted for the Media Studies Center in November/December 1995 show national journalists heavily Democratic in both party identification and presidential voting.[8] The idea that journalists, however disciplined professionally, can escape in their reporting the claims of their underlying political preferences, seems to me as silly as claims that those of us teaching American government and politics can approach our students unencumbered by our own political preferences. But journalists are surely right when they insist that their overriding guide is *not* loyalty to a political party. They see themselves in an adversarial relationship to parties generally. Today most Americans derive their political information from a source that tends to discourage rather than to encourage stable party loyalties.

Political parties just are not important institutions for most Americans today. Contrary to arguments advanced by Robert Putnam and others, I find evidence that "civic America" remains active and vital.[9] But political parties, never huge actors in civic America, are perhaps smaller ones now than ever before. There seems to be a general inclination across the public to reject the confines of "us and them" distinctions. We see this in religious group identification, where the proportion describing themselves as Protestant or Catholic is yielding to a growing proportion choosing the label "other Christian." Seventeen percent of voters interviewed by VNS on November 5, 1996 chose this "I don't want to be part of that old divide" response, as did 19 percent in the election day poll done by the *Los Angeles Times* nationally.[10] Similarly, being tied to the Republican or Democratic side seems to draw less favor than in times past.

Survey work done by the Roper Center for the Media Studies Center in 1996 reveals an electorate remarkably unanchored in partisan terms. Thus 65 percent indicated in the February 1996 poll that they "typically split [their] ticket—that is, vote for candidates from different parties." In 1942, Gallup had found that only 42 percent described themselves as ticket splitters. Sixty-three percent said, in 1996, that they had "voted for different parties for president" in past elections. Back in 1952, when the University of Michigan's Center for Political Studies first asked this question, just 29 percent reported having voted for different parties in past contests.

An experiment the Roper Center conducted in its February 1996 survey gives further indication of how weak party ties are for many voters, even when voters claim ties in some form. The Center asked the party identification question regularly used by the National Election Studies (NES): "Generally speaking, do you usually think of yourself as a Republican, a Democrat, an independent, or what?" Thirty-six percent identified with the Democratic party, 33 percent with the Republican party, and 24 percent claimed to be independents. The Center also asked another, different party identification question: "In your own mind, do you identify with one of the political parties or not?" If the respondent said yes, a follow-up asked, "Which party. . . ?"

The bivariate relationship between the NES question and the Roper question is instructive. Only three-quarters of Republican identifiers on the NES item were recorded as Republicans by the Roper Center question, and only two-thirds of Democrats on the NES measure remained Democrats in the Roper version. Overall, 32 percent of voters gave no consistent response—that is, were not Republican/Republican, Democrat/Democrat, or Independent/No Party—on the two questions. On both askings, only

TABLE 5 *In the same poll, on two occasions, at least one-fifth of those who called themselves Democrats or Republicans in the NES party identification question didn't identify with a party in the Roper Center question or party ID (Column percentages: read down)*

	NES ID (February 1996)				NES ID (September 1996)		
Roper Center ID	Rep.	Dem.	Ind.	Roper Center ID	Rep.	Dem.	Ind.
Yes, Rep.	76	1	11	Yes, Rep.	77	1	12
Yes, Dem.	2	69	11	Yes, Dem.	4	78	21
Don't identify	22	30	78	Don't identify	19	20	67

24 percent of registered voters identified with the Republicans and 24 percent with the Democrats. Thus, in both measures, a slight majority (52 percent) did not consistently identify with either major party. Even those who were "consistent" Democrats or Republicans said that they often do not vote the party line: about 60 percent of both groups typically vote split tickets.

In September 1996, the Roper Center recontacted more than 500 randomly selected voters from the February survey in this panel study. It again posed the party identification questions and found significant movement in the NES measure over this seven-month span. Eighteen percent of those calling themselves Republicans in the February survey said in September that they were Democrats or independents, and 24 percent of Democrats in February said they were Republicans or independents in the fall.[11]

Such erosion in party loyalties makes it appear unlikely that the U.S. will in its postindustrial era experience a majority party of the type that the Democrats had in 1836, the Republicans in 1900, or the Democrats in 1940. The electorate is too weakly tied to parties to sit still as the "sun and moon" model that Lubell used in describing the New Deal party system requires.

TABLE 6 *Roughly one in five who called themselves Republicans or Democrats in February rejected this description in September. (Column percentages: read down)*

		NES ID (February 1996)		
NES ID (September 1996)		Rep.	Dem.	Ind.
	Republican	81	4	9
	Democrat	7	76	15
	Independent	11	20	62

Divided Government

The U.S. historically has had two prolonged periods where divided government has been the rule not the exception: the half-century or so from the early 1840s through the mid-1890s, and the period from the mid-1950s to the present. In both eras major realignment was occurring. And in both, neither of the major parties had attained majority status. The first was a time of slow, incomplete realignment that left both parties at rough parity for an extended span. By the time of the Civil War, although the new Republican party had come far, the Democrats had "won" a truly solid South and retained substantial Jacksonian-era-type backing outside Dixie. Not until industrialization had progressed far enough to erode the socioeconomic fabric of Jacksonian America did national Republican ascendancy become possible.

The divided government of our era also reflects the fact that changes in party strength have been occurring slowly. The Republicans have again gained ground (not, of course, as a new party but by progressing from their weak number two position during most of the New Deal/Great Society years), but they have climbed only to parity. This relatively even, two-party balance doesn't mandate that control of government will be divided, but it makes split results more likely.

Today—in contrast to the late nineteenth-century experience—a growing segment of the electorate really doesn't belong to any party and is disinclined to place much long-term faith in either party's leadership or direction. Historic American political individualism has long helped sustain our Madisonian Constitution, through which governmental authority is divided among different institutions (presidency, Congress, federal courts; national government, state and local governments) each with powerful resources to resist the other. Madisonianism has now become overlaid with a new feature: the unwillingness of many voters to commit themselves to any party.

Why hasn't the postindustrial realignment yielded a new majority party? Will it in the future? My strong understanding is that large parts of both interpretations just reviewed are valid. Both major parties are groping for a satisfactory response to the electorate's changed outlook, following the decisive but subtle realignment of political outlook. Finding the right leadership and voice could advance either party toward majority status. But this said, today's postindustrial sociopolitical environment makes it exceedingly difficult for any party to establish stable, long-term loyalties across much of the population.

SOCIAL GROUP ALIGNMENTS

Republicans won the three presidential elections of the 1980s and have lost the two of the 1990s. But while the parties' presidential fortunes have waxed and waned with the popularity of their candidates and voter reactions to current conditions, the underlying structure of social group support has remained essentially unchanged. The groups that in 1996 were the Republicans' best had been their best in the immediately preceding elections; the same is true for the Democrats.

Data from the exit polls done by Voter News Service show how closely Clinton's 1996 coalition resembled that of 1992. His share of the popular vote was up among most groups because it climbed 6.2 percentage points for the entire electorate. Dole's popular vote percentage, compared to George Bush's, rose 3.4 points, and Ross Perot's declined 10.4 points. Perot's support base shrank massively but in even proportions across the various groups. His 1996 support was 11 points down among whites, who had given him a whopping 20 percent in 1992, down 3 points among African-Americans, among whom he had been extremely weak four years earlier; his support was cut roughly in half in both groups. VNS also found Perot's 1996 drop-off roughly comparable in each income stratum. In both elections he did better among men than among women and much better among independents than among Democrats or Republicans; he lost support between 1992 and 1996 in similar proportions in these groups.

Clinton made a big gain among voters of Hispanic background—presumably in reaction to highly publicized, Republican-led efforts on immigration reform, such as that by Governor Pete Wilson in California. The president strengthened his position among women voters more than among men. But on the whole, the Clinton, Perot, and Dole votes in 1996 reflected a "universality of trends" from the 1992 balloting—modest increases for both major party candidates among most groups as Perot plummeted everywhere.

Asking voters whether their financial situation was getting better, worse, or staying the same produced an instructive caution on the matter of what causes what. Those who in 1996 said their financial position was getting better gave Clinton a 42-percentage point higher share of their votes than did those who in 1992 had said their finances were improving. A Republican occupied the White House in 1992, a Democrat in 1996. It is likely that many people who had decided to vote for Bush in 1992 wanted to give *him* economic credit by declaring that their economic position was improving; and similarly, the very different group of voters who had wanted to reelect the incumbent Democrat in 1996 sought to give him economic credit. Whether one's financial situation was improving or getting worse was not perhaps the operative dimension here—that causality ran the other way. I suspect that many respondents wanted to square their description of their personal economic position with an otherwise-determined decision on how to vote.

RACE, REGION, AND RELIGIOSITY

The racial background of voters, the region in which they live, and the extent of their religious participation have become in the postindustrial party system especially powerful factors in differentiating such political choices and stances as vote for president and Congress, party identification, and liberalism/conservatism. Neither race nor religiosity had been key variables in the New Deal years; and though region was central then as now, today's regional alignment is virtually a mirror image of that in the preceding era.

Even in 1996, when their presidential nominee ran weakly, the Republicans received a plurality of the presidential ballots of non-Hispanic whites and a decisive majority of white voters' congressional ballots. African-Americans moved into Democratic ranks following the Great Depression; but they were not a major part of the New Deal electorate because their voting rights were denied in much of the South and because Republicans retained significant support in the African-American community. Since 1964, however, African-American voters have backed Democratic candidates overwhelmingly almost every time and everywhere. In 1996 congressional votings, Southern whites backed GOP candidates by nearly two to one, leaving the black vote the major support for Democrats in the region. This was the case in Louisiana, for example, when Democrat Mary Landrieu narrowly defeated Republican Woody Jenkins by winning 91 percent of the black vote (VNS exit poll), but only 32 percent of the white vote. Persons of Hispanic background were 4 to 5 percent of the electorate in 1996, according to the VNS exit poll. They backed Clinton and Democratic congressional candidates by roughly three to one—substantially greater margins than in past elections.

Religion—from Denomination to Religiosity

Historically, the religious factor has been central in American politics—but with religion operating largely as a surrogate for ethnicity in the form of denominational affiliation. Older ethnic groups (in time of arrival in the United States) tended (outside the South) to back the Republicans, newer groups the Democrats; the former are heavily Protestant, the latter Catholic. This historic ethnic/denominational dimension can still be seen, but it has greatly eroded. In the 1996 vote for the U.S. House of Representatives, for example, non-Hispanic Roman Catholics gave Republicans a small plurality for only the second time in U.S. history. They first did so in 1994.

Religiosity, not denomination, sharply divides the electorate. Table 7 shows the extraordinary power of just one measure of religious participation: frequency of religious service attendance. According to the *Los Angeles Times* exit poll, those who do not practice a religion (9 percent of the electorate) backed Clinton by 62-to-22 percent; those who attend services regularly (once a week or more) gave Dole a large margin. House voting, party identification, and liberalism-conservatism all show this same strong pattern.

The relationship between religiosity and the vote is strong for both non-Hispanic whites and for Hispanic-Americans. For example, 51 percent of the former who rarely ever attend religious services voted for Clinton on November 5, while just 31 percent of non-Hispanic whites who attend church regularly backed the president. Among Hispanics who rarely attend church services, 77 percent voted for Clinton, while among those who attend regularly, 64 percent voted for him. Among African-Americans, however, there is no relation whatsoever between frequency of church attendance and vote choice or party identification. According to the *Los Angeles Times* exit poll data, 87 percent of African-Americans who rarely or never attend church backed Clinton—and 89 percent who attend church regularly did so.

TABLE 7   *Frequency of Religious Attendance Sharply Differentiates Americans Politically (in percentages)*

Question: How frequently do you attend religious services, or do you never attend religious services?

	Presidential Vote			Congressional Vote	
	Clinton	Dole	Perot	Democrat	Republican
Never/Don't practice a Religion = 9%	62	22	12	63	29
Less than once a year = 9%	54	31	15	55	38
Once a year = 7%	57	30	11	56	39
Several times a year/Once a month = 27%	53	36	9	54	41
Several times a month = 13%	46	49	4	47	50
Once a week = 23%	43	49	7	45	51
Several times a week or more = 12%	33	60	6	35	61

	Party Identification of Voters			Self-Described Ideology of Voters		
	Demo-crat	Repub-lican	Indepen-dent	Liberal	Conser-vative	Middle-of-the-Road
Never/Don't practice a Religion = 9%	62	22	12	63	29	29
Less than once a year = 9%	42	29	28	16	24	60
Once a year = 7%	46	32	22	20	26	53
Several times a year/Once a month = 27%	44	32	23	19	29	52
Several times a month = 13%	41	37	20	14	40	46
Once a week = 23%	41	42	16	14	40	46
Several times a week or more = 12%	30	51	17	9	61	31

Source· Los Angeles Times Exit Poll, 5 November 1996.

Region

A solidly Democratic South was a key component of the New Deal Democratic majority, as it had been a major part of the Democrats' coalition in the preceding Republican era. The South has long since swung Republican, however; and in 1996 it solidified its position as the Republicans' best region. When the election was over, there were fifteen Republican senators from the eleven states of the old confederacy and only seven Democrats; seventy-one Republican members of the U.S. House and fifty-four Democrats; and eight Republican governors compared to three Democratic. In the state legislatures of the region, Democrats still outnumber Republicans (1,061 to 712), but the GOP has made huge gains since 1992.

At the same time, the Northeast in general and New England in particular have moved steadily Democratic. On November 5, 1996, Massachusetts and Rhode Island gave Bill Clinton his biggest margins among the fifty states, and Clinton's worst New

FIGURE 5   *Both New England and the South Leave Home*

The percentage-point margin by which the state's popular vote for the GOP candidate exceeded or trailed the Republican percentages nationally.

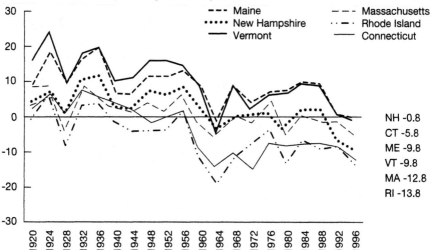

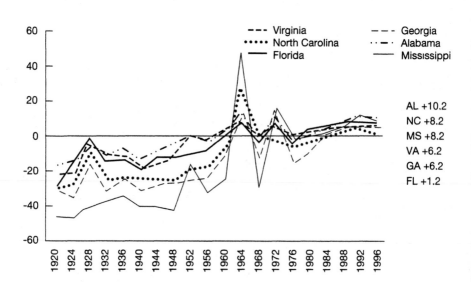

TABLE 8   *1996 Vote and Political Stance by Region and Religiosity (in percentages)*

Region	Frequency of Church Attendance	Presidential Vote			Self-Described Ideology		
		Clinton	Dole	Perot	Liberal	Conser-vative	Moderate
Northeast	Rarely	62	27	9	23	22	56
Midwest	Rarely	60	27	12	22	23	55
Northeast	Occasionally	56	39	4	19	26	55
West	Rarely	51	32	13	20	26	54
Northeast	Regularly	50	43	5	14	41	45
South	Rarely	50	38	11	19	32	50
Midwest	Occasionally	48	43	7	12	33	55
South	Occasionally	44	52	4	14	40	46
West	Occasionally	40	53	5	19	37	44
Midwest	Regularly	39	50	10	11	47	42
South	Regularly	37	56	6	13	49	39
West	Regularly	32	61	6	11	52	37

England state, New Hampshire, backed him by a margin roughly 3 points bigger than what he gained nationally. Figure 5 shows the long march of New England and the South away from their historic partisan homes.

Table 8 shows the powerful interaction of region and religiosity in shaping the contemporary electorate. The narrower frequency of church attendance categories used in Table 7 have been combined here into three broader groupings: persons who say they never attend religious services or do so rarely, those who attend occasionally (once a month to several times monthly), and those who attend at least weekly. Southerners who rarely or never participate in church services gave Bill Clinton a large plurality in 1996; those who attend regularly backed Bob Dole by a margin of roughly 20 points. Northeasterners who attend church regularly were the only group of regular attendees to give Clinton a plurality, but they gave him a much smaller margin (7 points) than those in the region who do not attend services (a 35-point Clinton margin).

THE GENDER GAP—AGAIN

The gender gap has become an important dimension of American politics in the postindustrial era in large part, probably, because of the big growth that has occurred in single-parent families, disproportionately female-headed, and the consequent feminization of poverty. But if gender is now an important discriminating variable— which it was not in the New Deal system—the divide it locates is by no means among the most prominent. Differences separating whites and blacks are, obviously, far larger; and so are many others, including those stemming from religiosity and regional subcultures.[12]

The VNS exit poll taken November 5 found women giving both Bill Clinton and Democratic House candidates solid margins; men split evenly in presidential voting and gave Republican House candidates an 8-point edge. White men backed Dole by an 11-point margin, and white women favored Clinton by 5 points. In U.S. Senate races, Democratic candidates, male and female alike, typically received higher proportions of women's than of men's votes in most states.

POSTINDUSTRIALISM'S POLITICAL STATUS QUO

The 1996 election results were momentous—and in one sense a sharp departure from modern U.S. political experience. Bill Clinton became the first Democrat to win election to the presidency and then reelection since FDR. And the Republicans won consecutive congressional elections for the first time since 1928.

Nonetheless, the continuities evident in the November 5 balloting are in many ways more striking than the above departures. Voters again elected a president of one party and gave congressional majorities to the other, though for the first time this century it was the presidency that was held by the Democrats and the Congress that remained in control of the Republicans. They again signaled a desire to curb the growth of national government, though not to cut it greatly. The social group alignments of the New Deal years have been so altered that "obliterated" is not too strong a verb. Indeed, today's alignment differs from the New Deal's more than the latter differed from the preceding Republican era's. Race, region, and religiosity continued in 1996 to split the U.S. electorate in ways without precedent.

Americans remained remarkably unanchored in partisan terms. Substantial numbers of those who still call themselves party adherents identify with one or the other party very weakly. Regular party identifiers are now too small a proportion for anyone to win the presidency largely on party terms. In this setting presidential elections, especially when an incumbent is running, hinge more than ever on short-term factors such as the perceived state of the economy, together with the comparative personal standing of the main contenders. Bill Clinton won decisively the vote of those uncommitted in partisan terms and thereby gained his victory.

NOTES

1. For an instructive description of this dimension of the contemporary party and elections system, see Lawrence K. Grossman, *The Electronic Republic: Reshaping Democracy in the Information Age* (New York: Viking, 1995).

2. Samuel Lubell, *The Future of American Politics,* 3rd ed. (New York: Harper & Row, 1965), p. 192.

3. I have discussed many of the distinguishing features of the social group alignment of the postindustrial system in my previous elections articles in the *PSQ.* See "The Brittle Mandate: Electoral

Dealignment and the 1980 Presidential Election," 96 (Spring 1981), pp. 1–25; "On Mandates, Realignments. and the 1984 Presidential Election." 100 (Spring 1985), pp. 1–25; "The 1988 Elections: Continuation of the Post-New Deal System," 104 (Spring 1989), pp. 1–18; "The 1992 Vote for President Clinton: Another Brittle Mandate?," 108 (Spring 1993), pp. 1–28; "The 1994 Congressional Elections: The Realignment Continues," (Spring 1995), pp. 1–23.

4. I have discussed these developments in a number of earlier publications, especially in *American Political Parties: Social Change and Political Response* (New York: W. W. Norton, 1970).

5. Daniel Bell, *The Coming of Postindustrial Society* (New York: Basic Books, 1973) I have elaborated on implications of Bell's underlying argument for the American party and election system and contemporary U.S. politics generally in "The 1994 Congressional Elections: The Realignment Continues," *PSQ,* 110 (Spring 1995), pp. 3–10.

6. Lamar Alexander, *The Wall Street Journal,* December 24, 1996, p. A12.

7. I have criticized this dimension of the realignment literature in "Like Waiting For Godot: The Uselessness of Realignment for Understanding Change in Contemporary American Politics." I meant by the title not realignment as major transformation of the party and election system but realignment in the "critical elections" New Deal model. This paper, first presented to the 1989 meeting of the American Political Science Association in Atlanta. was subsequently published in *Polity,* 22 (Spring 1990), pp. 511–525; and in Byron E. Shafer, ed., *The End of Realignment? Atrophy of a Concept and Death of a Phenomenon* (Madison: University of Wisconsin Press, 1991), chap. 2.

8. See Kenneth Dautrich and Jennifer Necci Dineen, "Media Bias: What Journalists and the Public Say About It," *The Public Perspective* (October/November 1996), pp 7–10.

9. The argument that "civic America," or the country's "social capital," is in decline has been variously advanced by a number of observers, most prominently by Robert D. Putnam, "Bowling Alone: America's Declining Social Capital." *The Journal of Democracy,* 6 (January 1995), pp. 65–78; and in a series of articles. "The Strange Disappearance of Civic America," *The American Prospect* 29 (Winter 1996), pp. 34–48; "Tuning In, Tuning Out: The Strange Disappearance of Social Capital in America," *PS: Political Science and Politics* 28 (December 1995), pp. 664–683. My colleagues and I have examined these articles and relevant data and reached conclusions that differ sharply from Putnam's. See Ladd, "The Data Just Don't Show Erosion of America's 'Social Capital,'" *The Public Perspective* 7 (June/July 1996). pp. 1, 5–22; and related articles by other authors in this same issue.

10. A small proportion of respondents (for example, Mormons) really aren't Protestant or Catholic Christians, but most "other Christians" belong to new, nondenominational churches.

11. For a further discussion of the party identification data from the Roper Center/Media Studies Center surveys, see Kenneth Dautrich, "Partisan Instability in the 1996 Campaign," *The Public Perspective* (October/November 1996), pp. 52–54.

12. I have discussed gender differences in contemporary politics in a number of other publications. See, in particular, Everett C. Ladd, "Media Framing of the Gender Gap." in *Women, Media, and Politics,* Pippa Norris, ed. (New York: Oxford University Press, 1997), pp. 113–128.

Ideological Realignment in the U.S. Electorate

Alan I. Abramowitz and Kyle L. Saunders

Since the publication of *The American Voter* in 1960, political scientists have generally divided the factors that influence voting decisions and election outcomes into two types: short-term forces and long-term forces (Campbell et al. 1960; Converse 1966). Short-term forces include the issues, candidates, and conditions peculiar to a given election, while the most important long-term force is the distribution of party identification within the electorate. Campbell et al. (1960) found that party identification was far more stable than attitudes toward issues and candidates. As a result, party identification exerted a strong influence on individual voting decisions both directly and indirectly, through its influence on attitudes toward the candidates and issues.

More recent research has confirmed that party identification is more stable than other political attitudes (Abramson and Ostrom 1991; Converse and Markus 1979; Fiorina 1981; Jennings and Niemi 1981) and exerts a much stronger influence on these attitudes than they exert on party identification during the course of a single election campaign (Green and Palmquist 1990, 1994). Therefore, the distribution of party identification remains a key influence on the outcomes of elections in the United States.

For nearly 50 years following the Great Depression and the New Deal, the Democratic Party enjoyed a major electoral advantage over the Republican Party because far more Americans identified with the Democrats than with the Republicans. Since the early 1980s, however, the Democratic advantage in party identification has been shrinking. Despite the Democrats' victory in the 1992 presidential election, the difference between the percentage of Democratic and Republican identifiers in the electorate declined from 19 points in 1980 to 10 points in 1992 (Wayne 1996, 73).

Political scientists have long recognized that party identification has a dynamic component. Major realignments, or shifts in the partisan orientation of the electorate, have occurred periodically throughout American history, and these party realignments have been extensively described and analyzed by electoral scholars (Burnham 1970; Clubb, Flanigan, and Zingale 1980; Key 1955, 1959; Sundquist 1983). Some scholars have argued that realignments primarily involve the conversion of voters' party loyalties in response to changes in the issue context or the social and economic environment (Ladd with Hadley 1978). Other scholars have argued that realignments mainly involve the disproportionate mobilization of new or previously disenfranchised voters (Andersen 1979; Beck 1976; Campbell 1985; Carmines and Stimson 1989).

Source: Alan I. Abramowitz and Kyle L. Saunders, "Ideological Realignment in the U.S. Electorate," *Journal of Politics,* 60 (August 1998), pp. 634–649, 651–52.
Alan I. Abramowitz is the Alben W. Barkley professor of political science at Emory University. Kyle Saunders is a graduate student in political science at the same institution.

Critical elections are sometimes seen as harbingers of a partisan realignment. These critical elections, characterized by severe stresses to the political system resulting from some cataclysmic event such as the Civil War or the Great Depression, may set off a realignment of party loyalties that continues for several election cycles (Beck and Sorauf 1992; Burnham 1970; Key 1955, 1959; Sundquist 1983).

In light of realignment theory, however, it is difficult to explain the outcome of the 1994 elections. Confounding almost all of the experts, the Republican Party picked up 53 seats in the House of Representatives and 8 seats in the Senate to gain control of both chambers of Congress for the first time in forty years. In winning majorities in both the House and Senate for the first time since the Eisenhower administration, Republicans won majorities of Senate and House seats from the South for the first time since the end of Reconstruction. Furthermore, two years later Republicans retained control of both chambers, winning consecutive terms as the majority party for the first time since the 1928–30 election cycle.

The outcome of the 1994 election clearly reflected more than normal voter dissatisfaction with the performance of the president at midterm. Yet the social and economic situation of the nation seemed bereft of any of the factors normally associated with a critical election. There seemed to be no cataclysmic event that could have triggered such a dramatic change.

Given the existence of peace and prosperity, how can we explain the outcome of the 1994 election? We argue that 1994 was not a critical election in the traditional sense; rather, the Republican takeover of Congress was the culmination of a secular realignment that had been occurring for several election cycles prior to the momentous Republican victory. This secular realignment reflected the increased ideological polarization of the two major parties and fundamental changes in public perceptions of the parties during this period. Our findings show that even without a cataclysmic precipitating event, changes in the parties' issue stances can produce dramatic changes in the distribution of party loyalties over the course of several election cycles.

THEORY: IDEOLOGICAL REALIGNMENT

Political scientists have discovered that partisan identification can be affected by a variety of short-term factors. This research has demonstrated that party identification at the individual level can be influenced by presidential vote choice (Markus and Converse 1979) as well as retrospective evaluations of party performance (Fiorina 1981; MacKuen, Erikson, and Stimson 1989). However, neither of these factors would seem to offer a satisfactory explanation for long-term shifts in the distribution of partisan identification within the electorate, as neither has consistently favored one party or the other.

The inability of either retrospective evaluations or presidential vote choice to explain long-term shifts in the party loyalties of the electorate leads us to consider a third explanatory variable: policy preferences. A considerable body of research has demonstrated that party identification can be influenced by policy preferences (Carmines, McIver, and Stimson 1987; Franklin 1992; Franklin and Jackson 1983; Luskin, McIver, and Carmines 1989; Page and Jones 1979). Although none of these studies attempted to explain long-term shifts in the distribution of partisanship, their findings imply that changes in the parties' policy stands or the salience of these policy stands could, over the course of several election cycles, alter the distribution of party loyalties in the electorate as individuals respond to these changes by bringing their party loyalties into line with their policy preferences.

We will demonstrate that the Republican victories in the 1994 and 1996 congressional elections reflected a long-term shift in the relative strength and bases of support of the two major parties and that this shift in the party loyalties of the electorate was in turn based on the increased ideological polarization of the Democratic and Republican parties during the Reagan and post-Reagan eras. Clearer differences between the parties' ideological positions made it easier for citizens to choose a party identification based on their policy preferences. The result has been a secular realignment of party loyalties along ideological lines.

The election of Ronald Reagan, the most prominent leader of the American conservative movement, resulted in a marked increase in ideological polarization among party leaders and activists in the United States (Stone, Rapoport, and Abramowitz 1990). Reagan's program of tax cuts, increased military expenditures, and reductions in domestic social programs divided the nation along ideological lines and produced the highest levels of party unity in Congress in decades. Liberal Republicans and conservative Democrats found themselves under increasing pressure to follow the party line on key votes. Some went along with their party's leadership at the risk of losing support in their own constituencies. Others switched parties or retired. The result was an increasingly liberal Democratic Party and an increasingly conservative Republican Party (Rohde 1991).

The results of the 1992 elections accelerated the movement toward ideological polarization. Although he campaigned as a "new Democrat" rather than traditional liberal, Bill Clinton moved quickly to reward liberal interest groups that had supported his candidacy by announcing policies such as permitting gay and lesbians to serve openly in the military and ending the ban on abortion counseling in federally funded health care clinics. The president further antagonized conservatives with his proposals to raise taxes on middle- and upper-income Americans and dramatically expand the role of the federal government in providing health insurance (Quirk and Hinchliffe 1996).

The actions of the Republican Party in the House of Representatives may have contributed even more to ideological polarization in the 1990s than President Clinton's policies. At the beginning of the 103rd Congress (1993–95), House Republicans chose Representative Newt Gingrich of Georgia as their minority whip. The election of Gingrich as the minority whip and heir apparent to Minority Leader Robert Michel (R-Illinois) reflected a long-term shift in the distribution of power within the House GOP. The older, relatively moderate wing of the party, based in the Midwest and the Northeast, and represented by accommodationist leaders such as

Michel, was gradually losing influence to a younger, more conservative wing, based in the South, and represented by leaders such as Gingrich who preferred confrontation to accommodation in dealing with the Democrats (Wilcox 1995).

The 1994 election campaign was a direct result of the Republican leadership changes in the 103rd Congress. The Contract with America, a compendium of conservative issue positions chosen for maximum public appeal, was the brainchild of Newt Gingrich and Richard Armey (R-Texas), another hard-line conservative and Gingrich's top lieutenant. They decided what issues to include in the Contract, and they persuaded the overwhelming majority of Republican House candidates to publicly endorse its contents. The result was one of the most unified and ideological campaigns in the history of U.S. midterm elections: Republican candidates across the country ran as members of a party team committed to enacting a broad legislative program (Gimpel 1996; Wilcox 1995).

One of the conditions for a party realignment is the emergence of party leaders who take sharply contrasting positions on the realigning issue or issues (Sundquist 1983, chap. 3). In order to choose a party based on issue positions, voters must recognize the differences between the parties' positions. We believe that the increased ideological polarization of Democratic and Republican party leaders and activists since 1980, and especially since 1992, has made it easier for voters to recognize the differences between the parties' positions and to choose a party based on its proximity to their own ideological position. The result has been an ideological realignment of party loyalties among the electorate—a realignment that contributed to the Republican takeover of Congress in 1994.

In order to demonstrate that an ideological realignment has taken place in the U.S. electorate since the late 1970s, we will present evidence showing that:

1. Since 1980, there has been a gradual increase in the proportion of Republican identifiers and a corresponding decrease in the proportion of Democratic identifiers in the electorate. While this shift in party loyalties has been gradual, it has resulted in a substantial reduction in the size of the Democratic advantage in party identification.

2. Republican gains have been very uneven among different groups of voters. The largest gains have occurred among groups with conservative policy preferences, such as white males and white southerners.

3. There has been a substantial intergenerational shift in party identification in favor of the GOP—today's voters are considerably more Republican and less Democratic than were their parents.

4. The largest intergenerational differences are found among those groups with conservative policy preferences, such as white males and white southerners, and among voters of relatively high socioeconomic status.

5. Since 1980, and especially since 1992, voters have become more aware of differences between the parties' issue positions.

6. Because they are more aware of differences between the parties' issue positions, voters in the 1990s are more likely to choose a party identification based on issue positions than were voters before 1980.

DATA

The study reported here is based upon survey data collected in the American National Election Studies (NES) between 1976 and 1994, including the 1992–94 panel survey. These datasets contain measures of partisan identification, parental partisan identification, policy preferences, perceptions of party positions on policy issues, socioeconomic status, and other social background characteristics.

We chose 1976 as the beginning date of our study to establish a baseline that allows us to measure the effects of the so-called Reagan Revolution and other polarizing forces that may have affected partisanship during the 1980s and 1990s. The study concludes with the Republican takeover of the House and Senate in the 1994 elections.

Many of the analyses that we report in this paper utilize data from the 1978 and 1994 election studies. There are two major reasons for this. First, the 1978 and 1994 studies included identical questions concerning respondents' policy preferences and their perceptions of the parties' positions. This makes it possible to compare respondents' awareness of party differences at the beginning and end of the time period of interest in our study. In addition, midterm elections may provide more accurate measures of the underlying partisan identification of the electorate than presidential elections. In presidential election years, strong positive or negative responses to the presidential candidates can result in substantial short-term fluctuations in the distribution of party identification (MacKuen, Erikson, and Stimson 1989).

In examining trends in party identification between 1976 and 1994, we have attempted to minimize the effects of short-term fluctuations in party identification by combining data from adjacent presidential and midterm elections that form a single election cycle. Thus, data from the 1976 and 1978 elections are combined to form a single data point, as are data from the 1980–82, 1984–86, 1988–90, and 1992–94 election cycles.

RESULTS

Trends in Partisanship

Since the New Deal realignment of the 1930s, Democrats have held an advantage in partisan identification. This advantage has manifested itself in almost continuous control of the Senate and House of Representatives since 1952. We have hypothesized, however, that the Democratic advantage in voter identification has decreased significantly since the end of the 1970s. Figure 1 presents data bearing on this hypothesis.

Figure 1 shows the trend in party identification over five election cycles, combining each presidential election with the subsequent midterm election, from 1976–78 to 1992–94. Over this time period, the proportion of Democratic identifiers in the electorate has fallen from 54 percent to 48 percent while the percentage of Republican identifiers has risen from 32 percent to 41 percent. As a result of these

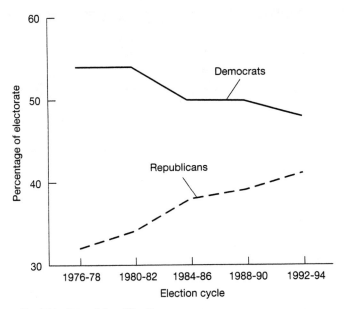

FIGURE 1 *Trend in Party Identification*

shifts, the Democratic advantage in voter identification was reduced by two-thirds: from 22 points in 1976–78 to only 7 points in 1992–94. These results strongly support our hypothesis.

The data in Figure 1 show a substantial decrease in the Democratic advantage in voter identification since the late 1970s. However, these data conceal the wide variation in the size of this shift across subgroups. Table 1 presents data on the party loyalties of several key groups within the electorate at the beginning and end of the time period of interest to our study.

TABLE 1 *Change in Party Identification among Subgroups between 1976–78 and 1992–94*

	Support for Democratic Party (%)			
	1976–78	*1992–94*	*Change*	*(n of cases)*
Blacks	93	90	–3	(442/500)
Whites	58	49	–9	(3,889/3,546)
Male	58	44	–14	(1,732/1,697)
Female	58	55	–3	(2,157/1,849)
North	56	51	–5	(2,946/2,570)
South	64	48	–16	(943/890)

Note: Support for Democratic Party is based on Democratic identifiers, including independent leaners, divided by combined total of Democratic and Republican identifiers.

Source: American National Election Studies, 1976–1994.

We have hypothesized that the largest shifts in party identification since the late 1970s have occurred among groups with conservative policy preferences, such as white males and white southerners. The data in Table 1 strongly support this hypothesis. While support for the Democratic Party in the entire electorate declined by 8 points, from 60 percent to 52 percent, support among white males declined by 14 points and support among white southerners plummeted 16 points.

The results of these trends were the emergence of a gender gap and a reversal of the traditional regional gap in party identification. In the late 1970s, white males and females supported the Democratic Party at identical rates. By the mid-1990s, white females were 11 points more Democratic than white males. Similarly, in the late 1970s, southern whites still identified with the Democratic Party at a higher rate than northern whites. By the mid-1990s, southern whites had become more Republican than their northern counterparts.

Intergenerational Change

According to students of political socialization, Americans generally learn their party identification from their parents during their preteen and adolescent years. Moreover, once formed, this party affiliation is usually resistant to change. The result is a high degree of continuity in party affiliation between generations (Campbell et al. 1960; Jennings and Niemi 1974). During a realigning era, however, this intergenerational continuity may be interrupted (Beck 1976). To the extent that citizens choose their party identification on the basis of current issues, the influence of parental partisanship should be attenuated.

In order to test for the occurrence of a partisan realignment since the late 1970s, we compared the party identification of survey respondents in 1994 with the recalled party identification of their parents when the respondents were growing up. We have hypothesized that the current generation of voters are more Republican than were their parents. Furthermore, we have hypothesized that the largest intergenerational shifts should be found among groups with conservative policy preferences, such as white males and white southerners, and among respondents of higher socioeconomic status. Table 2 presents data bearing on these hypotheses.

The data in Table 2 provide strong support for all of our hypotheses. The magnitude of the intergenerational shift toward the Republican Party is especially impressive considering that this sort of recall data is likely to underestimate change. There was a net gain of 13 points in Republican identification in the overall electorate, representing a major shift toward the Republican Party between generations. However, the pro-Republican shift was much larger among several subgroups: 22 points among upper-income whites, 24 points among white males, and 27 points among white southerners. White males were just as likely to report growing up in Democratic families as white females. In 1994, however, white males were 16 points more Republican than white females. Two-thirds of southern whites reported growing up in Democratic families. In 1994, however, three-fifths of these southern whites identified with the Republican Party. Thus, even though southern whites were much

TABLE 2   *Intergenerational Difference in Party Identification by Subgroups in 1994*

Group	Parents	Respondents	Difference	(n of cases)
	Support for Democratic Party (%)			
Overall	65	52	–13	(723)
Blacks	95	91	–4	(85)
Whites	61	46	–15	(597)
North	57	49	–8	(420)
South	68	41	–27	(177)
Male	62	38	–24	(294)
Female	60	54	–6	(303)
High School	63	54	–9	(261)
College	59	42	–17	(318)
Lower Income	65	67	+2	(122)
Middle Income	58	43	–15	(281)
Upper Income	59	37	–22	(160)

Note: Support for Democratic Party is based on Democratic identifiers, including independent leaners, divided by combined total of Democratic and Republican identifiers.

Source: 1992–94 American National Election Study Panel Survey.

more likely to report growing up in Democratic families than northern whites, by 1994 they were substantially more Republican in their party loyalties than northern whites.

Table 3 presents additional data on the movement toward the Republican Party by cross-tabulating respondent partisan identification with parental partisan identification in 1978 and 1994. In comparing the results from 1978 and 1994, we find little difference between respondents from Republican families. However, respondents from independent or Democratic families were much more likely to identify with the Republican Party in 1994 than in 1978. Whereas 73 percent of respondents with Democratic parents maintained their parents' Democratic legacy in 1978, only 65 percent followed their parents in 1994. While only 17 percent of respondents with Democratic parents had switched to the Republican Party in 1978, 29 percent had abandoned their parents' party affiliation and identified themselves as Republicans in 1994. At least among voters raised in Democratic families, the link between parental partisanship and party identification was considerably weaker in 1994 than in 1978.

Awareness of Party Differences

We have hypothesized that the connection between parental partisanship and party identification has weakened since the late 1970s because of the increasing importance of ideology. According to this hypothesis, with the growing polarization of the parties in the Reagan and post-Reagan eras, voters are more likely to choose a party identification based on their policy preferences, because they are more likely to recognize the differences between the parties' positions. As a result, many conservative whites who were raised as Democrats have moved into the Republican camp.

TABLE 3   *Party Identification by Parental Party Identification in 1978 and 1994*

	Parental Party Identification					
	Democratic		*None or Independent*		*Republican*	
Respondent Party Identification	*1978*	*1994*	*1978*	*1994*	*1978*	*1994*
Democratic	73%	65%	44%	38%	23%	23%
Independent	10	6	24	15	12	7
Republican	17	29	32	47	65	70
Total	100%	100%	100%	100%	100%	100%
(n of cases)	(1,136)	(353)	(559)	(179)	(549)	(191)

Source: 1978 American National Election Study and 1992–94 American National Election Study Panel Survey.

In order to test our hypothesis of growing awareness of ideological differences between the parties, we compared respondents' awareness of party differences on four issues (overall liberalism–conservatism, government responsibility for jobs and living standards, private vs. government health insurance, and government aid to blacks) in 1978, 1988, and 1994. These were the only years in which respondents were asked to place the parties on all four issues. Table 4 presents data bearing on this hypothesis.

The data in Table 4 strongly support our hypothesis of increasing public awareness of party differences. Respondents in the 1994 NES were much more likely to recognize the differences between the parties' positions on these four issues than respondents in the 1978 NES. Respondents in the 1988 NES fell between the 1978 and 1994 respondents on our measure of ideological awareness. In 1978, 59 percent of respondents were unable to differentiate between the parties' positions on more than one of the four issues; by 1994, only 37 percent of respondents displayed this

TABLE 4   *Awareness of Party Issue Differences in 1978, 1988, and 1994*

Awareness of Party Issue Differences	*1978*	*1988*	*1994*
Low (0–1)	59%	49%	37%
Moderate (2–3)	25	30	32
High (4)	16	21	32
Total	100%	100%	100%
(n of cases)	(2,304)	(2,040)	(1,795)

Source: 1978, 1988, and 1994 American National Election Studies.

level of ignorance of ideological differences. At the same time, the proportion of respondents who achieved a perfect score (4) doubled, from 16 percent in 1978 to 32 percent in 1994.

We have demonstrated that respondents were much more aware of differences between the parties' issue positions in 1994 than in 1978. But did this increased awareness of party differences lead to a closer connection between ideology and party identification? In order to address this question, we compared the correlations between party identification and ideology in 1978 and 1994 while controlling for awareness of party differences. The results of this comparison are presented in Table 5.

The data in Table 5 show that among all respondents the correlation between ideology and party identification increased dramatically between 1978 and 1994—going from .23 to .42. Furthermore, much of this increase was due to increased awareness of ideological differences between the parties. Among respondents with little or no awareness of party differences, there was no relationship between ideology and party identification in either year. However, this group made up a much larger proportion of the entire electorate in 1978 than in 1994.

Ideology and Partisan Change

Given increased awareness of ideological differences between the parties, the increase over time in the correlation between ideology and party identification could have been caused either by voters choosing a party identification based on their ideology (ideological realignment), or by voters shifting their ideological stance to bring it into line with their party identification (partisan persuasion). It is important to know which of these two processes was at work during the 1980s and 1990s.

We have already presented strong evidence of Republican gains in party identification in the overall electorate and especially in subgroups with conservative policy preferences, such as white males and white southerners, between 1978 and 1994. These shifts in the aggregate distribution of party identification are consistent with the ideological realignment hypothesis. However, in order to compare the relative importance of ideological realignment and partisan persuasion at the individual level,

TABLE 5   *Correlations between Party Identification and Ideology by Awareness of Party Differences in 1978 and 1994*

Awareness of Party Differences	1978	1994	(n of cases)
Low (0–1)	.06	.06	(1,295/579)
Moderate (2–3)	.37	.40	(568/544)
High (4)	.48	67	(361/589)
All Respondents	.23	.42	(2,224/1,712)

Note. Entries shown are Kendall's tau-b.

Source: 1978 and 1994 American National Election Studies.

we performed a path analysis, using data from the 1992–94 NES panel survey to compare the influence of 1992 ideology on 1994 party identification with the influence of 1992 party identification on 1994 ideology. We also performed a separate path analysis for ideologically sophisticated respondents because we would expect to find the strongest evidence of either ideological realignment or partisan persuasion among this group. The results of the path analyses are presented in Figure 2.

The results in Figure 2 show that among all panel respondents, and especially among ideologically sophisticated respondents, ideology was more stable than party identification; furthermore, the influence of 1992 ideology on 1994 party identification was much stronger than the influence of 1992 party identification on 1994 ideology. These results provide strong support for the ideological realignment hypothesis: the increase in the correlation between ideology and party identification between

FIGURE 2   *Path Analyses of Ideology and Party Identification in 1992–94 Panel Survey*

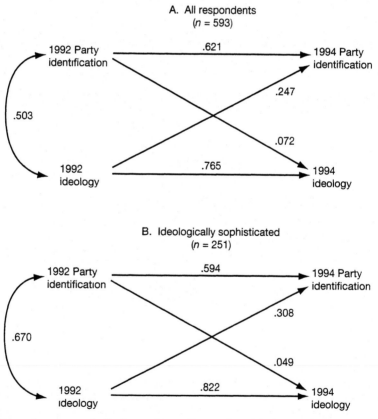

Note: Entries shown are standardized regression coefficients. Curved double-headed arrows represent correlation coefficients.

1992 and 1994 (from .50 to .58 among all respondents and from .67 to .75 among ideologically sophisticated respondents) was due almost entirely to respondents bringing their party identification into line with their prior ideological preference.

We have demonstrated that citizens were much more aware of differences between the parties' issue positions in 1994 than in 1978. But were they also more likely to choose their party identification on the basis of these issues, and does this explain Republican gains in voter identification? In order to address these questions, we compared the relationship between party identification and ideology for 1978 and 1994 among respondents raised by Democratic parents. The data are presented in Table 6.

The data presented in Table 6 show a stark contrast between the influence of ideology on party identification in 1978 and 1994. Liberals raised in Democratic families were just as loyal to the Democratic Party in 1994 as in 1978. For conservatives, however, the story was dramatically different. In 1978, conservatives raised by Democratic parents favored the Democrats over the Republicans by a 56 percent to 32 percent margin. In contrast, in 1994, conservatives raised by Democratic parents preferred the GOP over the Democrats by an overwhelming 63 percent to 28 percent margin. These data demonstrate that the intergenerational shift toward the Republican Party was based largely on ideology. Conservatives raised by Democratic parents were abandoning the party of their fathers and mothers and flocking to the GOP.

Liberals raised by Republican parents were also abandoning the party of their fathers and mothers: in 1994, 54 percent of these respondents indicated a preference for the Democratic Party while only 39 percent remained loyal to the GOP. However, this group was only about half the size of the group of conservatives raised by Democratic parents. Therefore, the net result of this intergenerational movement was a substantial increase in Republican identification in the electorate.

The results presented thus far indicate that the growing influence of ideology resulted in a weakening of the connection between parental partisanship and party

TABLE 6   *Party Identification by Ideology in 1978 and 1994, Respondents with Democratic Parents*

| | Ideology | | | | | |
| | Liberal | | Moderate | | Conservative | |
Party Identification	1978	1994	1978	1994	1978	1994
Democratic	85%	85%	78%	68%	56%	28%
Independent	9	5	10	6	12	10
Republican	6	10	13	26	32	63
Total	100%	100%	101%	100%	100%	101%
(n of cases)	(393)	(146)	(428)	(116)	(295)	(90)

Source: 1978 American National Election Study and 1992–94 American National Election Study Panel Survey.

TABLE 7   *The Effects of Parental Partisanship and Ideology on Party Identification in 1978 and 1994*

Independent Variable	1978	1994
Parental Partisanship	.531*	.397*
	(.024)	(.044)
Ideology	.115*	.197*
	(.009)	(.015)

Note: Entries shown are unstandardized regression coefficients with corresponding standard errors. Based on multiple regression analyses including age, gender, education, family income, race, and region as control variables.

*p < .001

Source: 1978 American National Election Study and 1992–94 American National Election Study Panel Survey.

identification in the electorate. In order to provide a more definitive test of this hypothesis, however, we conducted parallel multiple regression analyses, using data from the 1978 and 1994 election studies, with the 7-point party identification scale as the dependent variable. The independent variables in the regression analyses were the ideology scale and parental partisanship. Age, gender, education, family income, race, and region (South vs. non-South) were included in the regression analyses as control variables. The results of these regression analyses are presented in Table 7. For clarity of presentation, we have excluded the coefficients for the control variables from this table.

The data presented in Table 7 strongly support our hypothesis concerning the changes in the influence of ideology and parental partisanship between 1978 and 1994. The unstandardized regression coefficients in this table indicate that the influence of parental partisanship was about 25 percent weaker in 1994 than in 1978, while the influence of ideology was almost 75 percent stronger in 1994 than in 1978. Based on these results, it appears that voters in 1994 were less likely to maintain the party identification of their parents and more likely to choose a party identification based on their own policy preferences.

DISCUSSION AND CONCLUSIONS

The dramatic Republican victory in the 1994 midterm election and the reelection of a Republican Congress in 1996 reflected a long-term shift in the party loyalties of the U.S. electorate. Since the late 1970s, the electorate has undergone a secular realignment. As a result of this realignment, the advantage in voter identification that the Democratic Party enjoyed from the 1930s through the 1970s has been drastically reduced. Today's voters are considerably less inclined to identify with the Democratic Party than voters in the 1960s and 1970s. They are also considerably less likely to identify with the Democratic Party than were their own parents.

Republican gains in party identification since the late 1970s have varied widely across subgroups of the electorate. In general, GOP gains have been greatest among members of groups with conservative policy preferences, such as white males and white southerners. GOP gains have been much smaller among blacks, northern whites, and white females. Southern whites, whose parents overwhelmingly supported the Democratic Party, are now one of the most Republican segments of the electorate. College-educated and upper-income whites are also much more Republican than were their parents.

We have presented evidence in this study that the secular realignment of the electorate since the late 1970s was based largely on ideology. Although past research has shown that individuals can shift their party identification based on their policy preferences (Franklin and Jackson 1983; Page and Jones 1979), the overall distribution of partisanship in the electorate has been seen as highly stable except during periods of extreme social or economic distress (Green and Palmquist 1990, 1994). However, our findings show that even without a cataclysmic precipitating event, changes in the parties' issue stances can produce dramatic changes in the distribution of party loyalties over the course of several election cycles.

Our theory of ideological realignment has much in common with Carmines and Stimson's (1989) theory of "issue evolution." However, we disagree with Carmines and Stimson concerning both the timing of this realignment and the role played by racial issues. Carmines and Stimson argue that the process of realignment was set off by the growing polarization of the parties on the issue of civil rights during the 1960s; we argue that this process did not begin until the 1980s and that civil rights was only one of a host of issues involved in the realignment (see Abramowitz 1994).

The increasing ideological polarization of the Democratic and Republican Parties in the Reagan and post-Reagan eras made it easier for voters to recognize the differences between the parties' policy stands. As a result, voters have been choosing their party identification on the basis of their policy preferences rather than maintaining the party allegiance that they inherited from their parents. Conservatives who were raised by Democratic or independent parents have moved dramatically toward the Republican Party.

Our results show that the issue-based model of partisanship is the best explanation for changes that have occurred over the past few election cycles. The voting models (Markus and Converse 1979) would have predicted that the Democrats would have been assisted by the Clinton victory in the 1992 presidential election, but the Democrats continued to decline in 1994. The retrospective evaluation theory (Fiorina 1981; MacKuen, Erikson, and Stimson 1989) would have predicted that the 1991 recession and the poor performance evaluations that George Bush received from the public would have signaled the end of any Republican realignment, but the Republicans continued their secular advance after 1992.

The secular realignment of party loyalties since 1980 has not produced a new majority party in the U.S. Even in 1994, Democratic identifiers slightly outnumbered Republican identifiers. Moreover, there is no guarantee that the electorate will continue to move toward the Republicans. It is even possible that the Democrats will regain some of the ground that they have lost. However, the data presented in this study suggest that the era of Democratic domination of Congress is over. A new era of intense party competition for control of Congress as well as the White House has begun.

REFERENCES

Abramowitz, Alan I. 1994. "Issue Evolution Reconsidered: Racial Attitudes and Partisanship in the U.S. Electorate." *American Journal of Political Science* 38(1): 1–24.

Abramson, Paul R., and Charles W. Ostrom. 1991. "Macropartisanship: An Empirical Reassessment." *American Political Science Review* 85(1): 181–92.

Andersen, Kristi. 1979. *The Creation of a Democratic Majority, 1928–1936.* Chicago: University of Chicago Press.

Beck, Paul A. 1976. "Youth and the Politics of Realignment." In *Political Opinion and Behavior,* ed. E. C. Dreyer and W. A. Rosenbaum. Belmont, CA: Wadsworth Publishing.

Beck, Paul Allen, and Frank J. Sorauf. 1992. *Party Politics in America.* 7th ed. New York: Harper-Collins.

Burnham, Walter D. 1970. *Critical Elections and the Mainsprings of American Politics.* New York: W. W. Norton.

Campbell, Angus, Philip E. Converse, Warren E. Miller, and Donald E. Stokes. 1960. *The American Voter.* New York: John Wiley and Sons.

Campbell, James E. 1985. "Sources of the New Deal Realignment: The Contributions of Conversion and Mobilization to Partisan Change." *Western Political Quarterly* 38(3): 357–76.

Carmines, Edward G., John P. McIver, and James A. Stimson. 1987. "Unrealized Partisanship: A Theory of Dealignment." *Journal of Politics* 49(2): 376–400.

Carmines, Edward G., and James A. Stimson. 1989. *Issue Evolution: Race and the Transformation of American Politics.* Princeton: Princeton University Press.

Clubb, Jerome M., William H. Flanigan, and Nancy H. Zingale. 1980. *Partisan Realignment: Voters, Parties, and Government in American History.* Beverly Hills, CA: Sage Publications.

Converse, Philip E. 1966. "The Concept of a Normal Vote." In *Elections and the Political Order,* ed. Angus Campbell, Philip E. Converse, Warren E. Miller, and Donald E. Stokes. New York: John Wiley and Sons.

Converse, Philip E., and Gregory B. Markus. 1979. "Plus Ça Change: The New CPS Election Study Panel." *American Political Science Review* 73(1): 32–49.

Fiorina, Morris P. 1981. *Retrospective Voting in American National Elections.* New Haven: Yale University Press.

Franklin, Charles H. 1992. "Measurement and the Dynamics of Party Identification." *Political Behavior* 14(3): 297–310.

Franklin, Charles H., and John E. Jackson. 1983. "The Dynamics of Party Identification." *American Political Science Review* 77(4): 957–73.

Gimpel, James G. 1996. *Fulfilling the Contract: The First 100 Days.* Boston: Allyn and Bacon.

Green, Donald P., and Bradley Palmquist. 1990. "Of Artifacts and Partisan Instability." *American Journal of Political Science* 34(3): 872–901.

Green, Donald P., and Bradley Palmquist. 1994. "How Stable is Party Identification?" *Political Behavior* 16(4): 437–66.

Jennings, M. Kent, and Richard G. Niemi. 1974. *The Political Character of Adolescence.* Princeton: Princeton University Press.

Jennings, M. Kent, and Richard G. Niemi. 1981. *Generations and Politics.* Princeton: Princeton University Press.

Key, V. O., Jr. 1955. "A Theory of Critical Elections." *Journal of Politics* 17(1): 3–18.

Key, V. O. 1959. "Secular Realignment and the Party System." *Journal of Politics* 21(1): 198–210.

Ladd, Everett C., with Charles Hadley. 1978. *Transformations of the American Party System.* 2d ed. New York: W. W. Norton.

Luskin, Robert C., John P. McIver, and Edward G. Carmines. 1989. "Issues and the Transmission of Partisanship." *American Journal of Political Science* 33(2): 440–58.

MacKuen, Michael B., Robert S. Erikson, and James A. Stimson. 1989. "Macropartisanship." *American Political Science Review* 83(4): 1125–42.

Markus, Gregory B., and Philip E. Converse. 1979. "A Dynamic Simultaneous Equation Model of Electoral Choice." *American Political Science Review* 73(4): 1055–70.

Page, Benjamin I., and Calvin C. Jones. 1979. "Reciprocal Effects of Policy Preferences, Party Loyalties, and the Vote." *American Political Science Review* 73(4): 1071–89.

Quirk, Paul J., and Joseph Hinchcliffe. 1996. "Domestic Policy: The Trials of a Centrist Democrat." In *The Clinton Presidency: First Appraisals,* ed. Colin Campbell and Bert A. Rockman. Chatham, NJ: Chatham House.

Rohde, David W. 1991. *Parties and Leaders in the Postreform House.* Chicago: University of Chicago Press.

Stone, Walter J., Ronald B. Rapoport, and Alan I. Abramowitz. 1990. "The Reagan Revolution and Party Polarization in the 1980s." In *The Parties Respond,* ed. L. Sandy Maisel. Boulder, CO: Westview Press.

Sundquist, James L. 1983. *Dynamics of the Party System: Alignment and Realignment of Political Parties in the United States.* Rev. ed. Washington, DC: Brookings Institution.

Wayne, Stephen J. 1996. *The Road to the White House 1996.* New York: St. Martin's Press.

Wilcox, Clyde. 1995. *The Latest American Revolution? The 1994 Elections and Their Implications for Governance.* New York: St. Martin's Press.

The Passing of Realignment and the Advent of the "Base-Less" Party System

Daniel M. Shea

INTRODUCTION

Nearly half a century has passed since V. O. Key introduced students of American politics to critical realignment theory. At its core, this model holds that changes in the party system imply a good deal more than "new periods." Realignment theory posits important, long-term shifts in the partisan cleavages among the electorate and, accordingly, the balance of power within government. To Burnham, these events represent the "mainsprings" of American governance; something that snaps the political process back to its popular roots and forces the system to respond to the needs of average citizens. It is "a mode of behavior by which the electorate seeks to exercise its sovereignty over government" (Burnham 1970, p. 183).

This article examines the prospects of critical realignment given the turn party organizations have taken in the last two decades. The first section confronts the persistence of dealignment. Contrary to a number of studies, here it is argued that the dominant characteristic of American politics remains an unanchored electorate. Next, conventional explanations for the stubbornness of postalignment politics are rejected in favor of placing the burden on party organizations. Beginning in the 1970s, party organizations pointed in a new direction, focusing efforts on raising ever-larger sums of money and providing candidates cutting-edge services. They have become highly effective short-term service agents of the candidates. This shift has transformed the nucleus of party activities from better linkages with voters to greater assistance to candidates. Although candidates appreciate the new focus, "service-oriented" parties contribute to the movement away from partisan attachments and, in turn, the possibility of any realignment. The final section charts a few possible consequences of the seventh party era, referred to as the "base-less party" system.

THE PERSISTENCE OF DEALIGNMENT

The mid to late 1960s had many of the markings of a traditional realignment. It was on track with the generational change view of political eras (every 36 or so years) and

Source: Daniel M. Shea, "The Passing of Realignment and the Advent of the 'Base-Less' Party System," *American Politics Quarterly,* 27 (January 1999), pp. 33–57. Copyright © 1999 by Sage Publications. Reprinted by permission of Sage Publications, Inc.

Daniel M. Shea is assistant professor of government at Lafayette College and co-editor of *The State of the Parties.*

marked a shift in voter preferences for GOP presidential candidates. The South moved away from Democratic presidential candidates beginning in 1964, and in earnest 4 years later. Carmines and Stimson (1989) suggest the late 1960s marked a realigning period because Democrats became less tied to their Southern segregationist wing, the South became more Republican, and African-Americans became solidly Democratic. Reflecting on Nixon's win in 1968, Miller and Shanks (1996) write: "For the first time since systematic, modern measurement had dominated social scientific analysis of electoral behavior, the bedrock of party identification cracked" (p. 153).

But it was surely an incomplete realignment, if it was one at all. The House of Representatives remained in Democratic control from 1933 until 1995, with the brief exceptions of 1947–1949 and 1953–1955. The Senate followed a similar pattern, adding 1981–1987. In fact, the proportion of House and Senate Democrats declined only modestly in the 1960s. Most governorships and state legislatures, as well as most municipal offices, remained in Democratic hands. Only 19 percent of state legislative chambers were controlled by the GOP in 1966; a decade later, this figure actually drops to 14 percent.[1] Watergate had an effect throughout the 1970s, perhaps stunting GOP gains, but at no time during the decade—or in the 1980s for that matter—did the GOP come close to controlling most state legislative chambers. As for the "Southern realignment," there was undoubtedly a movement toward the GOP among party identifiers, but there was *also* a precipitous increase of independents (Beck 1999). Non-Southern Republican identifiers were no more common in the 1960s, 1970s, or 1980s than they were in the 1950s. As noted in Table 1, the number of self-identified Republicans nationwide actually dropped from about 30 percent in 1960 to about 22 percent in 1974. Finally, according to National Election Study (NES) data, ticket splitting between U.S. House and presidential candidates doubled between 1962 and 1972, going from 15 percent to 30 percent.

Several indicators suggest the early 1980s marked a sea change in American politics. Reagan came into office with a much different view of government, the Senate changed hands to a Republican majority, and the GOP made substantial gains in the House. There was a breakdown of the New Deal coalition with, for example, most blue-collar workers supporting Reagan in 1980 and 1984. The number of Republican identifiers grew a bit during this period, going from about 22 percent in 1978 to 28 percent 10 years later—as did the number of voters considering themselves "conservative" (Miller & Shanks 1996, Chap. 7). But the realignment was again incomplete: The number of Democrats in the House in 1978 (64%) increased to 71 percent by 1982, and then leveled off for the next 10 years at about 66 percent. Nor was there a dramatic change at the state legislative level, with most chambers remaining solidly Democratic. By the end of the 1980s, the number of state governments controlled by Republicans was nearly at an all-time low. Gains in Republican identification did not mean the GOP had become the majority party, even in the South (Miller & Shanks 1996, p. 166). Though Reagan was reelected in a landslide in 1984, the GOP lost the Senate 2 years later.

Perhaps the strongest case can be made for a critical realignment in the early 1990s. The Republican sweep into the House and Senate in 1994 marked a dramatic transformation, and few would dispute Burnham's (1996) claim that it was a "very

TABLE 1   Changes in Party Identification: Dealignment Continues, 1952–1998

	Gallup Surveys			National Election Studies		
	Democrat	Republican	Independent	Democrat	Republican	Independent
1952	51	29	20	47	28	23
1956	44	35	21	44	29	23
1958	—	—	—	49	28	19
1960	47	29	24	45	30	23
1962	—	—	—	46	28	21
1964	52	25	23	52	25	23
1966	—	—	—	46	25	28
1968	42	28	30	45	25	30
1970	—	—	—	44	26	31
1972	40	28	32	41	23	35
1974	—	—	—	39	22	37
1976	48	24	28	40	25	37
1978	—	—	—	29	22	38
1980	36	32	31	41	25	34
1982	—	—	—	44	24	30
1984	39	35	27	37	27	34
1986	—	—	—	40	26	33
1988	36	32	31	36	28	36
1990	—	—	—	36	28	36
1992	—	—	—	36	25	37
1993	36	30	32	—	—	—
1994	—	—	—	34	30	34
1995	28	31	37	—	—	—
1996	—	—	—	39	28	34
1997	31	29	33	—	—	—
1998	38	28	34	—	—	—

NOTE. M-dashes indicate that data were unavailable for that year.

Sources: Gallup Surveys, 1952–1998. Text of the question: "In politics, as of today, do you consider yourself a Republican, a Democrat, or an independent?"

National Election Study data, 1952–1996. Text of question: "Generally speaking, do you usually think of yourself as a Republican, a Democrat, an Independent, or what?"

big event indeed" (p. 370). Ten percent of House incumbents were thrown from office—a hefty number compared to prior years—and every one was a Democrat. In open seat House races, Republicans won 21 out of 31 contests, and the election marked the first time that the GOP held a majority of southern House seats. Many GOP House candidates carried with them into office a distinct policy plan—the *Contract With America*—and although most voters were unfamiliar with the document, survey evidence indicated a growing rejection of government as a preferred means to solve problems (Ladd 1997, pp. 5–10). Republican gains were also quite impressive at the state and local level: Before the election, Republicans controlled just 31 state legislative chambers; after it, they controlled 50 (1 is nonpartisan and 2 were deadlocked). They won 24 of 36 gubernatorial races. Finally, 2 years later, during the 1996 presidential race, ticket splitting had reached its lowest level since 1968.

Once more, however, there are numerous countertrends. As noted in Table 1, Gallup findings suggest that aside from the Goldwater disaster of 1964 and the post-Watergate election of 1976, there are today perhaps fewer GOP identifiers than at any point since their polls were conducted. Even though the Republicans control more state legislative chambers than do the Democrats, overall there are still more Democratic legislators. The *Contract* appeared to be a catalyst for change, but most of its provisions, especially those dealing with substantive policy choices, went no further than the House. The voters were apparently not completely sold on the Republican agenda and sent Bill Clinton back to the White House. To be sure, Republican leadership has been quite willing to set a middle-of-the-road course. As noted by *The New York Times* reporter Alison Mitchell (1998), "Three years after sweeping into office on their *Contract With America*, House Republicans are acting as if they now have a contract with their campaign consultants: to keep the revolution on hold" (p. A14). Perhaps GOP leaders are adept at reading public opinion polls, which suggested that although conservative positions were often popular, "radical" Republicanism was not. More government might be a bad thing, but that does not mean there should be markedly less (Ladd 1997).

What we are left with, then, is a complex list of trends and countertrends. Seeking a satisfactory middle ground, some scholars rely on a secular realignment explanation, but even here important modifiers are used. Paul Beck (1999), for instance, suggests the "uniqueness" of this secular transformation: "First, a more even balance in electoral strength between the two major parties than the nation has seen in the last century and, second, a more substantial portion of the electorate who can be said to be dealigned than probably ever before." Others draw a focus on increased levels of GOP identification among Southerners and young Americans. For example, Miller and Shanks devote an entire chapter of their impressive recent work (1996, Chap. 7) to suggest realignment-like changes have indeed occurred. Their silver bullet is a cohort analysis, which clearly demonstrates generational differences in party identification. However, their analysis of voting behavior—namely, the propensity of all voters, including the youngest, to split their vote choice—is less cogent. Another approach is to describe the events of the 1960s and 1970s as a dramatic turn away from the party system and consequently a realignment of different sorts (Blumenthal 1980; Burnham 1989, 1991). Aldrich and Niemi (1996) suggest a sixth party era began in the late 1960s, which they dub the "candidate-centered party system." Silbey (1990) goes one step further by submitting we have entered a "post-alignment" era. Still others hold firm to the Key/Burnham model, broadening it to compensate for growing nonpartisanship. Rhodes (1996) argues that the South has undergone a traditional, partisan-based realignment, but the rest of the nation has undergone a "punctuated change," where we have moved to a "post-party" state. Aldrich (1999) combines voter attitudes with changes in political elites and the conduct of politics in his model of realignment. He finds the late 1960s *and* the early 1990s are "critical" periods.

Although all these perspectives contribute to our understanding of recent politics, there is no escaping that the dominant characteristic of contemporary politics is an electorate unanchored—in a word, dealignment. Even for those citizens who declare an affiliation, which is a shrinking lot (Table 1), the attachment is becoming less meaningful. During the last presidential election, the Roper Center asked respondents two very similar party identification questions, one at the beginning and one at the end of the survey. Only 68 percent of partisan identifiers gave a consistent response to both questions. The same sort of mushiness was found in two waves of a panel study, 6 months apart (Ladd 1997, p. 15). What is more, the skepticism toward political parties as avenues for change has continued. In 1996, the National Opinion Research Center found that 85 percent of Americans believed PAC money had more influence on the parties than they did, an equal number said money bought a candidate's loyalty, and a whopping 82 percent thought "both parties are pretty much out of touch with the American people."

In the last presidential election, 24 percent of the electorate cast a ballot for a candidate of a different party than the House candidate they supported. Limiting the analysis to just the major party candidates, this figure is the lowest since 1968. Taken separately, this finding would encourage strong party advocates, even though the rate is more than double what it was during the 1950s. But there are a number of indicators suggesting this drop might be fleeting. As noted in Table 2, a majority of Americans typically split their vote choice. This is even true among voters who consider themselves to be a Democrat or a Republican. At first glance, the data might suggest a generational effect, with the youngest voters being less inclined to split-ticket vote.

TABLE 2   Split-Ticket Voting in 1996 (in percentages)

Social Group	Votes for Different Parties for President	Typically Votes Split Ticket	Typically Votes Straight Ticket	Very/Somewhat Likely to Vote for an Independent
Age				
18–29 years old	31	46	36	52
30–44 years old	59	65	27	41
45–59 years old	68	77	20	36
60+ years old	64	65	28	18
Education				
Less than high school	51	55	33	42
High school graduate	59	64	26	37
Some college	56	61	30	38
College graduate	59	68	25	32
Postgraduate	61	76	20	29
Party identification				
Republican	50	59	32	27
Democrat	51	56	37	29
Independent	74	84	9	58

Source: Survey by the Media Studies Center/Roper Center, February 1996. Text of question. "When voting in elections do you typically vote a straight ticket—that is for candidates of the same party, or do you typically split your ticket—that is vote for candidates from different parties? Have you always voted for the same party for president or have you voted for different parties for president? In 1996, how likely is it that you would vote for an independent candidate for president? Is it very likely, somewhat likely, not too likely, or not at all likely?" In Dougherty, Ladd, Wilber, and Zayachkiwsky (1996, p 190).

This would be a misunderstanding of the data: the reason why the youngest group scores lowest on the first three indicators in Table 2 is that these measures are predicated on having voted in a few elections. That only 31 percent of the respondents have voted for different parties for president is in large part because many have voted only in one election. The same can be said of the other two questions that examine "typical" voting choice. It is probably more illustrative that 52 percent of the youngest group are willing to vote for an independent.

Only 19 states had unified party control of the governorship and both legislative houses as of 1997. Of the 48 states that have a plural executive, only 8 had unified party control of these offices as of 1997. As Wattenberg (1998) writes,

> Fiorina sees a clear logic to outcomes such as the recent election of a Republican governor in Massachusetts and a Democratic governor in Alaska—namely that this is an easy way to counterbalance the long dominance of the other party in the state legislature. But what is the logic behind setting one part of the executive off against the other? (p. 230)

A governor is supposed to work with his or her lieutenant governor. Yet, of the 18 states that have separately elected lieutenant governors, only 10 were of the same party as the governor. Of the 43 states that elect a state attorney general, only 22 were of the same party as the governor. The same phenomena can be found at the municipal level.

Still another indication of a dealigned system is mounting interest in third-party candidates. Ross Perot's 19 percent showing in 1992 highlights this development, but it can be seen elsewhere. Collet and Hansen (1996) have found the number of third-party candidates for governor and Congress doubled from 1970 to 1994, and there has been an even more dramatic increase in the number of races with three, four, and five or more candidates. They also note that in one survey after another, roughly 65 percent of Americans would like to see viable third-party candidates join the act. A full 43 percent of respondents to a September 1995 CNN/*USA Today* poll thought it was "not too important" or "not at all important" for the president to be from one of the two major parties.

WHY DEALIGNMENT PERSISTS:
THE ADVENT OF SERVICE-ORIENTED PARTIES

Why has the American electorate remained dealigned, given its "ripeness" for a realignment since the 1970s? The most frequent explanation is that myriad forces have simply pushed voters away from parties. Failed presidencies, international frustrations, domestic turmoil, and the disruptive effects of civil rights protest, anti-Vietnam war demonstrations, and counterculture revolution pushed voters, especially those just entering the electorate, away from the party system. Their children, today's newest voters, were socialized to be nonpartisans. Ladd (1997) argues higher levels of education allow voters to "make political judgement independent of party cues," and "most Americans derive their political information from [the media,] a source that tends to discourage rather than encourage stable party loyalties" (p. 14). A related perspective is the candidate-centered view (Wattenberg 1991, among many others). Candidates have learned that they can run for office more effectively by downplaying their party affiliation—perhaps because voters have done the same. Consider that in his 57-minute nomination acceptance speech, Bill Clinton mentioned his own party by name only twice. Harry Truman, in very much the same political situation as Clinton, made reference to his party 27 times in 1948—in a speech less than half the length (Wattenberg 1998).

Traditional explanations of the growing neutrality toward party labels, and consequently the end of partisan-based realignments, are incomplete because they overlook the activities of party organizations. If anything, there is a mistaken belief that stronger party organizations are the product of growing partisanship in the electorate. The orientation of contemporary party organizations, what they do and seek to accomplish, is radically different than in the past. There has been a shift from community-based organizations to national, "service-oriented" units. This transformation has only exacerbated the public's disdain for party-politics, and consequently the inability of our system to realign.

The roots of the shift to service-oriented parties can be traced to the Republican National Committee (RNC) during the 1960s.[2] Headed by Ray C. Bliss and his "nuts and bolts" approach to party politics, the RNC began a concerted effort to raise money and to develop greater campaign prowess. During the 1970s, Bill Brock took GOP fundraising a step further with the refinement of direct mail, and on the Democratic side, Charles Manatt turned his organization to a similar path. The parties could once again be real players, they believed, by raising truckloads of money and by helping candidates. Ironically, this revitalization was occurring at the same time many journalists and scholars bemoaned the passing of party politics in America.

By the early 1980s, a growing chorus of scholars challenged the electorate-centered notion of party decay. The adjustments of Bliss, Brock, and Manatt had taken hold, and the parties were "responding." In the words of one team of scholars, "the phoenix has risen from the ashes" (Kayden & Mahe 1985, p. 3). It was becoming clear that American parties were "resilient creatures" (Bibby 1990, p. 27). Both parties were developing campaign-centered branch organizations, revamping their internal operations, and devising innovative ways to raise huge sums of cash. Additionally, the number of full-time party employees, the size of their operating budgets, their average financial contribution to individual candidates, and the range of services provided had vastly increased (Cotter, Gibson, Bibby, & Huckshorn 1984).

Even though the "revivalist perspective" challenged traditional wisdom, it was also clear that service-oriented party organizations were different. A flurry of works set their sights on redefining what parties were up to and how they might best be conceptualized. Leading the way was Arterton (1982) and his "Party as PACs" model, Frantzich's (1989) "service-vendor party," and perhaps most notably Herrnson's systematic reviews of the institutionalization of the parties' congressional committees during the 1980s (1988, 1990, 1994). Paralleling each other in many key aspects, these perspectives suggested that parties comprise a small group of elite campaign professionals that hold as their foremost goal raising ever-larger sums and becoming more technically advanced at campaigning. They have adopted "PAC politics" by serving as intermediaries between special interest groups and candidates. Although winning elections remained the most important outcome of party activity, "successful" parties are also those capable at aiding candidates with new-style elections.[3] After a period of decline, the parties had "attained a degree of institutional preeminence that they have never known before and [had] carved out a secure niche for themselves by virtue of their fundraising and campaign capabilities" (Price 1984, p. 297).

This transformation brought with it a collective sigh of relief because it was assumed the new focus would resonate throughout the political system. Among other things, there were hopes that the institutionalized party system would increase the cohesiveness of the party-in-government; increase the salience and importance of party cues in other areas of legislative politics; foster the development of a stronger, more nationally oriented sense of party identification among voters; lead to party-centered television commercials, radio advertisements, and press releases; strengthen the party's policy-based image; create a large group of new-style partisans—ones who were more committed to support a party than are traditional party identifiers; and make elections more competitive (see, for instance, Herrnson 1988, pp. 126–127).

After nearly two decades, the results are mixed. There have been modest improvements in some areas. For example, the number of citizens who believed that there is no significant difference between the two parties was roughly 45 percent throughout the 1960s. This percentage increased a bit in the 1970s, but by the 1980s and 1990s had lowered to about 40 percent (NES data). There has been an increase in party-line voting in Congress (Pomper 1998), apparently much related to the disappearance of conservative Southerners from the Democratic ranks and liberal Republicans from their roster (see also Kolodny 1999). There is also growing evidence that the ideological distinctiveness of the parties is growing (Jackson, Clayton, & Green 1999; Pomper 1999). It should be noted, however, that the latter two developments *might* be a product of declining turnout, something service-oriented parties could be contributing to by mobilizing only the most partisan voters. Ansolabehere and Iyengar (1995) write:

> Though the number of nonpartisans has grown in public opinion polls, Independents have not emerged as a great force in American politics because they do not vote in proportion to their numbers. . . . The hostile tenor of political campaigns contributes in no small part to the disaffection of the Independent voter. . . . As their bases of support become more partisan (or at least less Independent and centrist) members of Congress will work harder to represent those partisan interests. (p. 113)

Either way, other evidence suggests *voters* are more alienated from the party system than prior to the resurgence period. The near persistent state of divided government is obviously illustrative of weak parties, as is the shrinking percentage who take the time to vote. "Ross Perot may not be easy to explain in any context," writes John Colman (1996), "but within the celebration of party 'resurgence' and 'revitalization' in the party organization literature he becomes an enormous enigma" (p. 370). We might also look at public attitudes toward parties. For example, since the early 1970s, the NES has asked respondents which party they believe is best able to handle the nation's most important problem. If service-oriented parties have been successful at developing a stronger sense of purpose, the number of respondents suggesting there is "not much difference" or "don't know" should have declined. This is not the case: The number of those without a clear sense of which party would be more effective has remained quite stable since the 1970s. What is even more telling is that two-thirds of those born after 1959 believe neither party is best able to handle the nation's most pressing problem (1996 data).

What about public perceptions of the overall election process? Again, if service-oriented parties have been successful at cultivating a connection to voters, we might expect a more trusting, efficacious electorate since the 1970s. Table 3 suggests quite the contrary. It contains NES data from 1960 to 1996, for several election-oriented questions, averaged by decade. The trend is clear: fewer respondents see elections as important and their role in the political process as meaningful.

The New Clientele of Party Organizations

Why, then, has the electorate remained dealigned and skeptical about the election process at precisely the same time party organizations are providing more money and better services? The reason the voters have not returned to the parties is because the party organizations perpetuate individual-based politics. During the 1970s, parties became peripheral structures, as new technologies made personal contact unnecessary, interest groups dominated the policy process, and new-style campaign consultants sold their wares. Yet, electorates became unpredictable, and the costs of

TABLE 3 *Perceptions of the Role of the Citizen in Elections/Governance, National Elections Study, 1960–1996 (percentage, averaged by decade)*

Decade	1960s	1970s	1980s	1990s
Elections make government pay attention (percentage noting "a good deal")	63	54	40	43
How much does government listen to the people (percentage noting "a good deal")	26	15	13	12
People don't have a say in what the government does (percentage agreeing)	33	42	41	48
Public officials don't care what people think (percentage agreeing)	34	50	49	61

Note: Not every question was asked during every wave of the study. For example, the first two questions were not asked until 1964. The decade averages represent, nonetheless, at least three waves of data.

Source: National Election Study data, 1952–1996.

campaigns skyrocketed. These contextual changes made candidates fearful of election outcomes—not an irrational anxiety, given that the standard deviation of incumbent election margins mushroomed during this period (Jacobson 1987). Party adjustments were therefore made because candidates desperately needed help. Put a bit differently, it was because *voters* abandoned their party allegiances that *politicians* wanted stronger party organizations. Decline in one sphere triggered growth in another (Schlesinger, 1985). The outcome has been highly professional, nationalized campaign organizations. Parties have adapted to contemporary conditions but in the process have transformed what they have historically contributed to the political process. Instead of considering voters the primary client of the party, cultivating their loyalties and activating them on election day, service-oriented parties strive to please candidates.

One of the most significant changes to fulfill the new mandate has been to invigorate their office- and level-specific campaign organizations. Both parties have operations specifically geared to a single branch of the legislature. At the national level, these units are called the Hill Committees, and at the state level, legislative campaign committees (LCCs).[4] They use cutting-edge techniques and top-notch professionals to get *their* members elected, but rarely transfer money, share information, or conduct joint activities with members of the party running for different offices. Broad-based television, radio, or mail advertisements are highly unusual. As Frank Sorauf (1992) notes, these organizations serve "only the agendas and priorities of legislative partisans." This tends to "insulate them from the pressures of their party. Collective action has helped to bring legislative parties freedom from the agendas of presidential or gubernatorial parties" (p. 120). In an earlier study, I found only about 20 percent of LCCs work with their state party committee to raise and distribute funds, and even fewer work together on nonfinancial activities (Shea 1995, Chap. 6). It is also common for these units to encourage their clients (candidates) to run in opposition to an unpopular candidate of the *same* party. Perhaps realizing George Bush was in deep trouble, the director of the National Republican Congressional Committee (NRCC) (then Ed Rollins) sent a letter early in 1992 to all Republican House candidates telling them "not [to] hesitate to oppose the President's [budget agreement]" (Shea 1995, p. 16).

The rejection for broad-based party appeals by the Hill Committees took a new turn in 1996. During the waning weeks of the election, a decision was made by the NRCC to distance their clients from Bob Dole, with the hopes of maintaining a grasp on the House. They ran a series of advertisements that encouraged voters to split their vote choice. The operatives who devised the commercials would argue that they were not "throwing Dole overboard," as suggested by Wattenberg (1998), but merely doing all they could for *their* clients. Perhaps, but there is no question these spots were very different than any prior party activity and did little to encourage party-line voting. Republican operatives also recommended that their clients abandon the *Contract* if it suited their election efforts. Commenting on the blank check he gave GOP House candidates, Newt Gingrich suggested, "It's better to have a majority that's slightly confused than a minority that's thoroughly solid" (as cited in Wattenberg 1998, p. 223).

The growing rift between elements of the party structure could again be seen in 1998, this time within the Democratic ranks. During the waning days of the 1998 election, leaders of the House and Senate campaign committees became furious with the DNC. Apparently, the DNC was hoarding its funds to better position themselves for the 2000 presidential race, even though many House and Senate races were up for grabs. On top of this, Roy Romer, general chairman of the DNC, had commented to the media that he expected his party to lose about 25 seats in the House. To House leaders, this estimate was exceedingly pessimistic and hurtful to their cause. Commenting on the situation, Charles Rangel (D-NY), finance chair of the DCCC, noted: "Frankly, I don't know what the hell the DNC does. Let him do what he has to do for the President, but he's not entitled to an opinion on Congressional races . . . He's a nice man, but he's not giving us any damn money . . . Keep your money and shut your mouth" (Berke Oct. 27, 1998, A20). The idea that the leader of a national party committee should have no opinion on his party's congressional races is surely a dramatic turn.

As for which candidates to support, the Hill Committees and state LCCs provide assistance based solely on a candidate's ability to win elections; there is no concern for policy/party solidarity. Two comments are illustrative in this regard: Deborah Flavin, a former Republican House organization official, a few years ago noted, "At the NRCC our only ideology is that you have a 'big R' by your name. There is no litmus test on any issue" (as cited in Herrnson 1998, p. 78). Second, Tom Loftus, former Democratic Speaker of the Wisconsin House of Representatives, remarked, "Our only test is that the candidate is in a winnable seat and he or she is breathing, and those two requirements are in order of importance" (as cited in Shea 1995, p. 29).

Service-oriented parties have adapted to the hard-hitting, shrill campaign tactics that seem to win elections, but also alienate voters. Countless examples can be pointed to each election where party organizations conceive, produce, and sponsor profoundly negative campaign spots. They do this precisely because it is the best approach to win elections among a dealigned electorate, but it has had a disastrous effect on voter attitudes toward parties and levels of political participation. Ansolabehere and Iyengar (1995) note: "Unfortunately, negative campaigns only reinforce nonpartisans' disillusionment and convinces them not to participate in a tainted process" (p. 3). During the 1998 election, both parties spent record-breaking amounts on "issue advocacy." Nearly all of these spots were negative, leading some observers to call them "issue attacks" (Abramson Oct. 14, 1998).

Money has always been important, but prior to party "adaptation," many activities were labor-intensive—such as door-to-door canvassing and literature drops. Today, money itself drives party activities, and they do a great job raising it. Soft money made headlines in 1996. Huge contributions, upwards of $500,000, were given to the national party committees, which were then passed on to state committees. Combined, the two parties raised and disbursed more than $250 million in soft money, an increase of more than 200 percent from 1992 (Corrado 1997). This boosted the role of the parties in helping their needy clients, but it has led to even greater cynicism among voters. "An illness that has plagued previous elections," notes Anthony Corrado, "has developed into an epidemic" (1997, p. 151).

Despite the fact that many prominent Republicans have urged the Justice Department to investigate whether the DNC's soft money activities in 1996 were in violation of election laws, by 1998 the RNC had orchestrated a massive, record-breaking soft money plan. Called "Operation Breakout," the plan called for spending $20 million on congressional races, most channeled through state and local party organizations. In addition, $6 million was to be spent on issue advertisements. According to *New York Times* reporter Jill Abramson, the RNC has "resorted to pressure tactics" to raise the needed funds (Oct. 26, 1998, p. A14). It is little wonder that a recent *New York Times*/CBS poll found 75 percent of respondents agreeing that "many public officials make or change policy decision as a direct result of money received from major contributors" (Lehman 1997). Obviously, this does little to build public support for the party system.

The money-centered, technical party system has also discouraged local activism. There is simply little need for grassroots help. First, consider the thoughts of a would-be volunteer on his foray into local party politics in 1994:

> I'm young, I'm Ivy League Educated, and I'm politically disenfranchised. When I graduated from college this past December, I thought I would assume certain social responsibilities. But the conventional American political institutions— namely the political parties—can't use me. I don't know what gave me the idea that they could. Maybe it was the fact that I graduated in the top 2 percent of my class, or that I won the only award that the political science department gave out for the study of American politics. . . . But it seems that all of my academic achievements were self-indulgent tripe. When I went to the campaign headquarters of a mayoral race, something happened that I never expected: I was dissuaded from getting involved. . . . I was outright rebuffed. (Ferro 1996, p. 4)

Second, the decline of grassroots party activism is supported by survey data. According to the NES, during the 1960s and 1970s about 6 percent of Americans participated in party functions. In the 1990s, it was down to 3 percent. A nearly identical change can be seen for financial contributors to parties or candidates: In the 1970s, about 14 percent gave money. Today, it is about 7 percent.

Finally, let us consider how contemporary party politics is played out in the media. News coverage of politics is presented as if it were a contest among individuals, rather than between parties and sets of ideas. A premium is placed on character-based transgressions (often based on rumor and gossip). The outcome has been a reconfiguration of political news from partisan, policy-based skirmishes to personal breaches. This shift is not simply the media's doing, but something the parties also promote. Party leaders have found scandal politics more effective than slugging it out in the trenches of ideas and policy alternatives. Recent examples abound: When Gingrich was elected Speaker in 1994, the first attack from Democrats was *not* over elements of the *Contract,* but rather his lucrative book contract and possible illegalities made by his political action committee, GOPAC. When the Republicans became frustrated with Clinton, they simply turned up the heat on Whitewater, "Travelgate," "Filegate," and more recently Democratic National Committee fund-raising activities and an "improper relationship" with a White House intern. During the waning days of the 1996 presidential race, Gingrich emerged from the shadows *not* as an avid supporter of Dole or of the GOP supply-side platform, but to level new charges against Clinton, this time for accepting "illegal" campaign contributions from an Indonesian couple. "This scandal," suggested Gingrich, "will make Watergate look tiny."[5] Just 2 weeks after Clinton acknowledged an affair with Monica Lewinsky, RNCC operatives introduced a multimillion dollar ad campaign designed to exploit the president's fall from grace—even though polls show voters are more concerned with saving Social Security and improving education (Berke 1998). Partisan politics is now individual-centered scandal politics. This clearly does nothing to bind voters to a partisan badge or promote a coherent party platform.

In summary, although studies on the persistence of dealignment are mounting, few observers have set their sights on how party organizations have affected this process. The movement of voters away from parties is a product of myriad forces, including sociological changes in the Information Age, and it is also possible that party organizations have taken the only route left. But it seems only honest to admit that the disdain for "partisan politics" among voters has been intensified by service-oriented party organizations. So long as voters are encouraged to think of politicians as individuals, rather than as members of a ticket, and so long as candidates are encouraged by party operatives to pitch themselves in this light, partisan attachments will be sporadic and policy-based realignments unlikely.

A NEW POLITICAL ERA: THE BASE-LESS PARTY SYSTEM

Unlike the scholars Ladd (1991) suggests are "like waiting for Godot," I am not optimistic that a critical realignment will occur any time soon. We have moved beyond that. Those suggesting a sixth party era was ushered in during the late 1960s, a period characterized by a turn from party politics, were correct. Parties were peripheral organizations during the 1960s and 1970s, both in the minds of voters and as players in campaigns. And an "old-style partisan critical realignment" (Burnham 1996, p. 363) probably did not occur in the early 1990s, as there are simply too many indicators suggesting voters are leery of partisan attachments—a trend that is growing, not reversing. Yet, a new party period did begin in the mid-1980s, what might be labeled the "base-less" party system.

In this period, centralized, professional organizations vastly overshadow other elements of the party system, including party-in-government and certainly party-in-the-electorate. To a degree, Key's tripartite model no longer describes reality. There have been other periods in American history when organizations were similarly overwhelming, namely, the machine era, which spanned from about 1840 to 1920. Nevertheless, machine activities were designed first and foremost to develop partisan loyalties. Silbey (1991) writes, "Party organizations, symbols, issues and cues were powerful enough to catch, and keep loyal, the overwhelming number of American voters at every office level" (p. 12). It was assumed that once party brand loyalty was established, the particulars of candidate traits and campaign activities were secondary. We could say that first came the voters, and next came the candidates. It is little wonder that studies until the 1950s found minimal evidence of campaign effects (see, for example, Berelson, Lazarsfeld, & McPhee 1954; Lazarsfeld, Berelson, Gaudet 1948).

The "base-less" party period differs significantly. Confronting a wholesale abandonment of party loyalties during the 1970s, party operatives adopted a posture that put their organizations at the center of the electoral process, this time through greater services to candidates. Perhaps it was assumed voters would remain dealigned and that this was the only alternative. But it has become a self-perpetuating cycle: The more voters abandon partisan cues and the more erratic elections become, the more aggressive and professional party organizations grow. Aggressive party organizations strive to win elections at any cost, including helping candidate's downplay their partisan tag and by abandoning unpopular members of the ticket. Voters are left with little reason to form a partisan allegiance, which again leads to organizational innovation.

Characterizing the party system as base-less does not imply a void of policy concerns. The current system has a strong policy element, and much of the financial brawn that parties now boast comes from ideological individuals and groups. Nonetheless, it is elite centered: Contributors and activists in the organization, such as state and local party officials and delegates to the national conventions (and to some extent self-labeled partisans), are concerned about scores of issues, but little of what party organizations do cultivates a similar affect at the mass base of the structure. The gap between what activists desire and what the voters care about is growing, and is even wider when it comes to the interests of nonvoters (Jackson et al. 1999). This ideological component is further muted by party operatives who measure success by the number of victories on election day.

The idea that the party system can be simultaneously headed in two directions presents an anomaly for most theories of realignment. As noted by Cotter and his colleagues (1984), "If party in the electorate is in process of erosion, and parties as organizations are stronger now than in the past, this conjunction of trends does not conform to the expectations derived from theories of party transformation" (p. 159). Their landmark study not only forced scholars to reevaluate the unidimensional party decline assumption but also to contemplate how revitalized party organizations might affect the renewal process. They raise a number of possibilities but seem to speculate that vibrant organizations will yield a "counter-realigning" effect (p. 164). That is, parties will exert ever-greater organizational prowess to overcome any electoral disadvantage, and as one party develops an edge, the other quickly plays catch up. This makes good sense.

After two decades, we are now in the position to ponder what impact the base-less party system has had (and will have) on our political system more generally. It seems clear that service-oriented parties foster a more competitive election process, as conjectured by Herrnson and others. By implicitly encouraging voters to devalue partisan cues, they contribute to idiosyncratic electorates. And where it appears a race is up for grabs (which is increasingly likely, given such an electorate), the party is likely to infuse the race with money and other sophisticated services. The outcome is a growing number of hotly contested races. The number of competitive congressional races, for instance, has grown almost to the level found in the 1960s, and the average incumbent surge has plummeted. Much related, concerns that partisan affiliations would be traded for mere incumbency cues, leading to a steadfast advantage for those already in office, seem to have been counterbalanced by the saturation approach used by parties. Phenomenal sums are spent to oust "marginals."

We can also imagine that elected officials will better heed the wishes of constituents. Because party operatives place victory at the top of their agenda, they encourage elected officials to take positions contrary to the mainstream of the party if it will help please folks back home. Given the growing chorus that government is aloof to the concerns of average citizens, this shift toward ambassador-type representation might be welcome. Others, of course, would lament this shift as a move toward collective irresponsibility.

Divided government will be the norm in a base-less party system. As noted above, few party activities are geared toward promoting the ticket. This implies accountability judgments will remain difficult, fueling lower turnout and more nonpartisans. It could also leave the electorate confused, frustrated, and more cynical. Mayhew (1991) and others have suggested shifts in policy *are* indeed possible during periods of divided government, particularly when there is public consensus on an issue. I would suggest that even though incremental change might occur during periods of divided government, these shifts are not likely to quench the public's thirst for "action." That is to say, policy disputes are reduced to middle-of-the-road measures that appease constituencies without affording long-term solutions. The public remains dissatisfied with government outputs, but not irate. In his powerful book, *Why Americans Hate Politics*, E. J. Dionne (1991) puts it a bit differently: "Wracked by contradiction and responsive mainly to the needs of their various constituencies, liberalism and conservativism *prevent* the nation from settling the questions that most trouble it" (p. 11). The voters are afforded, he argues, a set of false choices.

Which brings us to what could be the most serious ramification of the base-less party system; the nature of the democratic process may be shifting toward the elite pole. Scholars have, for some time, noted a conflict between elite and popular democracy (see Bachrach 1967; Dahl 1989; Lappe 1989; Walker 1966; White & Shea in press). Elite democracy, or what might be dubbed the "Hamiltonian" model, holds that so long as there are guarantees of fairness and political opportunity, the system is healthy. After elections, public officials should be left to conduct the business of government. It is best for average citizens to stay out of the way because governance is complex. Popular democracy, or the "Jeffersonian" approach, is based on the Rousseauian model and places a premium on civic involvement in the conduct of government. This implies an ongoing, meaningful involvement in the affairs of the state. When this occurs, citizens develop an affinity for the system because they have a stake in the outcome.

Advocates of Jeffersonian party politics might argue that periodic realignments give citizens a means of becoming involved in the direction of the government—albeit sporadically. During these elections, voters head to the polls with a clear view of what should be done and which party is best suited to accomplish it. They become "partisan" because the parties have slugged it out in a battle of ideas. "In such a pressure cooker, the ideological element of politics is very greatly highlighted, and ideologically linked polarization reaches abnormal levels on all sides" (Burnham 1996, p. 372). Regardless of who wins, voters feel reassured that they have been players. It matters little how truly informed they are or what actual bearing their vote had on the outcome, only that their involvement had the *potential* to shape the direction of the nation. Realignments give voters a reason to believe in the political system—a reason to like politics. Even though contemporary party organizations afford candidates with cutting-edge services, little of what they do fosters a party ideology or an affinity for politics among those at the base of the political system. Perhaps Dionne overstated things a bit when he noted that "a nation that hates politics will not long thrive as a democracy" (1991, p. 355), but certainly the advent of this new party system should give students of popular government pause.

NOTES

1. This information was compiled from *The Book of the States*. I used data from volumes 12 through 22 (1959 through 1979).
2. Others might stretch things back a bit further, perhaps to the election of 1916. Jensen (1969) suggests this election marked a shift from "militarists" party activities, focused on grass-roots organizations, to "mercantilists" campaigning, where a premium is placed on the manipulation of symbols and the strategies of advertising.
3. Scores of scholars and journalists commented on the power and sophistication of the Republican National Committee during the 1980s, even though their electoral success was limited.
4. Although it is true that the Hill Committees emerged in the 1860s, they were not significant players until the 1970s.
5. This comment was made on *Meet the Press*, Sunday, October 13, 1996.

REFERENCES

Abramson, J. (October 26, 1988). "Political parties channel millions to issue attacks." *The New York Times*, pp. A1, A14.

Aldrich, J. H. (January 1999). "Political parties in a critical era." *American Politics Quarterly*, 27(1): 9–32.

Aldrich, J. H., & Niemi, R. G. (1996). "The sixth American party system: Electoral change, 1952–1992." In S. C. Craig (ed.), *Broken contract: Changing relationships between Americans and their government*. Boulder, CO: Westview, pp. 87–109.

Ansolabehere, S., & Iyengar, S. (1995). *Going negative: How political advertisements shrink and polarize the electorate*. New York: Free Press.

Arterton, C. F. (1982). "Political money and party strength." In J. L. Fleishman (ed.), *The future of American political parties: The challenge of governance.* Englewood Cliffs, NJ: Prentice Hall, pp. 101–139.

Associated Press. (October 4, 1996). Speaker puts House races first.

Bachrach, P. (1967). *The theory of democratic elitism: A critique.* Boston: Little, Brown.

Beck, P. A. (1999). "The changing American party coalitions." In J. C. Green & D. M. Shea (eds.), *The state of the parties: The changing role of contemporary* (3rd ed.). Lanham, MD: Rowman and Littlefield.

Berelson, B. R., Lazarsfeld, P. F., & McPhee, W. N. (1954). *Voting.* Chicago: University of Chicago Press.

Berke, R. L. (September 2, 1998). "Lewinsky issue inspires theme for GOP ads." *The New York Times,* p. A22.

Berke, R. (October 27, 1998). "Financial debate divides Democrats as elections near." *The New York Times,* pp. A1, A20.

Bibby, J. F. (1990). "Party organization at the state level." In L. S. Maisel (ed.), *The parties respond: Changes in the American party system.* Boulder, CO: Westview, pp. 21–40.

Blumenthal, S. (1980). *The permanent campaign: Inside the world of elite political operatives.* Boston: Beacon.

Burnham, W. D. (1970). *Critical elections and the mainsprings of American government.* New York: Norton.

Burnham, W. D. (1989). "The Reagan heritage." In G. Pomper (ed.), *The election of 1988.* Chatham, NJ: Chatham House, pp. 1–32.

Burnham, W. D. (1991). "Critical realignment: Dead or alive?" In B. E. Shafer (ed.), *The end of realignment? Interpreting American electoral eras.* Madison: University of Wisconsin Press, pp. 101–140.

Burnham, W. D. (1996). "Critical realignment lives: The 1994 earthquake." In C. Campbell & B. A. Rockman (eds.), *The Clinton presidency: First appraisals.* Chatham, NJ: Chatham House, pp. 363–396.

Carmines, E. G., & Stimson, J. A. (1989). *Race and the transformation of American politics.* Princeton, NJ: Princeton University Press.

Collet, C., & Hansen, J. (1996). "Minor parties and candidates in sub-presidential elections." In J. C. Green & D. M. Shea (eds.), *The state of the parties: The changing role of contemporary American parties* (2nd ed.). Lanham, MD: Rowman and Littlefield, pp. 239–255.

Colman, J. J. (1996). "The resurgence of party organization? A dissent from the new orthodoxy." In D. M. Shea & J. C. Green (eds.), *The state of the parties: The changing role of contemporary American parties.* Lanham, MD: Rowman and Littlefield, pp. 370–384.

Corrado, A. (1997). "Financing the 1996 elections." In G. M. Pomper (ed.), *The election of 1996: Reports and interpretations.* Chatham, NJ: Chatham House, pp. 135–172.

Cotter, C. P., Gibson, J. L., Bibby, J. F., & Huckshorn, R. J. (1984). *Party organizations in American politics.* New York: Praeger.

Dahl, R. A. (1989). *Democracy and its critics.* New Haven, CT: Yale University Press.

Dionne, E. J. (1991). *Why Americans hate politics.* New York: Simon & Schuster.

Dougherty, R., Ladd, E. C., Wilber, D., & Zayachkiwsky, L. (eds.). (1997). *America at the polls, 1996.* Storrs, CT: Roper Center for Public Opinion Research.

Ferro, M. V. (March/April 1996). "Where's the party." *The Humanist,* p. 4.

Frantzich, S. E. (1989). *Political parties in the technological age.* New York: Longman.

Herrnson, P. S. (1988). *Party campaigning in the 1980s.* Cambridge, MA: Harvard University Press.

Herrnson, P. S. (1990). "Reemergent national party organizations." In L. S. Maisel (ed.), *The parties respond: Changes in the American party system.* Boulder, CO: Westview, pp. 41–66.

Herrnson, P. S. (1994). "The revitalization of national party organizations." In L. S. Maisel (ed.), *The parties respond: Changes in the American party system* (2nd ed.). Boulder, CO: Westview, pp. 50–82.

Herrnson, P. S. (1998). *Congressional elections: Campaigning at home and in Washington* (2nd ed.). Washington, DC: Congressional Quarterly.

Jackson, J. L., Clayton, N., & Green, J. C. (1999). "Issue networks and party elites in 1996." In J. C. Green & D. M. Shea (eds.), *The state of the parties: The changing role of contemporary American parties* (3rd ed.). Lanham, MD: Rowman and Littlefield.

Jacobson, G. C. (1987). "The marginals never vanished: Incumbency and competition in elections to the U.S. House of Representatives, 1952–1982." *American Journal of Political Science, 31:* 126–141.

Jensen, R. (1969). "American election analysis." In S. M. Lipset (ed.), *Politics and the social sciences.* New York: Oxford University Press, pp. 136–159.

Kayden, X., & Mahe, E., Jr. (1985). *The party goes on: The persistence of the two-party system.* New York: Basic Books.

Kolodny, R. (1999). "Moderate partisan in the 1990s: Withering away or digging in?" In J. C. Green & D. M. Shea (eds.), *The state of the parties: The changing role of contemporary American parties.* (3rd ed.). Lanham, MD: Rowman and Littlefield.

Ladd, E. C. (1991). "Like waiting for Godot: The uselessness of 'realignment' for understanding change in contemporary American politics." In B. E. Shafer (ed.), *The end of realignment? Interpreting American electoral eras.* Madison: University of Wisconsin Press, pp. 24–36.

Ladd, E. C. (1997). "1996 vote: The 'no majority' realignment continues." *Political Science Quarterly, 112:* 1–28.

Lappe, F. M. (1989). *Rediscovering America's values.* New York: Ballantine.

Lazarsfeld, P. F., Berelson, B., & Gaudet, H. (1948). *The people's choice: How the voter makes up his mind in a presidential campaign.* New York: Columbia University Press.

Lehmann, C. (May 12, 1997). "In the end: Cynical and proud." *The New York Times,* p. 40.

Mayhew, D. R. (1991). *Divided we govern: Party control, law making, and investigations, 1946–1990.* New Haven, CT: Yale University Press.

Miller, W. E., & Shanks, J. M. (1996). *The new American voter.* Cambridge, MA: Harvard University Press.

Mitchell, A. (March 11, 1998). "House G.O.P. content to make ripples." *The New York Times,* p. A14.

Pomper, G. M. (1999). "Parliamentary government in the United States?" In J. C. Green & D. M. Shea (eds.), *The state of the parties: The changing role of contemporary American parties.* (3rd ed.). Lanham, MD: Rowman and Littlefield.

Price, D. (1984). *Bringing back the parties.* Washington, DC: Congressional Quarterly.

Rhodes, T. L. (1996). "The year of the elephant—1994: Realignment and/or punctuated change?" *Southeastern Political Review, 24:* 319–336.

Schlesinger, J. A. (1985). The new American political party. *American Political Science Review, 79:* 1152–1169.

Shea, D. M. (1995). *Transforming democracy: Legislative campaign committees and political parties*. Albany: State University of New York Press.

Silbey, J. H. (1991). "Beyond realignment and realignment theory: American political eras, 1789–1989." In B. E. Shafer (ed.), *The end of realignment? Interpreting American electoral eras*. Madison: University of Wisconsin Press, pp. 3–23.

Sorauf, F. J. (1992). *Inside campaign finance: Myths and realities*. New Haven, CT: Yale University Press.

Walker, J. L. (1966). "A critique of the elitist theory of democracy." *American Political Science Review, 60:* 285–295.

Wattenberg, M. P. (1991). *The rise of candidate-centered politics*. Cambridge, MA: Harvard University Press.

Wattenberg, M. P. (1998). *The decline of American political parties: 1952–1996*. Cambridge, MA: Harvard University Press.

White, J. K., & Shea, D. M. (in press). *Parties in the information age*. New York: St. Martin's.

Parties, Elections, and Governance

Political parties seek control of government so that their goals and programs will be converted into public policy. Elections are the forum in which parties compete to win that right to govern. In this final chapter, we consider what implications elections have for the governing that comes after them.

In the first selection, Robert Dahl examines presidential claims that their election to office bestows upon them a "mandate" to pursue the policies they advocated during the campaign. Although Dahl focuses on this claim most directly in connection with the Reagan administration, he acknowledges that President Reagan was scarcely the first president to hold this view; nor will he be the last. But does it really matter? In Dahl's judgment, it matters a great deal, for not only does the idea of an election mandate run directly counter to how the Framers viewed elections, but the empirical evidence simply does not support the claim that voters are providing the victorious presidential candidate with a policy mandate. Furthermore, the very idea of a presidential election mandate has, in Dahl's view, contributed to the *pseudodemocratization* of the presidency—a development harmful both to the institution itself and the principle of balanced government.

The second article by Gerald Pomper considers the extent to which the behavior of our political parties is taking us closer to a parliamentary form of government. As Pomper is quick to note, of course, constitutional strictures preclude our government from ever becoming truly parliamentary in character. The president, after all, is chosen separately from the House and the House separately from the Senate; and each is elected to a fixed term. In a parliamentary system, on the other hand, the prime minister is chosen by the legislature and is subject to removal by that body through a vote of "no confidence." This said, Pomper nevertheless finds that our political parties are acting in ways reminiscent of those in parliamentary systems. More specifically, they are espousing reasonably specific programs (a result of greater coordination *across* branches); they are doing a creditable job in fulfilling their promises; unity and discipline within the congressional parties has increased significantly; they play a major role in campaigning; and they serve as a recruitment ground for presidential candidates. Pomper concludes by predicting that, given ideological changes within the parties, these parliamentary tendencies will likely persist.

Whereas Pomper focuses on change within parties and the implications for governing, Morris Fiorina considers the relationship between parties and its impact on government. He points out first that the phenomenon of divided government, so prevalent over the last forty years, is likely to continue into the future, but not necessarily following the pattern of the past, whereby the Republicans controlled the presidency and the Democrats, the Congress. The ability of the Democrats to win back the presidency in 1992, and the Republicans to gain control of Congress for the first time since 1954, suggests that both institutions may now be up for grabs. Although a number of scholars and commentators lament the prevalence of divided government, asserting that it greatly limits efficiency and effectiveness, Fiorina rejects the claim that a Congress and executive controlled by the same party is able to accomplish more. Furthermore, to suggest that the alleged failings of our government should be laid at the doorstep of our "political-institutional processes" is, in his view, to overlook the more fundamental cause—a divided public.

Myth of the Presidential Mandate

Robert A. Dahl

On election night in 1980 the vice president elect enthusiastically informed the country that Ronald Reagan's triumph was

> . . . not simply a mandate for a change but a mandate for peace and freedom; a mandate for prosperity; a mandate for opportunity for all Americans regardless of race, sex, or creed; a mandate for leadership that is both strong and compassionate . . . a mandate to make government the servant of the people in the way our founding fathers intended; a mandate for hope; a mandate for hope for the fulfillment of the great dream that President-elect Reagan has worked for all his life.[1]

I suppose there are no limits to permissible exaggeration in the elation of victory, especially by a vice president elect. He may therefore be excused, I imagine, for failing to note, as did many others who made comments in a similar vein in the weeks and months that followed, that Reagan's lofty mandate was provided by 50.9 percent of the voters. A decade later it is much more evident, as it should have been then, that what was widely interpreted as Reagan's mandate, not only by supporters but by opponents, was more myth than reality.

In claiming that the outcome of the election provided a mandate to the president from the American people to bring about the policies, programs, emphases, and new directions uttered during the campaign by the winning candidate and his supporters, the vice president elect was like other commentators echoing a familiar theory.

ORIGIN AND DEVELOPMENT

A history of the theory of the presidential mandate has not been written, and I have no intention of supplying one here. However, if anyone could be said to have created the myth of the presidential mandate, surely it would be Andrew Jackson. Although he never used the word mandate, so far as I know, he was the first American president to claim not only that the president is uniquely representative of all the people, but that his election confers on him a mandate from the people in support of his policy. Jackson's claim was a fateful step in the democratization of the constitutional system of the United States—or rather what I prefer to call the pseudodemocratization of the presidency.

Source: Robert A. Dahl, "Myth of Presidential Mandate," *Political Science Quarterly,* 105 (Fall 1990), pp. 355–371.

Robert A. Dahl is the Sterling professor emeritus at Yale University and past president of the American Political Science Association. He is author of numerous books, the most recent of which is *On Democracy.*

As Leonard White observed, it was Jackson's "settled conviction" that "the President was an immediate and direct representative of the people."[2] Presumably as a result of his defeat in 1824 in both the electoral college and the House of Representatives, in his first presidential message to Congress, in order that "as few impediments as possible should exist to the free operation of the public will," he proposed that the Constitution be amended to provide for the direct election of the president.[3]

> To the people," he said, "belongs the right of electing their Chief Magistrate: it was never designed that their choice should, in any case, be defeated, either by the intervention of electoral colleges or by . . . the House of Representatives.[4]

His great issue of policy was the Bank of the United States, which he unwaveringly believed was harmful to the general good. Acting on this conviction, in 1832 he vetoed the bill to renew the bank's charter. Like his predecessors, he justified the veto as a protection against unconstitutional legislation; but unlike his predecessors in their comparatively infrequent use of the veto he also justified it as a defense of his or his party's policies.

Following his veto of the bank's charter, the bank became the main issue in the presidential election of 1832. As a consequence, Jackson's reelection was widely regarded, even among his opponents (in private, at least), as amounting to "something like a popular ratification" of his policy.[5] When in order to speed the demise of the bank Jackson found it necessary to fire his treasury secretary, he justified his action on the ground, among others, that "The President is the direct representative of the American people, but the Secretaries are not."[6]

Innovative though it was, Jackson's theory of the presidential mandate was less robust than it was to become in the hands of his successors. In 1848 James Polk explicitly formulated the claim, in a defense of his use of the veto on matters of policy, that as a representative of the people the president was, if not more representative than the Congress, at any rate equally so.

> The people, by the constitution, have commanded the President, as much as they have commanded the legislative branch of the Government, to execute their will. . . . The President represents in the executive department the whole people of the United States, as each member of the legislative department represents portions of them. . . . The President is responsible not only to an enlightened public opinion, but to the people of the whole Union, who elected him, as the representatives in the legislative branches . . . are responsible to the people of particular States or districts. . . .[7]

Notice that in Jackson's and Polk's views, the president, both constitutionally and as representative of the people, is on a par with Congress. They did not claim that in either respect the president is superior to Congress. It was Woodrow Wilson who took the further step in the evolution of the theory by asserting that in representing the people the president is not merely equal to Congress but actually superior to it.

Earlier Views

Because the theory of the presidential mandate espoused by Jackson and Polk has become an integral part of our present-day conception of the presidency, it may be hard for us to grasp how sharply that notion veered off from the views of the earlier presidents.

As James Ceaser has shown, the Framers designed the presidential election process as a means of improving the chances of electing a *national* figure who would enjoy majority support. They hoped their contrivance would avoid not only the populistic competition among candidates dependent on "the popular arts," which they rightly believed would occur if the president were elected by the people, but also what they believed would necessarily be a factional choice if the president were chosen by the Congress, particularly by the House.[8]

In adopting the solution of an electoral college, however, the Framers seriously underestimated the extent to which the strong impulse toward democratization that was already clearly evident among Americans—particularly among their opponents, the anti-Federalists—would subvert and alter their carefully contrived constitutional structure. Since this is a theme I shall pick up later, I want now to mention only two such failures that bear closely on the theory of the presidential mandate. First, the Founders did not foresee the development of political parties nor comprehend how a two-party system might achieve their goal of insuring the election of a figure of national rather than merely local renown. Second, as Ceaser remarks, although the Founders recognized "the need for a popular judgment of the performance of an incumbent" and designed a method for selecting the president that would, as they thought, provide that opportunity, they "did not see elections as performing the role of instituting decisive changes in policy in response to popular demands."[9] In short, the theory of the presidential mandate not only cannot be found in the Framers' conception of the Constitution; almost certainly it violates that conception.

No president prior to Jackson challenged the view that Congress was the legitimate representative of the people. Even Thomas Jefferson, who adeptly employed the emerging role of party leader to gain congressional support for his policies and decisions

> was more Whig than . . . the British Whigs themselves in subordinating [the executive power] to "the supreme legislative power". . . . The tone of his messages is uniformly deferential to Congress. His first one closes with these words: "Nothing shall be wanting on my part to inform, as far as in my power, the legislative judgment, nor to carry that judgment into faithful execution.[10]

James Madison, demonstrating that a great constitutional theorist and an adept leader in Congress could be decidedly less than a great president, deferred so greatly to Congress that in his communications to that body his extreme caution rendered him "almost unintelligible"[11]—a quality one would hardly expect from one who had been a master of lucid exposition at the Constitutional Convention. His successor, James Monroe, was so convinced that Congress should decide domestic issues without presidential influence that throughout the debates in Congress on "the greatest political issue of his day . . . the admission of Missouri and the status of slavery in Louisiana Territory," he remained utterly silent.[12]

Madison and Monroe serve not as examples of how presidents should behave but as evidence of how early presidents thought they should behave. Considering the constitutional views and the behavior of Jackson's predecessors, it is not hard to see why his opponents called themselves Whigs in order to emphasize his dereliction from the earlier and presumably constitutionally correct view of the presidency.

Woodrow Wilson

The long and almost unbroken succession of mediocrities who succeeded to the presidency between Polk and Wilson for the most part subscribed to the Whig view of the office and seem to have laid no claim to a popular mandate for their policies—when they had any. Even Abraham Lincoln, in justifying the unprecedented scope of presidential power he believed he needed in order to meet secession and civil war, rested his case on constitutional grounds, and not as a mandate from the people.[13] Indeed, since he distinctly failed to gain a majority of votes in the election of 1860, any claim to a popular mandate would have been dubious at best. Like Lincoln, Theodore Roosevelt also had a rather unrestricted view of presidential power; he expressed the view then emerging among Progressives that chief executives were also representatives of the people. Yet the stewardship he claimed for the presidency was ostensibly drawn—rather freely drawn, I must say—from the Constitution, not from the mystique of the mandate.[14]

Woodrow Wilson, more as political scientist than as president, brought the mandate theory to what now appears to be its canonical form. His formulation was influenced by his admiration for the British system of cabinet government. In 1879, while still a senior at Princeton, he published an essay recommending the adoption of cabinet government in the United States.[15] He provided little indication as to how this change was to be brought about, however, and soon abandoned the idea without yet having found an alternative solution.[16] Nevertheless, he continued to contrast the American system of congressional government, in which Congress was all-powerful but lacked executive leadership, with British cabinet government, in which parliament, though all powerful, was firmly led by the prime minister and his cabinet. Since Americans were not likely to adopt the British cabinet system, however, he began to consider the alternative of more powerful presidential leadership.[17] In his *Congressional Government,* published in 1885, he acknowledged that "the representatives of the people are the proper ultimate authority in all matters of government, and that administration is merely the clerical part of government."[18] Congress is "unquestionably, the predominant and controlling force, the center and source of all motive and of all regulative power." Yet a discussion of policy that goes beyond "special pleas for special privilege" is simply impossible in the House, "a disintegrate mass of jarring elements," while the Senate is no more than "a small, select, and leisurely House of Representatives."[19]

By 1908, when *Constitutional Government in the United States* was published, Wilson had arrived at strong presidential leadership as a feasible solution. He faulted the earlier presidents who had adopted the Whig theory of the Constitution.

> ... (T)he makers of the Constitution were not enacting Whig theory. . . . The President is at liberty, both in law and conscience, to be as big a man as he can. His capacity will set the limit; and if Congress be overborne by him, it will be no fault of the makers of the Constitution, — it will be from no lack of constitutional powers on its part, but only because the President has the nation behind him, and Congress has not. He has no means of compelling Congress except through public opinion. . . . (T)he early Whig theory of political dynamics . . . is far from being a democratic theory. . . . It is particularly intended to prevent the will of the people as a whole from having at any moment an unobstructed sweep and ascendancy.

And he contrasted the president with Congress in terms that would become commonplace among later generations of commentators, including political scientists:

> Members of the House and Senate are representatives of localities, are voted for only by sections of voters, or by local bodies of electors like the members of the state legislatures.[20] There is no national party choice except that of President. No one else represents the people as a whole, exercising a national choice. . . . The nation as a whole has chosen him, and is conscious that it has no other political spokesman. His is the only national voice in affairs. . . . He is the representative of no constituency, but of the whole people. When he speaks in his true character, he speaks for no special interest. . . . (T)here is but one national voice in the country, and that is the voice of the President.[21]

Since Wilson, it has become commonplace for presidents and commentators alike to argue that by virtue of his election the president has received a mandate for his aims and policies from the people of the United States. The myth of the mandate is now a standard weapon in the arsenal of persuasive symbols all presidents exploit. For example, as the Watergate scandals emerged in mid-1973, Patrick Buchanan, then an aide in the Nixon White House, suggested that the president should accuse his accusers of "seeking to destroy the democratic mandate of 1972." Three weeks later in an address to the country Nixon said:

> Last November, the American people were given the clearest choice of this century. Your votes were a mandate, which I accepted, to complete the initiatives we began in my first term and to fulfill the promises I made for my second term.[22]

If the spurious nature of Nixon's claim now seems self-evident, the dubious grounds for virtually all such pretensions are perhaps less obvious.[23]

CRITIQUE OF THE THEORY

What does a president's claim to a mandate amount to? The meaning of the term itself is not altogether clear.[24] Fortunately, however, in his excellent book *Interpreting Elections*, Stanley Kelley has "piece[d] together a coherent statement of the theory."

> Its first element is the belief that elections carry messages about problems, policies, and programs—messages plain to all and specific enough to be directive. . . . Second, the theory holds that certain of these messages must be treated as authoritative commands . . . either to the victorious candidate or to the candidate and his party. . . . To qualify as mandates, messages about policies and programs must reflect the *stable* views both of individual voters and of the electorate. . . . In the electorate as a whole, the numbers of those for or against a policy or program matter. To suggest that a mandate exists for a particular policy is to suggest that more than a bare majority of those voting are agreed upon it. The common view holds that landslide victories are more likely to involve mandates than are narrow ones. . . . The final element of the theory is a negative imperative: Governments should not undertake major innovations in policy or procedure, except in emergencies, unless the electorate has had an opportunity to consider them in an election and thus to express its views."[25]

To bring out the central problems more clearly, let me extract what might be called the primitive theory of the popular presidential mandate. According to this theory, a presidential election can accomplish four things. First, it confers constitutional and legal authority on the victor. Second, at the same time, it also conveys information. At a minimum it reveals the first preferences for president of a plurality of votes. Third, according to the primitive theory, the election, at least under the conditions Kelley describes, conveys further information: namely that a clear majority of voters prefer the winner because they prefer his policies and wish him to pursue his policies. Finally, because the president's policies reflect the wishes of a majority of voters, when conflicts over policy arise between president and Congress, the president's policies ought to prevail.

While we can readily accept the first two propositions, the third, which is pivotal to the theory, might be false. But if the third is false, then so is the fourth. So the question arises: Beyond revealing the first preferences of a plurality of voters, do presidential elections also reveal the additional information that a plurality (or a majority) of voters prefer the policies of the winner and wish the winner to pursue those policies?

In appraising the theory I want to distinguish between two different kinds of criticisms. First, some critics contend that even when the wishes of constituents can be known, they should not be regarded as in any way binding on a legislator. I have in mind, for example, Edmund Burke's famous argument that he would not sacrifice to public opinion his independent judgment of how well a policy would serve his constituents' interests, and the argument suggested by Hanna Pitkin that representatives bound by instructions would be prevented from entering into the compromises that legislation usually requires.[26]

Second, some critics, on the other hand, may hold that when the wishes of constituents on matters of policy can be clearly discerned, they ought to be given great and perhaps even decisive weight. But, these critics contend, constituents' wishes usually cannot be known, at least when the constituency is large and diverse, as in presidential elections. In expressing his doubts on the matter in 1913, A. Lawrence Lowell quoted Sir Henry Maine: "The devotee of democracy is much in the same position as the Greeks with their oracles. All agreed that the voice of an oracle was the voice of god, but everybody allowed that when he spoke he was not as intelligible as might be desired."[27]

It is exclusively the second kind of criticism that I want now to consider. Here again I am indebted to Stanley Kelley for his succinct summary of the main criticisms.

> Critics allege that 1) some particular claim of a mandate is unsupported by adequate evidence; 2) most claims of mandates are unsupported by adequate evidence; 3) most claims of mandates are politically self-serving; or 4) it is not possible in principle to make a valid claim of a mandate, since it is impossible to sort out voters' intentions.[28]

Kelley goes on to say that while the first three criticisms may well be valid, the fourth has been outdated by the sample survey, which "has again given us the ability to discover the grounds of voters' choices." In effect, then, Kelley rejects the primitive theory and advances the possibility of a more sophisticated mandate theory according to which the information about policies is conveyed not by the election outcome but instead by opinion surveys. Thus the two functions are cleanly split: presidential elections are for electing a president, opinion surveys provide information about the opinions, attitudes, and judgments that account for the outcome.

However, I would propose a fifth proposition, which I believe is also implicit in Kelley's analysis:

> 5) While it may not be strictly impossible *in principle* to make a reasoned and well-grounded claim to a presidential mandate, to do so *in practice* requires a complex analysis that in the end may not yield much support for presidential claims.

But if we reject the primitive theory of the mandate and adopt the more sophisticated theory, then it follows that prior to the introduction of scientific sample surveys, no president could reasonably have defended his claim to a mandate. To put a precise date on the proposition, let me remind you that the first presidential election in which scientific surveys formed the basis of an extended and systematic analysis was 1940.[29]

I do not mean to say that no election before 1940 now permits us to draw the conclusion that a president's major policies were supported by a substantial majority of the electorate. But I do mean that for most presidential elections before 1940 a valid reconstruction of the policy views of the electorate is impossible or enormously difficult, even with the aid of aggregate data and other indirect indicators of voters' views. When we consider that presidents ordinarily asserted their claims soon after their elections, well before historians and social scientists could have sifted through reams of indirect evidence, then we must conclude that before 1940 no contemporary claim to a presidential mandate could have been supported by the evidence available at the time.

While the absence of surveys undermines presidential claims to a mandate before 1940, the existence of surveys since then would not necessarily have supported such claims. Ignoring all other shortcomings of the early election studies, the analysis of the 1940 election I just mentioned was not published until 1948. While that interval between the election and the analysis may have set a record, the systematic analysis of survey evidence that is necessary (though perhaps not sufficient) to interpret what a presidential election means always comes well after presidents and commentators have already told the world, on wholly inadequate evidence, what the election means.[30] Perhaps the most famous voting study to date, *The American Voter,* which drew primarily on interviews conducted in 1952 and 1956, appeared in 1960.[31] The book by Stanley Kelley that I have drawn on so freely here, which interprets the elections of 1964, 1972, and 1980, appeared in 1983.

A backward glance quickly reveals how empty the claims to a presidential mandate have been in recent elections. Take 1960. If more than a bare majority is essential to a mandate, then surely Kennedy could have received no mandate, since he gained less than 50 percent of the total popular vote by the official count—just how much less by the unofficial count varies with the counter. Yet "on the day after election, and every day thereafter," Theodore Sorensen tells us, "he rejected the argument that the country had given him no mandate. Every election has a winner and a loser, he said in effect. There may be difficulties with the Congress, but a margin of only one vote would still be a mandate."[32]

By contrast, 1964 was a landslide election, as was 1972. From his analysis, however, Kelley concludes that "Johnson's and Nixon's specific claims of meaningful mandates do not stand up well when confronted by evidence." To be sure, in both elections some of the major policies of the winners were supported by large majorities among those to whom these issues were salient. Yet "none of these policies was cited by more than 21 percent of respondents as a reason to like Johnson, Nixon, or their parties."[33]

In 1968, Nixon gained office with only 43 percent of the popular vote. No mandate there. Likewise in 1976, Carter won with a bare 50.1 percent. Once again, no mandate there.

When Reagan won in 1980, thanks to the much higher quality of surveys undertaken by the media, a more sophisticated understanding of what that election meant no longer had to depend on the academic analyses that would only follow some years later. Nonetheless, many commentators, bemused as they so often are by the arithmetical peculiarities of the electoral college, immediately proclaimed both a landslide and a mandate for Reagan's policies. What they often failed to note was that Reagan gained just under 51 percent of the popular vote. Despite the claims of the vice president elect, surely we can find no mandate there. Our doubts are strengthened by the fact that in the elections to the House, Democratic candidates won just over 50 percent of the popular vote and a majority of seats. However, they lost control of the Senate. No Democratic mandate there, either.

These clear and immediate signs that the elections of 1980 failed to confer a mandate on the president or his Democratic opponents were, however, largely ignored. For it was so widely asserted as to be commonplace that Reagan's election reflected a profound shift of opinion away from New Deal programs and toward the new conservatism. However, from this analysis of the survey evidence, Kelley concludes that the commitment of voters to candidates was weak; a substantial proportion of Reagan voters were more interested in voting against Carter than for Reagan; and despite claims by journalists and others, the New Deal coalition did not really collapse. Nor was there any profound shift toward conservatism. "The evidence from press surveys. . . . contradicts the claims that voters shifted toward conservatism and that this ideological shift elected Reagan." In any case, the relation between ideological location and policy preferences was "of a relatively modest magnitude."[34]

In winning by a landslide of popular votes in 1984, Reagan achieved one prerequisite to a mandate. Yet in that same election, Democratic candidates for the House won 52 percent of the popular votes. Two years earlier, they had won 55 percent of the votes. On the face of it, surely the 1984 elections gave no mandate to Reagan.

Before the end of 1986, when the Democrats had once again won a majority of popular votes in elections to the House and had also regained a majority of seats in the Senate, it should have been clear and it should be even clearer now that the major social and economic policies for which Reagan and his supporters had claimed a mandate have persistently failed to gain majority support. Indeed, the major domestic policies and programs established during the thirty years preceding Reagan in the White House have not been overturned in the grand revolution of policy that his election was supposed to have ushered in. For eight years, what Reagan and his supporters claimed as a mandate to reverse those policies was regularly rejected by means of the only legitimate and constitutional processes we Americans have for determining what the policies of the United States government should be.

What are we to make of this long history of unsupported claims to a presidential mandate? The myth of the mandate would be less important if it were not one element in the larger process of the pseudodemocratization of the presidency—the creation of a type of chief executive that in my view should have no proper place in a democratic republic.

Yet even if we consider it in isolation from the larger development of the presidency, the myth is harmful to American political life. By portraying the president as the only representative of the whole people and Congress as merely representing narrow, special, and parochial interests, the myth of the mandate elevates the president to an exalted position in our constitutional system at the expense of Congress. The myth of the mandate fosters the belief that the particular interests of the diverse human beings who form the citizen body in a large, complex, and pluralistic country like ours constitute no legitimate element in the general good. The myth confers on the aims of the groups who benefit from presidential policies an aura of national interest and public good to which they are no more entitled than the groups whose interests are reflected in the policies that gain support by congressional majorities. Because the myth is almost always employed to support deceptive, misleading, and manipulative interpretations, it is harmful to the political understanding of citizens.

It is, I imagine, now too deeply rooted in American political life and too useful a part of the political arsenal of presidents to be abandoned. Perhaps the most we can hope for is that commentators on public affairs in the media and in academic pursuits will dismiss claims to a presidential mandate with the scorn they usually deserve.

But if a presidential election does not confer a mandate on the victor, what does a presidential election mean, if anything at all? While a presidential election does not confer a popular mandate on the president—nor, for that matter, on congressional majorities—it confers the legitimate authority, right, and opportunity on a president to try to gain the adoption by constitutional means of the policies the president supports. In the same way, elections to Congress confer on a member the authority, right, and opportunity to try to gain the adoption by constitutional means of the policies he or she supports. Each may reasonably contend that a particular policy is in the public good or public interest and, moreover, is supported by a majority of citizens.

I do not say that whatever policy is finally adopted following discussion, debate, and constitutional processes necessarily reflects what a majority of citizens would prefer, or what would be in their interests, or what would be in the public good in any other sense. What I do say is that no elected leader, including the president, is uniquely privileged to say what an election means—nor to claim that the election has conferred on the president a mandate to enact the particular policies the president supports.

THE DEMOCRATIZATION OF THE PRESIDENCY

It was inevitable that the executive designed by the Framers would be fundamentally altered in response to the powerful influence of democratizing impulses. If the Framers had intended a chief executive whose election and capacity for governing would not require him to compete for popular approval and who therefore would not depend on "the popular arts" of winning public support,[35] they seriously underestimated both the strength of the democratic impulses among their fellow citizens and its effects on the presidency. Nothing reveals this more clearly than the amazing speed with which the Framers' design for the executive was replaced by a presidency dependent on popular election and popular approval.

The consequences of democratization were evident almost at once and gained strength with the passage of time. I have already described one aspect of this process of democratization in some detail: the invention of the theory of the presidential mandate. Jackson's invention was, however, preceded by decades of democratization that gave plausibility to the theory.

By Jackson's time the presidency had long since become an office sought by partisan candidates in popular elections. Though political parties had existed in Britain and Sweden as elite organizations in systems with a severely limited suffrage, under the leadership of Jefferson and Madison the Republican party became an instrument by which popular majorities could be organized, mobilized, and made effective in influencing the conduct of government. Henceforth a president would combine his role as a presumably nonpartisan chief executive with his role as a national leader of a partisan organization with a partisan following.[36]

If the presidential office was to be attained by partisan contestation, then in order to reach that office a serious presidential candidate would ordinarily need to gain the endorsement and support of a political party. Though the story of the evolution of the presidential nominating process has often been told, it so vividly reveals the impact of democratizing impulses that I want to summarize it briefly.

The Nominating Process

The first organized system for nominating candidates for president and vice president was the congressional caucus, which both the Republicans and the Federalists introduced in 1800.[37] Yet given the emerging strength of democratic ideology, a system so obtrusively closed to participation by any but a small group of congressional politicians was clearly vulnerable. Democratic sentiments we would find familiar in our own time were expressed in a resolution passed in the Ohio legislature in 1823:

> The time has now arrived when the machinations of the *few* to dictate to the *many* . . . will be met . . . by a people jealous of their rights. . . . The only unexceptional source from which nominations can proceed is the people themselves. To them belongs the right of choosing; and they alone can with propriety take any previous steps.[38]

By 1824, when the candidate of the congressional caucus of Democratic Republicans trailed a bad fourth in the election behind Jackson, John Quincy Adams, and Henry Clay, who all ran without benefit of a blessing by the caucus, the outrage to democratic sentiments was easily exploited, most notably by Jackson and his supporters. The congressional nominating caucus came to an end.[39]

In an obvious extension of democratic ideas, which by then had thoroughly assimilated the concept of representation, in 1831 and 1832 the nominating convention came into existence. But in due time,

> [j]ust as once the democratic passions of the people were roused against the Congressional caucus, so now they were turned against the convention system. . . . Away therefore with the delegates, who can never be trusted, and back to the people![40]

So in a further obvious extension of democratic ideas to the nominating process, from 1901 onward the direct primary was introduced, initially for state and congressional nominations, and soon for presidential candidates. The presidential primary system was in turn subjected to the democratizing impulse. "By the election of 1972," Ceaser remarks, "the election process had been transformed into what is essentially a plebiscitary system."[41]

Reducing Intermediate Forces

The democratization of the nominating process is instructive for many reasons—among others because after almost two centuries of trials employing three major forms with many variations, a sensible method of nominating presidential candidates still seems beyond the reach of Americans. The present system has its defenders no doubt, but they seem to be rapidly diminishing.

The democratization of the nominating process is also instructive because it shows how the relations between the public and presidents or presidential candidates have become increasingly direct. Jeffrey Tulis has described the enormous change that has taken place in the way presidents address the public—presidential speech, if you like. The view that prevailed during the early years of the republic, and for much of the nineteenth century, tended to follow "two general prescriptions for presidential speech." First, proposals for laws and policies would be written and directed principally to Congress; although public, they would be fashioned for congressional needs and not necessarily for general public understanding or approval. Second, when presidential speech was directed primarily to the people at large it would address general principals rather than specific issues.

> The inaugural address, for example, developed along lines that emphasized popular instruction in constitutional principle and the articulation of the general tenor and direction of presidential policy, while tending to avoid discussion of the merits of particular policy proposals.[42]

Presidents rarely directly addressed the general public, except possibly on official occasions. From Washington through Jackson, no president gave more than five speeches a year to the general public, a total that was not exceeded by half the presidents from Washington through William McKinley. When they did address the general public the early presidents rarely employed popular rhetoric or discussed their policies.[43] The great exception was Andrew Johnson, who, however, scarcely served as a model for his successors.[44] Moreover, Gil Troy has recently discovered that until Woodrow Wilson no president had ever "stumped on his own behalf." Until the 1830s, even presidential candidates did not make stump speeches. "Such behavior," Troy has written, "was thought undignified—and unwise. Presidential candidates, especially after nomination, were supposed to stand, not run, for election."[45]

What we now take as normal presidential behavior is a product of this century. The innovators were Theodore Roosevelt and to an even greater extent Woodrow Wilson.[46] Since their day and particularly in recent decades, the task of shaping presidential speech to influence and manipulate public opinion—if necessary by appealing over the heads of Congress in order to induce the Congress to support the president's policies—has become a central element in the art and science of presidential conduct.

THE PRESIDENT AND THE CONSTITUTIONAL SYSTEM

Thus the presidency has developed into an office that is the very embodiment of the kind of executive the Framers, so far as we can discern their intentions, strove to avoid. They did not wish an executive who would be a tribune of the people, a champion of popular majorities; who would gain office by popular election; who as a consequence of his popular election would claim a mandate for his policies; who in order to mobilize popular support for his policies would appeal directly to the people; who would shape the language, style, and delivery of his appeals so as best to create a public opinion favorable to his ambitions; and who whenever it seemed expedient would by-pass the members of the deliberative body in order to mobilize public opinion and thereby induce a reluctant Congress to enact his policies. That is, however, a fair description of the presidency that emerged out of the intersection of the Framers' design with the strongly democratic ideology that came to prevail among politically active Americans.

One response to this kind of presidency is to argue that these developments are, on the whole, good. They are good, it might be said, because democracy is good. more democracy is better than less democracy, and a more democratized presidency is better than a less democratized presidency. In the immortal cliché of the 1970 McGovern-Fraser Commission, "the cure for the ills of democracy is more democracy."[47] Yet this response does not seem to quiet the fears of a growing number of critics. In Arthur Schlesinger's now popular term, the presidency was transformed into the imperial presidency.[48] James Ceaser, Theodore Lowi, and others have referred to development of the plebiscitary presidency.[49] Lowi has also dubbed it the personal presidency, remarking that "the new politics of the president-centered Second Republic can best be described as a plebiscitary republic with a personal presidency."[50] Jeffrey Tulis calls the presidency that was seeded by Wilson and cultivated by his successors the rhetorical presidency.[51]

In criticisms of the modern presidency I want to distinguish several different perspectives. From one, what is lamentable is the break with the doctrines, intentions, and designs of the Founders. A rather different perspective, one more pragmatic and functional, emphasizes that the presidency is simply no longer working satisfactorily in its existing constitutional setting. For example, a president claiming a mandate for his policies may be blocked in one or both houses of Congress by a majority of members who in effect also claim a mandate for their policies. The result is not constructive compromise but deadlock or contradictions in policies. Examples are the recent conflicts over the deficit and over American policies in Central America.

From a third perspective, however, the presidency has come to endanger the operation of democratic processes. It is this perspective that I want to emphasize here.

I have alluded to the developments over the past two centuries as the *pseudodemocratization* of the presidency. I have no wish, much less any hope of adding to the other epithets another even more cumbersome and more ugly; but the term does speak directly to my concerns. By pseudodemocratization I mean a change taken with the ostensible and perhaps even actual purpose of enhancing the democratic process that in practice retains the aura of its democratic justification and yet has the effect, intended or unintended, of weakening the democratic process.

In the case of the presidency, I have two adverse consequences in mind. One, the more obvious, is a loss of popular and congressional control, direct and indirect, over the policies and decisions of the president. A president endowed with the mystique of a mandate—which may sometimes be deepened in a democratic country by the majesty and mystery generated by his popularity and his capacity to evoke and reflect popular feelings, yearnings, and hopes—may encounter resistance to a particular policy in Congress, perhaps even in the public. So the president exploits all the resources of his office to overcome that resistance: his rhetorical resources, his unique capacity to influence or even manipulate public opinion, and all the power and authority derived properly or factitiously from the Constitution—including his power as commander-in-chief, his unique authority over foreign affairs, his right or claim to executive privilege and secrecy, his authority and influence over officials in the executive branch, over the objectives they are obliged or induced to seek, and over the moneys and other resources necessary to reach those objectives. Whatever term we may wish to apply to an executive like this, we can hardly call it democratic.

The other consequence, though more elusive and not wholly independent of the first, is equally important. Now on one view—which I would describe as either simplistic or hostile—democracy means rule by public opinion. This view is mistaken both historically and theoretically. Democracy cannot be justified, I think, and its advocates have rarely sought to justify it as no more than the triumph of raw will. It can be and is justified because more than any feasible alternative it provides ordinary people with opportunities to discover what public policies and activities are best for themselves and for others, and to insure that collective decisions conform with— or at least do not persistently and fundamentally violate—the policies they believe best for themselves and for others.

I cannot undertake to explicate the complexities in the notion of discovering what is best for themselves and for others, nor do I need to. For it is obvious that discovering what is best for oneself or others requires far more than announcing one's raw will or surface preferences. Imagine this extreme situation. Suppose we were called upon to vote in a national plebiscite on a proposed treaty governing nuclear weapons that had been secretly negotiated between the president and the leader of the Soviet Union. Suppose further that the plebiscite is to be held one day after the agreement between the two leaders, and that we are to vote yes or no. The very perversity of this example serves to emphasize the crucial importance of opportunities for *understanding* as a requirement in the democratic process and illustrates why in the absence of such opportunities we should speak instead of a pseudodemocratic process.

Many writers have stressed the importance of *deliberation*. While some associate it with classical republicanism, deliberation is surely central to the idea of democratic decision making. What I have referred to elsewhere as enlightened understanding is an essential criterion for the democratic process. Deliberation is one crucial means, though I think not the only means, to enlightened understanding. Others include systematic research and analysis, experimentation, consultation with experts, orderly discussion, casual and disorderly discussion, day-dreaming, and self-inquiry.

The modern presidency all too often impairs not only deliberation but also other means to a more enlightened understanding by citizens and the Congress. Nelson Polsby's conclusions about the presidential selection process should be extended to the presidency as a whole. The increasing directness of relationships between a candidate or president and the public means that the traditional "intermediation processes," to use his term, have become less effective. Face-to-face groups, political parties, and interest groups are less autonomous and now rely heavily on the mass media.[52] For example, some nice experiments have recently shown that in assessing the relative importance of different issues, citizens are strongly influenced by television news.[53] I share Polsby's judgment that not only are deliberative processes weak in the general public's consideration of candidates and presidents, but they are also insufficiently subject to extensive review and appraisal by their peers.[54] I also share his judgment that "the directness of direct democracy in a very large scale society seems . . . illusory."[55]

CONCLUSION

How serious a matter is the pseudodemocratization of the presidency? What, if anything, can and should we do about it? To answer those questions responsibly would obviously take us far beyond the slender limits of an article. Among friends and colleagues I think I detect rather sharply differing perspectives. Let me list several.

First, the problem is not serious.

Second, though the problem is serious, the solution is to elect one more great president.

Third, the problem is serious but there isn't much we can do about it.

Fourth, the problem is serious but can be corrected by fairly modest incremental changes, possibly including a constitutional amendment, say one providing for an American equivalent to the question hour in the British or Canadian parliaments.

Last, the problem is so profoundly built into the interaction between the constitutional framework and democratic ideology that it cannot be solved without a fundamental alteration in one or the other. This is the conclusion to which I find myself increasingly drawn.

However, given that conclusion, a solution—assuming one is attainable—could require either that Americans transform their constitutional framework or give up their democratic beliefs. I think some critics may hope that Americans will reject their democratic ideology in favor of what these critics believe to be eighteenth-century republican doctrines that would restore the Constitution to its pristine condition in the form the Framers presumably intended. I think this alternative is not only morally wrong but politically and historically illusory.

A goal more suitable to the democratic beliefs of Americans would be to begin the arduous task of rethinking constitutional needs in order to determine whether they may not design a form of government better adapted to the requirements of democracy and less conducive to pseudodemocratization. Among other rethinking, Americans need to consider how to create better opportunities for deliberation and other means by which citizens might gain a more enlightened understanding of their political goals.

To achieve the daunting goal of rethinking the Constitution will not be easy and no one should believe that, properly done, it can be accomplished quickly. But begun now, it might be achieved before this century is over. It would be an appropriate undertaking to commence now that the bicentennial of the American Constitution is behind us.*

*This article is based on *The Tanner Lectures on Human Values*, vol. 10, edited by Grethe B. Peterson, University of Utah Press.

NOTES

1. Stanley Kelley, Jr., *Interpreting Elections* (Princeton, NJ: Princeton University Press, 1983), p. 217.

2. Leonard D. White, *The Jacksonians: A Study in Administrative History, 1829–1861* (New York: Free Press, 1954), p. 23.

3. Quoted in ibid., p. 23.

4. Cited in James W. Ceaser, *Presidential Selection: Theory and Development* (Princeton, NJ: Princeton University Press, 1979), p. 160, fn. 58.

5. White, *Jacksonians,* p. 23.

6. Ibid., p. 23.

7. Ibid., p. 24.

8. Although Madison and Hamilton opposed the contingent solution of a House election in the event that no candidate received a majority of electoral votes, Gouverneur Morris and James Wilson accepted it as not too great a concession. Ceaser, *Presidential Selection,* pp. 80–81.

9. Ibid., p. 84.

10. Edward S. Corwin, *The President: Offices and Powers, 1789–1948,* 3rd. ed. (New York: New York University Press, 1948), p. 20.

11. Wilfred E. Binkley, *President and Congress* (New York: Alfred A. Knopf, 1947), p. 56.

12. Leonard D. White, *The Jeffersonians: A Study in Administrative History, 1801–1829* (New York: Free Press, 1951), p. 31.

13. Lincoln drew primarily on the war power, which he created by uniting the president's constitutional obligation "to take care that the laws be faithfully executed" with his power as commander-in-chief. He interpreted the war power as a veritable cornucopia of implicit constitutional authority for the extraordinary emergency measures he undertook during an extraordinary national crisis. (Corwin, *The President,* pp. 277ff.)

14. "Every executive officer, in particular the President, Roosevelt maintained. 'was a steward of the people bound actively and affirmatively to do all he could for the people. . . .' He held therefore that, unless specifically forbidden by the Constitution or by law, the President had 'to do anything that the needs of the nation demanded. . . .' 'Under this interpretation of executive power,' he recalled, 'I did and caused to be done many things not previously done. . . . I did not usurp power, but I did greatly broaden the use of executive power,'" See John Morton Blum, *The Republican Roosevelt* (New York: Atheneum, 1954), p. 108.

15. Woodrow Wilson, *Cabinet Government in the United States* (Stamford, CT: Overbrook Press, 1947), orig. publication in *International Review,* 1879.

16. "He seems not to have paid much attention to the practical question of how so radical an alteration was to be brought about. As far as I know, Wilson's only published words on how to initiate the English system are in the article, *Committee or Cabinet Government*, which appeared in the *Overland Monthly* for January 1884." His solution was to amend Section 6 of Article I of the Constitution to permit members of Congress to hold offices as members of the Cabinet, and to extend the terms of the president and representatives. See, Walter Lippmann, *Introduction to Congressional Government* (New York: Meridian Books, 1956), pp. 14–15.

17. Wilson's unfavorable comparative judgment is particularly clear in *Congressional Government: A Study in American Politics* (New York: Meridian Books, 1956; reprint of 1885 ed.), p. 181. Just as Jackson had proposed the direct election of the president, in his first annual message Wilson proposed that a system of direct national primaries be adopted. See Ceaser, *Presidential Selection*, p. 173.

18. Wilson, *Congressional Government*, p. 181.

19. Ibid., pp. 31, 72–73, 145.

20. The Seventeenth Amendment requiring a direct election of senators was not adopted until 1913.

21. Woodrow Wilson, *Constitutional Government in the United States* (New York: Columbia University Press, 1908), pp. 67–68, 70, 202–203.

22. Kelley, *Interpreting Elections*, p. 99.

23. For other examples of claims to a presidential mandate resulting from the election, see William Safire, *Safire's Political Dictionary* (New York: Random House, 1978), p. 398; and Kelley, *Interpreting Elections*, pp. 72–74, 126–129, 168.

24. See "mandate" in *Oxford English Dictionary* (Oxford, England: Oxford University Press, 1971, compact edition); Safire, *Political Dictionary*, p. 398; Jack C. Plano and Milton Greenberg, *The American Political Dictionary* (New York: Holt, Rinehart and Winston, 1979), p. 130; Julius Gould and William L. Kolb, *A Dictionary of the Social Sciences* (New York: The Free Press, 1964), p. 404; Jay M. Shafritz, *The Dorsey Dictionary of American Government and Politics* (Chicago: The Dorsey Press, 1988), p. 340.

25. Kelley, *Interpreting Elections*, pp. 126–128.

26. Cited in ibid., p. 133.

27. Cited in ibid., p. 134.

28. Ibid., p. 136.

29. Paul F. Lazarsfeld, Bernard Berelson, and Hazel Gaudet, *The People's Choice* (New York: Columbia University Press, 1948).

30. The early election studies are summarized in Bernard R. Berelson and Paul F. Lazarsfeld, *Voting* (Chicago: University of Chicago Press, 1954), pp. 331ff.

31. Angus Campbell et al., *The American Voter* (New York: Wiley, 1960)

32. Quoted in Safire, *Political Dictionary*, p. 398.

33. Kelley, *Interpreting Elections*, pp. 139–140.

34. Ibid., pp. 170–172, 174–181, 185, 187.

35. Ceaser, *Presidential Selection*, pp. 47ff.

36. As Ceaser remarks, *Presidential Selection*, pp. 88, 90: "The nonpartisan selection system established by the Founders barely survived a decade By the election of 1796, traces of partisanship were already clearly in evidence, and by 1800 the contest was being fought on strictly partisan lines." Like many other innovations, Jefferson's had unintended consequences. "Jefferson . . . had an abiding distrust of national elections and, except in the case of his own election, never regarded them as the proper forum for making decisive changes. . . . The paradox of Jefferson's election in 1800 was that while he was chosen for partisan reasons, he did not intend to institute a system of permanent party competition."

37. Noble E. Cunningham, Jr., *The Jeffersonian Republicans: The Formation of Party Organization, 1789–1801* (Chapel Hill: University of North Carolina Press, 1957), pp. 163–165.

38. M. Ostrogorski, *Democracy and the Party System in the United States* (New York: Macmillan, 1926), p. 12, fn. 1.

39. Though Jackson gained more votes than Adams, both popular and electoral, he was denied victory in the House of Representatives.

40. Ostrogorski, *Democracy,* p. 342.

41. Ceaser describes three phases in the evolution of the presidential selection process since the introduction of the primaries: 1912–1920, a period of the expansion of the primaries and the "plebiscitary model"; 1920–1960s, which saw the decline of primaries and the resurgence of parties; and the period since 1972. See *Presidential Selection,* pp. 215ff.

42. Jeffrey K. Tulis, *The Rhetorical Presidency* (Princeton, NJ· Princeton University Press, 1987), pp. 46–47.

43. Ibid., p. 64, table 3.1 and 66, table 3.2.

44. Ibid., pp. 87ff.

45. *New York Times,* January 17, 1988.

46. On Theodore Roosevelt, see Tulis, *Rhetorical Presidency,* pp. 95–116; on Wilson, see ibid., pp. 118–137.

47. Ceaser, *Presidential Selection,* p. 275.

48. Arthur Schlesinger, Jr., *The Imperial Presidency* (Boston: Houghton Mifflin, 1973).

49. Ceaser, *Presidential Selection,* p. 5; Theodore J. Lowi, *The Personal President: Power Invested, Promise Unfulfilled* (Ithaca, NY: Cornell University Press, 1985), pp. 97ff, 134ff.

50. Lowi, *Personal President,* p. xi.

51. Tulis, *Rhetorical Presidency.*

52. Nelson W. Polsby, *Consequences of Party Reform* (New York: Oxford University Press, 1983), pp. 134, 170–172.

53. Shanto Iyengar and Donald R. Kinder, *News That Matters: Television and American Opinion* (Chicago: University of Chicago Press, 1987).

54. Polsby, *Consequences,* pp. 134, 170–172

55 Ibid., p. 147.

Parliamentary Government in the United States?

Gerald M. Pomper

In 1996, the important political decision for American political warriors was not the contest between Bill Clinton and Robert Dole. "For virtually all of the powerful groups behind the Republican Party their overriding goal of keeping control of the House stemmed from their view that that was where the real political power—near- and long-term—lay." Moreover, "Sitting in his office on the sixth floor of the AFL-CIO building on 16th Street, political director Steve Rosenthal said that labor, too, saw the House elections as the most important of 1996—more important than the contest for the Presidency" (Drew 1997: 2, 72).

These informed activists alert us to a major shift in the character of American politics. To baldly summarize my argument, I suggest that the United States is moving toward a system of parliamentary government, a fundamental change in our constitutional regime. This change is not a total revolution in our institutions, and it will remain incomplete, given the drag of historical tradition. Nevertheless, this trend can be seen if we look beyond the formal definition of parliamentary governments, the union of legislature and executive.

The parliamentary model is evident in both empirical and normative political science. Anthony Downs begins his classic work by defining a political party virtually as a parliamentary coalition, "a team of men seeking to control the governing apparatus by gaining office in a duly constituted election" (Downs 1957: 25). Normatively, for decades, some political scientists have sought to create a "responsible party system" (American Political Science Association Committee on Political Parties 1950), resembling such parliamentary features as binding party programs and legislative cohesion.

Significant developments toward parliamentary government can be seen in contemporary American politics. The evidence of these trends cannot be found in the formal institutions of the written (capital C) Constitution. Institutional stability, however, may disguise basic change. For example, in formal terms, the president is not chosen until the electoral college meets in December, although we know the outcome within hours of the closing of the polls in early November.

Let us go beyond "literary theory"[1] and compare the present reality of U.S. politics with more general characteristics attributed to parliamentary systems. In the ideal parliamentary model, elections are contests between competitive parties presenting

Source: Gerald M. Pomper, "Parliamentary Government in the United States?" in John C. Green and Daniel M. Shea, eds., *The State of the Parties,* 3rd ed. (Lanham, MD: Rowman and Littlefield Publishers, 1999), pp. 252–270.

Gerald M. Pomper is Board of Governors professor of political science at Rutgers University. He is author of *The Election of 1996.*

alternative programs, under leaders chosen from and by the parties' legislators or activists. Electoral success is interpreted as a popular mandate in support of these platforms. Using their parliamentary powers, the leaders then enforce party discipline to implement the promised programs.

The United States increasingly evidences these characteristics of parliamentary government. This fundamental change is due to the development of stronger political parties. In particular, I will try to demonstrate transformations of American politics evident in the following six characteristics of the parties:

- The parties present meaningful programs;
- They bridge the institutional separations of national government;
- They reasonably fulfill their promises;
- They act cohesively under strong legislative leadership;
- They have assumed a major role in campaigning; and
- They provide the recruitment base for presidential candidates.

PARTY PROGRAMS

A parliamentary system provides the opportunity to enact party programs. By contrast, in the American system, observers often have doubted that there were party programs, and the multiple checks and balances of American government have made it difficult to enact any coherent policies. For evidence, I examine the major party platforms of 1992–1996, the 1994 Republican Contract with America, and the 1996 Democratic Families First Agenda.

In previous research (Pomper and Lederman 1980: chapters 7 and 8), we argued that party platforms were meaningful statements and that they were good forecasts of government policy. We found, contrary to cynical belief, that platforms were composed of far more than hot air and empty promises. Rather, a majority of the platforms were relevant defenses and criticisms of the parties' past records and reasonably specific promises of future actions. Moreover, the parties delivered: close to 70 percent of their many specific pledges were actually fulfilled to some degree.

Furthermore, parties have differed in their programs. Examining party manifestos in the major industrial democracies over forty years, 1948–1988, Budge concludes, "American Democrats and Republicans . . . consistently differentiate themselves from each other on such matters as support for welfare, government intervention, foreign aid, and defense, individual initiative and freedom. . . . Indeed, they remain as far apart as many European parties on these points, and more so than many" (1993: 696f.).

In recent years, we might expect platforms to be less important. National conventions have become television exercises rather than occasions for party decision making. The expansion of interest groups has made it more difficult to accomplish policy intentions. Candidate-centered campaigning reduces the incentives to achieve collective, party goals and appears to focus more on individual characteristics than on policy issues.

The party platforms of 1992 provide a test. An independent replication confirms our previous research on platform content. Perhaps surprisingly, this new work indicates that the most recent platforms, like those of previous years, provide significant political and policy statements. These manifestos meet one of the tests of a parliamentary system: meaningful party programs.

The 1992 platforms[2] can be divided into three categories: puff pieces of rhetoric and fact, approvals of one's own party policy record and candidates or disapproval of the opposition, and pledges for future action. The pledges, in turn, can be categorized as being simply rhetorical or general promises or more useful statements of future intentions, such as promises to continue existing policies, expressions of party goals, pledges of action, or quite detailed promises.[3]

As seen in Figure 1, there is much in the platforms that induces yawns and cynicism. The Democrats were fond of such rhetorical statements as "It is time to listen to the grassroots of America." (Actually a difficult task, since most plants are speechless.) The Republicans were prone to vague self-congratulation, as when they boasted, "Republicans recognize the importance of having fathers and mothers in the home." (Possibly even more so if these parents are unemployed, not distracted by jobs?)

Nevertheless, these documents—while hardly models of rational discussion—did provide useful guides to party positions. When the Democrats criticized "the Bush administration's efforts to bankrupt the public school system . . . through private

FIGURE 1   *Platform Content, 1992*

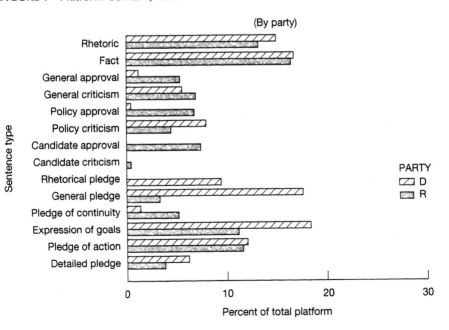

school vouchers," and when the Republicans declared that "American families must be given choice in education," there was an implicit policy debate. Comparison was also facilitated by the similar distributions of platform statements across policy areas. Each party tended to devote about as much attention to particular or related policy areas as its opposition. The only important difference is that Democrats gave far more attention to issues involving women and abortion. Overall, about half of the platforms were potentially useful to the voters in locating the parties on a policy continuum.[4]

The 1994 Contract with America was even more specific. It consisted entirely of promises for the future, potentially focusing attention on public policy. Moreover, the large majority of its fifty-five sentences were reasonably specific promises. Pledges of definite action comprised 42 percent of the total document, and detailed pledges another 27 percent, while less than 4 percent consisted of only vague rhetoric. From the promise of a balanced budget amendment to advocacy of term limits, the Republicans foreshadowed major innovations in American institutions and law. This high degree of specificity can facilitate party accountability to the electorate.

PARTY AS PROGRAMMATIC BRIDGE

The great obstacle to party responsibility in the United States has always been the separation of national institutions, the constitutional division between the executive and legislative branches. Party has sometimes been praised as a bridge across this separation (Ford 1914), and party reformers have often sought to build stronger institutional ties, even seeking radical constitutional revision to further the goal (Ranney 1954). Despite these hopes and plans, however, the separation has remained. Presidential parties make promises, but Congress has no institutional responsibility to act on these pledges.

In a parliamentary system, the most current research argues—contrary to Downs—"that office is used as a basis for attaining policy goals, rather than that policy is subordinated to office" (Budge and Kerman 1990: 31, chapter 2). In the United States as well, party program rather than institutional discipline may provide the bridge between the legislature and its executive. In previous years, however, we lacked a ready means to compare presidential and congressional programs. Now we have authoritative statements from both institutionalized wings of the parties. The Republican Contract with America marks a major first step toward coherent, interinstitutional programs.

The 1994 contract was far more than a campaign gimmick or an aberrational invention of Newt Gingrich. It was actually a terse condensation of continuing Republican Party doctrine, as can be seen in the left-hand columns of Table 1, a comparison of its specific pledges with the 1992 and 1996 Republican platforms. A majority of these promises had already been anticipated in 1992 and the party endorsed five-sixths of its provisions in 1996.

For example, the 1992 national platform criticized the Democratic Congress for its refusal "to give the President a line-item veto to curb their self-serving porkbarrel

TABLE 1 *Inclusion of Congressional Pledges in National Party Platforms*

	Republican "Contract" Party Platform of		Democratic "Agenda" Party Platform of	
	1992	*1996*	*1992*	*1996*
Mentioned only	5 (12)	3 (7)	5 (6)	1 (1)
Took credit	2 (5)	16 (38)	0 (0)	16 (18)
Future promise	16 (38)	16 (38)	36 (40)	48 (53)
No mention	19 (45)	7 (17)	49 (54)	25 (28)

Note: N = 42 for "Contract;" *N* = 90 for "Agenda." Percentages appear in parentheses.

projects" and promised adoption of the procedure in a Republican Congress. The 1994 contract repeated the pledge of a "line-item veto to restore fiscal responsibility to an out-of-control Congress," while the 1996 platform reiterated, "A Republican president will fight wasteful spending with the line-item veto which was finally enacted by congressional Republicans this year over bitter Democrat opposition."[5] Republicans built on traditional party doctrine, specified the current party program, and then affirmed accountability for their actions. Building on this achievement in party building, and their claims of legislative "success," the Republicans have already promised to present a new contract for the elections at the turn of the century.

The Democrats imitatively developed a congressional program, the Families First Agenda, for the 1996 election. Intended primarily as a campaign document by the minority party, it is less specific than the Republican contract. Still, 90 of its 204 statements were reasonably precise promises. The legislative Democrats also showed significant and increasing agreement with their presidential wing and platform. By 1996, as detailed in the right-hand columns of Table 1, three-fourths of the congressional agenda was also incorporated into the Clinton program, and the official platform specifically praised the congressional program. The agenda's three sections—"security," "opportunity," and "responsibility"—paralleled those of the national platform (which added "freedom," "peace," and "community"—values presumably shared by congressional Democrats), and many provisions are replicated from one document to another.

The Republican Contract with America and the Democratic Families First Agenda, then, can be seen as emblems of party responsibility and likely precedents for further development toward parliamentary practice in American politics. Party doctrine has become a bridge across the separation of institutions.

PROGRAM FULFILLMENT

Both Democrats and Republicans, as they held power, followed through on their election promises, as expected in a parliamentary model. Despite the clumsiness of the Clinton administration, and despite the Democrats' loss of their long-term control of Congress in their catastrophic election defeat in 1994, they actually fulfilled most of the 167 reasonably specific pledges in their 1992 manifesto (see Figure 2).

A few examples illustrate the point. The Democrats promised negative action, in opposing major change in the Clean Air Act—and they stood fast. In their 1993 economic program, the Democrats won action similar to their platform pledge to "make the rich pay their fair share in taxes." Through executive action, the Clinton administration redeemed its promise to reduce U.S. military forces in Europe. The Democrats achieved full action on their promise of "A reasonable waiting period to permit background checks for purchases of handguns."

To be sure, the Democrats have not become latter-day George Washingtons, unable to tell an untruth. There clearly has been no action on the pledge to "limit overall campaign spending and . . . the disproportionate and excessive role of PACs." In other cases, the Democrats did try but were defeated, most notably in their promise of "reform of the health-care system to control costs and make health care affordable." (It is obviously too early to judge fulfillment of 1996 Democratic pledges, made in either the presidential platform or the congressional party Families First Agenda.)

Most impressive are not the failures but the achievements, illustrated in Figure 2. Altogether, Democrats did accomplish something on nearly 70 percent of their 1992 promises, in contrast to inaction on only 19 percent. In a completely independent analysis, another researcher came to remarkably similar conclusions, calculating Clinton's fulfillment of his campaign promises at the same level, 69 percent (Shaw 1996).[6] I do not believe this record is the result of the virtues of the Democratic Party, which I use for this analysis simply because it controlled the government, nor can this record be explained by Bill Clinton's personal qualities of steadfast commitment to principle. The explanation is that we now have a system in which parties, whatever their names or leaders, make and keep promises.

FIGURE 2 *Fulfillment of 1992 Democratic Platform Pledges*

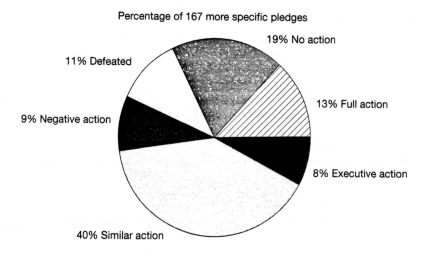

Percentage of 167 more specific pledges

11% Defeated

19% No action

9% Negative action

13% Full action

8% Executive action

40% Similar action

This conclusion is strengthened if we examine the Republicans. While the GOP of course did not hold the presidency, it did win control of Congress in 1994. In keeping with the model of parliamentary government, Republicans interpreted their impressive victory as an endorsement of the Contract with America, and then they attempted to implement the program. We must remember that the 1994 election cannot be seen as a popular mandate for the Republican manifesto: two-thirds of the public had not even heard of it in November, and only 19 percent expressed support. The contract expressed party ideology, not voter demands.

Despite its extravagant tone and ideological character, the Republicans delivered on their contract, just as Democrats fulfilled much of their 1992 platform (see Figure 3). Of the more specific pledges, 69 percent were accomplished in large measure[7] (coincidentally, perhaps, the same success rate as the Democrats'). Even if we include the rhetorical and unspecific sentences in our test, as in Figure 3, more than one-half of this party program was accomplished.

Despite the heroics of vetoes and government shutdown, despite bicameralism and the vaunted autonomy of the Senate, and despite popular disapproval, the reality is that most of the Contract with America was implemented. The Republicans accomplished virtually all that they promised in regard to congressional reform, unfunded mandates and welfare, as well as substantial elements of their program in regard to crime, child support, defense, and the social security earnings limit. Defeated on major economic issues, they later achieved many of these goals, including a balanced budget agreement in place of a constitutional amendment, a children's tax credit, and a reduction in capital gains taxes. On these questions, as indeed on the general range of American government, they won the greatest victory of all: they set the agenda for the United States, and the Democratic president eventually followed their lead. Such initiative is what we would expect in a parliamentary system.

FIGURE 3   *Fulfillment of "Contract" Pledges*

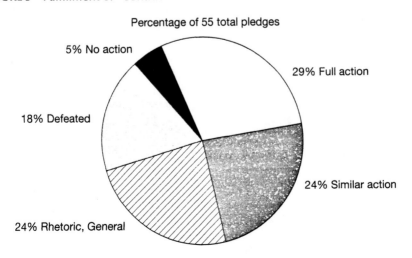

Percentage of 55 total pledges

5% No action

29% Full action

18% Defeated

24% Similar action

24% Rhetoric, General

Congressional performance on the Contract with America also carries significant implications for the theory of political parties. Monroe and Bernardoni (1995) test its implementation against two party concepts: responsible parties and a Downsian spatial model. Overall, the implementation of the contract lends support to a different "cleavage" model developed by Page (1978), in which the parties "offer ideologically distinct positions . . . on those issues which have historically divided the parties and are related to support from voting blocs and interest groups" (Monroe and Bernardoni 1995: 2). This model fits well with that developed through the Manifestos Research Project, comparing party programs across Western democracies. In this model, "what parties offer electors thus seems to be a choice between selective policy agendas, not between specific alternative policies addressed to items on a universal agenda" (Klingermann, Hofferbert, and Budge 1994: 25).

PARTY COHESION

Program fulfillment results from party unity. The overall trend in Congress, as expected in a parliamentary system, is toward more party differentiation.[8] One indicator is the proportion of legislative votes in which a majority of one party is opposed to a majority of the other (i.e., "party unity" votes). Not too long ago, in 1969, such party conflict was evident on only about one-third of all roll calls. By 1995, nearly three-fourths of House votes and over two-thirds of Senate roll calls showed these clear party differences.

Figure 4 shows another trend—the increasing commitment of representatives and senators to their parties. The average legislator showed party loyalty (expressed as a "party unity score") of less than 60 percent in 1970. In 1996, the degree of loyalty had climbed to 80 percent for Democrats and to an astounding 87 percent for Republicans. Cohesion was still greater on the thirty-three House roll calls in 1995 on final passage of items in the Contract with America. Republicans were unanimous on sixteen of these votes, and the *median* number of Republican dissents was but *one*. Neither the British House of Commons nor the erstwhile Supreme Soviet could rival this record of party unity.

The congressional parties now are ideologically cohesive bodies, even with the occasional but significant split among Democrats on such issues as trade and welfare reform. We need to revise our political language to take account of this ideological cohesion. There are no more "Dixiecrats" or southern conservative Democrats, and therefore there is no meaningful "conservative coalition" in Congress. Supportive evidence is found in the same roll call data: the average southern Democrat supported his or her party 71 percent of the time in 1996, and barely over a tenth of the roll calls found Dixie legislators in opposition to their own party and in alliance with a majority of Republicans. It also seems likely that "liberal Republican" will soon be an oxymoron restricted to that patronized minority holding a pro-choice attitude on abortion, confined to the back of the platform or, so to speak, to the back of the party bus.

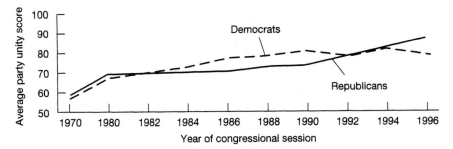

FIGURE 4   *Partisan Unity in Congress*

Republicans have been acting like a parliamentary party beyond their ideological unity on a party program. The "central leaders efforts during the Contract period were attempts to *impose* a form of party government," which succeeded in winning cooperation from committee chairman and changed roll call behavior as "many Republicans modified their previous preferences in order to accommodate their party colleagues" (Owens 1997: 259, 265). Beyond programmatic goals, the Republicans have created strong party institutions in Congress, building on previous Democratic reforms (Rohde 1991).

Even after the Contract with America is completely passed or forgotten. these institutions will likely remain. In their first days in power, as they organized the House, the Republicans centralized power in the hands of the Speaker, abolished institutionalized caucuses of constituency interests, distributed chairmanships on the basis of loyalty to the party program and in disregard of seniority, and changed the ratios of party memberships on committees to foster passage of the party program. Instruments of discipline have become more prevalent and more exercised, including caucus resolutions, committee assignments, aid in securing campaign contributions, and disposition of individual members' bills.

The building of parliamentary party institutions continues. Some of the structural changes in the House have now been adopted by both the Senate and the Democrats, perhaps most significantly the rotation of committee chairmanships, curbing the antiparty influence of seniority. The Republicans have insisted that committees report party bills, even when opposed by the chair, as in the cases of term limits and telecommunications. The party record became the major issue in the 1996 congressional elections, with party leaders Newt Gingrich and Richard Armey doing their best to aid loyalists—but only loyalists—through fund-raising and strongarming of ideological allies among political action committees.

The party differences and cohesion in Congress partially reflect the enhanced power of legislative leaders. The more fundamental reason for congressional party unity—as in parliamentary systems—is not discipline as much as agreement. Party members vote together because they think the same way. Republicans act as conservatives because they *are* conservatives; Democrats act like liberals or, as they now prefer, progressives because they believe in these programs.

Supportive evidence on the ideological consistency of party elites can be found in studies of other partisans. In research conducted nearly forty years ago, Herbert McClosky and his students (1960: 406–27) demonstrated the large ideological differences among the two major parties' national convention delegates. Continuing party differences are also shown in more recent studies of convention delegates. John Kessel and his students (Bruce, Clark, and Kessel 1991: 1089–1106) have drawn the ideological structures of these party representatives. Though not monolithic, they are sharply distinct between the parties. These divisions persist among broader layers of party activists, such as contributors and campaign workers (Bruzios 1990: 581–601). Similarly, extensive surveys of state party convention delegates show consistent ideological differences, independent of state cultures (Abramowitz, McGlennon, and Rapoport 1986: chapter 3). There is a difference, consistent with the expectations of a parliamentary system.

The most recent nominating conventions provide further support for the ideological cohesion of the national parties. The CBS/*New York Times* Poll found massive differences between Republican and Democratic delegates on questions involving the scope of government, social issues, and international affairs (see Table 2). A majority of these partisans opposed each other on *all* of ten questions; they were remotely similar on only one issue—international trade—and were in essentially dif-

TABLE 2   *Percentages for 1996 Convention Delegates' Issue Attitudes*

	Democratic		Republican		All
	Delegates	*Voters*	*Delegates*	*Voters*	*Voters*
Scope of government:					
Government should do more to:					
Solve the nation's problems	76	53	4	20	36
Regulate the environment and					
safety practices of business	60	66	4	37	53
Promote traditional values	27	41	56	44	42
Social issues:					
Abortion should be permitted					
in all cases	61	30	11	22	27
Favor a nationwide ban on					
assault weapons	91	80	34	62	72
Necessary to have laws to					
protect racial minorities	88	62	30	39	51
Affirmative action programs					
should be continued	81	59	9	28	48
Organized prayer should be					
permitted in public schools	20	66	57	69	66
International:					
Trade restrictions necessary to					
protect domestic industries	54	65	31	56	60
Children of illegal immigrants					
should be allowed to attend					
public school	79	63	28	46	54

Source: CBS News/*New York Times* Poll, *The New York Times,* August 26, 1996, A12.

ferent political worlds (fifty or more percentage points apart) on issues of governmental regulation, the environment, abortion, assault weapons, civil rights, affirmative action, and immigration.

PARTY ORGANIZATION

Party unity has another source, related to the recruitment of individual candidates with a common ideology. Unity is also fostered by the development of strong national party organizations, precisely measured by the dollars of election finance. Amid all of the proper concern over the problems of campaign contributions and spending, we have neglected the increasing importance of the parties in providing money, "the mother's milk of politics."

There are two large sources of party money: the direct subsidies provided by the federal election law, and the "soft money" contributions provided for the parties' organizational work. Together, even in 1992, these funds totaled $213 million for the major candidates and their parties.[9] Underlining the impact of this party spending, the Republican and Democratic presidential campaigns in 1992 each spent twice as much money as did billionaire Ross Perot, whose candidacy is often seen as demonstrating the decline of the parties.

An enhanced party role was also evident in the other national elections of 1992. Beyond direct contributions and expenditures, the parties developed a variety of ingenious devices, such as bundling, coordinated spending, and agency agreements, to again become significant players in the election finance game. Overall, in 1992, the six national party committees spent $290 million. (For comparison, total spending in all House and Senate races was $678 million.[10]) The party role became even more evident in 1994, with the victory of a Republican majority originally recruited and financed by Newt Gingrich's GOPAC, a party body disguised as a political action committee.

The party role expanded hugely in 1996, bolstered by the Supreme Court, in its 1996 *Colorado* decision.[11] The Court approved unlimited "independent" spending by political parties on behalf of its candidates. Moreover, four justices explicitly indicated that they were prepared to approve even direct unlimited expenditures by parties, and three other justices are ready to rule on that issue in a future case.

The parties quickly took advantage of the Court's opening. Together, Republican and Democratic party groups spent close to a billion dollars, conservatively 35 percent of all election spending, without even counting the $160 million in federal campaign subsidies for the presidential race.[12] Despite the commonplace emphasis on "candidate-centered" campaigns, the parties' expenditures were greater than that of all individual House and Senate candidates combined. In discussions of election finance, political action committees receive most of the attention, and condemnation, but the reality is that PACs are of decreasing importance. PACs' money has barely increased since 1988, and they were outspent 2 to 1 by the parties in 1996.[13] The parties now have the muscle to conduct campaigns and present their programs, to act as we would expect of parliamentary contestants.

PARTY LEADERSHIP

Parties need leaders as much as money. In parliamentary governments, leaders achieve power through their party activity. That has always been the case even in America when we look at congressional leadership: a long apprenticeship in the House and Senate has usually been required before one achieves the positions of Speaker, majority and minority leader, and whip. A strong indication of the development of parliamentary politics in the United States is the unrecognized trend toward party recruitment for the presidency, the allegedly separated institution.

The conventional wisdom is quite different. Particularly since the "reforms" of the parties beginning with the McGovern-Fraser Commission after 1968, presidential nominations have apparently become contests among self-starting aspirants who succeed by assembling a personal coalition that appeals directly to the voters in a series of uncoordinated state primaries. We have come to assume the disappearance of party influence in presidential nominations.

In reality, however, the parties have become important sources of leadership recruitment. Since 1980, as specified in Table 3, we have seen ten presidential nominations, all of them the choice of an established party leader, even in the face of significant insurgencies. These selections include four renominations of the sitting party leader, with only one facing a strong challenge (Carter in 1980); four selections of the leader of the established dominant faction of the party; and two selections of the leader of a major party faction.

Presidential nominations certainly have changed, but the trend is toward different, rather than less, party influence. Look back at the "traditional" convention system, as analyzed by Paul David and associates (1960). Historically, some presidents retired voluntarily or involuntarily after one term, but every chief executive since 1972 has been renominated, including Gerald Ford, never elected to national office. When nominations have been open, inheritance and factional victory have become the universal paths to success. In contrast, past patterns of inner-group selection or compromise in stalemate have disappeared.[14]

TABLE 3   *Recent Presidential Nominations*

Year	Party	Candidate	Type
1980	Democrat	Carter	Renomination of incumbent
1980	Republican	Reagan	Dominant factional victory
1984	Democrat	Mondale	Dominant factional victory
1984	Republican	Reagan	Renomination of incumbent
1988	Democrat	Dukakis	Factional victory
1988	Republican	Bush	Dominant factional victory
1992	Democrat	Clinton	Factional victory
1992	Republican	Bush	Renomination of incumbent
1996	Democrat	Clinton	Renomination of incumbent
1996	Republican	Dole	Dominant factional victory

The selection of presidential nominees still evidences influence by leaders of the organized parties or its factions, even if these choices have not been made primarily by the formal party leadership (such as Democratic "superdelegates" and similar Republican officials). These decisions are quite different from the selection of such insurgents as Goldwater in 1964 or McGovern in 1972, the typical illustrations of the asserted decline of party. While insurgents do now have access to the contest for presidential nominations, the reality is that they fail in that contest, as shown by the examples of Democrats Edward Kennedy in 1980, Gary Hart in 1984, and Jesse Jackson in 1988 and the virtual absence of any Republican insurgents throughout the period until 1992.

The presidential nominations of 1992 and 1996 particularly evidence the party basis of recruitment. There were notable insurgent candidates: Republican Pat Buchanan twice attempted to reincarnate Barry Goldwater, Jerry Brown imitated McGovern, and Paul Tsongas eschewed partisanship. In contrast to earlier years, however, all were soundly defeated by established party figures. George Bush not only was the incumbent leader but also typified the career of a party politician, securing his nomination as the heir of the retiring leader, Ronald Reagan. Robert Dole was the quintessence of a parliamentary party leader, achieving nomination on the basis of his past service as national chairman, vice-presidential candidate, and legislative leader of the Senate and, moreover, against very pallid opposition, including a Buchanan insurgency even weaker than in 1992.

Bill Clinton came to party leadership from the position of governor, reflecting the variety of career opportunities available in a federal system, but Arkansas was hardly a robust power center. Clinton's real base was the Democratic Leadership Council (DLC), which provided much of his program, his source of contacts and finances, and his opportunity for national exposure. The DLC, composed of party officials and officeholders, is an organized party faction (Hale 1994: 249–63). Clinton's 1992 success is a testament to the influence of that faction, far more than evidence of the decline of party and the substitution of unmediated access to the voters. The absence of any challenge to the president in 1996 underlines the renewed importance of party leadership, despite his political vulnerabilities and intraparty discontent with his turn away from party orthodoxy.

Contrary to the fears of many observers (Polsby 1983), the new presidential nominating system has developed along with new institutions of party cohesion. Front-runners have great advantages in this new system (Mayer 1995: chapter 2), but that means that prominent party figures—rather than obscure dark horses stabled in smoke-filled rooms—are most likely to win nomination. Contrary to fears of a personalistic presidency, the candidates chosen in the postreform period tackle tough issues, support their party's program, and agree with their congressional party's leaders on policy positions as much, or even more, than in the past (Patterson and Bice 1997).

Contemporary presidential nominations have become comparable—although not identical—to the choice of leadership in a hypothetical U.S. parliamentary system. Is the selection of Reagan in 1980 that different from the British Tories' choice of Margaret Thatcher to lead the party's turn toward ideological free market conservatism? In a parliamentary system, would not Bush and Dole, Reagan's successors, be the ideal analogues to Britain's John Major? Is the selection of Mondale as the liberal standard-bearer of the liberal Democratic Party that different from the lineage of left-wing leaders in the British Labour Party? Is the Democratic turn toward the electoral center with Clinton not analogous to Labour's replacement of Michael Foot by Neil Kinnock, John Smith, and Tony Blair?

To be sure, American political leadership is still quite open, the parties quite permeable. Presidential nominations do depend greatly on personal coalitions, and popular primaries are the decisive points of decision. Yet it is also true that leadership of the parties is still, and perhaps increasingly, related to prominence within the parties.

TOWARD PARLIAMENTARY GOVERNMENT?

Do these changes amount to parliamentary government in the United States? Certainly not in the most basic definitional sense, since we will surely continue to have separated institutions, in which the president is elected differently from the legislature, and the Senate differently from the House. Unlike a formal parliamentary system, the president will hold his office for a fixed term, regardless of the "votes of confidence" he wins or loses in Congress. By using his veto and the bully pulpit of the White House, Bill Clinton has proven that the president is independent and still "relevant." It is also true that we will never have a system in which a single political party can both promise and deliver a complete and coherent ideological program. As Jones correctly maintains, American government remains a "separated system," in which "serious and continuous in-party and cross-party coalition building typifies policy making" (1996: 19). These continuing features were strikingly evident in the adoption of welfare reform in the 104th Congress.

But parliaments also evidence coalition building, particularly in multiparty systems. British parliamentarians can be stalemated by factional and party differences on issues such as Northern Ireland just as the Democrats and Republicans were on health care in the 103d Congress. Achieving a consensual policy on the peace process in Israel's multiparty system is as difficult as achieving a consensual policy on abortion among America's two parties.

In the 105th Congress, we have already seen more open coalition building. With a close division among the parties in the House, more frequent use of filibusters in the Senate, and the president's veto threats, the necessities of politics and government have forced compromise, most notably in the budget-balancing agreement. Nevertheless, the party basis of parliamentary government will continue, because the ideological basis of intraparty coherence and interparty difference will continue and even be increased with the ongoing departure of moderate legislators of both parties. The need for strong party institutions in Congress will also be furthered by new policy problems, more rapid turnover of membership, and the continuation of split-party control of government (Owens 1997: 269–72).

Of course, the presidency will remain relevant, yet it may also come to be seen as almost superfluous. A principal argument on behalf of Bob Dole's candidacy was that he would sign the legislation passed by a Republican Congress—hardly a testament to presidential leadership. President Clinton fostered his reelection by removing himself from partisan leadership, "triangulating" the White House between congressional Democrats and Republicans, and following the model of patriotic chief of state created by George Washington and prescribed in *The Federalist:* "to guard the community against the effects of faction, precipitancy, or of any impulse unfriendly to the public good" (Madison 1941: 477).

In keeping with this restrictive model, Clinton has become less involved in controversial issues, newly emphasizing the less partisan area of foreign policy, while appealing to consensual attitudes such as "family values" and school achievement. He adopted Republican programs, even changing previous positions on many issues, most prominently the balanced budget and welfare reform. He succeeded in winning reelection, but at the cost of the loss of policy initiative.

Political ambition, immodestly evidenced by President Clinton, Senator Dole, and their peers, is no sin. But the implications of the 1996 election campaign for American government remain important. The presidency is already a diminished office because the end of the Cold War has removed a principal support of its power, the predominance of foreign and defense policy. The limits on federal funds, created by the emphasis on budget balancing and the burden of middle-class entitlements, restrict the energy of the executive. Clinton's pieties on children and Dole's condemnation of drugs and pornography evoked no mandate for meaningful policy initiatives.

The absence of presidential initiative is more than a problem of the Clinton administration. Throughout American history, the president has persistently provided the energy of American government, the source of new "regimes" and policy initiatives (Skowronek 1993). Perhaps the lassitude of contemporary politics is only the latest example of the recurrent cycle of presidential initiative, consolidation, and decline. Or, more profoundly, perhaps it marks the decline of the executive office itself as a source of creativity in the government of the United States.

America needs help. It may well be time to end the fruitless quest for a presidential savior and instead turn our attention, and our support, to the continuing and emerging strengths of our political parties. We are developing, almost unnoticed, institutions of semiparliamentary, semiresponsible government. To build a better bridge between the past and the future, perhaps this new form of American government is both inevitable and necessary.

NOTES

I gratefully acknowledge the help of Andrea Lubin, who performed the content analyses of party platforms included in this essay.

1. The phrase is from Walter Baghot's (1928: 1) classic analysis of the realities of British politics.
2. The texts are found in *The Vision Shared* (Washington, DC: Republican National Committee, 1992) and for the less loquacious Democrats, *Congressional Quarterly Weekly Report* 50 (July 18, 1992): 2107–13.
3. Each sentence, or distinct clause within these sentences, constituted the unit of analysis. Because of its great length, only alternate sentences in the Republican platform were included.

No selection bias is evident or, given the repetitive character of the platforms, likely. In total, there are 426 units of analysis in the Democratic platform, 758 in the Republican. For further details on the techniques used, see Pomper and Lederman (1980: 235–48). To avoid contamination or wishful thinking on my part, Lubin did the analysis independently. My later revisions tended to classify the platform sentences as less specific and meaningful than hers, contrary to any optimistic predisposition.

4. The "useful" categories are policy approval and policy criticism, candidate approval and candidate criticism, and future policy promises classified as pledges of continuity, expressions of goals, pledges of action, and detailed pledges.

5. *The Vision Shared* (1992 Republican Platform), p. 46; "Contract with America," in Wilcox (1995. 70); *Restoring the American Dream* (1996 Republican Platform), p. 25.

6. Using the same content categories, Carolyn Shaw (1996), of the University of Texas, lists 150 presidential campaign promises of 1992 in the more specific categories. In regard to fulfillment, she employs the methods of Fishel (1985). With this method, she finds that there was "fully comparable" or "partially comparable" action on 69 percent of Clinton's proposals. This record is higher than that found by Fishel for any president from Kennedy through Reagan.

7. Even this figure underestimates the impact of the Contract with America. I have counted the failure to pass term limits as a defeat, although the Republicans actually promised no more than a floor vote, and I have not given the party credit for achievements in the following Congress.

8. These data are drawn from *Congressional Quarterly Weekly Report* 54 (December 21, 1996): 3461–67.

9. *Congressional Quarterly Weekly Report* 51 (May 15, 1993): 1197.

10. *Congressional Quarterly Weekly Report* 51 (March 20, 1993): 691; Federal Election Commission, *Record* 19 (May 1993): 22.

11. *Colorado Republican Federal Campaign Committee et al. v. Federal Election Commission* (No. 95-489, 1996 U.S. LEXIS 4258).

12. The parties spent $628 million directly, plus at least $263 million and up to $400 million in soft money. For detailed figures, see *Congressional Quarterly Weekly Report* 55 (April 5, 1997): 767–73.

13. For an excellent discussion of 1996 election spending, see Corrado (1997).

14. The only exception to the trend away from inner party selection or compromise since 1924 is Alf Landon's designation at the Republican candidate in 1936. The last president "voluntarily" to decline a second term was Lyndon Johnson in 1968.

REFERENCES

Bruce, John M., John A. Clark, and John H. Kessel. 1991. "Advocacy Politics in Presidential Parties." *American Political Science Review* 85: 1089–1106.

Bruzios, Christopher. 1990. "Democratic & Republican Party Activists & Followers." *Polity* 22: 581–601.

Budge, Ian. 1993. "Parties, Programs and Policies: A Comparative and Theoretical Perspective." *American Review of Politics* 14: 696.

Budge, Ian, and Hans Keman. 1990. *Parties and Democracy.* Oxford: Oxford University Press.

David, Paul T., Ralph M. Goldman, and Richard C. Bain. 1960. *The Politics of National Party Conventions.* Washington, D.C.: Brookings.

Downs, Anthony. 1957. *An Economic Theory of Democracy.* New York: HarperCollins.

Drew, Elizabeth. 1997. *Whatever It Takes: The Real Struggle for Political Power in America.* New York: Viking.

Ford, Henry Jones. 1914. *The Rise and Growth of American Politics.* New York: Macmillan.

Hale, Jon F. 1994. "The Democratic Leadership Council: Institutionalizing Party Faction." In *The State of the Parties: The Changing Role of Contemporary American Parties*, ed. Daniel M. Shea and John C. Green. Lanham, MD: Rowman & Littlefield.

Jones, Charles O. 1996. "The Separated System." *Society* 33: 18–23.

Klingemann, Hans-Dieter, Richard Hofferbert, and Ian Budge. 1994. *Parties, Policies, and Democracy*. Boulder, CO: Westview.

Madison, James. 1941 [1787]. *The Federalist*. New York: Modern Library.

Mayer, William. 1995. *In Pursuit of the White House*. Chatham, NJ: Chatham House.

Monroe, Alan D., and Brian A. Bernardoni. 1995. "The Republican 'Contract' with America: A New Direction for American Parties?" Paper presented at the annual conference of the Southern Political Science Association, Tampa, FL.

Owens, John E. 1997. "The Return of Party Government in the US House of Representatives." *British Journal of Political Science* 27: 247–72.

Page, Benjamin. 1978. *Choices and Echoes in Presidential Elections*. Chicago: University of Chicago Press.

Patterson, Kelly, and Amy Bice. 1997. "Political Parties, Candidates, and Presidential Campaigns: 1952–1996." Paper presented at the annual meeting of the American Political Science Association, Washington, D.C.

Polsby, Nelson. 1983. *Consequences of Party Reform*. New York: Oxford University Press.

Pomper, Gerald M., with Susan L. Lederman. 1980. *Elections in America*, 2d ed. New York: Longman.

Ranney, Austin. 1954. *The Doctrine of Responsible Party Government*. Urbana: University of Illinois Press.

Rohde, David W. 1991. *Parties and Leaders in the Postreform House*. Chicago: University of Chicago Press.

Shaw, Carolyn. 1996. "Has President Clinton Fulfilled His Campaign Promises?" Paper presented at the annual meeting of the American Political Science Association, San Francisco.

Skowronek, Stephen. 1993. *The Politics Presidents Make*. Cambridge, MA: Belknap.

The Causes and Consequences
of Divided Government: Lessons of 1992–1994

Morris P. Fiorina

This essay updates the discussion in my 1992 book (*Divided Government*). First, it looks at the election results that unified control in 1992, then redivided it in 1994. Not surprisingly, I conclude that the era of divided government is still very much with us. Second, this essay considers the implications of the 1992–1994 performance of the Clinton administration for arguments about the consequences of divided government. Little in this two-year performance suggests that divided control is to blame for the various perceived ills that beset the nation.

THE 1992 AND 1994 ELECTIONS

The 1992 National Elections

For the media and for many popular commentators on American politics, the main story of the 1992 elections was a story of change. Bill Clinton broke the supposed Republican "lock" on the presidency, only the second time since 1964 that a Democrat had been able to poll more votes than a Republican at the presidential level. Certainly that was a noteworthy change from recent electoral history, and understandably it became the focus of a news establishment that defines news largely in terms of things that change.

To those who looked closely at the underlying reality, however, the story was as much a story of continuity as of change. Like his regional predecessor in 1976, Clinton won under exceptional conditions.[1] Although his popular vote margin over Bush was a comfortable 5.6 percent, and his electoral vote margin overwhelming, the presence of Ross Perot in the race clouded matters considerably. Clinton won a majority of the popular vote only in his home state of Arkansas. The most detailed analyses that have been done conclude that Perot took about as many votes from Clinton as from Bush, suggesting that Clinton's popular vote margin over Bush in a two-way race would have been about the same as Bush's 1988 margin over Dukakis, but there is no denying the relative unpopularity of both major party candidates in 1992.[2]

Source: Morris Fiorina, "The Causes and Consequences of Divided Government: Lessons of 1992–1994," in Peter F. Galderisi, ed., with Roberta Q. Herzberg and Peter McNamara, *Divided Government. Change, Uncertainty, and the Constitutional Order* (Lanham, MD: Rowman and Littlefield Publishers, 1996), pp. 35–59.

Morris P. Fiorina is professor of political science at Harvard University and author of *Divided Government*.

Whatever the uncertainties and ambiguities, Clinton won, and given that the Democratic "lock" on Congress continued, unified government was restored to the national level. There had been much speculation in the media about 1992 being the "year of the outsider." Congress had been buffeted by a series of scandals—the Keating Five, the House Post Office, the House Bank, Danny Rostenkowski—and popular esteem for the institution was at historic lows. Approval of the performance of Congress, for instance, was below 20 percent, in contrast to more normal (albeit still low) levels of about 35 percent.[3] Disgust with the campaign finance system was widespread. Term limit proposals passed wherever they got on the ballot.

Despite such a generally negative view of Congress, constituents continued to view their own representatives and senators much more favorably than they viewed the collective Congress, although 1992 approval levels in the 50 to 60 percent range for individual members of Congress were lower than the 60 to 70 range that was normal in the 1970s and 1980s.[4] As a consequence of this continued differentiation between individuals and the collectivity, the year of the outsider was much less apparent than feared by some Democrats and hoped for by some Republicans. In the House, many of the more tainted incumbents either retired or were defeated in primaries, leading to a relatively quiet general election.[5] Eighty-eight percent of all incumbents were reelected, clearly lower than the 1980s average of 95 percent, but a figure not suggestive of any wholesale rejection of Washington.[6] Republicans had put much effort into the redistricting process after the 1990 census, and hoped to make significant gains, but in the end they gained only ten seats.

The Senate results were even more disappointing for the Republicans. Twenty of the thirty-five contested seats were held by Democrats. Given that Senate elections in this era are highly competitive, and that incumbency counts for less in the Senate than in the House, on statistical grounds alone the Republicans expected to make gains.[7] When all the votes were counted, however, the Republicans actually lost one seat, leaving them on the short side of a 57 to 43 division.

In sum, in 1992 the voting decisions made by millions of Americans brought back unified government, a significant change from the recent past. But a look at the voting decisions that accomplished that result does not reveal major shifts in the way Americans were making their choices. Counting Perot voters, a record 36 percent of those voting split their tickets between the parties' candidates for the presidency and the House. Not counting Perot voters, 22 percent of those voting split their tickets, a figure just three points below the 1972–1988 average.[8]

The 1994 National Elections

Political conditions changed as much between 1992 and 1994 as they had between 1990 and 1992. According to the polls, the electorate that had wavered in its preference for divided over unified national government in the fall of 1992 decided after two years of experience with unified government that it really preferred divided government after all.[9] Whether out of an actual preference for divided government or for a host of other reasons, the electorate restored divided national government with the only means at its disposal: electing Republican majorities to Congress.

If the main story of 1992—electoral change—was something of an exaggeration, few will make a similar claim about the main story of 1994 —electoral change in the form of the Republican capture of the House of Representatives. Not since 1952 had the Republicans won a majority of House seats, the longest period of one-party control in American history. And not since 1952 had the Republicans received a majority of the nationwide popular vote cast for House candidates. The gain in the party's national popular vote between 1992 and 1994 was 7 percent, not large in absolute terms, but relatively speaking, very large—the largest shift in either party's House vote since 1948.[10] With a loss of fifty-four House seats and eight Senate seats, the "earthquake," "tsunami," and other geological and meteorological metaphors that filled the media were understandable. The House figure, in particular, was a throwback to the first half of the twentieth century: not since 1946 had a party lost so many seats in one election.

Despite the common tendency to paint the Republican victory as a "tsunami" that washed away all the Democrats in its path, in reality the voting patterns were more complex and their causes more differentiated than such metaphors suggest. The House results had at least four significant components, although as yet there is little research on how important they were and how they interacted with one another: the normal midterm loss, the secular realignment in the South, unpopular issue stands, and reapportionment and redistricting.

First, in every midterm election since the Civil War, save one (1934), the party of the president has lost seats. Given the state of the economy in 1992 (according to the traditional indicators, it was pretty good), most statistical forecasting models predicted these "normal" losses to be relatively small. But given Clinton's low approval ratings and the fiasco in Congress created by his health care plan, most analysts expected losses somewhat larger than the historical norm.

Second, the Republicans made their first breakthroughs in the South in the 1960s. During the intervening thirty years, many southern states had become downright Republican at the presidential level and at least competitive statewide, but the Democrats had been hanging on at the congressional level and holding firm at the state legislative level. The 1994 elections showed significant breakthroughs at these levels.

Third, national Democrats continue to get burned by a variety of symbolic issues on which they are at odds with constituencies who have traditionally supported the Democrats on economic grounds.[11] Such issues contribute to a popular impression that the Democrats are out of step with the values and aspirations of ordinary middle Americans, an impression the Republicans have been happily exploiting for nearly a generation.

In the fourth component of the House results, reapportionment and redistricting, two distinct factors are at work. One is that following the past two decennial censuses, there has been a reallocation of congressional districts from the Frost Belt to the Sun Belt—from areas more heavily Democratic to areas less so. In the 1990 reapportionment, Sun Belt states gained eighteen seats. The other factor is majority–minority redistricting. In recent years, Republicans have joined civil rights groups to press for redistricting plans that create the maximum number of seats with African-American and Hispanic majorities. This practice increases the likelihood of electing minority members to Congress but marginally weakens adjacent Democratic districts that lose minority voters. David Lublin estimates that majority–minority redistricting cost the Democrats twelve seats in 1992 and 1994, an estimate he calls "conservative."[12]

The important point to notice is that losses from these two distinct sources probably should have occurred entirely in 1992, the first election after the census, but the poor showing of George Bush may have enabled some Democratic incumbents to hang on in weakened districts and some Democratic challengers to win in others where they were not expected to. When such districts belatedly fell to the Republicans in 1994, they added to the impression of a national Republican tide.

A close look at the congressional voting reveals some important elements of continuity, as well as the major instances of change that we have noted. In particular, 90 percent of all running House incumbents were reelected, a slight increase over 1992, but 5 percent below the average of the previous decade. Still, the incumbent reelection rate in 1994 was higher than the *average* for the elections between 1946 and 1966, suggesting that even in 1994, incumbency was of a different order of importance than a generation ago. To be sure, with the electoral tide running in the Republican direction, not a single Republican incumbent lost, while thirty-five Democratic incumbents did. The latter is an unusually large number but one that still left the Democrats with an 85 percent success rate. Using one widely accepted method of calculation, the incumbency advantage in 1994 was something over 12 percent for Republicans and something over 8 percent for Democrats; the advantage of incumbency certainly did not disappear in 1994.[13]

In the Senate, the Republicans also enjoyed great success, although their takeover there was much less of a surprise. For the second election in a row, the Democrats were heavily exposed in Senate races: twenty-two of the thirty-four seats up for election in 1994 were held by Democrats. Because Senate races have become highly competitive in recent years, few observers thought it was out of the question that the Republicans would gain enough seats to win control, despite their failure to do so when the Democrats were similarly exposed in 1992. The Republicans needed a net gain of seven seats and got eight (plus Richard Shelby of Alabama, who defected from the Democrats shortly after the election). Only two Democratic incumbents lost, but every single open seat was captured by the Republicans.

Whatever the policy consequences of the Republican victories (at the time of this writing, there has been much sound and fury in the House, but not much has made it into law, or even through the Senate), the 1994 election results make it clear that the Democratic "lock" on the House of Representatives has been broken. Taken in combination with the 1992 results wherein the Democrats at least picked the Republican lock on the presidency, the 1994 elections indicate that either party can capture any one of the three elected branches of the national government, given circumstances that we have seen transpire in a three- or four-year span of time. This suggests that divided government at the national level will be common in years to come, although it may take patterns different from the Republican president/Democratic Congress that had been the norm between 1954 and 1992. In particular, the present division of Democratic president/Republican Congress is the first instance of such a pattern since 1948.

THE CONSEQUENCES OF DIVIDED GOVERNMENT REVISITED

During the 1992 presidential campaign, a new issue came to the fore. It was not a policy issue like reducing the deficit, "ending welfare as we know it," or admitting gays into the military. Nor was it an issue of personal or institutional performance like Bush's handling of the economy or the apparent venality of Congress. The issue was broader than either policy or performance and was blamed for shortcomings in both. The issue was *gridlock*. According to many commentators—by no means all of them Democrats—the United States had taken a long look at Sundquist's "new era of coalition government" and, like him, they found it wanting.[14] Years of Republican presidents cohabiting with Democratic congresses had generated an indictment that charged divided government with "bitter partisanship, poor governmental performance, policy incoherence, nondecisions, showdowns, standoffs, checkmate, stalemate, deadlock, and in the most recent nomenclature, *gridlock*."[15]

In *Divided Government*, I noted that there was little empirical support for the strong claims that have been made about the negative effects of divided control. Whether one looked closely at deficits, at legislative productivity, at interbranch conflict, or at presidents' ability to conduct foreign affairs or staff their administrations, there was little in the empirical record that pointed to significant differences between years of unified government and years of split control.[16] That may have been the case as of 1988, but had the picture changed during the Bush Administration? Had the divided government chickens finally come home to roost? Many Democrats suggested as much, many pundits agreed with them, and even voters became less supportive of divided government than they had been earlier.[17]

Efficiency and Effectiveness under Unified Government in 1993–1994

When Bill Clinton was elected, advocates of activist government breathed a sigh of relief. With unified government restored, the country could once again expect innovative programs, decisive government action, and efficient institutional performance. Such expectations were not just the exaggerated expectations of naive observers. Experienced congressional leaders convinced President-elect Clinton that he should ignore moderate Republicans and adopt a legislative strategy that relied exclusively on the Democratic majorities in Congress. For his own part, Clinton indiscreetly suggested that his first hundred days would be the most productive period since Franklin Roosevelt.

Things do not seem to have worked out that way. Almost immediately, President Clinton was slapped down by Congress when he attempted to end discrimination against gays by the military. Not only did his own party not stand behind him, but Democrats made it clear that they would provide enough votes to override his veto if he sought to block a joint resolution overturning his proposed executive order. This was hardly an auspicious beginning. The finale of his first two years was far worse. Health care reform, the planned centerpiece of the Clinton administration, died a long, noisy, and messy death in Congress, some months after the congressional Democrats rejected the president's plan and attempted to substitute various ones of their own.

In between, there was considerably more of the same. Many of the president's victories recalled the "perils of Pauline" stories of the silent movie era. His budget passed by a single vote in the House, as conservative Democrats abandoned ship. The president won on the North American Free Trade Agreement (NAFTA) only because Republican Speaker-to-be Newt Gingrich delivered the Republican votes to make up for Democratic defections. Dissident Democrats joined with Republicans to hold up the crime bill, forcing the president to make concessions on spending. A Democratic senator, Fritz Hollings, held up a vote on the General Agreement on Tariffs and Trade (GATT) until after the 1994 elections, at which time President Clinton was forced into embarrassing negotiations with the newly empowered Republican minority. But on these matters, at least Clinton won in the end, however difficult and damaging the process.

Other policymaking episodes did not have happy endings. The president's economic stimulus package died in the Senate as the strategy of relying exclusively on Democratic votes in Congress encouraged Republicans to adopt a "take no prisoners" approach to the president's program. The campaign finance reform package also died in the Senate, but not before complacent House Democrats had delayed it for a year. Congress rejected the president's proposal to reform grazing rights in the West, and Superfund died as well. Environmental spokespersons labeled the 103rd Congress a disappointment.[18]

Faced with such developments, the high hopes expressed only two years earlier now turned to disappointment. Rank-and-file House Democrats rushed to adjourn, suggesting a desire to get out of Washington before they did any further political damage.[19] Polls found that voters once again overwhelmingly saw the virtues of divided control. Some in the media could scarcely contain their disgust:

> This will go down in the record books as perhaps the worst Congress—least effective, most destructive, nastiest—in 50 years. The wisdom of the moment is that the dismal record represents a victory for the Republicans. . . . But it's also a myth to claim that they bear the entire responsibility for the failure that has occurred. The Democrats brought a major part of the wreckage on themselves. . . . The only good news as this mud fight finally winds down is that it's hard to imagine much worse.[20]

Certainly things were not as bad as that. The disappointment and disillusion expressed in late 1994 were no more justified than the hope and anticipation expressed in late 1992. Unified government should not have been expected to work miracles, and a fair review of the record suggests that unified control in 1993 and 1994 was by no means the disaster suggested by some.

After updating the research reviewed in his earlier book, David Mayhew judged the 103rd Congress as "relatively productive . . . good . . . respectable. . . . I think with five year's perspective we'll say this is an average first Congress for a president. . . . It's like Truman's first Congress, or Carter's first, maybe a little bigger than Kennedy's first."[21] To be sure, Mayhew by no means was retreating from his earlier conclusion that divided government was as productive as unified government. He went on to say, "Once you step back and look, you wonder whether it adds up to more than Bush's first Congress. . . . I don't think it's in a class with Ronald Reagan's first Congress."[22]

Contrary to much of what has been written in the media, most academic observers of Congress judge that the two years of unified government under Clinton were reasonably productive. In addition to deficit reduction, NAFTA, and GATT, one finds amidst the various defeats and embarrassments significant policy initiatives such as the Family and Medical Leave Act, the National Service Corps, the Brady (handgun control) Bill, and the Anticrime Bill, as well as procedural reforms such as "motor voter" registration, Hatch Act revisions, and reform of government procurement. Moreover, Charles O. Jones, James Thurber, and other scholars point out "negative" accomplishments, including termination of giant pork-barrel projects such as the superconducting super collider.[23]

All in all, the lessons to be drawn from the 1993–1994 episode of unified national control appear quite consistent with those drawn from previous episodes. There were plenty of instances of gridlock and stalemate, but also instances of legislative accomplishment. Despite hyperbolic newspaper editorials and bitter partisan commentary, the experience of the 103rd Congress suggests no need to revise the earlier conclusions regarding the relative unimportance of divided control. This episode of unified government seems well within the historical range of what one could expect from either a unified or a divided government.

Recent research supports that verdict about the relative unimportance of split versus unified control. Although their approaches and methodologies could not be more different, important studies by Charles Jones and Keith Krehbiel reach very similar general conclusions.[24] Based on an extensive empirical study of post–Second World War presidents, Jones finds that divided government is only one of many factors that determine legislative productivity and other measures of presidential success. Indeed, split-party control may not even be a major factor in many cases; only when it occurs in combination with other considerations does divided control have the popularly assumed negative effects.

Jones identifies four patterns of presidential–congressional relations.[25] In the first, *partisanship,* split control can indeed lead to gridlock, as in the final two years of the Bush administration. But Jones concludes that gridlock was not inevitable; the perceived weakness of both sides led them to eschew compromise in favor of an all-out attack on the opposing party/institutional actor. In contrast, when both parties have acknowledged strengths, a pattern of *copartisanship* may develop, in which parties compromise their positions—even very different positions. Jones points to the 1990 budget deal as a prime example. Democrats swallowed budget cuts and accepted restraints they swore they would never accept, and Bush abandoned his "read my lips, no new taxes" pledge.[26]

An even kinder, gentler form of executive–legislative relations is *bipartisanship*, by which Jones means that parties cooperate and compromise, not just at the final-passage stage of the legislative process, but in the development of legislative proposals. Foreign relations, especially the Marshall Plan under Truman and congressional Republicans, is the classic example. Finally, *crosspartisanship* occurs when a segment of one congressional party joins with the other party to form a majority. Thus, although formally divided, was the government practically unified when the southern "boll weevils" gave Reagan "ideological control" of the House in 1981 and enabled him to win passage of far-reaching budget and tax proposals? Although formally unified, was the government practically divided when defections by southern Democrats blocked some parts of the agendas of Democratic presidents such as Roosevelt and Kennedy?

All in all, in his major extension of Mayhew's work, Jones finds little merit in the traditional argument that American government functions best when a strong president actively leads a Congress controlled by his party. Reading Jones's account, any disinterested observer will find examples of ineffective and effective government, successful and unsuccessful presidents, and good and bad legislation, under both unified and divided governments.

Krehbiel arrives at strikingly similar conclusions via an entirely different route. He sets up a sequential game-theoretic model of the national policymaking process, then solves the game for the equilibria that exist under different configurations of the institutional actors. The elements of the configurations in Krehbiel's formal model are three: the position of the president, the position of the median voter in the legislature, and the positions of legislators empowered by extramajoritarian features of the national policymaking process, that is, the one whose vote, when added to those of one-third of a chamber, makes a veto override impossible and the one whose vote, when added to those of two-fifths, makes a filibuster succeed. Krehbiel finds that divided or unified control makes little difference. Under a wide range of parameter values, both unified and divided configurations have gridlock equilibria. Even when Krehbiel assumes, contrary to fact, that the majority party is perfectly cohesive, gridlock still characterizes the equilibria of the unified government game. Krehbiel does identify one important factor that determines legislative movement: the position of the status quo ante. Where the status quo is far from the preferences of all the important actors—president, party or legislature median, and filibuster and veto pivots—the legislature passes and the president signs legislation. But this happens with either divided or unified control!

Divided Government and Executive–Legislative Conflict

The studies reviewed thus far examine the impact of divided government on legislative productivity: does divided control result in a lower level of legislative output? Such a clear, direct effect is not the only logically possible one, of course; divided control might have other, more subtle, more indirect effects on the political process, such as raising the level of executive–legislative conflict. For example, the historical record clearly indicates that presidents veto more legislation when government is divided than when unified. Consistent with that record, President Clinton vetoed no bills during his first two years in office, whereas President Bush vetoed twenty-five during the preceding two years.

Sean Kelly recently has shown that interbranch conflict on roll call votes is greater during periods of divided government. Policy agreement between the president and congressional majorities is more than 20 percent lower when the institutions are controlled by different parties.[27] Significantly, the effect seems to be a step function reflecting the presence or absence of control, not a linear function of the number of seats controlled by the president's party. These findings support Sundquist's argument that under divided control congressional majorities are loath to do anything that would enhance the president's standing; on the contrary, they will bring matters the president opposes to a vote precisely to demonstrate their disagreement.[28]

On the other hand, examination of another congressional arena—committee hearings—reveals no difference between unified and divided control. Paul Peterson and Jay Greene find that hostile questioning of executive branch witnesses has declined in the postwar period even as divided control has become more common.[29] Congressional members of the president's party have become friendlier over time, whereas congressional members of the opposition are no more hostile now than in earlier decades. Peterson and Greene suggest that the common perception of increased interbranch conflict is a misperception. One way of reconciling Kelly's findings based on roll call votes and Peterson and Greene's based on committee hearings is to suggest that partisan conflict will be more likely to emerge in more public arenas such as the floor of the House and Senate than in more private arenas such as the committee rooms. This would also help to reconcile findings of greater conflict with findings of little or no difference in legislative productivity. Legislators might posture when the cameras are on but continue to do the work of government when out of the spotlight.

Divided Government and Budget Deficits

Many observers have attributed the huge deficits of the 1980s to divided government. More systematic research over a longer period of time has raised doubts. What is the current state of opinion? The national experience of recent years does little to settle the question. President Bush and the Democratic Congress negotiated a budget package/tax increase in 1990 that significantly lowered the growth of the deficit. And in 1992, the Democratic congressional leadership rammed through President Clinton's budget package/tax increase without a single Republican vote in either chamber. Whatever the electoral cost to Bush of violating his "no new taxes" pledge and to Clinton of appearing to be an "old Democrat," most analysts judged both Bush's and Clinton's tax increase to have been among the significant accomplishments of their respective administrations. The former is an example of what Jones calls crosspartisanship; the latter, of partisanship. One was produced by divided government; one by unified government. At the national level, the relationship between divided government and budget deficits is as unclear as before.

ACCOUNTABILITY UNDER UNIFIED CONTROL: THE LESSONS OF 1993–1994

Beyond questions of governmental efficiency and effectiveness, critics of divided government have charged that divided control confuses the lines of responsibility in American politics. With different institutions controlled by different parties, how can voters hold parties collectively responsible for their performance? Moreover, knowing that it is hard for voters to assess responsibility, elected officials have less reason to worry about their performance; even if they have nothing to show by way of tangible accomplishments, they can resort to the "blame game," posturing about what they support and blaming the other party for their inability to deliver.

Certainly, the 1994 congressional elections are consistent with the notion that unified control enhances electoral accountability. For two decades, election observers had marveled at the ability of congressional incumbents to insulate themselves from larger issues of national policy and performance, but many of these incumbents evidently found their insulation insufficient in 1994. Speaker of the House Tom Foley, Judiciary Chair Jack Brooks, Senate Majority Leader heir-apparent Jim Sasser—these and many others found themselves too closely tied to the policies and performance of the Clinton administration for a majority of their constituents. As usual, they ran, but this time they couldn't hide. Unified Democratic control may well have been the difference.

Still, it is easy to exaggerate the extent to which the election was dominated by an angry electorate exacting its revenge on the Democrats. That image takes too literally the earthquake, tidal wave, and tsunami metaphors that dominated postelection commentary. As noted above, a variety of important considerations underlay the election results. Certainly, I will not be surprised if subsequent research shows that national issues and presidential performance affected the congressional voting in 1994 to a greater extent than in other recent elections. But that still leaves open the question of why? Why were the Republicans able to "nationalize" the 1994 elections? Was the answer simply "unified Democratic control"? If so, why were they not able to nationalize the 1978 elections against a floundering Carter administration? Do the 1994 results indicate that collective accountability was there all along, just lying dormant and waiting for unified control to revive it—despite the Republicans' inability to capitalize in 1978—or was 1994 an aberration? If unified control has revived collective responsibility, then we might see an older pattern of politics reassert itself, a pattern wherein one party or the other expects to gain unified control in the presidential elections, and divided government occurs as a consequence of losing one or both houses at the midterm. If this were to happen, proponents of unified government would have the chance to test their beliefs against contemporary reality. As citizens, we can only hope that in such an eventuality, the optimism of the advocates of unified government would be justified. But as analysts, it is far too early to conclude either that the era of candidate-centered elections has reverted to an older party-centered era or that if it has, conditions will necessarily improve.

CONCLUSION: DIVIDED GOVERNMENT OR DIVIDED CITIZENRY?

All in all, there is little in the record of the mid-1990s to support the stronger claims of the critics of divided government. To the extent that the effects of divided government can be identified at all, they appear quite limited. Critics and commentators have been too quick to lay the blame for the perceived failings of governments on political–institutional processes, while ignoring other, more important factors.

Prominent among those other factors are the preferences of the voters. If citizens condemn budget deficits while overwhelmingly opposing cuts in entitlements and/or increases in taxes, there is not much that even a unified government can do to reduce the deficit. If citizens want a zero-risk society but resent bureaucratic intrusion and red tape, they are unlikely to be satisfied with the regulatory process. If citizens want guaranteed health care for all, choice of doctors and facilities, and cheaper insurance premiums for health care than they currently pay, they are unlikely to be happy with any conceivable national health care plan. Does it make sense to blame political–institutional processes for failing to satisfy incompatible wants?

Of course, the fault may lie with our leaders. After all, if we had inspiring, charismatic leaders who could educate the voters, inform their preferences, and dispel the illusions and contradictions, then the political process would work better. Perhaps, but I will not hold my breath waiting for such leaders, and I suspect that there have been few of them in the past. Such demigods are created after the fact in the panegyrics of palace historians. The times make the leader more than the leader makes the times.[30]

Even more than before, I believe that the prevailing dissatisfaction of Americans with their governments largely reflects their lack of agreement on what, if anything, should be done. If almost no one likes the status quo but different groups strongly disagree over what direction policy should move in, no one is going to be very happy. Consider the suggestive data in Table 1. Over the course of the past generation, Americans' views of the power of the federal government have polarized. When Lyndon Johnson and the Eighty-ninth Congress were adopting Great Society initiatives, a plurality of the electorate expressed satisfaction with the level of activity of the federal government, and a significant minority favored additional activity. In contrast, when Bill Clinton and the 103rd Congress were trying to pass a national

TABLE 1　*Americans' Opinions on Federal Power*

	1964	*1992*
Too much federal power	26%	39%
About right	36%	12%
Not enough federal power	31%	40%

Note: Respondents were asked: "Which one of these statements comes closest to your own views about governmental power today? (1) The federal government has too much power. (2) The federal government is using about the right amount of power for meeting today's needs. (3) The federal government should use its powers more vigorously to promote the well-being of all segments of the people."

Source: American National Election Studies.

health care program, only a tiny minority were satisfied with the federal government as is, while large and equal-sized pluralities wanted to go in opposite directions. In both cases, government was unified, but it acted in the former case and gridlocked in the latter. The difference was the size of the center relative to the opposed extremes in the 1960s versus the 1990s.

Those who yearn for energetic, effective government probably should shift their focus away from the simple question of party control to the more complicated question of how to build majorities for the ends they espouse. If both divided control and government inaction reflect the absence of popular consensus, attention should shift toward explaining the lack of consensus. Does this lack result from the decline of consensus-building actors such as parties and the rise of consensus-destroying actors such as single-issue groups, conflict-obsessed media, and ideologically rigid political elites? Or are these developments, too, just symptoms, not causes? Or both? In the final analysis, we are talking about the ability of a nation to govern itself democratically, and no single factor operating in simple, straightforward fashion will determine how well or poorly we do. It would have been nice if political scientists could have shown to everyone's satisfaction that unified control is the answer to most of our problems. Unfortunately, the world is not so simple.

NOTES

1. In 1976, Carter was running against the *appointed* vice-president of a president who had resigned in disgrace, in the aftermath of a serious recession. Under such conditions, it was less noteworthy that a Democrat won than that he won by such a narrow margin—less than 1 percent

2. Paul R. Abramson. John H. Aldrich, and David W. Rohde, *Change and Continuity in the 1992 Elections* (Washington, DC: Congressional Quarterly Press, 1994); Herbert F. Weisberg and David C. Kimball, "Attitudinal Correlates of the 1992 Presidential Vote: Party Identification and Beyond," in, *Democracy's Feast: Elections in America,* ed. Herbert F. Weisberg (Chatham, NJ: Chatham House, 1995), pp 72–111.

3. David Magleby and Kelly Patterson. "The Polls—Poll Trends: Congressional Reform," *Public Opinion Quarterly* 58 (1994), pp. 419–27.

4. Compare Magleby and Patterson, p. 423, with Kelly Patterson and David Magleby. "Public Support for Congress," *Public Opinion Quarterly* 56 (1992), p. 549.

5. Gary C. Jacobson and Michael Dimock, "Checking Out: The Effects of Bank Overdrafts on the 1992 House Elections," *American Journal of Political Science* 38 (1994), pp 601–24.

6. Norman Ornstein, Thomas Mann and Michael Malbin, *Vital Statistics on Congress, 1993–1994* (Washington, DC: Congressional Quarterly Inc., 1994), table 2–7.

7. If every race were a toss-up, then the Republicans would have expected to win seventeen or eighteen of the thirty-five seats. Incumbency would have dampened such expectations somewhat, but the situation still looked highly promising for the Republicans. On statewide competitiveness, see Alan Abramowitz and Jeffrey Segal, *Senate Elections* (Ann Arbor: University of Michigan Press, 1995), chapter 8.

8. Calculated from the 1994 American National Election Study. These data were made available through the Interuniversity Consortium for Political and Social Research.

9. In the autumn of 1992, support for divided government in the *Wall Street Journal*/ABC poll dropped below a majority for the first time since the question was asked in 1984. By the autumn of 1994, a comfortable majority supported divided government once again.

10. Everett Carll Ladd, ed., *America at the Polls: 1994* (Storrs, CT: The Roper Institute. 1995), p. 2.

11. For example, gun control is an issue that is political poison in southern and western states and even in states like Pennsylvania where the National Rifle Association has a large membership. While I have no systematic evidence on this point, my reading of campaign reports and my conversations with various local observers suggest that gun control may have made the difference in at least a half-dozen seats in 1994, including the defeats of longtime incumbents like Jack Brooks of Texas and Dan Glickman of Kansas. For a comprehensive treatment of the gun control issue, see Robert Spitzer, *The Politics of Gun Control* (Chatham. NJ: Chatham House, 1995).

12. David Lublin, "Costs of Gerrymandering," *New York Times*, December 13, 1994, letter to the editor. Lublin's estimates are based on analyses described in "Gerrymander for Justice? Racial Redistricting and Black and Latino Representation" (Ph.D. diss., Harvard University, 1994). At a panel held during the 1991 American Political Science Association meetings in Washington, D.C., Gary C Jacobson, a leading expert on House elections, predicted a loss of between twenty and twenty-five seats, based in large part on the delayed impact of the 1991 redistricting. This was well before Congress took up health care, and a year before Clinton's approval ratings hit bottom.

13. The method is set forth in Andrew Gelman and Gary King, "Estimating the Incumbency Advantage without Bias," *American Journal of Political Science* 34 (1994), pp. 1142–64. Thanks to Gary King for the 1994 figures.

14. James L. Sundquist, "Needed: A Political Theory for the New Era of Coalition Government in the United States," *Political Science Quarterly* 103 (winter 1988–89), pp. 613–35

15. This pithy summation of the bill of particulars aimed at divided government is due to Keith Krehbiel, "Institutional and Partisan Sources of Gridlock: A Theory of Divided and Unified Government," *Journal of Theoretical Politics* 8 (1996), pp 7–40.

16. The exception to this summation is vetoes: presidents were significantly more likely to veto bills and resolutions when Congress was controlled by the other party. Consistent with this finding, President Clinton cast no vetoes during his first two years.

17. See note 9 above.

18. David S. Cloud, "Health Care's Painful Demise Cast Pall on Clinton Agenda," *Congressional Quarterly Weekly Report,* November 5, 1994, 3144.

19. David S Cloud, "End of Session Marked by Partisan Stalemate," *Congressional Quarterly Weekly Report,* October 8, 1994, 2849.

20. "Perhaps the Worst Congress," *Washington Post National Weekly Edition.* October 17–23. 1994, 27.

21. David R. Mayhew, *Divided We Govern: Party Control, Lawmaking, and Investigations, 1946–1990* (New Haven: Yale University Press, 1991). For Mayhew's update see Stephen Gettinger, "View from the Ivory Tower More Rosy than Media's," *Congressional Quarterly Weekly Report,* October 8. 1994, 2850–51.

22. Gettinger, "View from the Ivory Tower," 2850.

23. Ibid., 2851.
24. Charles O. Jones, *The Presidency in a Separated System* (Washington, DC: Brookings Institution, 1994); Krehbiel, "Sources of Gridlock."
25. Jones, *The Presidency,* pp. 19–23.
26. See also Weatherford's analysis of an earlier budget deal, the national response to the 1958 recession. M. Stephen Weatherford, "Responsiveness and Deliberation in Divided Government: Presidential Leadership in Tax Policy Making," *British Journal of Political Science* 24 (1994), pp. 1–31.
27. Policy agreement is calculated from a subset of important votes included in *Congressional Quarterly*'s presidential success scores. See Sean Q Kelly, "The Institutional Foundations of Inter-Branch Conflict in the Era of Divided Government," *Southeastern Political Review* (forthcoming).
28. Sundquist, "Needed: A Political Theory."
29. Paul E. Peterson and Jay P. Greene, "Why Executive-Legislative Conflict in the United States Is Dwindling," *British Journal of Political Science* 24 (1994). pp. 33–55.
30. Stephen Skowronek, *The Politics Presidents Make: Leadership from John Adams to George Bush* (Cambridge: Harvard University Press, 1993).